Belfast Studies in Language, Culture and Politics

General Editors
John M. Kirk and Dónall P. Ó Baoill

1: *Language and Politics: Northern Ireland, the Republic of Ireland, and Scotland*
published 2000 ISBN 0 85389 791 3

2: *Language Links: the Languages of Scotland and Ireland*
published 2001 ISBN 0 85389 795 6

3: *Linguistic Politics: Language Policies for Northern Ireland, the Republic of Ireland, and Scotland*
published 2001 ISBN 0 85389 815 4

4: *Travellers and their Language*
published 2002 ISBN 0 85389 832 4

5: Simone Zwickl, *Language Attitudes, Ethnic Identity and Dialect Use across the Northern Ireland Border: Armagh and Monaghan*
published 2002 ISBN 0 85389 834 0

6: *Language Planning and Education: Linguistic Issues in Northern Ireland, the Republic of Ireland, and Scotland*
published 2002 ISBN 0 85389 835 9

7: Edna Longley, Eamonn Hughes and Des O'Rawe (eds.) *Ireland (Ulster) Scotland: Concepts, Contexts, Comparisons*
published 2003 ISBN 0 85389 844 8

8: Maolcholaim Scott and Róise Ní Bhaoill (eds.) *Gaelic-Medium Education Provision: Northern Ireland, the Republic of Ireland, Scotland and the Isle of Man*
published 2003 ISBN 0 85389 847 2

9: Dónall Ó Riagáin (ed.) *Language and Law in Northern Ireland*
published 2003 ISBN 0 85389 848 0

10; *Towards our Goals in Broadcasting, the Press, the Performing Arts and the Economy: Minority Languages in Northern Ireland, the Republic of Ireland, and Scotland*
published 2003 ISBN 0 85389 856 1

Other volumes in preparation
www.bslcp.com

Queen's University
Belfast

Towards our Goals in Broadcasting, the Press,
the Performing Arts and the Economy:
Minority Languages in Northern Ireland, the
Republic of Ireland, and Scotland

Edited by

John M. Kirk and Dónall P. Ó Baoill

Cló Ollscoil na Banríona
Belfast 2003

First published in 2003
Cló Ollscoil na Banríona
Queen's University Belfast
Belfast, BT7 1NN

Belfast Studies in Language, Culture and Politics
www.bslcp.com

The publication of this book has been supported by Foras na Gaeilge and Tha
Boord o Ulstèr-Scotch.

British Library Cataloguing-in-Publication Data
A catalogue record for this book is available from the British Library.

ISBN 0 85389 856 1

Typeset by John Kirk in Times New Roman

Cover design by Colin Young
Printing by Optech, Belfast

Editorial Disclaimer

The views expressed in each paper are those of the author. Publication in this volume does not signify either editorial agreement or disagreement or editorial responsibility for these views.

Publisher Disclaimer

The publisher has used its best endeavours to ensure that the URLs for external websites referred to in this book are correct at the time of going to press. However, the publisher has no responsibility for the websites and can make no guarantee that a site will remain live or that the content is or will remain appropriate.

CONTENTS

CONTRIBUTORS

Dr. Esmond Birnie, MLA was born in Edinburgh and grew up in Ballymena. He is a graduate of the University of Cambridge and currently on leave of absence as a Senior Lecturer in Economics at Queen's University. In 1998, He was elected to the Northern Ireland Assembly to represent Belfast South for the Ulster Unionist Party. He is currently the UUP's spokesperson on Employment and Learning. His numerous co-authored books deal with the economies of Northern Ireland, Republic of Ireland, Germany, European Union and Eastern Europe, including (with P.J. Roche) *An Economics Lesson for Irish Nationalists & Republicans* (1995), (with David Hitchens) *The Northern Ireland Economy: Performance, Prospects, Policy* (1999, Ashgate), and (with John Bradley) *Can the Celtic Tiger cross the Irish Border?* (2001, Cork University Press, for the Centre for Cross-Border Studies, Armagh).

Neil Blain is Professor of Media and Culture and Associate Dean at the School of Media, Language and Music at the University of Paisley. Recent work includes *Media, Monarchy and Power* (Intellect, 2003, with Hugh O'Donnell) and *Sport, Media, Culture: Local and Global Dimensions* (Frank Cass, 2003, with Alina Bernstein). He has written numerous journal articles and book chapters focusing in particular on the media, cultural politics and collective identity; on cultural theory; on Scotland and on Europe. He is Secretary of the Scottish Media and Communication Association and represents Scottish higher education on the Scottish Industry Skills Panel. Other activities have included producing large-scale audience research and policy reports for the broadcasting industry during the 1990s, and frequent broadcasting on topical, cultural, arts and political matters since the 1980s. Current research includes empirical work on citizenship issues, and writing on place and sovereignty. He is an Editor of the forthcoming *International Journal of Media and Cultural Politics*, which will be published from 2005.

Dr. Janice Carruthers is a native of Belfast and a graduate in French and Linguistics from the University of Cambridge. She is a senior lecturer in French at Queen's University and a former Associate Dean of the Faculty of Humanities. She has co-authored (with Wendy Ayres-Bennett) *Problems and Perspectives: Studies in the Modern French Language* (2001, Longman) and is an Editor of the *Journal of French Language Studies*. Her main research interests and most of her other publications lie in the areas of tense and aspect in the French verb, the structure of spoken French, sociolinguistics (particularly variation) and discourse-pragmatics; she is currently working on time and tense in oral narration.

Dr. Douglas Chalmers is a native of Dundee and is currently a Lecturer in the Division of Economics and Enterprise at Glasgow Caledonian University. In 2003, he completed a PhD thesis on the Economic Impact of Gaelic Arts and Culture, and was joint author in 1998 of the report 'The Demand for Gaelic Artistic and Cultural Products and Services: Patterns and Impacts' produced by Glasgow Caledonian University.

Dr. John Corbett is a native of Ayr and a graduate of the Universities of Glasgow and New Brunswick. He is currently a Senior Lecturer in English Language at the University of Glasgow. He works primarily in modern Scots language studies, although he also has long-established interests in Scottish literary studies and English Language teaching. He is the author of: *Language and Scottish Literature* (1997), *Written in the Language of the Scottish*

Nation: A History of Literary Translation into Scots (1999) and *An Intercultural Approach to English Language Teaching* (2003). With Derrick McClure and Jane Stuart-Smith, he co-edited and contributed to *The Edinburgh Companion to Scots* (2003), launched at the symposium. John is Co-director of the research project producing the Scottish Corpus of Texts and Speech (SCOTS), and the active Chair of the Language Committee of the Association for Scottish literary Studies.

Dr. Mike Cormack is Course Director for the BA in Gaelic and Media Studies at Sabhal Mòr Ostaig, Isle of Skye. When the papers included here were presented, he was a Senior Lecturer in the Department of Film and Media Studies at the University of Stirling and a member of the Stirling Media Research Institute. Book publications include *Ideology* (University of Michigan Press, 1992) and *Ideology and Cinematography in Hollywood 1930-39* (Palgrave Macmillan, 1994). His current research interests include Gaelic in the media, minority language media, and media representations of the highlands and islands. Over the past ten years, he has published a series of academic papers on issues concerning Gaelic in the media, Scots in the media, and, more generally, minority language media. He is currently co-editing a book to be entitled *Minority Language Media: Concepts, Critiques and Case Studies*.

Maggie Cunningham has spent her entire career with the BBC. She started her career as a producer in BBC Highland in 1979, worked as a freelance journalist from 82 to 89, returning to the BBC as Executive Producer, Radio nan Gaidheal. She became Editor, Radio nan Gaidheal in 1992 and was responsible for developing daily output from Inverness for Radio Scotland. She became Secretary, BBC Scotland in 1995, returned to production in 1997 to set up BBC Scotland's talent pool, ensuring effective deployment and development of staff in a bi-media world. In 1999, she became Head of Features, Education and Religion in BBC Scotland, and in November 2000, she became Head of Radio, Scotland, the post which currently holds.

Dr. Fiona Douglas is a native of Lanarkshire and completed all her studies at the University of Glasgow, culminating in a PhD on the use of Scots in the present-day Scottish press. From 2001 to 2003 she was the Research Assistant on the Scottish Corpus of Texts and Speech (SCOTS) at the University of Glasgow. She took up a lectureship in English Language at the University of Leeds in August 2003. Recent articles include 'The role of Scots lexis in Scottish newspapers' in *Scottish Language*, 21 (2002), and 'The Scottish Corpus of Texts and Speech: Problems of corpus design' in *Literary & Linguistic Computing* 18:1 (2003).

Dr. Sheila Douglas was born in Yorkshire and grew up in Paisley and graduated in English from the University of Glasgow. She published much of the material collected for her University of Stirling PhD as *The King o the Black Art and other folk tales* (1987, AUP). More of her research on travellers appeared in *Travellers and their Language* (2002, Cló Ollscoil na Banríona) and will be continued in her forthcoming edited anthology *Our Destiny: a Treasury of Travellers Verse*. For many years, she taught English at Perth Academy and is currently Tutor in Scots and Folklore at the Royal Scottish Academy of Music and Drama. Sheila is one of Scotland's leading traditional singers, and a collection of her own songs was published as *Lines upon the Water* in 1997 (Ossian). Sheila is a tireless campaigner for the recognition of Scots in all its varieties and with a view to promoting Scots better in schools she has, in recent years, edited and proof read *Ma Sledgin*

Granny and *Mixter Maxter* (two anthologies of Scottish children's writing, one for primary. one for secondary) and written two unpublished children's novels, *The Speaking Birds of Renfrew* and *The Torque of Dreams*, all still awaiting publication.

Robert Dunbar is a Canadian who studied Law at Osgoode Hall Law School, York University, in Canada and at the London School of Economics and is currently Senior Lecturer in Law at the University of Glasgow. His main area of research is with respect to the law and minority peoples in international law and select national legal systems, and he is particularly interested in minority language rights, language legislation and language policies. For his pre-eminence in those fields, his advice is regularly sought from throughout the world. He has advised a number of Gaelic language organisations and public sector bodies in Scotland, Irish language organisations in Northern Ireland, and the Northern Ireland Human Rights Commission working group on language rights on language law, legislation and policy. He has recently co-authored a report for the Kurdish Human Rights Project, a London-based human rights organisation, on Kurdish language rights in Turkey. He assists the Council of Europe in providing expert advice to governments with respect to the European Charter for Regional or Minority Languages. He is the author of numerous outstanding papers, renowned for the clarity of their exposition, several of which are published or to be published by Cló Ollscoil na Banríona. In Rob Dunbar, Scotland is exceptionally privileged to have such a distinguished internationally-renowned advocate for Gaelic.

Aled Eírug was born in London and was brought up in Mid and South Wales. He has worked for the BBC for the past twelve years, initially as Head of News for BBC Wales and, for the past year, has been leading the BBC's work in developing its services for minority indigenous languages in Wales, Scotland and Northern Ireland. Aled's academic background is a BA in History at UC Aberystwyth, and an M.Sc. in Urban and Regional Planning at the London School of Economics. He is also an external examiner in the Journalism School at Cardiff University.

Jean-Luc Fauconnier is a native of Walloon. He is a linguist, dialectologist, writer and currently works for Direction Générale de la Culture et de la Communication at the Conseil des Langues Régionales Endogènes de la Communauté Française de Belgique He is also a Filolec at the Université Libre de Bruxelles He is Président du Conseil des Langues Régionales Endogènes de la Communauté Française de Belgique and a member of the Board of Directors of the European Bureau for Lesser-used Languages. He is renowned for his work on Walloon, that dialect of the Langue d'oïl (French) which is indigenous to the greater part, but not the whole of, Wallonia, the French-speaking part of Belgium.

Dr. Bill Findlay is a native of Culross in Fife. He is Research Fellow in the School of Drama and Creative Industries, Queen Margaret University College (QMUC), Edinburgh. He is a graduate in English Studies from the University of Stirling, undertook postgraduate work at Edinburgh University, and obtained his PhD from QMUC on the topic of Scots translations for the stage. He is editor of *A History of Scottish Theatre* (1998, Polygon), *Scots Plays of the Seventies* (2000, Scottish Cultural Press), and *Frae Ither Tongues: Essays on Modern Translations into Scots* (forthcoming February 2004, Multilingual Matters). He has published widely on the use of Scots in drama, and has translated into Scots for professional production in Scotland over a dozen contemporary and classic plays. Nine of these translations have been from Quebec-French, mostly plays by Quebec's national dramatist Michel Tremblay. The Royal Lyceum Theatre in Edinburgh staged this spring the eighth Tremblay play translated into Scots by Bill and his Montreal collaborator Dr. Martin Bowman.

Anne Gifford taught English in secondary schools in Glasgow and Ayrshire before joining the Faculty of Education in the University of Paisley. Currently, she is Associate Dean for learning and teaching in the School of Media, Language and Music based at the Ayr Campus of the University. The main focus of her teaching and research is in language, literature and cultural theory, with a particular interest in Scottish culture. She also does work for the Scottish Qualifications Authority, setting and vetting papers for Advanced Higher Language and Scottish Language and Media Studies. Recent publications include: Gifford, A. (1998), 'Dialect in the Classroom', *The Secondary English Magazine*, vol. 2 no.2, Garth Publishing; Gifford, A. (1999), The poetry section in *Using Scottish Texts* ed. David Menzies, Scottish CCC; Gifford, A. and Liddell, G. (2001) *New Scottish Poetry*, Heineman; Gibson, G. and Gifford, A. (2001), *Standard Grade English*: Pupil and Teacher Books, Heineman; Gifford, A. and Robertson E.J. (2002), *Contemporary Scottish Plays for Higher English and Drama*, Hodder and Stoughton.

David Grant is a native of Co. Antrim and a graduate in Law from the University of Cambridge. During the past twenty years, has worked extensively in theatre throughout Ireland as a director and critic. He has been Managing Editor of *Theatre Ireland* magazine, Programme Director of the Dublin Theatre Festival, Director of Ulster Youth Theatre and Artistic Director of the Lyric Theatre, Belfast. He is now Head of Drama at Queen's University. His research interests include the development of youth theatre, theatre-in-education and theatre for young audiences and its impact on mainstream work, and Irish theatre in the twentieth century, with a special emphasis on recent new writing from the north of Ireland. He is author of 'Playing the Wild Card: Community Drama and Small Scale Theatre in Northern Ireland', and edited *The Crack in the Emerald*, a collection of new Irish plays for Nick Hern Books. He has directed more than 100 theatre productions in contexts ranging from Her Majesty's Prison Maghabery to London's Royal National Theatre. Most recently he directed a stage adaptation of Seamus Heaney's *Beowulf*, and directed a Hungarian-language production of Brian Friel's *Translations* for the Hungarian Theatre of Cluj in Romania. He is currently working on a book entitled *The Stagecraft of Brian Friel* for Greenwich Exchange Books.

Professor François Grin is a native of Switzerland. He is Professor of Economics at the School of Translation and Interpretation at the University of Geneva and Adjunct Director of the Education Research Unit. He has served as the Deputy Director of the European Centre for Minority Issues (ECMI) in Germany and taught in Canada and the United States. He is the author of numerous publications in language and education policy evaluation, including his new book *Language Policy Evaluation and the European Charter for Regional or Minority Languages*, which is published by Palgrave and receiving its UK launch at the symposium. (The book has a chapter by Dónall Ó Riagáin providing an overview of the Charter, and a chapter by Regina Jensdóttir on the procedures of ratification and monitoring of the Charter.)

Kieran Hegarty works for the BBC with responsibilities and duties for Irish-medium broadcasting and education.

Dr. Steven King is a graduate of both Queen's University and, for his PhD, the University of Ulster. Stephen a political adviser to David Trimble and as such a senior member of the Ulster Unionist Party. He writes a trenchant weekly column in the *Belfast Telegraph* and for other newspapers. He was once described as 'the Republic's favourite Unionist'. He is a member of Queen's University Belfast Senate.

Dr. John Kirk is a native bairn of Falkirk and a graduate of the Universities of Edinburgh, Sheffield, where he did a PhD on Scots grammar, and Queen's University Belfast. He taught in Bonn and Sheffield before coming to QUB where is currently a Senior Lecturer in English. With Jeffrey Kallen (TCD), he is Co-director of the International Corpus of English Ireland Project and Co-director of a major AHRB-funded research project investigating the sociolinguistics of standardisation of English in Ireland. With a preliminary beta version of the ICE-Ireland corpus now finished, analysis and interpretation has begun for publications including the *ICE-Ireland Handbook* (Benjamins). Previously, he has edited books on linguistic geography and corpus linguistics. With Dónall Ó Baoill, he organises what has become an annual symposium on language and politics currently as a constituent project of the AHRB Research Centre for Irish and Scottish Studies. Dónall and John are the publishers and general editors of Cló Ollscoil na Banríona; together, they have edited *Language and Politics* (2000), *Linguistic Politics* (2001), *Language Planning and Education* (2002) and *Travellers Language* (2002). In 2003, he was appointed as a consultant on the new English-Irish bilingual dictionary commissioned by Foras na Gaeilge and managed by Lexicography MasterClass.

Dr. Alex Law is a native of Parkhead in the east side of Glasgow and is a graduate of the Open University and the University of Edinburgh, where he completed a PhD. He is currently a lecturer in Sociology at the University of Abertay Dundee. His research addresses social, cultural and technological change, with a particular focus on the framing of national identity in Scotland. He co-edited a book on some of these themes, *Boundaries and Identities: Nation, Politics and Culture in Scotland* (2001). His recent articles include studies of newspapers and the reproduction of national consciousness in Scotland, both contemporary, 'Near and Far: banal national identity and the press in Scotland' (2001), and historical 'Tabloid Nation'(2002). Other work includes, the 'Sociology of Culture in Scotland' (2003), a paper on punk culture and British nationalism, 'Jubilee Mugs' (2002), an examination of childhood and film in the movie *Ratcatcher* in 'Magical Urbanism' (2003), and the contradictions of mobile communications in 'Base Station Fears' (2003). He is currently working on a book on the time-spaces of modernist culture.

John Law is a native of Fife and a graduate in English Literature and Moral Philosophy from the University of Glasgow. He is a teacher of English by profession. For most of us, however, he is known as Editor of *Lallans*, the twice-yearly magazine for writing in Scots, as Chair of the Management Committee of the Scots Language Resource Centre in Perth, as one of the most experienced writers of Scots, with a clear sense of how standardisation might be achieved, and as one of Scotland's foremost advocates on behalf of recognition and rights of Scots.

Patricia McAlister is a native of Northern Ireland and a graduate in Italian from Queen's University. Her entire career has been with the Civil Service. Upon devolution, she was appointed Head of the Linguistic Diversity Branch within the Department of Culture, Arts and Leisure. In this role, Pat holds the most strategic position in the devising and implementation of language policy for Government in Northern Ireland. We admire her willingness to consult and to engage in open discussion – far more so than we've experienced with civil servants in Scotland – and are grateful for all her support and participation in all four Language and Politics symposia.

Tómas Mac An Iomaire is a native of Conamara, Co. Galway and is currently Ceannaire with Raidió na Gaeltachta, the national Irish language radio service which forms part of RTÉ's public broadcasting service. The station was first established to provide a comprehensive radio service for the people of the Gaeltacht (Irish-speaking region) and for Irish speakers nationwide and began broadcasting at 3pm on Easter Sunday, 2 April 1972. Raidió na Gaeltachta celebrated its 30th anniversary in 2002. Since 1st October 2001 the station broadcasts 24 hours a day, with a wide range of news and current affairs, magazine programmes, music, sport, discussion and entertainment. *An Ceannaire*, Tomás Mac Con Iomaire has played a central role in their development.

Dr. Gordon McCoy grew up in Saintfield, Co. Down, and is a graduate of Queen's University Belfast, where he completed a PhD on Protestants and the Irish language. He is currently Development Officer with the ULTACH Trust and co-editor of *Gaelic Identities* (Institute of Irish Studies, 2000).

Charles MacDonald is a native of Arisaig completing a PhD on the function of language in Celtic media under Mike Cormack's supervision. He teaches Gàidhlig at beginners level for Stirling and Clackmannan Councils, and chairs an association of organisations aiming to promote Gàidhlig and Scots in Central Region.

Seosamh Mac Donncha is a native of Co. Galway and Chief Executive of Foras na Gaeilge. Formerly, he was Chief Executive of the Gaelic Athletic Association. He is currently Chair of Comhairle Theilifís na Gaeilge, the advisory board for TG4.

Stuart McHardy has been rightly called 'a lad o pairts'. He is a writer, musician, storyteller, poet, researcher, lecturer, broadcaster and activist. When, for five years during the mid-late 90s, he was Director of the Scots Language Resource Centre in Perth, he emerged as one of the most forthright campaigners for the recognition of Scots and its restoration as a national language. His interest in the older Pictish and Celtic Mythology of Scotland is reflected in his books *The Strange Secrets of Ancient Scotland, Scotland: Myth, Legend and Folkore, The Quest for Arthur* and *The Quest for the Nine Maidens* published in March 2003. His interest in drink is reflected in his invaluable *Edinburgh and Leith Pub Guide* and in *Tales of Whisky and Smuggling* – true tales from the eighteenth and nineteenth centuries, which he continues to research. For children, he has written the story of *The Wild Haggis* and *The Greetin-faced Nyaff*. He is currently working on a series of folk tale collections. As a compiler, he has compiled the highly commendable anthology, *Scots Poems to be Read Aloud*. All of Stuart's recent books are published by the Luath Press in Edinburgh.

Dr. Kenneth MacKinnon is Visiting Professor and Emeritus Reader in the Sociology of Language at the University of Hertfordshire, Honorary Fellow in Celtic at the University of Edinburgh, and an Associate Lecturer in Social Sciences, Education and Language Studies of the Open University. From 2000-2002, he served as a member of the Ministerial

Advisory Group on Gaelic (MAGOG) and co-authored *A Fresh start for Gaelic*. He is internationally known for his work in demo- and ethno-linguistics, and language planning and development. His research interests include a focus on Celtic language groups, the Gaelic language and Cornish.

Ishbel MacLennan is a native of the Island of Lewis in Scotland and a graduate in Gaelic from Glasgow University. Her entire career has been in broadcasting with the BBC. She joined BBC Radio nan Gaidheal, in 1987 and is currently Editor Gaelic Programmes, based in Inverness with BBC Craoladh nan Gaidheal. This is a multi-media department which transmits an average of 65 hours per week on radio and 150 hours annually on television. Amongst her current responsibilities are the scheduling of programmes and the management of independent production for the department.

Dr. Wilson McLeod is an American by birth and a graduate of the Haverford College in Pennsylvania, Harvard University, where he studied law, and the University of Edinburgh, where he took his PhD in Celtic studies.. His research interests are in language policy and planning issues in Scotland and internationally; language legislation and language rights; the cultural politics of Irish and Scottish Gaelic literature from the late medieval period to the present day. From his many recent articles, those relevant to the symposium include 'Language Planning as Regional Development? The Growth of the Gaelic Economy', *Scottish Affairs* (2002), 'Gaelic in the New Scotland: Politics, Rhetoric and Public Discourse', *Journal on Ethnopolitics and Minority Issues in Europe* (Summer 2001).

Catherine Ann McNeil is a Research Officer and Team Leader at the Lèirsinn Research Centre which provides research services to the people of the Highlands and Islands, and Gaelic communities of Scotland. Research work is commissioned from a variety of sponsoring bodies in the areas of: Education, Social and Economic Development, European Minority languages, Culture, Heritage and Community, and Broadcasting. Currently, Lèirsinn is undertaking four pieces of media research: two are sponsored by sponsored by The Gaelic Broadcasting Committee: The Gaelic Television Audience Response Project, and a Longitudinal Analysis; two are sponsored by BBC Scotland: the Provision of Reach Figures for Gaelic Radio and Television; and Response to Service Developments on BBC Radio nan Gàidheal. With all this research behind her, Catherine Anne McNeil is in a strong and rather privileged position for providing a critical assessment of the state of Gaelic-medium Broadcasting in Scotland.

Mairéad Ní Nuadháin is a native of Ballaghaderreen, Co. Roscommon. She lived for many years in Galway, where she was a founder member of the Druid Theatre. Much of her career has been in broadcasting. Since 2000, she has been Commissioning Editor for Irish Language, Multi-cultural and Educational Programmes.. Before that, she had been originator and series producer of *Léargas*. She has also produced entertainment programmes and documentaries. Her department contributes current affairs, sport, magazine and childrens' programmes to TG4 and originated RTE's first inter-cultural series, *Mono*.

Dr. Dónall Ó Baoill is a native of West Donegal and a graduate of UCG and the University of Michigan. For 25 years, he worked at the ITÉ, Dublin. Since 1999, he has Professor of Irish at Queen's University Belfast and, since 2002, Head of the School of Languages, Literature and Arts. He has published on all aspects of language pertaining to Ireland, especially Irish, and including Travellers' language and Sign language. He is also co-author of *The Irish Deaf Community* Volume 2, *The Structure of Irish Sign Language* (ITÉ, Dublin 2000), and his recent edited books include *TEANGA 19* (IRAAL, Dublin 2000*)* and *Integrating Theory and Practice in LSP and LAP* (ALC & IRAAL, Dublin 2000). With John Kirk, he organises what has become an annual symposium on language and politics currently as a constituent project of the AHRB Research Centre for Irish and Scottish Studies. John and Dónall are the publishers and general editors of Cló Ollscoil na Banríona; together, they have edited *Language and Politics* (2000), *Linguistic Politics* (2001), *Language Planning and Education* (2002) and *Travellers Language* (2002). In 2003, he was appointed Editor-in-Chief of the new English-Irish bilingual dictionary commissioned by Foras na Gaeilge and managed by Lexicography MasterClass.

Pádhraic Ó Ciardha is a native of Cois Fharrige in the Connemara Gaeltacht and a graduate in Celtic Studies (BA) and Modern Irish (MA) from St Patrick's College Maynooth. His entire career has been in broadcasting where he held a number of posts in broadcast journalism in Irish and English before being seconded to act as Advisor to the Ministers of Broadcasting responsible for establishing Teilifís na Gaeilge. He joined TG4 in 1995 and is currently Leascheannasaí (Deputy Director).   TG4 was established and currently operates under the corporate and statutory wing of RTÉ. Since the outset, it has been envisaged that the service will ultimately be set on an independent corporate footing. The Broadcasting Act 2001 contains provisions that enable the Minister for Arts, Heritage, Gaeltacht and the Islands to do this, although, to date, no Minister has not made an order to activate this section of the Act. The service is overseen by Comhairle Theilifís na Gaeilge; an advisory body of the RTÉ Authority which comprises a thirteen member board and which is currently chaired by Seosamh Mac Donncha

Seosamh Ó Cuaig (Joe Cooke) is a well known public figure in the Gaeltacht Community as he has always been very active in Gaeltacht affairs and politics down through the years, as well as being a reporter with Radio na Gaeltachta. Joe was born in Aill na Brún, Cill Chiaráin, Connemara in 1949. He attended Kieran's National School before attending Meánscoil Sheosamh in Carna, where he sat his Leaving Certificate in 1967. He started his first job the same year for the *Mayo News* newspaper. He also worked for the Irish language newspaper *Inniu*. Joe was involved in the establishment of Saor Raidio Chonamara, a pirate community radio station in the late sixties. It was around this time that he first went on-air. Joe was also one of the founders of the Gaeltacht Civil Rights Movement. He fought for the rights of, not alone the Connemara Gaeltacht community, but the Gaeltacht community in general throughout the country. He also spent several years working for Cló Chois Fharraige, where he translated and edited books. Joe initially started working for Raidió na Gaeltachta as a freelance journalist in the news department when the station first opened in 1972. He stayed with the station for several years on a contract basis but is now working there permanently as a news journalist. He is frequently to be heard on the radio reading national and international news. Joe is also involved with television and he has made several TV documentaries, including, 'Na Connemaras of Minnesota' and 'Taibhsí na Staire'. Joe began his official political career in 1988/89 when he ran for the Údarás na Gaeltachta election on behalf of the 'Cumhacht' (i.e. 'power') party. He was easily elected that year. He ran again in December 1999 on his own initiative as an independent candidate and was once again elected to the Board of An tÚdarás. He is still living in his native Aill na Brún, Cill Chiaráin.

Ciarán Ó Duibhín is a native of Newry and a graduate of QUB in Applied Mathematics and of UU in Linguistics. In his time as a lecturer in Computer Science at Queen's University, he facilitated the introduction of computing techniques into numerous research projects in the humanities. He has developed the textbase of Modern Gaelic *Tobar na Gaedhilge*, and a bibliography of Gaelic in East Ulster, and he acts as a computing adviser to Foclóir na Nua-Ghaeilge at the Royal Irish Academy. Web site: www.smo.uhi.ac.uk/~oduibhin .

Ciarán Ó Pronntaigh is a native of Omagh and a graduate of Coleraine in 1989. He has been editor of the Irish language newspaper *Lá* since September2000, when he replaced Eoghan Ó Néill. Before this, Ciarán was editor of the magazine *An tUltach* and also worked with the Council for Curriculum and Educational Assessment (CCEA) in Belfast.

Dr. Des O'Rawe is a native of Belfast and a graduate in English from Queen's University Belfast. Prior to his appointment as a Lecturer in Film Studies at Queen's, he had taught at various further and higher education institutions. He has published articles on Irish film, literature and cultural politics and his co-edited book *Ireland (Ulster) Scotland: Concepts, Contexts, Comparisons* appeared from Cló Ollscoil na Banríona in 2003.

Dónall Ó Riagáin is a native of Dublin and is an Honorary Fellow of Trinity College, Carmarthen. He was a founding member and first President of the European Bureau for Lesser Used Languages (1982-1984) and served as the organisation's Secretary General from 1984 until 1998 – a post which he held with great distinction. He is now a freelance consultant, whose advice is regularly sought world-wide. He is the author of numerous papers on planning and developing minority languages and implementing policy, and is one of the world's most pre-eminent authorities in those fields. Most recently, he was written the chapter on organisational issues arising from implementing the European Charter in Francois Grin's book *Language Policy Evaluation* and edited the papers from the symposium held at Stormont in February 2003 for publication as *Language and Law in Northern Ireland* (2003, Cló Ollscoil na Banríona). He is a member of the International Advisory Committee of Linguapax (UNESCO).

Janet Paisley is a versatile short story writer, poet and playwright who relishes the different disciplines of the different forms. She set-up and co-ordinated the first Scottish PEN Women's Committee which inaugurated the Naomi Mitchison Memorial Lectures and has has published five collections of poetry: *Pegasus in Flight* [1989], *Images* [1990], *Biting through Skins* [1992], *Alien Crop* [1996], *Reading the Bones* [1999], the prose collection, *Wild Fire* [1993], and a collection of her poetic monologues, *Ye Cannae Win* [2000] in the Chapman Wild Women series. A leading Scottish writer of drama for stage, television, radio, and cinema, she was a member of the Working Party for a Scottish National Theatre and has held numerous writing fellowships. Her work has been translated into Russian, Italian, Spanish, Bulgarian, Hungarian and Slovakian and she has spoken and read at many international literary events. One of her play scripts, *Refuge*, won the prestigious Peggy Ramsay Award in 1996. Her short film, *Long Haul*, won nominations for BAFTA's best new screenwriter 2001 and RTS best TV drama 2002. In 2000, she won a Creative Scotland Award to write *Not for Glory*, a collection of linked short stories in Scots, set in Glen Village near Falkirk, where she lives. The project involved working with young people in the community, encouraging them to realise that 'literature comes from your own doorstep and in voices that you know'.

Ian James Parsley is a native of Groomsport and a graduate in Germanic Languages and Spanish from the University of Newcastle-upon-Tyne. In 1999, he launched the ULLANS-L emailing list and accompanying website, and since then he has founded the Ulster-Scots Research Centre and Ultonia. With the demise of the Northern Ireland Assembly, his career as a lobbyist became suspended, but his translation, editing and PR services continue unabated.. Ian has been a consultant to the Ulster-Scots Agency, a regular commentator on Ulster-Scots as well as general minority-language issues.

Dr. David Purves is a native of the Scottish borders and is an academic in biochemistry by training and profession. His absorption of borders Scots into his veins as a child combined with his considerable literary talents has made him into one of Scotland's foremost writers in Scots during the past half-century. As editor of *Lallans* magazine, with he gained unrivalled experience for editing and standardising Scots which came to be reflected in his extremely sound *A Scots Grammar*, a second edition of which was launched in at last year's symposium. David Purves has written eight plays, including *The Puddock an the Princess* (based on the Frog prince theme), *Whuppitie Stourie* (based on Rumplestiltskin) and several translations including *The Tragedie o MacBeth* (from Shakespeare), *The Thrie Sisters* (from Chekhov), and *The Ootlaw* (from Strindberg), all of which deserve to be better known and more often performed. He has also written countless poems.

Christine Robinson is a native of Perth. She studied English Language and Literature at the University of Edinburgh where she completed a PhD in English Language at Edinburgh in 1988. Her publications include an edition of the *Speculum Vitae* and studies on Older Scots and Modern Scots. With Carol Ann Crawford, she wrote *Scotspeak* (Perth: Scots Language Resource Centre, 2001), a guide intended for use by actors, on the accents of Glasgow, Edinburgh, Dundee and Aberdeen. She is currently teaching part-time in the Department of English Language at Edinburgh University and also lectures on Scots for the University of the Highlands and Islands. She is Director of Outreach and Administration for Scottish Language Dictionaries and has recently launched their Scots website for schoolchildren, www.scuilwab.org.uk, which she is continuing to develop, with the help of teachers, with a view to making it a significant Scots teaching resource.

Prof. Dr. Eduardo J. Ruiz Vieytez is a native of the Basque Country and a graduate in Law. He is currently Director of the Pedro Arrupe Institute of Human Rights at the University of Deusto-Bilbao (Basque Country), which was founded in 1997 in response to the pressing social demand for an academic contribution to the promotion of human rights and long-lasting peace in a democratic society. He has been juridical assessor to the Ombudsman in the Basque Parliament and he is the author of several publications in the fields of environmental law, the Basque electoral system, immigration law and minority rights. He has been a member of the Spanish Board on Immigration and has participated as expert in several missions of the Council of Europe on linguistic minorities. He has also been invited to teach in other European universities such as Derby (UK), Tilburg (Netherlands) and Lyon 3 (France). His main publications include *The History of Legal Protection of Minorities in Europe (XVIIth–XXth centuries)* (Derby: University of Derby, 1999).

Chris Spurr is Yorkshire-born and a graduate in English from the University of Leeds. He recently received an MA in Media Management, also from Leeds. Apart from an early flirtation with theatre in England and Ireland, his entire career has been in broadcasting with the BBC. He is Head of BBC Northern Ireland's Ulster-Scots Unit. for Ulster-Scots broadcasting and is the producer of highly-acclaimed Ulster-Scots magazine programme *A Kist o Words*. Within the BBC, he holds one of the few central positions within the corporation for the development of broadcasting both in and about Scots. At the Celtic Film and Television Festival held in Belfast in April 2003, Chris took part in a debate on Ulster-Scots culture entitled 'Ar Yis Taakin Tae Me?'

Dr. Alan Titley is a native of Cork and was educated at St. Patrick's College, Drumcondra, where is now Ceann Roinne (Senior Lecturer) in Gaelic. His *Pocket History of Gaelic Culture* appeared in 2000 (O'Brien). He has published numerous novels in Irish including *Méirscrí na treibhe* (1978), *Stiall Fhial Feola* (1980) and *An Fear Dána* (1993) based on the life of Muireadhach Albanach.

John Walsh is a native of Dublin and a graduate in Irish and Welsh of University College Dublin and in International Relations of Dublin City University. He is currently working on PhD research at DCU on the Irish language and socio-economic development, and he works as lecturer in Applied Irish at the same university. Formerly, he was a journalist with RTÉ with whom he continues to broadcast occasionally. His book *Díchoimisiúnú Teanga: Coimisiún na Gaeltachta 1926* was published in Dublin by Cois Life in 2002. He is also a contributor on the Irish language to the newly-published *Encyclopaedia of Ireland* (Gill & Macmillan).

ACKNOWLEDGEMENTS

Many people have helped us with ideas and suggestions which led to the programme at the symposium and subsequently to the papers in this volume. We are grateful to:

- Tom Devine and George Watson, Arts and Humanities Research Board's Research Centre for Irish and Scottish Studies, University of Aberdeen, for supporting, indeed championing, the symposia and the edited proceedings as one of the Centre's constituent projects
- Derrick McClure, and the Forum for Research on the Languages of Scotland and Ulster Committee for their unflinching support and on whose behalf the symposia are organised
- to Iomairt Cholm Cille, which enabled the participation of so many Scottish Gaels, and to Foras na Gaeilge and Tha Boord o Ulstèr-Scotch, for additional funding, without which we could not meet participants' and other expenses of the event
- each of the contributors for their willingness and co-operation in writing to our agenda and accepting our editorial style
- Minister Éamon Ó Cúiv, TD for his coherent and candid reflection of the views of Republic of Ireland's Government on Irish, in a talk at the symposium dinner on 19 September 2003.
- John Hume, MP, MEP, who will launch this volume early in 2004
- John Corbett for enabling the inclusion of papers from the conference on *Language and News Media* organised by the Language Committee of the Association for Scottish Literary Studies and held fortuitously at the University of Stirling on 15 November 2003, and to those contributors (Neil Blain and Anne Gifford, Alex Law, and Christine Robinson) for letting us have such polished papers so soon afterwards
- Gordon McCoy for originally offering his paper on *Ros na Rún* for the symposium and for kindly letting us include it in the present volume
- Dónall Ó Riagáin for his numerous suggestions and very practical help throughout the year
- our simultaneous translators: Philip Campbell for Irish, Doileag Nic Leoid for Gaelic, and Máire Ó Baoill for French, and to Doileag Nic Leoid for the generous donation
- the skill, patience and advice of our printers at Optech, especially to John Doherty and Nigel Craig and to their staff
- all those many others, including our colleagues at Queen's University Belfast, who have patiently answered our queries or simply wished us well
- Colin Neilands and Máire Ó Baoill for their patience and loving support

Our biggest debt, as always, is to each other – without each other, we simply could not have done this or any of symposia or volumes of edited papers involving either the three *stewartries* of Northern Ireland, the Republic of Ireland, and Scotland or the two *Sprachbunde* of the Gaeltacht and Scotstacht.

John M. Kirk   *Dónall P. Ó Baoill*
December 2003

Towards our Goals in Broadcasting, the Press, the Performing Arts and the Economy: Minority Languages in Northern Ireland, the Republic of Ireland, and Scotland

John M. Kirk and Dónall P. Ó Baoill

The papers in this volume arise from the Fourth Symposium on Language and Politics,[1] which was held at Queen's University Belfast from 16-20 September 2003.[2] They are supplemented by three papers from a conference on Language and the Media in Scotland, held at the University of Stirling on 15 November 2003 and organised by the Language Committee of the Association for Scottish Literary Studies.[3]

One of the most imaginative and far-reaching cross-community aspects of the *Belfast (Good Friday) Agreement* of 1998 was its recognition of the importance of language issues – especially Irish and Ulster Scots. This provision led in 1999 to acts of implementation and the creation of two cross-border bodies, Foras na Gaeilge and Tha Boord o Ulstèr-Scotch. Those bodies were established with remits of language promotion and development, much of which had been inspired by the *European Charter for Regional or Minority Languages*, administered by the Council of Europe. In 2000, the UK government signed the Charter with regard to Irish and Scots in Northern Ireland, and Gaelic and Scots in Scotland, but no corresponding action was taken by the Dáil – no doubt because of as well as in spite of its status as the Republic's 'first official language'. In 2001, the UK Government ratified the Charter and a submitted a report of progress in 2002. That report was investigated by an ad hoc Committee of Experts appointed by the Council of Europe who visited Scotland and Northern Ireland in January 2003. Their report is awaited with keen interest.

In ratifying the European Charter, the UK Government and its Executives and Agencies in Northern Ireland and Scotland had to acknowledge that certain provisions were in place to promote Scots in Scotland and Northern Ireland, and a lot more provisions were in place to promote and develop Gaelic in Scotland and Irish in Northern Ireland. Those provisions have proved to be hugely controversial, as both submissions to and meetings with the Committee of Experts showed. For some, the provisions were considered to be a restatement of a minimalist status quo, in effect complacently rubber-stamping inadequate current practice. For

---

[1] Volumes of previous symposium papers are published by Cló Ollscoil na Banríona as John M. Kirk and Dónall P. Ó Baoill eds. *Language and Politics: Northern Ireland, the Republic of Ireland, and Scotland* (2000), John M. Kirk and Dónall P. Ó Baoill eds. *Linguistic Politics: Language Policies for Northern Ireland, the Republic of Ireland, and Scotland* (2001), *and* John M. Kirk and Dónall P. Ó Baoill eds. *Language Planning and Education: Linguistic Issues in Northern Ireland, the Republic of Ireland, and Scotland* (2002).

[2] Presentations by Alex Hijmans (*Foinse*), Malcolm MacLean (Pròiseact nan Ealan), Geared Ó Cairealláin (Aisling Ghéar, An Chultúrlaan) Pól Ó Múirí (Irish Editor, *Irish Times*) and the symposium dinner address by Minister Eamon Ó Cúiv, TD, have not led to submissions to this volume.

[3] On that occasion, the following papers were also presented: 'BBC Scotland: Language and the Web, by Jill Adair, and "Broadcasting and Public Discourse' by David Hutchison.

others, the provisions were considered to be a statement of a lack of intentions to undertake any promotion and development, much to the annoyance of activists and practitioners who argued just the opposite – that considerably more initiatives would be needed if promotion and development were to made in any constructive way. For many Scots activists on both sides of the North Channel, the Government's most controversial decision was to deny Scots and Ulster-Scots Part III recognition alongside Gaelic, since when strong arguments in terms of discrimination, rights and equality have been advanced by activist groups.

Four areas of the Charter's provision – status, discrimination, rights, and education – formed the focus of our previous symposia. This present symposium focuses on those other areas of provision in Part III of the European Charter which we have not yet visited – 'The Media', 'Cultural Activities and Facilities' and 'Economic and Social Life', which domains for practical purposes we have divided into 'broadcasting' (i.e. radio and television), 'the press', 'the performing arts' (for our purposes, we have interpreted those as drama and film and the related activity of script-writing), and 'the economy'. From the outset, it was clear that, in all of those domains, the provisions in the Republic of Ireland are completely different – despite the obvious linguistic continuities across the Northern Ireland border.

Broadcasting and the performing arts form a natural pair. Each involves the use of speech; but whereas each reflects naturally-occurring speech, each is distinctive because of its functional uses, often quite different from naturally-occurring speech. Moreover, much broadcast or performed speech is first written for that purpose, so that questions of standardisation quickly arise. Broadcasting and the performing arts are not quite about ordinary people speaking naturally – yet it is to the status and impact of broadcasting and the language used on the stage, on television and on the big screen, that many will turn for legitimation and reinforcement of their everyday speech patterns and their use. Although they reflect ordinary speech, it is the heightened generic uses of broadcasting, drama and film which come to regarded as models and standards of acceptability.

By their ubiquity and popularity, television and radio have enormous impact on people's lives; on the other hand, drama and film have the potential to heighten and aggrandise the language into memorable, sometimes powerful, virtuoso works of art. Each can generate confidence. Given that the language policies of the European Charter and the implementation bodies in Northern Ireland are about language promotion and development, it is appropriate and timely to initiate a critical review of the roles of television, radio, the press, and scripts for the stage and film in the context of minority language development so that we may better come to understand their impact upon speakers and questions of status. To this end, we formulated five questions, which we wanted to have addressed at this symposium, and which were also circulated to speakers.

The symposium title *Towards Our Goals: The media, the performing arts, and the economy in minority language and personal development in Northern Ireland, the Republic of Ireland, and Scotland* sums up the overall developmental theme in those key domains which we had in mind. Those invited to speak were asked to consider the following questions:

1. How do the Media, the Performing Arts, and the Economy contribute to minority language development? How do they contribute to the personal development of those languages' speakers? In each of those areas, what is

being done in the context of language development? And where are those efforts leading? How far, in respect of each area, is the *European Charter for Regional or Minority Languages* being implemented in Scotland and Northern Ireland, and how far does the Charter fall short? What should be done? What are the obstacles to anything being done? What are the solutions to those obstacles? How does the Languages Equality Bill address those issues in the Republic of Ireland? And, again, the same questions may be asked: how far does the Bill fall short? What should be done? What are the obstacles to anything being done? What are the solutions to those obstacles?

2. For whom are minority language outputs from broadcasting and the media and the performing arts intended? Who decides? And with what success?

3. By using minority languages, what questions are broadcasting, the press, the performing arts addressing? How coordinated is the policy for broadcasting, the press, the performing arts coordinate with language development policy?

4. How far, with regard to minority languages, is the notion of the Economy restricted to those very areas under discussion: the media and the performing arts? And how much further might that notion of Economy stretch?

5. In broadcasting, the press, and the performing arts: What cross-current themes are being addressed by using minority languages? Are those cross-current themes educational or cultural or developmental? Are those themes coordinated between broadcasting, the press and the performing arts?

6. How far do minority languages in broadcasting, the press and the performing arts express or substantiate culture, and how far is their use merely symbolic?

7. How far is the use of minority languages in broadcasting, the press and the performing arts simply an educational issue? Or where do the boundaries fall?

Those seven sets of questions struck us as the key questions for the presentations at the symposium and those written papers.

Inevitably, not everybody addressed those themes and no-one addressed all of them. Nevertheless, we were greatly encouraged both by the extent to which they were addressed and handled explicitly and also by the creativity in many papers which added to the questions which we had identified. In this introduction, we provide for each contribution a summary which includes, where proposed, any answers or solutions. Finally, attempt to bring the entire book together in a short synthesis.

Broadcasting

There are no fewer than 14 contributions on this topic covering The Republic of Ireland, Northern Ireland and Scotland.

The first contribution is by **Patricia McAlister**, Head of Language Diversity, DCAL. She outlines the policy framework directing the department's work, describes what is being done regarding broadcasting of minority indigenous language in Northern Ireland (NI), and gives some indication of future developments. Their work is being driven by provisions within the *Belfast (Good Friday) Agreement*, the work of the North/South Implementation Bodies, the application of the provisions of the *European Charter for Regional and Minority Languages* and the *Communications Act 2003*. Working with the broadcasting industry is a crucial and central element in achieving respect, tolerance and understanding of the problems associated with the promotion of minority languages. Although the BBC has made lasting contributions to Irish and Ulster-Scots through radio broadcasting, there has been no comparable support historically from BBC Northern Ireland or UTV for Irish-language broadcasting on a similar level as is provided for Welsh in Wales and for Gàidhlig in Scotland. DCAL agreed that a report produced for the ULTACH Trust about broadcasting and the Irish language in NI should be taken as a starting point to test demand, and a two phased pilot programme was initiated at a cost of £250,000 each, to run over a period of two years. The project is expected to identify training priority requirements and hence to develop suitable training courses. Having consulted widely in NI, Scotland and elsewhere a multi-skilling course was run and successfully completed by 14 participants. The Government is committed to broadcasting provisions in respect of Article 11 (Part III of the Charter) but it is awaiting the Council of Europe's first report about the implementation of the Charter. A draft Bill published in May 2002 referred to the commitments in the *Belfast (Good Friday) Agreement* and indicated it would give effect to these commitments in order to promote understanding, respect and tolerance for linguistic diversity within NI. The passing of the UK *Communications Act 2003*, however, was greeted by astonishment and disbelief as it contained no reference at all to the promotion of Irish in NI. After much subsequent debate at Westminster and Stormont, a training and production fund of £12 million was to be made available over 3 years, subject to the preparation of an acceptable business plan. A draft report is presently under consideration.

Aled Eírug has been involved in a review of minority language provision within NI for the BBC and reports on his findings in his article. He makes certain comparisons with the Welsh language broadcasting situation. He admits, however, that the language situation in NI is more polarized but creating a consensus imposes a responsibility to reflect differing cultures and languages as long as the demand for them is real and reflects a social reality. The BBC has an abiding commitment to representing this linguistic and cultural diversity in its programmes. All services and programming related to Irish and Ulster Scots are to be increased on television, radio and online, including existing programmes. The BBC recognizes, however, that there are differences in the linguistic and cultural development of both languages and in their domains of usage. Irish is an accepted medium of communication in an extensive variety of formal and informal contexts, including broadcasting and education in particular. Audience research is underway, which will influence and inform the scope and range of suitable programming in the future. Funding for the new training initiatives has already been alluded to and is fully supported by the BBC and will fund television, radio and online programming. This will be done in collaboration with TG4 and other broadcasting services. TG4 in particular must be able to transmit fully into NI and if and when the Production Fund is created, it will become incumbent on all parties to ensure TG4's availability throughout NI is secured. Language services are provided within broadcasting because they form a precious and, at this point, valuable part of our heritage. The commitment by the Government to the creation of the fund is an important first step and producers and broadcasters must ensure that these good intentions are converted into successful and creative programming.

Kieran Hegarty from BBC Northern Ireland's Education Unit addresses the particular question of how broadcasting can contribute to the welfare and development of minority languages. The media plays an important role in all our lives and its contribution to minority languages has the ability to synthesise scarce resources and increase interactivity along various parameters. Irish always had limited access to many spheres and domains of usage because the needs of the majority monoglot English language development is no exception. Digital media offers great scope, and choice of access to speaking population came first. With the new proliferation of output channels, there are far more new possibilities and openings coming on stream. Shared traditional and cultural values before the impact of television were imparted through family and local community activities. At present, the individual is more at the mercy of outside influences through media and technological advances. He/she may have no particular traditional allegiance to any of those influences. Media in minority languages has an important role to play in the personal development of speakers and learners of minority languages, especially in the fields of education and entertainment. This will give the media the chance to respond to the real needs of individuals and society, including minority language speakers. There are signs of a more comprehensive service for minority languages in the very near future and the creation of the film and television fund will create opportunities of increasing relevance to the welfare of minority languages in broadcasting. Minority language outputs are addressed to a wide range of people, including fluent speakers, advanced learners, All-Irish school pupils and adult learners. Programmes addressed at minority language populations much have wide appeal, provide a distinctive and different angle and world view of various events that impinge on our daily lives. Professional broadcasters aided by good consultation practices and audience feedback should be able to make decisions about the content of relevant programming. This should help broadcasters to get closer to communities and individuals and to the issues that impact on their lives. Addressing regional linguistic and cultural diversity is a big challenge and, if done well, will contribute substantially to work being done by other educational, cultural and community organizations. In this way, learning becomes embedded in many aspects of media output. The use of the latest technologies and methodologies of broadcasting, as well as developments concerning language learning and maintenance among language minorities, coupled with increasing accessibility and interaction for communities should bring better quality programming.

In his paper, **Chris Spurr**, Producer and Head of BBC Northern Ireland's Ulster-Scots unit, reports on the BBC NI's contribution to Ulster Scots. In doing so, Spurr stresses that the views presented are his own, and secondly that he prefers to avoid the 'inaccurate' term *language* in referring to Ulster Scots. It is important for folk to hear their tongue being broadcast on BBC as it adds credence to its use as an alternative medium to English. Ulster Scots programming became a reality on 6th March 2002 when Conal Gillespie presented his first A *Kist o Wurds*. As much Ulster Scots as is possible is used on the programmes depending on how comfortable and confident speakers are in using it and expressing themselves freely in it. What is important, however, is that, once it is heard on radio, it reinforces its usage else where and especially in classroom discussions. Decisions about programming are made at senior level within the BBC and, while suggestions may be put forward, there is no guarantee that they will be implemented. What is of relevance and significant is the development of people's understanding of Ulster Scots among native speakers and learners. This also leaves scope for a radio series for Ulster Scots learners and genuinely interested parties. Programmes presented so far have been well received by a wide cross-section of the population of NI and demonstrate above all the living quality of Ulster Scots. Various documentaries and a dedicated website established under the pan-BBC *Voices* Project will make access to Ulster Scots voices available to all these with internet facilities. At present, the use of Ulster Scots is not an educational issue, but future developments may change all of that. The majority of cross-current themes veer towards the cultural. Better co-ordination is required between broadcasting, the press and media in general and drama has not featured on either television or radio. There is no agreement so far on a formal language development policy and input from professionals with teaching and linguistic expertise is a necessary next step if we are to further the cause of Ulster Scots. Although the number of programmes is small, they are making a genuine contribution to the development Ulster Scots speech and usage. At present, there is no sign of a dedicated radio or TV channel for Ulster Scots, and it is subject to debate whether or not the small number of broadcasting hours satisfies the implementation referred to in the provisions of the European Charter.

Seosamh Ó Cuaig has had extensive experience as a broadcaster with Raidió na Gaeltachta and has researched and presented several well-received documentaries on television (TG4). He is well placed to evaluate and comment on the importance of radio work and its impact on the Irish language and its future development. He has often asked himself the question whether all the broadcasting is having an affect on the community and who exactly is listening in. Through meeting and talking to various people from different sociolinguistic backgrounds and domains, both here in Ireland and to the Irish diaspora throughout the world, but particularly in the United States and Canada, he has come to a clearer understanding of the importance of his work and how many of the listeners find the themes and discussions uplifting and encourages further development and pride in the native indigenous language. Above all he feels that Raidió na Gaeltachta must present its own particular view on world and home affairs through the medium of the Irish language. This 'methodology', as he calls it, is best represented by the phrase 'Súil Eile' ('Another Eye View'). It must be a genuine heart felt view not driven by consumerism or homogenization or imperialism or many of the other ills associated with modern society. There is a constant fight between modernity and old ideas, but it should be obvious to any keen observer that there are many features within both that should be preserved and cultivated. He insists that we should be aware of 'translating' American propaganda and he gives the fine example of the fall of Saigon and how he dealt with this particular news item. Above all we must have the highest regard and respect for the language – otherwise it is all in vain. It is a fact of life here in Ireland that the people in charge at senior level in broadcasting are people who have learned Irish but, at times, not very well. They tend to impose their own norms on more competent speakers, including native speakers. This should be resisted by all the means at our disposal.

Tomás Mac An Iomaire is Director of Raidió na Gaeltachta. He gives a clear and succinct presentation in his paper on the philosophy behind the programming on Raidió na Gaeltachta. He poses several questions – is it worth having as a service? Could we do without it? How is it contributing to our life and personal development? We watch programmes, which we enjoy and which fill a certain need or void in our lives. He is fully convinced that there is a large cohort of listeners out there that feel we can't do without the services provided by Raidió na Gaeltachta. Raidió na Gaeltachta believes in what it does and above all in the medium through which it provides its services to the public – the Irish language. We must keep out listeners informed of all matters in which they have an interest and since that interest in wider than the local community, we need to complement our local service so as to encompass national and international news and events. Above all the provision must check language development. Raidió na Gaeltachta has never outlined a planned programme to develop Irish or to save the language. This is not its role. However, through the high standards of its programming and through its secondary role in supporting the Irish language come to terms with modern idiom and usage, it performs an important role in securing the language's future. It has also advanced the cause of Irish music in general and has provided a platform for top class artists and people with national and international reputations. While it doesn't teach Irish, it nevertheless provides through its programmes a rich database of authentic materials to be accessed by learners at different levels of language development. It has connections with BBC Radio Ulster and with BBC Radio nan Gaedhal and in the latter case present a weekly bilingual programme in Irish and Scottish Gaelic. It is of crucial importance for minority language media to be independent of political and governmental pressure and pressures being exercised by minority language organizations. The media have an important role in cultivating and developing languages and cultures. It is, therefore, important that we initiate proper and ongoing debate about the role of the media involved in broadcasting to minority language groups. This symposium initiated this process.

Mairéad Ní Nuadhain from RTÉ addresses many of the issues raised by the symposium and concludes that language development per se is not part of RTÉ's brief and the *Language Bill* will have very little direct impact on their work. Her prime role at present is to commission Irish medium programmes for RTÉ and 182.5 hours of programmes in Irish for TG4. It is also her brief to ensure that Irish is spoken on special occasions. Those competent in Irish have been very successful within RTÉ's structure as the previous and present Director Generals exemplify. Recently, a series of 20 half-hour programmes have been commissioned for Irish language learners. The series will contain a real-life soap opera drama – five minutes per programme. All the work and preparation is being done in Irish, including work by camera crews. The 2001 *Broadcasting Act* sates that RTÉ must reflect in its programme the cultural diversity of the island of Ireland and cater for the expectations of the community with special minority interests and facilitate, encourage and promote innovation. In regard to the Irish language more programmes of a bilingual nature and those aimed at learners of all ages should be available on RTÉ and TG4. She is in the privileged position of being able to make many of the decisions herself and the most fruitful recommendation that she made was to have open subtitling throughout the programme. This has been facilitated by ongoing developments in TG4. Programmes are aimed at the highest audiences one can get at a particular time at night. It was never the intention of general programmes to revive Irish or to address all the needs of Gaeltacht audiences. Circumstances have changed over the years and because of the widespread choice available today, one can not make meaningful comparisons with successful programmes such as *Féach*, which had audiences of 600,000 at its peak. Audiences on the whole form a good cross-section of society, economic classes and age groups. RTÉ must provide Raidió na Gaeltachta with 365 hours of programming a year according to section 47 of the *Broadcasting Act*. They are divided equally between news and commissioned or bought in programmes. Last year 2002, RTÉ spent 8.578 million euro on those two services, which is no small feat.

Pádraic Ó Ciardha of TG4 said that the time is now ripe to undertake broadcasting in all of the Celtic languages of these islands. His proposals and recommendations are based on the results contained in Don Anderson's report, copies of which were distributed to all those attending the symposium. Broadcasting was denied over the geographical and time limitations were imposed on the areas in which there was a right to broadcast. That era is now coming to an end – the digitalization is with us – national and international regulations are being relaxed – one satellite can send a signal all over Europe. Two people have taken a pivotal role in these recent developments Rupert Murdoch and Greg Dyke – the former by establishing Sky television and BSkyB – the latter by setting up the Freestat system within the BBC in 2003 – all radio and television programmes can now be had unencrypted without rent or yearly subscriptions. All you have to do is buy the relevant equipment with a once off payment. The logical outcome of all this is that TG4 should be made easily and freely available throughout NI. This is what the *Belfast (Good Friday) Agreement* recommended. Irish speakers throughout the UK have language rights – those in Liverpool, Huddersfield, London or Glasgow. TG4 being available on Freestat would solve this problem of distribution and make the channel available in all corners of the UK. We must always remember that speakers of minority languages also speak a major language, and that it is they who ultimately make the choice which channel they watch. Audience research must constantly bear this in mind in analyzing their data.

Catherine Ann MacNeil talks about the critical issues affecting broadcasting in Scottish Gaelic. Recent advances in technology and the communications industry have advanced consumer choice and are beginning to break down geographical barriers. However, this brings in its wake a greater emphasis on homogeneity and the introduction of a globalised culture. The paper focuses on the strengths and weaknesses of Gaelic Broadcasting in Scotland within the context of the European Charter. A dedicated radio station broadcasts Gaelic programmes regularly as well as established slots for television at peak times on digital. Core audience research is available since 1993 and shows that the response to all new developments has been extremely positive. The sustained loyalty to the provision on television is due to wider expectations among its viewers such as support for language at home, access to authentic idiomatic Gaelic, the promotion of Gaelic culture both traditional and contemporary and acting as a standard bearer for the language. Various gaps appear in the provision for children, young people and learners of the language. Television seems to have no control over its destiny. Audiences have expressed concern about scheduling, quality and diversity of Gaelic programming. Continuity of output is an issue of concern – programming at its peak during autumn and winter and very little available during the summer. Regular slots are important in order to built up audiences. The range of programmes broadcast at present is insufficient to appeal to a whole spectrum of viewers. Viewers would like to see the wide and diverse interests of bilingual and bicultural communities being catered for. Integrated strategies are needed to help Gàidhlig survive in Scotland. Further marginalisation can only be prevented by providing a Gaelic channel where the needs of the target audience takes precedence.

Ishbel MacLennan outlines the work being done by BBC Craoladh nan Gàidheal. The BBC has a commitment to the language for over 80 years, and it is hoped that a Gaelic television channel will be delivered soon. Gaelic audiences have similar expectations to others, and it is crucial that sufficient resources are made available with the new service. It is also suggested that it is the audience, which now includes those watching and interpreting content with the help of subtitles, that decides what programmes are broadcast and when. There is a need to have a clearer strategy and co-ordination all round. It has proven difficult to attract certain age cohorts, teenagers for example and even older age groups, while considering Gaelic programming important, are still of the opinion that they should be focused on those over 45. It is also necessary to reach those who are not at present part of the general listenership in order to inform them of the entire provision. Media is considered an important tool for language development as it draws the scattered Gaelic community closer together, which develops better understanding and communication. This is done through courses for learners, development programmes for staff, education programmes for schools, which helps to greatly expand the range of resources available to students and teachers alike. In the past Gaelic was the language of the home and local community but as we enter the 21st century, it needs to reach into many other domains relevant to a modern vibrant language community. Radio and particularly television have a huge impact on people's attitudes to and view of language and consequently affects their usage pattern and personal development. The audience gets the feeling that they belong to a more cohesive society and this strengthens sociolinguistic ties and creates new and lasting networks of speakers.

The paper by **Robert Dunbar** reflects on the legal framework within the context created by the *Communications Act 2003*. Despite a prolonged and protracted campaign by activists and organizations for a stand alone Gaelic television channel, this was not delivered with the publication of the Act. Instead, it has provided for a new body, the Gaelic Media Service (GMS), which will have expanded statutory powers and people are hopeful that this will eventually result in the development of a service similar to what was envisaged by the Gaelic Broadcasting Task Force. The content of various programmes can easily be challenged as being 'old' and failing to portray and help create a modern healthy and vibrant culture. This raises several questions about whom or for what is the broadcasting intended, and who owns or controls it. These questions are not easily answered even for a small minority language such as Gàidhlig. At present, an ever-increasing number of programmes are commissioned and broadcast by commercial broadcasters, who argue quite reasonably that their aim should be to reach the biggest market share possible. This can only be done by using subtitling, as some Gaelic-medium programming has been sold abroad and rebroadcast in an other Celtic language. This has consequences which go beyond the needs and interests of the Gaelic-speaking population. The legislative framework within which Gaelic-medium broadcasting operates offers very little guidance about who the provision is meant to be for. Many of the answers we seek will depend on whether or not we are talking about commercial or public service broadcasting –

the former wants primarily to attract large audiences, whereas the latter's existence is justified by other considerations. The BBC, for example, may endeavour to reflect the diversity of the societies within which they operate and may also decide to strengthen social cohesion by creating and protecting a national culture and identity. Broadcasting can play an important ideological role by exploring identity and reinforcing a minority language community's core values. Language planning issues and the provision of a wide range of high quality programmes on broadcasting networks are not always compatible in reaching their target goals. The presence of non-Gaelic-speaking production staff is a problem that needs to be addressed and, in doing so, language planning considerations must be recognized within the statutory framework, which is not the case at present. A truth that is acknowledged by almost everyone is that the broadcasters own the programming. The new GMS will be able to finance programme making, but more importantly it may engage in making programmes, provide and engage in the training of personnel and carry out essential audience research. However, a grey cloud still hangs over the financing of GMS itself.

Mike Cormack asks what kind of programming should appear on dedicated Gaelic digital television channel and what underlying aims should direct and inform such programming. The *Communications Act 2003* has created a new organization, GMS, which takes over from the earlier Comataidh Craolaidh Gàidhlig (CCG) in January 2004. Although the Government are committed to a digital channel, there is no indication where the finances might come from. Current Gaelic broadcasting is quoted at £8.5 million. The new digital channel was estimated at £44 million in 2001 – a sum which will have increased further since then. This will undoubtedly be seen as expensive. The plan at present is for up to three hours of new programming each day, presumably news and current affairs. Digital television would create access to a much larger audience of Scottish Gaelic speakers outside of Scotland, which is another factor that might complicate programming schedules. The new channel will have to have an acceptable number of viewers and the actual content must be meaningful and attractive to a Gaelic audience. The role and value of television in promoting language maintenance and use is subject of much debate, and may in some cases interfere with the intergenerational transmission of language. Television may only be one factor within a network of factors, which help preserve and cultivate endangered languages. CCG has recently published a list of five primary objectives regarding content and range of programmes and recruitment and training of staff. The question of community and identity must be central to all digital television programming in a minority language, otherwise it will prove difficult to see how it differs from other channels replicating standard formats. The availability of a limited pool of programme makers and limited finances can only add to the difficulties.

Maggie Cunningham, Head of BBC Radio Scotland, discusses the role of Scots on BBC Radio Scotland. With changes in patterns of inward migration and a fall in the number of Scots speakers, it becomes more difficult and challenging to reflect the world from a Scottish perspective. Many technological innovations help people to listen to radio online and many indeed do so. Presenters are encouraged to use words and phrases they are comfortable with in whatever context they find themselves, whether on weekly shows, gardening programmes or documentary scripting. It is intended to continue with the commitment to the language and present regular series which look at the development of the language and initiate debate among contributors and broadcasters alike.

Stuart McHardy raises many interesting questions about developing policies that shows respect for Scots as it is used today in Scotland. The language as it is spoken much be the medium and broadcasters must reflect this reality of common usage. Decision makers are in the most part ignorant of what constitutes Scottish culture and the role of the Scots language as an expression of that culture. Thinking based on English class system values rests uneasily in Scotland, but it is within the educational system that this has its greatest effect. Clear policies are needed that will allow the expression of both cultural and linguistic identity in all indigenous minority languages in Scotland. It is imperative that Part III of the European Charter be implemented immediately for Scots and the BBC in Scotland should give the lead on this. Initiatives meant to address the needs of deprived communities, almost all of whom use Scots as their normal daily vernacular, are printed and written in standard educated English. Variety of speech must be represented on radio and television – teachers must be trained in the Scots language and how to teach and impart it to those who already use it. Perhaps it time to stop being too polite!

The Press

Of the six papers on the press, only one is devoted to the Irish-medium press; of the five devoted to Scotland, two deal with the Gaelic Press and three deal with Scots.

Ciarán Ó Pronntaigh, in his introductory remarks, attempts to describe the 'conceptual ideology' philosophy behind the publication of the Irish-medium newspaper, *Là*, as a weekly newspaper originally and, in the last year, as a daily. Since this latter move, *Là* has become part of a bigger newspaper group 'Nuachtáin' and this has brought much needed administrative and printing support. It is essential for minority languages to have daily access to news and events of importance to their survival and well-being. A weekly newspaper is more of a cultural tool and readers do not rely on it as a news vehicle. *Là* receives a generous grant in aid from Foras na Gaeilge and finances the rest of its activities through revenue from advertising and the issuing of shares among the Irish speaking community. Distribution has always been and still is the biggest difficulty facing the newspaper. While it is available in many outlets throughout Ireland on a daily basis, it was also necessary to introduce a new subscription option whereby readers can pay an annual fee and collect their paper without payment at their local shop or outlet. Such subscriptions are cheaper than paying the full price for the paper on a daily basis. In order to maximize and diversify news items, materials for publication are prepared and forwarded from three separate offices, Galway, Dublin and Belfast. News of national and international interest is published and information about Irish and its the Irish speaking community. Questions were raised during the debate on overreliance on Foras na Gaeilge's grant in aid and overemphasis on news about the Irish language itself.

With regard to the press and Scottish Gaelic, **Mike Cormack** argues forthrightly that newspapers in Gaelic with a full news and reflective editorial function would develop the Gaelic-community sense of itself and the building of its identity and would also provide a vehicle for self-representation and for control over that development. For Cormack, and inevitably his approach has to be forward-looking and idealistic, newspapers entirely in Gaelic have advantages over broadcasting in Gaelic: physically through their accessibility, portability, permanence, and socially as a sign of personal regional, national and political identity. The present reality is very different: newspapers use Gaelic no more than as a symbol of cultural display and tend to address topics of linguistic or only cultural interest; by contrast, broadcasting in Gaelic presents a lively and confident community with considerable emphasis on youth. Now that Northern Ireland has *Là*, surely the time has come for such a paper – even on a weekly basis – in Gaelic. Cormack considers that a clear obstacle is funding and we would support him in looking to the new Bòrd Gàidhlig na h-Alba and the new Seirbheis nam Meadhanan Gàidhlig for leadership and constructive initiatives and solutions.

The present use of Gaelic in Scottish Sunday newspapers is critiqued by **Chas Mac Donald** who considers that, until a substantial proportion of Scottish readers are able read Gaelic, it will remain symbolic in and of itself. His corpus of Press Gaelic from 2002-03 shows predominance in either Gaelic as a subject (including Michael Russell's Private Member's Bill, which was in itself a news item,) or by certain journalists (notably Murchadh Mac Leòid and Stuart Cosgrove). We agree with Mac Donald that the appropriation of Gaelic by *Scotland on Sunday* may not only be imitative of earlier Lowland adoptions of Highland culture but, if Gaelic is truly to become a *national* cultural asset, then it is in the Edinburgh press where the language needs to be 'accorded most significance'. As for broadcasting, Mac Donald urges policy to be as light as possible and talks up the interesting notion of 'mid-Minch Gàidhlig' as a way of accommodating the greatest number of speakers of the language, no matter how little is known about the audiences for Gaelic.

By contrast, **Alex Law** and, separately, **Neil Blain** and **Anne Gifford,** consider the question of nationhood in the context of the language expressing that national identity and do not find it in literary Scots; rather, they find it in the Scots that is spoken and which may on occasions be represented in the English of the Scottish tabloids such as the *Daily Record*. In an illuminating, theoretically-focussed interpretation of standardised Scottish Press English – tabloidese – from the *Daily Record*, Law carefully shows how it does not need literary – or any other written – Scots to construct or substantiate the Scottishness of national identity. For the deictic nature of such texts, heavily imbued with pronouns of solidarity and identity or distance and disaffection, are read with unmistakably Scottish – usually strong working-class – accents. For such readers are primarily oral rather than literate communicators, bringing to the reading of newspapers an accent, not a lexicon of obsolete vocabulary. The standardised English of tabloids functions as a sign with which speakers of differently oriented accents can intersect and respond – by actively participating in the reading of those newspaper reports, with their accents silently mouthing the texts running through their minds and thereby inferring the deictic references to themselves. Following Volosinov, Law argues that "newspaper reading is not a passive process but one where language is both repressive and expressive, and both at the same time. As such, all utterances carry an evaluative accent. Readers do not simply say or hear words, such as 'Irish', 'British' or 'Scottish', so much as say or hear the meaning, significance and truth-content that the word has for them." For Law, "a newspaper written in English might in fact prove 'more' fully Scottish and more fully national in its empowering proficiency than the written Scots that language activists would have Scottish newspapers adopt." To substantiate his case, Law provides an original analysis of three excerpts from the *Daily Record* spanning a 25 year period.

Like A. Law, **Neil Blain** and **Anne Gifford** are concerned with the constructedness of identity and in the use of labels to categorise an individual, and that, in the formation of Scottish political identity, language plays a defining role, but traditional Scots maybe a handicap and ridiculed. Their exploration of such themes arise from the need to prepare teachers for new Scottish Higher Still examination in Language, in which components include language in the media and linguistic characteristics of tabloid journalism, both of which relate to the study of Scottish political identity. In the present-day Scottish school, it is no longer a question of being 'Scottish' or 'Scottish and British', each requiring their own discourse of identity, for there is now the issue of post-British identity to include immigrant groups such as Scottish-Pakistani and Scottish-Muslims and such like whose hyphenated names reflect a bicultural focus between host culture and ethnic origin. With such labels of identity regularly featuring in tabloid newspapers, Blain and Gifford attempt a further distinction between labels of national character (e.g. being Scottish) and labels of political identity (e.g. being nationalist), trying to show how the linguistic constructedness of such notions in the *Daily Record* can be handled in the classroom.

In the final paper on the press, **John Law** treats the press in a way that the press does not write itself: in dense literary Scots. He presents six press excerpts about the Scots tongue between 1966 and 2000 and deconstructs the ideological presuppositions of the writers about Scots. Although the comments written or reported come from distinguished Scottish men of letters, much comment is negative: the lexicographer David Murison reportedly regards Scots as 'a dying language', the philosopher and dramatist Stanley Eveling is 'depressed' by Billy Kay's *Our Mother Tongue*, the poet Don Paterson finds Scots 'couthy' and detects 'a bad taste', the novelist Allan Massie finds 'Gaelic and Scots ... too fragile to have been the basis of a nationalist movement', and so on. Law denounces the easiness of dismissal and derogation; even if it is increasingly hard to hear good Scots spoken, and even if, for some, it is difficult to speak it spontaneously, there are many who are well read in Scots – such as those enjoying his very paper – who will recognise that what they are understanding is their *guidlie heirskep* or rich linguistic inheritance.

The Performing Arts

As a theatre director, **David Grant** pours scorn over the categorisation of language into unreal categories for the theatre is concerned with stimulating 'the auditory imagination', which is essentially oral and conveyed through a fluidity and confluence of accents which resist categorisation. In rehearsal, it is his experience that actors need to discover a native understanding of local voices and feel confident and comfortable about their rendition. Consequently, Grant is just as scornful about over-phoneticised, orthographically highly non-standard playscripts for they make meaning inaccessible and considers the phonetic rendition of essentially oral material unviable. Moreover, over-phoneticised scripts becomes reduced to parody. In the Irish context, Grant points out that some of the most effective recent plays have been built around the rendering of the oral tradition *in English*, not Irish, from the works of Synge, Brian Friel's *Translations*, to Kavanagh's *Tarry Flynn*, to McGuinness's *Observe the Son of Ulster Marching Towards the Somme,* with accent 'the crucial semiotic'. Throughout, Grant draws striking parallels from his experience with the very different situation in Romania, where translations was performed in Hungarian but listened to in a Romanian translation.

It is with films only in Irish that **Des O'Rawe** is concerned. Although Irish-language filmmaking has only ever been on a small scale, it provides important support for the development of the language, even although the quality and success of films is attributable not to the accents and voices of the actors (unlike the theatre) but to the non-acting parts, the "composing, framing, cutting and juxtaposing of shots". O' Rawe finds that, in films, the role of Irish has changed – from being the language of narration and documentary, as in *Amharc Éirean*, to becoming the language of political debate, as in *Caoineadh Airt Uí Laoghaire*, and that dissident ideas alongside critical images are all the more compelling if they are in Irish. Consequently, O'Rawe supports criticisms of certain recent films such as *Éireville*, which may be in Irish but merely imitative mainstream cinema forms and ideas, in the belief that Irish-language films should be the vehicle of an independent film culture.

Although he was prevented at the last moment from participating in the symposium, **Alan Titley**, renowned novelist in Irish as well as English, and great man of letters, provides a linguistically playful tour-de-force on the effects of broadcasting on the language on all of us. Pure fun!

Trevor Ó Clochartaigh explores the importance of the spirit and morale of people as demonstrated through language, culture and respect for their own identity as a people. To protect and cultivate this communal spirit, Ó Clochartaigh finds it necessary to give full scope to dramatic, literary and artistic endeavours. This will also help to forge links with other linguistic minorities throughout Europe and the rest of the world. There is, at present, a developing gap between providers of creative artistic programmes and those supporting them financially. Providers must engage more fully with the bureaucracy surrounding applications, and there is a great need for go-between organisations to assist and train people in relevant procedures. The standard of written and spoken Irish has fallen disastrously in recent years among young people within the Gaeltacht, and the educational seems unable to stop this deterioration in language competence and usage. There is a need for urgent action on this matter. From his own personal experience, he feels that people learn better through participation in activities they like such as drama, which allows them the scope to use a variety of talents including knowledge of language. Ó Clochartaigh feels this applies to all minority language and perhaps we here in Ireland have a role to play in formulating interesting new adventures, which can be disseminated and shared with others especially those involved with Scottish Gaelic and Welsh. Drama encompasses the use of literature, the visual arts, music, multimedia, acting and many other language related domains. It belongs to the community and is community based. Drama and dramatic activities focus people to reflect more deeply on the meaning of life, it develops the imagination, feelings and emotions and helps the promotion of various skills such as writing, acting, theatre production and design. Drama can be used as a vehicle in many domains but none more so than in education. It is felt that the promotion of drama in the primary school sector has been very much neglected. There is a need to bring drama to the schools by having access to professional drama companies, and the Gaeltacht and All-Irish medium schools should be a primary focus. Such activities would have a huge impact on language usage and competence among young people. Proper financial and human resources are necessary to make this a success as well as proper training in the relevant skills for those imparting and teaching drama. Theatre in Education has been happening in Ireland for over 30 years. Professional companies produce and present plays appropriate to particular age groups in educational establishments throughout Ireland. This has proved extremely successful and there is urgency about expanding the facility to Gaeltacht and all-Irish medium teaching schools. There is a further need to follow on after secondary school and provide young people in the 18-23 age bracket who want to pursue a professional career in drama. Courses such as 'Lasair', supported and organised by Iomairt Cholm Cille, for young people from Ireland and Scotland, should be an annual event in order to promote the forging of important links between the two countries. There is an urgent need for the introduction of a comprehensive course in Drama through Irish in one of the universities in Ireland. We must find and recruit people with the necessary interest to undertake all these new developments and to develop policies in order to attract appropriate state support.

The changing role of Irish identified by O'Rawe in film finds echoes in the Irish-language soap opera, *Ros na Rún*, the flagship series of TG4, of which Ó Clochartaigh is the producer. In a brilliant critical synthesis, **Gordon McCoy** teases out the contradictions both of the series and of its use of Irish. Against a theoretical background of essentialising and dynamic ideologies whereby language revival is considered to preserve, freeze and reify culture inevitably stereotypically, or to modify, adapt and change culture in line with contemporary post-modern society, McCoy finds *Ros na Rún* both real, unreal and surreal, "an alternative universe", raising but shattering romantic stereotypes at almost every turn. At the heart of, and as the vehicle of, this process lies the series' use of Irish – no uniform or national dialect, but a mixture of Ulster, Connemara, Munster, occasionally anglicised and also learner Irish, including L1-influenced learner Irish, where everyone is shown to manage to understand each other without difficulty or comment (not so in real life!), and where no-one switches to English even upon the encountering of strangers. Because absolutely everyone is shown to speak Irish all the time in the series, Irish is not a topic of conversation – unlike the press in Irish or Gaelic, as Ó Pronntaigh and Mac Donald show. "*Ros na Rún* is a microcosm of an unproblematically bilingual Ireland in which Irish is unremarkably spoken in *every* context, including by emergency services, hospital and hotel staff, and artists in Dublin art galleries. ... [It] has radically transformed the image of the language." McCoy argues that the serial is part of a process of cultural and linguistic hybridity which reconciles the old and the new, English and Irish cultures and languages. "The fact that these alternatives to traditional models not only exist, but attract a wide audience, indicates a revolution in attitudes to the Irish language, no longer the sole preserve of the conservative idealogues or a key to a purer past." McCoy concludes by the two contrasting images in the Republic of Ireland which the Irish language has. "One is that of officialdom and state cultural restoration, and undoubtedly a state-sponsored Irish language soap is part of this process. Another is that of counter-culture and subversion; a fundamental contradiction in Irish society is that although the state endorses Gaelic revivalism and the constitution recognises Irish as the first official language, Irish speakers are marginalised in many aspects of civil and political culture and, as such, often must use minority rights discourses to campaign for the status of the language." McCoy's important paper shows clearly that "the mixture of linguistic and cultural fantasy and reality in *Ros na Rún* reveal the competing essentialising and dynamic ideologies at play in the Irish language movement, and demonstrate a paradigm shift in favour of the latter without entirely deconstructing the former. Tradition and innovation exist concurrently as the cultures of rural native speakers and urban learners meet and create a synthesis, or a least an engaging stand-off, in the effort to represent and revive the Gaelic world."

In addressing the question of language planning for Scots in the context of the theatre, **Bill Findlay** champions the considerable body of dramatic writing which has emerged in Scots since the 1970s, although there are earlier precedents. This Scots is urban so-called demotic Scots, real and realistic vernacular Scots from the central belt and particularly from west-Central Scotland, the voice of daily speech scripted for performance. It is the speech realism of such plays which persuades Findlay that, in the formulation of our original questions, they will express and substantiate contemporary Scottish culture, not merely symbolise it, and that upon the beneficial consequences of those plays that language planners for Scots should build – not artificial re-imagined Lallans, neo-Lallans, or cod-Lallans, not traditional, conservative, country-inflected 'ideal' Scots, not 'Costume Scots', not so-called 'good' Scots of the past, which does not reflect the living speech and speech-habits of Scottish audiences. By the careful documentation and interpretation of those comparisons, Findlay's paper masterly charts "the sea-change" both in form and in attitude from 'historical' Scots to 'contemporary' Scots, showing that it is now the latter which has become a new kind of 'standard' Scots "in both naturalistic and non-naturalistic forms in terms of its ubiquity on our stages and in radio and television comedy and drama (and, indeed, in contemporary literature)", showing that it is living Scottish *speech*, not artificial, written, never-was-naturally-spoken Lallans, that since the 1970s has empowered Scottish drama, after all that most speech-based of genres, made Scottish theatre more popular than ever before, and above all "consolidates and advances Scots as an integral and high-profile part of Scottish culture". The recognition of the importance of speech for effective playwriting echoes not only A. Law's explanation of the use of Scots in the tabloid press but also Grant's experience in Ireland.

The opposite view is presented by **David Purves**, to whose *A Scots Grammar* we are all indebted for a listing of lexical, idiomatic, morphological and some syntactic features of traditional, conservative spoken Scots as spoken by his grandparents in the Scottish Borders. For it is for the revival of historical, literary and unspoken Scots that Purves urges as the way forward as, for him, that is the only authentic Scots, ignoring the ongoing dynamic and realities of present-day speech as documented by Findlay. Moreover, Purves urges that 'proper' Scots is the Scots which should be taught prescriptively in schools and be supported through the Scottish Executive's National Cultural Strategy, and a great many people would agree with him. This Scots is used in his own plays, translations of *MacBeth*, Chekhov's *The Thrie Sisters*, Strindberg's *The Ootlaw*, among other works.

Janet Paisley's Scots shows that she writes as she speaks, and the presence of Scots forms of lexical and grammatical items in her writing are sufficient for the categorisation as Scots rather than English. Scots, she claims, is spoken by 4million people and understood by almost the entire population, now approaching 6million. Although "the spoken language of the majority of Scotland's inhabitants is Scots", she finds little interest and few opportunities in the media for representing it. Whereas she has written and had performed TV scripts in Scots, producers prefer scripts in English and sometimes insist on the replacement of Scots words or forms with their English equivalents, leaving it up to the actors to provide the Scots largely through accent – not dissimilar to Grant's experience in Ireland. Paisley echoes Maggie Cunningham's policy by urging its mainstreaming in the media in mere (but actually more accurate) reflection of its use in society so that, by hearing their own voice coming back, it will provide confidence to speakers to use their own tongue, to which they have every right to do so.

The quality of Scots in the Scottish soap opera *River City* is developed further in the next paper by **Christine Robinson**. She finds that many Scottish characters are not given to utter the Scots form of many syntactic constructions even where these exist; that Asian characters from England are given odd constructions, too, so that the diversity which exists in real life and would mark character differences is not as exploited as they should be. On the other hand, certain characters such as Jim McRoberts, Shellsuit Bob, and the North-East character Rosine, are given some Scots to utter, but from Robinson's examples it strikes us as rather 'light'. Robinson then analyses a *River City* script by Janet Paisley; although differences such as between the North-east character and Glasgow characters are written in, Robinson finds that the Scots is so limited that it gives no more than "a flavour to an English text", and that the opportunity to create a Scots programme for a Scots-speaking society is missed. Robinson's analysis of the actors' accents reveals some distinctively Glasgow features, albeit (because this is acting for television) in an unrealistic, highly articulated setting, but not the homogeneity of place to be found in *Taggart*.

Sheila Douglas explores the contradiction that what has put the traditional arts at the forefront of Scottish culture has been its use of Scots – particularly in songs and story-telling – yet, although the majority language, spoken everywhere throughout Scotland and heard every time the Scottish Parliament is in session, the Scottish Executive cannot extend to it official recognition because of difficulties over definition and, she believes, over funding.

The Public Sphere

John Corbett and **Fiona Douglas** provide a fresh critical synthesis of recent achievements in the use of spoken and written Scots. They find that there is now substantive evidence to show that, over the last few years, Scots has come to fulfil virtually all the functions and functional domains of a full national language, as identified by Stewart in 1968: official, provincial, wider communication, international, capital, group, educational, school subject, literary, and religious, to which Corbett and Douglas add an eleventh: media. Gratifyingly, the present series of symposia have contributed to some of these categotries, including some of the papers in this volume which are cited as evidence. For **Corbett** and **Douglas,** Scots is closer to being a full national language than it was in 1968 or at any point since 1603. At the heart of this development, **Corbett** and **Douglas** identify what they call "Public Domain Scots" or "Civil Service Scots", a Scots which is message-oriented, transactional, practical, free of literary style or pretension, and also free from ridicule, although they recognise that its use particularly in translation serves a symbolic, identity-celebrating function. Against this background, **Corbett** and **Douglas** take a just as refreshing look at Scots in the current press, the former thus complementing the present treatments by A. Law, J. Law and Blain and Gifford. Press Scots has yet to find itself and be consistent – Press Scots is not the Civil Service Scots just described for it is not used in serious reporting of hard news (where English remains predominant); rather, it occurs in restricted domains, for which the traditional vocabulary is appropriate, it verges on the literary variety, and in the transferred context its purpose is to entertain and creative a sense of shared Scottshness and identity – *we're aa Jock Tamson's bairns*. **Corbett** and **Douglas** identify a second area of Press Scots: the reporting of contemporary politics. Here, the press is reporting what politicians have *said* and also, in some case, their appearance, and the press may be approving or disapproving. In such contexts,and with texts dealing with Rosie Cowan, MSP, and Helen Liddell, MP, **Corbett** and **Douglas** show how Scots can perform either ideological function – solidarity or criticism, with a view to eliciting readers' approval. **Corbett** and **Douglas** conclude by recognising that, as a result largely of linguist activism, Civil Service Scots has come of age, that, in the press, but also in kirks, education, broadcasting and other situations of dissemination, it has a marked ideological impact; but that those various impacts need to be researched as part of the ongoing language planning initiatives.

In what we might call Civil Service Ulster-Scots', **Ian Parsley** presents his own critical perspective of current policy and ongoing developments for Scots in Northern Ireland.

The papers on Scots in this volume represent the tension in the present debate about the nature and character of Scots, including Scots in Northern Ireland. For the one camp, the vitality of Scots rests with the speech of the present day and with the realistic representation of such speech in literature (as Findlay describes) or in non-literary contexts (as Corbett and Douglas describe as 'Civil Service Scots' and as demonstrated in Paisley's contribution to this volume); for the other, the vitality of Scots rest is based on the literature of the past and any present-day vitality rests with the continuation of that literary tradition, including the extension of such Scots to non-literary contexts. Each camp appears to be reinforced by a class bias and each has strong followers. Both camps agree that Scots plays a fundamental role in the substantiation of Scottish cultural identity but differ in the form and manner in which Scots reveals that identity. Much more could be said about each view, but it is no doubt the existence of these two fundamentally opposing or defining views that impedes political progress with Scots.

2001 Census

The release of Census results is recurrently a source of primary demographic and sociolinguistic information about the Celtic minority languages in the U.K. With the release of the 2001 UK Census results in the Spring of 2003, it was appropriate that those results be addressed as part of the symposium; little had we expected that they would need to be so critically addressed as they are by **Kenneth MacKinnon**. In this paper, MacKinnon's focus is on Northern Ireland, not only for its own sake, to compare differences with the 1991 Census, but also to draw comparisons with the 2001 results for Gaelic in Scotland and Welsh in Wales. His main criticism is the impossibility of establishing answers to such central questions as: how many speakers of Irish in Northern Ireland are there? According to MacKinnon: 115,731 (compared with 131.974 in 1991). He criticises the grouping of age categories over figures for single years for it prevents an accurate assessment of the success and seffects of Irish-medium education among those under 25; the single age category of 16-74 for a knowledge of Irish on the basis of sex and highest level of qualification for it prevents actual numbers of speakers to be inferred (whereas, for a knowledge of Irish in relation to community background and religion, numbers are presented in terms of seven age groups); the lack of social, economic, way-of-life, quality-of-life theme tables for a knowledge of Irish (it is either *any* knowledge or *no* knowledge) thus preventing comparison with Welsh and Gaelic, where this information is presented for some 17 such themes. Throughout all the tables, he regrets that totals for those who can read, write or understand Irish are simply not given.

MacKinnon's biggest criticism is that, from 37 age categories in 1991 and only 7 in 2001, a strict comparison speakers of Irish between 1991 and 2001 is not possible without a considerable loss of detail; that as not all 2001 age data has been been published, it is not possible to produce actual number of speakers on the basis of age. By incorporating information from other tables, MacKinnon suggests his Figure 3 is the best result so far; nevertheless, by the way age-data has been differently presented with regard to Welsh and differently yet again to Gaelic, a comparison of age-groups and of the effects of education in the language over the last ten years between Irish, Gaelic and Welsh speakers is simply not possible. A further casuality is the possibility of measuring inter-generational differences in order to identify patterns interpretable as a reversal of language shift. MacKinnon concludes with a set of recommendations so that those very cenral questions central to all Celtic languages in the UK can be addressed in future Census tables.

Ciaran O Duibhin expends MacKinnon's criticisms by taking up the central question of speaker numbers, not least because to the three questions (*do you speak Irish, read Irtish, write Irish?*) in 1991 was added a fourth in 2001: *do you understand spoken Irish?* To this combination of aural and visual, active and passive skills, Ó Duibhin shows that there are 16 possible responses. MacKinnon's figure of 115,731 speakers of Irish in 2001 is revised by Ó Duibhin to 167,490 speakers with some skills (or 10.35% of the population). That the central question is so hard even to infer or induce an answer suggests there there is a case to answer here by Northern Ireland's official statistics organisation, the Northern Ireland Statistical Research Agency.

Economics and Linguistic Diversity

François Grin's seminal paper discusses the historical and ongoing debate about the relationship between language diversity and economic prosperity. Very little is known in concrete terms about the causal links through which language and economic processes influence each other. It is difficult, however, to generalize the findings found in many tightly argued in-depth contributions published since the mid 1980s. There is no general model of the economic values of linguistic diversity in general or in reference to a particular language. However, we have available to us a framework that will help us structure the analysis. This approach rests on a benefits and cost comparison of the market/non-market value of a language, on the one hand, as opposed to private/social value, on the other. It is difficult to find empirical evidence to support non-market values – direct enjoyment, etc. resulting from linguistic diversity. In summary, it can be shown that there is growing evidence that there is economic value in linguistic diversity. However, the case needs to be strengthened before it can be advocated and successfully argued that public policy, backed up by social resources, should be made available to support and promote the use of small languages and linguistic diversity. There is also strong evidence that the benefits arising from linguistic diversity exceed its costs and that linguistically diverse communities and societies should promote and protect such diversity. Economic analysis, when viewed from the distributive aspect, linguistic diversity can be shown to be a matter of socio-economic justice across a wide spectrum of society. There is a need for further detailed research in order to tease out all the interconnections between language and the economy. This should help deepen our understanding of the important links between linguistic diversity and economic success. The analytical distinctions addressed in this paper should help us come to grips with many of the key issues and factors affecting the relationship between languages, including minority language, and the general economy.

Esmond Birnie, MLA and **Steven King** in their reply to Grin's paper and to other works of his, agree with his emphasis that there is an valuable and central economic aspect to language, and that this should be transparent in any language policy involving minority and lesser used languages. Decline within minority languages, they argue, has been the result of different factors, e.g. modernization, economic investment in learning, support and cultivation from local institutions, including the Church and the forging of new states/nations. They argue further that, despite the provisions within the European Charter regarding economic regulations and languages, the burden imposed by language regulations should be in direct proportion of the demand for services through the minority languages. They note and agree with Professor Grin's contention that we are still unable to quantify the impact of language policy in any detail. Wherever ethnic divisions and conflicts occur, they feel there is a greater need to address linguistic diversity in order to further stability and peace within national minorities. Economic growth is enhanced by and through linguistic diversity, but details of the cost involved is less clear. The authors endorse linguistic diversity on a philosophical level, in the same way in which we agree that biodiversity is a good thing. However, the opportunity cost of the language policy must be constantly borne in mind. They point out that language skills are as much a reflection of cultural preferences as they are a necessity to operate as part of an individual's acquired economic capability. While they agree that language is a matter of fundamental human rights, they return again and again to the cost involved in applying these rights in the economic sphere. They support the measured and proportional approach taken and implied by the Charter and, while agreeing with the political and cultural benefits of linguistic diversity, argue that the benefits are less clear on the economic side.

John Walsh's contribution is a historical overview of the debate about the interconnections between language and (economic) development in Ireland over the last hundred years or so. The results of his investigation reveal that the Irish language is not merely a communications code, but a more powerful force whose influences are felt on society in general and within the social and economic spheres, in particular. There also may be links between the survival of the native indigenous language, Irish and socio-economic development. It is obvious from much recent research in the field of sociolinguistics, in particular, that there is a strong connection between language, culture and the symbolism arising from speakers' beliefs about the rightful status of their language. The basic weakness of sociolinguistic research is that it seldom deals with developmental issues, especially economic development. New insights into the links between language and society are provided from the detailed analysis of the work of the writers surveyed, but it also reveals the total absence of an explicit theoretical basis for the language/bilingual policies pursued by the state. There is a need on a wider scale to link into theoretical frameworks being developed and applied successfully elsewhere, before we can come to a deeper understanding of the complicated interconnections between language diversity and cultural and economic development.

In his contribution, **Seosamh Mac Donncha** argues that any language is a valuable and precious resource and minority languages are no exception. He outlines the expanded role of Foras na Gaeilge when it was established on 2 December 1999. As part of developing that role, it has initiated and published a strategic plan. Within that plan, the importance of language within the marketing and economic context is strongly emphasized. Subsequently, a decision was taken to establish a specialised section within Foras na Gaeilge to deal with marketing and communication issues. Business organizations acknowledge that Irish is an economic asset, and that from this various benefits accrue: improvements to services, attraction of new customers, respect for the community and the strengthening of loyalty and allegiance to the language itself. Irish has great potential for employment within the Public Service. Certain gaps remain especially in technological training, but these are being addressed. Employment within Local Authorities is also high and, with the forthcoming legislation, the *Official Languages Act 2003*, there will be distinct advantages accruing to speakers and users of Irish. This will increase the demand for competent Irish speakers across a wide range agencies, as well as people competent to deal with legislation and legal procedures. The role of Údarás na Gaeltachta in creating and supporting employment in Gaeltacht areas is not to be overlooked in our review of the economic impact of Irish on local communities. Languages must adapt to new technological advances or otherwise perish. Great strides have been taken to equip workers and the Irish language itself to come to terms with the new technological advances and the future looks promising. Foras na Gaeilge is also responsible for the development and implementation of initiatives involving the use of Irish throughout the whole island of Ireland. Its success in dealing with future developments will benefit Northern Ireland and its economy as it has done elsewhere in Ireland and much of this is likely to be achieved through education provision and training. Economic developments and initiatives must become part and parcel of linguistic plans and strategies. Everyone will support initiatives involving Irish, which bring economic benefits in terms of jobs and training. The language and its speakers are an economic, artistic, cultural and social asset and must be supported and cultivated in order to achieve its full potential.

Wilson McLeod in his response addresses the ongoing debate in Scotland regarding the economic impact of Gaelic on its own communities and on the national level. The media, especially the English language media, are sporadic in their reporting and the content of their reporting is at a very superficial and predictable level. Why should we 'waste' money on a dying language when other serious problems require attention? Or some such question is the usual response. Those responsible for policy making in Scotland do not seem to reflect too deeply on issues relevant to minority languages and their impact on local communities and economic development, which is in direct contrast with other bilingual countries throughout the world. The majority/minority dichotomy is the subject of much debate – the majority supporting the subsidized minority. It can be shown that money spent on Gaelic, particularly within the local Gaelic–speaking community, has had a major impact in stimulating business and economic growth and most importantly creating jobs. This is a welcome development and challenges the older viewpoint that the language was a hindrance to economic growth and achievement. The number of jobs where Gaelic was an essential element is quite small, and the language remains as a peripheral requisite within an ever-increasing English-only economy. There is a great need for a fundamental change of attitude on these matters if the language is to make any progress and survive as a vehicle of communication and economic activity.

Douglas Chalmers, an economist, states that he is reluctant to enter the fray at multi-disciplinary conferences of any kind. However, he feels that our main speaker, François Grin, has given a focus to the discussion by posing some relevant and important questions. Arguing for the economic benefits of linguistic diversity might be better achieved by adopting a Gramscian approach, where the process is long term rather than a once-off victory. Evidence is emerging that a business oriented or market approach is failing to work in peripheral areas such as the Highlands and Islands of Scotland. There is increasing recognition of late that the approach that is most likely to be of utmost benefit is one where the potential of language, arts and culture are explicitly used and developed within an overall regional plan. Research relating to the artistic and cultural industry has shown that some 250 full-time jobs have been created, which is significant in a isolated peripheral geographical area such as the Highlands and Islands. The effect of participation in Gaelic-related artistic and cultural events and products are perceived to be promotion of cultural distinctiveness, improved self-confidence, attachment to local communities, a huge impact on tourism and the purchase of goods and services provided in and through Gaelic. It was also felt that, in future, migration could be lessened and the enhancement of tourism is likely to continue. It is therefore essential that the language and associated arts and culture undergo regeneration in order to promote social and economic development.

Two European Comparisons: Basque and Walloon

A further goal of these symposia and volumes is to draw fresh critical comparisons between the linguistic situation in Ireland and Scotland and with similar situations in Europe and beyond, and to bring recognised experts in those fields to Belfast.

At previous symposia, there were comparisons with Swiss German,[4] Frisian, Low German,[5] NyNorsk[6] and Meänkieli.[7] This present volume contains fresh comparisons between the situations between Basque and Walloon and those in Ireland and Scotland – in contributions by Eduardo J. Ruiz Vieytez and Jean-Luc Fauconnier, and in response to Fauconnier by Dónall Ó Riagáin and Janice Carruthers.

Eduardo Ruiz Vieytez presents the case for linguistic human rights with great succinctness and clarity. "We consider linguistic rights as human rights because language is one of the most important aspects of the human identity and a necessary tool for the development of the personality. … In this sense, the defence of cultural and linguistic equality of opportunities must be regarded, as it is the idea of promoting equality between men and women or in respect of wealth differences. … To put it in a nutshell, there is a common core of linguistic rights of the people belonging to linguistic minorities that must be regarded as human rights. These rights are not in a lower position in respect to other fundamental rights or civil liberties. On the contrary, their recognition and guarantee is a condition sine-qua-non to ensure a real protection of the human dignity of those people. As with other human rights, the public authorities of the State have the responsibility of ensuring the necessary conditions to make possible that members of linguistic minorities enjoy that core of rights and can develop their cultural and linguistic spheres in a proper environment." Ruiz then describes the complex linguistic situation of The Basque Country (*Euskal Herria*) which is one of the richest areas of Spain with a poulation of 2,800,000. The Basque Country comprises the Southern Basque Country (in Basque *Hegoalde*), within the Spanish Kingdom, and the Northern Basque Country (in Basque *Iparralde*), within the French Republic. The Southern Basque Country is divided in four historical territories or provinces: *Bizkaia/Biscay* (capital in *Bilbao*), *Araba/Alava* (capital in *Gasteiz/Vitoria*), *Gipuzkoa/Gipuscoa* (capital in *Donostia/San Sebastián*) and *Nafarroa/Navarra* (capital in *Irunea/Pamplona*). The number of speakers, the uses of the language, and the legislative provision thus differs in each area. There is no legal framework in the Northern Basque Country; in the Southern Basque Country, there are different frameworks in the Basque Autonomous Community from Navarra. Both are covered by the Spanish Constition which decrees that Spanish is the official language of State, but that the other Spanish languages may also be official in the Autonomous Communities. The official

---

[4] Andreas Fischer, 'Language and Politics in Switzerland', in John M. Kirk and Dónall P. Ó Baoill eds. *Linguistic Politics: Language Policies for Northern Ireland, the Republic of Ireland, and Scotland* (2001), 105-122.

[5] Manfred Görlach, 'Frisian and Low German: Minority Languages in Hiding', in John M. Kirk and Dónall P Ó Baoill eds. *Linguistic Politics: Language Policies for Northern Ireland, the Republic of Ireland, and Scotland* (2001), 67-87.

[6] Kevin McCafferty, 'Norway: Consensus and Diversity', in John M. Kirk and Dónall P. Ó Baoill eds. *Linguistic Politics: Language Policies for Northern Ireland, the Republic of Ireland, and Scotland* (2001), 89-103.

[7] Tove Skutnabb-Kangas, 'Irelands, Scotlands, Education and Linguistic Human Rights: Some International Comparisons', in John M. Kirk and Dónall P. Ó Baoill eds. *Language Planning and Education: Linguistic Issues in Northern Ireland, the Republic of Ireland, and Scotland* (2002), 221-266.

status of Basque in the Basque Autonomous Community from Navarra. is reinforced by various statututes and acts.

Ruiz then describes how Basque is used in Public Adminstration and Justice (not a lot, but it varies), Education (well provided for at all three levels by statutes), the Mass Media (also well provided for, with TV and radio broadcasting exclusively in Basque, and a daily newspaper in Basque), culture, sport and religion (where use is all widespread). He speculates on those problems remaining for Basque: resistance to its adoption by significant sectors of the population, processes of globalisation and the impact of new technologies, the lack of social use, its absence from technical, commercial and business domains and from the world of work, although he finds scope for improvement through the provisions now in place for education across all levels – those taught and trained in Basque might well want to practice in Brasque. Ruiz concludes that "the legislation in force in the BAC is near to the top of its possibilities. […] very few changes could be reached in the legislation and practice depending on the autonomous powers." He seems confident that the measures adopted for education will ensure the language in the medium term.

Ruiz then compares the situation of Basque with that of Irish in both the North and the South of Ireland under three headings: 'sociolinguistic elements', 'political factors' and 'legal status' and finds more similarities than differences. Sociolinguistic similarities are questions of linguistic distance in respect of the majority language, of minorityhood within their respective communities, of their medium size, of the absence of monolingual speakers, and of their limited social usae. Political similarities are questions of their being politically divided languages, of their living within a conflictive political framework, of their being an important element of nation al identity, of their lack of social and political prestige, of the existence of self-government powers to encourage and promote the language, of the positive attitude of the population towards the language, and of the existemce of political debate. Legal similarities are questions of their being official languages within a limited area, of their being languages pritected under the European Charter, of their being official legislated for, and of only the public sector being afected by statutory law.

Sociolinguistic differences are questions of different linguistic affiliations, different numbers of native speakers, the geographical predominance, and different social use. Political differences are different state political frameworks, different political attitudes, and different attitudes within the Catholic Church. Legal status differences are question of status both within and of each State (Irish is a treaty language of EU, Basque is merely a regional language; Irish is 'the first official and national language', Basque is the 'own language' of the BAC), the existence of an Ombudsman for Irish (compared with an Advisory Council for Basque), and the approaches of statutory acts (acts on Irish place obligations and commitments on public bodies, acts on Basque describe citizens' linguistic rights).

Ruiz concludes that "Although Basque has a greater amount of L1 speakers in comparison with Irish Gaelic, the current linguistic landscape in most of the Basque Country can be considered as similar to that of Ireland. In particular, looking to the social attitudes and political powers acting in favour of the minority language, situations in the Republic of Ireland and in the Basque Autonomous Community show a significant degree of similarity." But he sees comon dangers:

"Having more L1 speakers and a wider geographical area where the native language is predominant, Basque language authorities must try to stop the process of loosing the language via intergenerational transmission and protecting the Basque-speaking environments from the input of the state language. For both cases, Basque and Irish, the most important challenge nowadays would be to encourage the social use of the minority language among L2 speakers, providing them the necessary opportunities to get involved in a Basque/Irish linguistic environment. This must be tried not only for the traditional fields of social and familiar relations but also in respect to other aspects of every day's life." Here, legal and institutional frameworks can play a role, but so too can social pressure, political consciousness and citizen attitudes. It is a masterful comparison, with clarity and succinctness; it offers as much a critical guide to the status of present-day Irish as it does to the illuminating comparison between the two languages.

Jean-Luc Fauconnier relates the comparison between Walloon and Scots to a wider taxonomy of language varieties: nation-state languages which are used by a minority in another nation-state country (e.g. German as used by minorities in Belgium, Denmark, France and Italy, etc.), languages which are not nation-state languages (e.g. Scottish Gaelic), and what he calls *collateral languages*. We interpret *collateral* to mean 'of common ancestry but not of the same parents', 'descended through a different line'; for Walloon and Scots, we find *collateral language* a plausible notion (more so than Ó Riagáin and Parsley's *hidden language* or Ó Riagáin's *eclipsed language*) because it allows for independent, autonomous development and related but differentiated outcomes in the present day, as between Walloon and French and also Scots and English. *Collateral language* may thus be considered a linguistic or philological notion, to join such other notions as *dialect, jargon, patois, sociolect* and *regiolect*, much loved by scholars. Such terms are avoided by legislation – *dialects* (i.e. of major nation-state languages), for instance, are explicitly excluded from such influential instruments as the *European Charter for Regional or Minority Languages*. The Charter's orientation is personal and psychological or apperceptional – 'a language is a language if its speakers decide that what they speak is a language'. Nevertheless, criteria for regional languages are provided: the existence of dictionaries and grammar books, a standardised orthography, educational instruction both about and in the language, used broadcasting and the press, and used in literary works and folksongs. Fauconnier urges that those criteria for *regional languages* are also the criteria for *collateral languages*, so that Walloon and Scots, and that, therefore, *ipso facto*, each is both. Those arguments are accepted by Carruthers.

However, the matter does not rest there. Fauconnier considers it the responsibility of regional or devolved governments to promote and defend regional or collateral languages – and, indeed, the two developments in the case of Northern Ireland and Scotland have arisen simultaneously and, through the *Belfast (Good Friday) Agreement* and subsequent legislation and through the Scottish Parliament's Cross-Party Group on the Scots Language, such measures are being undertaken. Fauconnier recognises that regional/collateral languages can also be 'cross-border' or, to the European Charter's term, 'trans-frontier', and that, in some cases, only on one side of the border is the regional language indigenous whereas, on the other, it remains a dialect. Such a contra-distinction raises the designation of Scots both across the North Channel (indigenous only to Scotland?) and across the Northern Ireland border (regional language in Northern Ireland, no status whatsoever in the Republic of Ireland). Here lies a good explanation of why the bi-lateral, Anglo-Irish *Belfast (Good Friday) Agreement* is deliberately vague about the notion of 'Ulster-Scots'.

Fauconnier concludes by reminding us, in the area of language development, that nothing replace the attitudes of native speakers towards their regional languages and the dignity and true human values which they encode and express, although they might never have dreamt of resorting to legislative measures or considered any economic consequences.

In response to Fauconnier, **Dónall Ó Riagáin** proposes that the notion of *collateral language* should be the subject a future conference. And **Janice Carruthers** draws attention to the unhelpfulness of the clash between established linguistic terminology and recent legislative terminology for the classification of language variety, and to Fauconnier's identificaion of collateral languages with that of regional languages. Whereas, linguistically, all *langue d'oïl* languages are collateral languages with French, she considers that, by not fulfiling thecriteria, not all *langue d'oïl* languages to be regional languages. In any case, France has not signed the European Charter; with France's insistence on French as the language of State, little wonder that Fauconnier can remark about how delighted the Walloons are that Scots is recognised as one of the Charter's regional languages.

Towards Our Goals

The papers in this volume show collectively that each of the domains under consideration contributes constructively to language development and that the legislative measures such as the *European Charter for Regional or Minority Languages* and the *Languages Equality Bill* may be showing their beneficial effects towards the goals of better development and use.

Irish-language broadcasting both on radio and television is the most developed and best supported. Gaelic-medium broadcasting is advanced but, through new arrangements, in a state of flux and transition. Scots-language broadcasting is only weakly provided for in Scotland, despite a policy of mainstreaming, and paradoxically in terms of dedicated programming (with the likes of *A Kist o Wurds*) maybe marginally better off in Northern Ireland (*pace* McCausland 2003).[8]

Irish-language press in the form of *Foinse* and *Lá* published daily is considerably further developed than the Gaelic-language press in the form of *An Gàidhlig Ur* published monthly or single columns published weekly in the Sunday or daily national press. Scots-language journalism has hardly begun to be developed for serious hard news or expository editorial reflection, but in any case it was shown how effectively Scots-influenced tabloid English reflects Scottish national identity when read with strong Scottish accents. Those columns such as 'The Crack' in the Saturday issue of the *News Letter* tend to restrict themselves to subject matter for which traditional vocabulary is suited.

---

[8] Nelson McCausland, 'Ulster-Scots and the BBC: The Current Situation', in Dónall Ó Riagáin ed. *Language and Law in Northern Ireland* (Belfast, Cló Ollscoil na Banríona, 2003) 113-121.

In the performing arts, although there is no contribution on Irish-language drama, Irish drama as a whole has adopted English with consider virtuosity and success. Scots-language drama has been sustained throughout the twentieth century, although artificial literary Scots has been replaced by a realistic demotic vernacular.

At the same time, the popularity of the soap opera *Ros na Rún* is due to many factors other than its Irish language component, such as discussion of many societal problems, drugs, marital breakdown, planning issues, homosexuality, and so forth. The programme has succeeded in introducing Irish into many new domains unfamiliar to its speakers, a fact that has caused it to experiment with multiple dialectal forms and registers amongst a huge cross-section of its speakers – from the use of learner interlanguage, code-switching and genuine modern Irish as used by colloquial and educated native speakers.

All those measures, which contribute to language development, contribute to economic development. Contributions in this volume, which discussed language diversity and its impact on economic success, all agree that there is ample evidence that this is the case. Present theories are unable to pinpoint directly how we are describe this complicated connection in a way that would remove any remaining doubts persisting in the literature. Tangible evidence is available to indicate ongoing success in Ireland, both North and South, and in the Highland and Islands of Scotland. There is a general call for more interdisciplinary and cross-disciplinary research by both linguists and economists into the positive elements, which seem to contribute to success as indicated in various recent publications.

What emerges from these papers is the exertion of considerable control over language development by institutions and by Government, despite encouraging and enabling legislation. If those domains reflect the voice of the people back at them, it is not without filtering, selection and design in the process. Institutions and Government have, of course, helped, and there are good success stories like *Raidio na Gaeltachta* and *Ros na Rún*. But where there lingers a lack of motivation and will, as with the Scottish Executive and Scots-language broadcasting, there must remain causes for concern. Particularly alarming is the fact that in post-devolution Scotland and now the Executive's second-term, broadcasting remains a power reserved to Westminster and that even local production where it could be most influential does not appear to be in Scottish hands.

The papers here also indicate that there is little co-ordinated policy either between or within countries, or between any of the domains and a conscious policy in language development. Nevertheless, there seems to be some correlation between the levels of Government support and levels of development, with the republic of Ireland leading the way, a point not lost on Eamon Ó Cúiv in his symposium address.

Few papers addressed our question of cross-current themes, although those which did provided telling examples – the use of *Ros na Rún* for instruction in Irish in schools; the use of press texts for linguistic manifestations of Scottishness and nationhood, etc.; the role of Scots-language drama in the cultural strategy, and so on. Yet again, however, there was little evidence of co-ordination.

Finally, there is universal support that minority languages in broadcasting, the press and the performing arts should substantiate culture, but so far, in many instances, that support is shown to be merely symbolic; and that these issues are not primarily matters of education but form key issues as much for devolved Executives as for national Governments. The fulfilment of our goals in Broadcasting, the Press, the Performing Arts and the Economy and in each of Northern Ireland, the Republic of Ireland, and Scotland remains a vital question of language and politics.

The Department of Culture, Arts and Leisure's Language Diversity and Broadcasting Policy

Patricia McAlister

I'm a civil servant with the Department of Culture, Arts and Leisure where I've been heading up the Linguistic Diversity Branch since it was set up in 1998. The Department has lead responsibility for linguistic diversity policy in the Northern Ireland administration and the role of the Branch is to provide advice, support and guidance to Ministers, colleagues and others on linguistic diversity issues.

In this short presentation, I'd like to do three things. First, I'd like to set out briefly the policy framework within which the Department has been dealing with linguistic diversity. Secondly, I'd like to give you, by reference to the policy framework, some information on what we have been doing in relation to broadcasting and minority indigenous languages in Northern Ireland. Thirdly, I'd like to give some indication of what we see as the next steps in relation to broadcasting and the key issues facing us.

First, the policy framework. There are four instruments which we see as of particular significance in relation to minority indigenous languages and broadcasting:

1. the *Belfast (Good Friday) Agreement*
2. the *North/South Co-operation (Implementation Bodies) Northern Ireland Order 1999*;
3. the *European Charter for Regional or Minority Languages*
4. the *Communications Act 2003*.

The *Belfast (Good Friday) Agreement* provides the overarching, general policy objective for work in relation to linguistic diversity, in as much as it commits the Government of the United Kingdom and the Government of the Republic of Ireland to:

"respect, tolerance and understanding for linguistic diversity which in Northern Ireland includes Irish, Ulster Scots and the languages of the minority ethnic communities."

Although it doesn't specifically mention British and Irish sign languages, the Department recognises them too as languages for the purpose of that definition. We believe it is self-evident that communicating and progressing the Government's policy objective of achieving respect, tolerance and understanding in relation to Irish and Ulster Scots must involve engaging with and working through the broadcasting industry – it hasn't been called the most powerful industry in the world for nothing. In particular, it *must* involve television broadcasting, which is arguably the most influential shaper of popular opinion and most effective tool of mass communication in our culture.

In addition to that general commitment the *Belfast (Good Friday) Agreement* contains *two specific references* to broadcasting, both of which relate only to Irish and both of which are set in the context of the *European Charter for Regional or Minority Languages* which the Government was preparing to sign at the time of the Agreement. The Agreement states:

"In the context of active consideration being given to the UK signing the Council of Europe *Charter for Regional or Minority Languages* the British Government will in particular in relation to the Irish language, where appropriate and where people so desire explore urgently with the relevant British authorities and in cooperation with the Irish broadcasting authorities, the scope for achieving more widespread availability of Teilifis na Gaeilge [now TG4] in Northern Ireland."

Since *the regulation* of broadcasting and telecommunications is a reserved rather than a transferred matter, the obligation to implement this particular commitment rests with the UK Government and Whitehall rather than with local Northern Ireland Departments. In particular it is the responsibility of the UK Department for Trade and Industry, the Department for Culture, Media and Sport and, of course, the Northern Ireland Office.

Although responsibility for implementing the commitment rests in Whitehall, the practical implications of the commitment for Northern Ireland's minority languages are significant, and it is important for us here to see it fulfilled as soon as practicable. The reasons are clear. Wales has both its own Welsh language TV station, and Welsh language programming is provided by the BBC. Scotland's Gàidhlig TV programming is supported financially and is carried by English language broadcasters. For various reasons, there has historically been no comparable level of support by BBC Northern Ireland or UTV for Irish language television broadcasting in Northern Ireland.

The commitment in the Agreement effectively recognizes that TG4 is, has been and is likely to remain for the foreseeable future the principal supplier of television programming to meet the needs and demands of the Irish-speaking community in Northern Ireland. It is therefore important to ensure that coverage by TG4 is expanded to reach as many of them as possible.

Having said that, we would recognise the contribution which the BBC has made to Irish and Ulster-Scots language radio broadcasting and online programming and the role which Raidió na Gaeltachta has played. Extension of TG4 coverage could also have benefits for Ulster-Scots since the broadcaster has indicated that it is willing to explore the possibility of carrying quality programmes of interest to that community also. The Agreement goes on to say that the UK Government will also:

"seek more effective ways to encourage and provide financial support for Irish language film and television production in Northern Ireland."

The Government was fortunate in that there was no shortage of views among broadcasters, independent producers, the broad Irish language community, officials and others as how this commitment should be implemented – and they were more than willing to share them with us. Iontaobhas ULTACH / the Ul TACH Trust, in particular, has produced several very useful reports over a number of years. We considered these and we talked to broadcasters, independent producers, and Irish speakers with a wide range of interests. Our then Minister, Michael McGimpsey, agreed that the report produced by Don Anderson for the ULTACH Trust entitled "How to Broadcast the Irish Language in Northern Ireland" should be taken as the starting point for further development. The two recommendations of the report were for training provision for Irish speakers and a production fund in the region of £3m per annum. The then Secretary of State agreed that a two phase pilot project, costing £250,000 pounds per phase over two years should be run to test demand. The objectives of the pilot project were to identify priority training requirements and liaise with training providers to develop suitable training courses and a pilot course leading to NVQ2/3 or equivalent for a specified number of applicants

- to help put together a support package to ensure production of a number of Irish language films or television programmes
- to produce a report with recommendations for draft strategy
- and action plans for future development of the Irish-mediu sector.

After discussion with a wide range of expert opinion throughout the island, including representatives from the Gaelic and Gàidhlig broadcasting industries and the independent production sector, a multi-skilling course based on the successful Údaras na Gaeltachta course was run between February and April 2002. 14 participants successfully completed the course, which was managed by Iontaobhas ULTACH. Of those, many have now gained commissions, had programmes broadcast by TG4 or obtained employment in the industry. The first phase of the pilot has now been evaluated, and a report produced, which will shortly go to Ministers. It would not be appropriate to go into detail about the findings of the evaluation here. I can say, however, that it had many positive things to say about the course and made several useful recommendations about how a second course could be improved.

The Department of Culture, Arts and Leisure is considering these recommendations at present [September 2003]. I would say that the Department recognizes that it has been a cause of frustration to many that follow-up action has been so slow in coming.

In line with the *Belfast (Good Friday) Agreement, the North South Co-operation (Implementation Bodies) Northern Ireland Order 1999* established the North-South Language Body, which is jointly funded by both Governments.

The Body has two agencies, Foras na Gaeilge, the Irish Language Agency and Tha Boord o Ulstèr-Scotch, the Ulster-Scots Agency. Foras has been given the task of promoting the Irish language. Tha Boord has the function of promoting greater use and awareness of Ulster Scots language *and* culture.

Neither agency has been given a specific function in relation to broadcasting, but it is within their remit to take forward appropriate work if they choose. Both agencies have indeed indicated their interest in this area.

Under the *European Charter for Regional or Minority Languages*, the UK Government is committed, in accordance with Part II, to take resolute action to promote, maintain and safeguard both Irish and Ulster Scots. This is reflected in the remit given to North-South Language Body which I've just mentioned.

In accordance with Part III of the Charter, which applies only to Irish at this stage, the Government has made the following commitments in respect of Article 11 which includes broadcasting:

1d encourage or facilitate the production of audio and audiovisual works in Irish;

1 f ii apply existing measures for financial assistance also to audiovisual productions in Irish;

1g to support the training of journalists and other staff for media using regional or minority languages.

As work on broadcasting progresses, the Government will continue to review what provisions we can apply. We currently await with interest the Council of Europe's first report on how it feels the UK Government is implementing the Charter.

I mentioned the UK *Communications Act 2003*, which received Royal Assent this summer. Despite being the most radical overhaul of broadcasting legislation in recent decades, in terms of minority language broadcasting in Northern Ireland it has been widely regarded as the dog that didn't bark.

The draft Bill was published in May 2002 and was preceded in December with a White Paper entitled "A New Future for Communications". The White Paper acknowledged that Irish language broadcasting in Northern Ireland was much less developed than Celtic language broadcasting in Wales and Scotland. It also referred to the commitments given by government in the *Belfast (Good Friday) Agreement* and elsewhere, to promoting and facilitating the use of Irish language, and to Irish language broadcasting. It indicated that Government's aim was to give effect to these commitments without adversely affecting English language broadcasting. It went on to say that, in addition to the Good Friday commitments, future planning would need to reflect the broader commitment to promote understanding, respect and tolerance for linguistic diversity, including Ulster Scots.

Naturally, these comments raised expectations all round. Many saw them as a strong indication that practical help, in the form of statutory underpinning and resources for a Gaelic television fund would soon follow.

The First and Deputy First Minister and many others contributed to the subsequent consultation process on the Bill by underscoring the need to have regard to all of the *Belfast (Good Friday) Agreement* commitments on linguistic diversity.

Given this climate of expectation, it was not surprising that the total absence of any reference to the commitments in the ensuing Bill was greeted with astonishment, disbelief and exasperation. The next development was, of course, a strong campaign to have the Bill amended.

This did not succeed but matters did improve when, following debates in Westminster and Stormont, the Secretary of State for Culture, Media and Sport indicated that consideration would be given to establishing an Irish-medium production and training fund in Northern Ireland. The Northern Ireland Office endorsed this and latterly, in the recent Joint Declaration, the Secretary of State announced that, subject to the production of a satisfactory business case, a fund in the region of up to £12m over 3 years would be made available. The Department tendered earlier this year for a consultant to produce a business case and is currently considering a draft report which will shortly to go Ministers.

All that said, we will seek to work with the new regulatory framework and with the broadcasters to ensure that the issues of Irish and Ulster Scots broadcasting are kept to the fore.

Towards the BBC's Minority Languages Policy

Aled Eirug

In case you're wondering why a Welshman is speaking to you, perhaps I should explain that, for the past six months, I have been working on behalf of the BBC's Nations and Regions's Director of Nations and Regions, Pat Loughrey, and that I have been involved in a review of language provision in Northern Ireland, in particular related to Ulster Scots and Gaelic.

Before speaking about that work, I would like to explain the context of the study, and the relevance of the Welsh experience to the linguistic position in Northern Ireland. I feel that recognition and development of broadcast services in languages other than English is critically important. I count myself fortunate to have lived in Wales through a sea change in public policy towards the Welsh language, which has partly come about in response to political pressure, but also as a result of widespread public sympathy towards the language.

That combination has led to the creation of the Welsh language Fourth Channel, S4C; the creation of a statutory body to propagate the use of Welsh – the Welsh Language Board; the introduction of Welsh as a compulsory subject in the curriculum and an attempt to "mainstream" the language so that it come an integral part of the consideration of any policy area – whether it be health or housing, by the National Assembly for Wales.

That progress has been marked by a largely positive response by institutions, when they are pressed by parents for Welsh medium education, or by consumers for services in Welsh.

Now the situation in Northern Ireland of course, is very different – at the risk of understatement, it is certainly more polarised; support for the Irish language is seen by many within the Loyalist or even the wider Protestant community as opposition towards the other identities of Northern Ireland. However, the difficulty of creating consensus doesn't absolve us of the responsibility to reflect differing cultures and languages within broadcasting, as long as it reflects a real demand and a social reality.

The BBC has a deep and abiding commitment to reflect the diversity of its audience and recognises its responsibility to reflect the richness and diversity of the languages and identities of Northern Ireland, part of which is the Irish language and the culture associated with the Ulster Scots identity.

In the past six months, we have given serious thought to what our commitments should be towards Irish language broadcasting and Ulster Scots. The results of that review are that BBC Northern Ireland will increase its programmes and services related to Irish and Ulster Scots across television, radio and online, and will fund an unprecedented programme of research into defining the requirements and needs of the audience in Northern Ireland.

In the short term, in 2003-04, Irish language television output will include a 4 x 30 minutes observational documentary series on a year in the life of an Armagh GAA club, and a new 10-part magazine series for young people will be broadcast from January, 2004.

A language learning project for Irish, Ulster Scots, and Scots Gaelic is being developed in collaboration with BBC Wales and BBC Scotland.

BBC Northern Ireland's Ulster Scots series *A Kist of Wurds*, on Radio Ulster, will double from twelve programmes to 24 programmes per year, while a landmark event on TV documentary celebrating Ulster Scots culture will be held to coincide with Burns Night 2004.

A demand for "parity of esteem" for Ulster Scots is often made to the BBC; to quote one lobby group, in order "to address cultural imbalance and to *comply* with the principles of diversity, equality and inclusivity".[1] (my emphasis)

Whilst the demand is understandable, the BBC does recognise there is a historical difference in the development of both languages; Irish has a rich written and oral tradition, is taught in a substantial number of schools, and is an accepted medium of communication in many formal and informal settings. In contrast, Ulster Scots is in what has been termed as "severe decline" and rarely heard. The proposed establishment of an academic institution, the Ulster Scots Academy, which will have the same proposed level of funding as the Broadcast Production Fund for the Irish language, is a reflection of the difference in the development of both languages.

BBC Northern Ireland has commissioned a substantial piece of audience research in order to analyse the nature of the Irish language and Ulster Scots audience, and to inform the scope and range of our programming. The research, which is being commissioned from Price Waterhouse Coopers, includes focus group research in both the Irish language and Ulster Scots communities, quantitative research, and interviews with key stakeholders, the results of the survey which will be made available to interested groups.

BBC's Role

This work will help inform the proposed new Broadcast Production Fund due to be established next year with a commitment from Government for funding of £12 million over 3 years The BBC supports the creation of the Fund and will actively work to make the Fund a success, through working in collaboration with TG4, independent producers and the Northern Ireland Assembly's Department of Culture, Arts and Leisure, in particular.

The BBC is the biggest producer of Irish language programming in Northern Ireland, and it has 7 staff dedicated to Irish language broadcasting at present. We believe that the Broadcast Production Fund should not only fund television programmes, but also online and radio services. Our online learners's site, BLAS, for instance gets at least 5,000 hits every week. Interactive TV offers a range of opportunities for versioning programmes in more than one language, so that a GAA game, for instance could have commentary in English, and have Irish on the digital channel at a touch of a red button.

BBC Northern Ireland is part of the Television Broadcasters in Ireland Group

---

[1]   Cf. Nelson McCausland, 'Ulster-Scots and the BBC: The Current Situation', in Dónall Ó Riagáin, ed. *Language and Law in Northern Ireland* (Belfast, Cló Ollscoil na Banríona, 2003) at 66.

(TBIG), which includes the two regulatory agencies, the Broadcasting Council of Ireland, and the Independent Television Commission (Northern Ireland). TBIG's view of access in the Northern Ireland context is that broadcasters should work together to ensure that the necessary arrangements are put in place so that the "regulated to-air television services of each jurisdiction – namely BBC One and Two Northern Ireland, UTV, RTE and Network 2, TV3 an TG4 should be made available, at the earliest possible date, *equally* on all distribution platforms to viewers throughout the island of Ireland. However, although this matter has been discussed between the broadcasters, there has been no action taken to enable TG4 to be broadcast in Northern Ireland.

TG4 is at present available through transmission overspill into large parts of Northern Ireland, and covers up to half of the geographical area of Northern Ireland. TG4's difficulty in not being able to transmit fully into Northern Ireland is largely a problem associated with their inability to clear rights for much of their programming, such as sport, film rights, and soap series. If and when the Production Fund is created, it will be incumbent on all parties to ensure that TG4 is fully accessible in Northern Ireland.

In contrast to TG4, BBC Northern Ireland is primarily, and overwhelmingly an English language service, and has rarely broadcast Irish language programming during peak viewing hours.

The number of Irish language programmes on BBC One or Two NI will have to be considered in the context of a displacement factor, by which viewers would be deprived of English language programmes which they would expect to see. In Wales, much of the support for a solely Welsh language channel in the late nineteen seventies came from non-Welsh speakers who resented the scheduling of Welsh language programmes in peak viewing on BBC Wales and HTV.

Language services are not provided solely because it is in the interest of Irish or Welsh, or Ulster Scots speakers to do so. It is because we as a society feel that it is a valuable and precious part of our heritage – whether we speak that language or not. The joint commitment by the Governments of the UK and Ireland in the Belfast / Good Friday Agreement to the creation of the Broadcast Production Fund in Northern Ireland is an important step for the Irish language. It is now for the broadcasters and producers to ensure that good intentions are translated into practical and creative action.

BBC Northern Ireland and Irish

Kieran Hegarty

This paper addresses the questions set by the symposium organisers in the symposium prospectus and in the Introduction to the present volume.

How does the media contribute to minority language development and the personal development of minority language speakers?

If media is playing an increasingly central and important role, for better or worse, in the life and culture of all of us, at governmental, societal, economic and individual levels, it is obvious that it has an important contribution to make to minority language development. If it is the major channel of communication, information, education, commerce and culture then minority languages need access to it as much as core or mother languages. Media is the main dissseminator of common culture to a far greater extent than was previously the case, which poses both threats and opportunities for minority language culture.

The pace of change is increasing exponentially with rapid paradigm shifts which can be to the advantage of the previously disadvantaged. So minority languages don't have to get increasingly left behind and forced to play catch up or start at the ground floor. Digital media offers greater choice and democratisation through 24/7 access, the synthesis of scarce resources, increasing interactivity, differentiated material, etc.

Irish has traditionally suffered because of its minority situation with its limited access to the world of government, law, commerce, education, media – because media resources were comparatively limited and the needs of the majority monoglot section of population had to be met first. Where all cultural outputs were channelled through a limited number of media outlets, an inevitable homogeneity occurred which was antipathetic to minority differences. It was Darwinian – survival of the biggest and fittest. Where now there is a proliferation of output channels, diversity is much more possible – though not inevitable because of the disproportionate power the big players can yield.

At the same time, and conversely, society is becoming increasingly individualised with communal groupings and activities losing their impact. Before tv and the media became so powerful there were other centres of gravity – the family, local community, wider community, interest groups, etc. which affirmed and ensured the continuity of shared values and cultures. They have now lost much of their power and the individual is now much more at the mercy of new influences to which he has had no traditional allegiances. It should however be noted that there is already a countermovement against this based on the notion of the importance of social capital and an awareness of the danger of loss of individuality and uniqueness in cultural terms. This tendency is already inherent in adherents of minority cultures and will find new allies in those reacting against current trends.

In this context, media in minority languages can have an important role in minority language development and in the personal development of minority language speakers – which, as we have seen, is increasingly the area of focus. Educate, entertain, inform, celebrate, challenge – these are all crucial roles broadcasting can play in minority language development. Taking education for example, as the media is becoming important in so many aspects of our lives, so it is with education. There is increasing emphasis on the provision of online interactive materials for individualised and group learning, on the one hand, and an increasing emphasis on embedding learning in much of what we broadcast, on the other. This has been seen in the BBC's social action and learning campaigns which tackle issues from basic numeracy and literacy to computer literacy to domestic violence, fitness etc. The media in certain aspects is increasingly responding to the real needs of individuals and society. As well as providing relevant output, the development of learning centres, the roll-out of learning buses and the development of partnerships with other learning providers ensures multiple access points and develops long term relationships. With the increased choice which multi-platform and multi-channel offerings should bring, including 24/7 online access, that service is also available to minority language individuals and communities.

How far is the European Charter being implemented and where is it falling short?

There has been some movement towards complying with the European Charter in general in that there is greater recognition of the needs and rights of minority language groups and more support for minority language broadcasting but, obviously, there is much more that could be done. With increased programming in Irish from BBCNI and greater availability of TG4 in NI and the prospect of a film and television fund, there are positive signs of a more comprehensive service being on offer in the relatively short term. There is also a lot more that could be done in the field of radio and specifically new media that is particularly appropriate and relevant for minority languages.

For whom are minority language outputs intended and who decides and with what success?

In the context of BBCNI, our minority language outputs are intended for speakers of those languages and those interested in the languages and culture. That's a pretty wide range of groupings – in terms of Irish language, the latest Census figure [2001] of 168,000 represents a vast number of learners of varying abilities and includes a core grouping of fluent speakers. Outside of that are those with no knowledge of but some interest in the language and aspects of the culture. So our output is for a very disparate range from many schoolchildren learning the language, to adult learners of varying abilities to fluent speakers to non-linguists. And that's just the linguistic ability sorted! There are then the bewildering variety of demographics that the scheduler/commissioner of the main English language output seeks to serve. Young/old/single/young parents/old rockers, etc.

Minority language output in ways has to stretch further than mainstream output, meet more needs and have wider appeal. Partly that's balanced by the fact that we are not chasing jaded palates but are providing '*súil eile, teanga eile, cluas eile*' – a distinctive and different way of looking at and presenting the world. That gives a certain advantage but the output has to be to the same standards that people have become used to with more mainstream programming.

Who decides?

In the end, professional broadcasters should decide, but only after wide ranging consultation with the end users. There are two main ways of doing it – audience insight beforehand or figures and feedback afterwards. But also there are fundamental changes evolving in the way broadcast output is envisaged and produced where broadcasters are looking to mediate less and empower more, to get closer to individuals and communities and let them raise their own issues, tell their own stories, not only creating the broadcast space for this but giving the actual skills to capture, edit, present their material. It is a gradual process of deconstruction and democratisation which is going on, not across all output, but in a growing percentage of it.

By using minority languages what questions are broadcasters addressing? How coordinated is the policy for broadcasting with language development policy?

Minority language broadcasters are obviously attempting to reflect in a more comprehensive and public service way the diverse linguistic and cultural make up of the region in question. They are not always directly pursuing the same aims as language development organisations though much of what they do may contribute to the achievement of those aims. Public service broadcasters should seek to meet the broadcast needs of the diverse population which they serve, inform, entertain and educate (in Reithian terms), reflect, celebrate, challenge and, as the BBC is increasingly attempting to do, build long term links with various communities, to enable people to tell their own stories, to embed learning in many aspects of the output. If we do that job right, it obviously has a very positive effect on language development.

What cross-current themes are being addressed by using minority languages?

Inherent in minority language broadcasting, there are obvious ideas of identity, belonging, diversity, owned and participative as opposed to commodified culture, the affirmation of cultures, the role of the local or minority language in an increasingly internationalised and homogenised cultural context.

Are those themes educational or cultural or developmental?

Many are culturally based but with educational and developmental aspects. The degree to which they are one and/or the other varies between minority languages and their circumstances. Here we are talking of a vibrant language which is used in a variety of settings and also a form of cultural expression which is being consciously repossessed.

Are those themes coordinated between broadcasters, press and the performing arts?

Not in any systematic or regular fashion. But it is happening e.g. with the latest language learning model being developed by the BBC which shows a number of relevant developments – using cutting edge technology and methodologies, the latest research from language learning experts, co-operation between production centres, multi-media models and links to other language providers in more traditional settings, etc.

How far do minority languages in broadcasting, etc., express or substantiate culture, and how far is their use merely symbolic?

I hope we have moved beyond that consideration by now – it is clearly a question of reflecting in as wide and positive and challenging a way what is there and considering what should be there. Nor is it tokenistic, even if the actual quota of programming is not as high as many would wish. We do not produce as much Irish language material as many speakers would wish – for a variety of reasons and causes some of which are clearly being addressed – but the range and quality of what is there and the increasing accessibility and potential for interaction with that means that you do have to consider the quality at least as much as the quantity.

The BBC Northern Ireland Ulster-Scots Unit

Chris Spurr

I have been impressed by the quality and breadth of the speakers I have already heard at this symposium discussing broadcasting in Irish or Scots Gaelic, and not only by the breadth, but also by the width, in that there have been so many distinguished speakers, many of them the heads of their particular broadcasting organisations. In contrast, with regard to Ulster-Scots broadcasting within BBC Northern Ireland, it is not precisely "myself alone", but it is not too far removed from that. At present, we are a small group of three, our broadcast assistant, Fionnuala Wilson, our presenter, Conal Gillespie, and myself, as producer. It is small, but it is a start.

In addressing you at this symposium, I need initially to mention two important things. First, that the views and opinions expressed here are my own, gained over several years experience as a programme maker working in the area of Ulster-Scots, but they are not the official views of the BBC with regard to Ulster-Scots broadcasting, although I will of course allude to some of the management strategy which has led to the current position. Secondly, I shall attempt to avoid the linguistically inaccurate term "language" for referring to Ulster-Scots speech, although the more accurate term "the dialect of Scots, as spoken in Ulster" is quite a mouthful – *At fair fills tha mooth wi wurds.*

Even as revelations at the Hutton Inquiry imply that the BBC has some journalistic feet of clay, there still remains the feeling that the Corporation offers a quality benchmark as a broadcaster. "I heard it on the BBC" suggests some imprimatur of authority and worth. For speakers of or adherents to a minority language to hear their tongue spoken "on the BBC" renders that tongue, if not equal to English, at least a credible alternative to the nation's dominant speech. For speakers of Ulster-Scots, and for those who do not speak the tongue, but who either aspire to speak it, or who strongly believe in the need for Ulster-Scots programmes on radio and television here in Northern Ireland, to hear the tongue used in the context of a broadcast, introducing topics, linking items, in interviews and in reports, demonstrates to them and to the world that Ulster-Scots does indeed possess a contemporary relevance. After a period of doubt and scepticism on several parts: that of speech activists, many of whom had thought for a long time that BBC Northern Ireland would not deliver any Ulster-Scots programmes, and that of many people within the BBC, who thought that programmes in Ulster-Scots would be an impossibility, all were confounded on Sunday March 6th, 2002, when this was heard on BBC Radio Ulster:

> *Fair fa ye, yin an aa, tae A* Kist o Wurds *wi mesel, Conal Gillespie.
> Theday's skailin is a kist fu o music, wittins an crack, wi fowk baith
> young an auld, frae the Airds o Down, tae the shores o the Foyle. A'll
> be haein a yairn wi James Fenton frae Belnaloob; Sally Young frae
> Ballywalter chats about toonland names around whar she wes reared
> ben the Airds; Willie Drennan is fer telling us what the Ulster-Scots
> Fowk Orchestra is aa about, an forby aa that, there's a wheen mair
> things in the kist theday.*[1]

The first series of *A Kist o Wurds* ran for four programmes. Presented by Conal Gillespie, it ranged through a variety of topics and personalities, from "aa tha`Scotch colloguing airts" of Ulster, including, of course, east Donegal. The title is thought particularly apt, and I am sometimes asked to explain it to colleagues within the BBC. A *kist* is, of course, 'a chest used to store or keep things', and so within the programme the notion of 'opening up' or 'discovering' items can be employed. It was thought important to point up that the series was about language, so *the kist hed tae be fu o wurds*. The programmes are topical, in magazine format, and do not rely heavily on bygone reminiscence. From the start, I felt that the series had to be by Ulster-Scots, for Ulster-Scots, and have within the programmes as much Ulster-Scots language as possible. All Conal's presentation and some of his interviews are conducted in Ulster-Scots, of which he is an accomplished and confident speaker. Many contributors, though, are less comfortable or confident in their speech, and so use standard or "Ulsterised" English. A programme totally in Ulster-Scots is an aspiration, and as and when more speakers and contributors can converse at ease, this will no doubt happen. This next extract features Sally Young, from Ballywalter, down the Ards peninsula. We are back with Sally at her parent's farm, looking over the Co Down countryside, and across to Scotland.

> *If ye go by Portavogie, an go doon by sort o Cloughy, Ratallagh, it's different because it wes mair English settlers settled there. An ye can hear the difference – like we wud taak aboot a* dug *'dog', an* stray, *for* 'straw'; *but they wud taak aboot* strow *and a* doag. *There is a difference. They wud nae hae that same Ulster-Scots in it. But if ye go on roond bi Kirkiston, and in tae Kirkubbin, an all tha, it's pure Ulster-Scots up there, the whole thing. An A suppose wi the secondary schools it's sort o, it's hammered oot o ye a bit in the schools; for the teacher dinnae hauf time know whit A wes taakin aboot. If A wes taakin aboot a whaup, he hed nae a notion o wha A wes taakin aboot.[2]*

People like Sally are the essence of what *A Kist o Wurds* is about, and by extension what Ulster-Scots broadcasting on BBC Northern Ireland is about also. This is not just for people of Sally's generation [she is a proud grandmother] who were castigated in school for calling a curlew a *whaup*, and who now feel they can use their own speech publicly and freely, but for young folk too, who are increasingly encouraged by enthusiastic teachers to celebrate the Ulster-Scots dimension in their speech and culture. A presence on radio re-enforces the message in the classroom, and contributes to language development across society.

Any decision about provision for language broadcasting is taken at senior management level. A producer or editor can make suggestions or recommendations for specialised broadcasts, based on their knowledge of an area, but the ultimate decision is at senior level. For example, I might consider that there is an audience within the community of interest that Ulster-Scots embraces to justify at least one radio programme a week. I can suggest this to management,

---

[1] Gillespie introduces the first *A Kist o Wurds*, BBC Radio Ulster, Sunday 6 March 2002
[2] Sally Young, Ballyfrench,/Ballywalter, Co Down, *A Kist o Wurds*, BBC Radio Ulster, Sunday 6 March 2002

with appropriate reference and evidence to make the case, but the decision to implement the suggestion is ultimately not mine. What should be realised, and what influences the thinking of the BBC[3] and its strategy on this, is that in any "like for like" debate, between provision for Irish language programmes and for Ulster-Scots, there is the understanding that the two tongues are at different stages of development. Irish is seen as being a complete written language, with a large literature, both historical and contemporary, with a significant and established presence across all three educational levels, possessing a large cohesive body of speakers, employing both formal and informal use, and having an established grammar and vocabulary. In contrast, Ulster-Scots speech is seen as being fragmented, and at a very different stage of development. What is of interest and relevance is how the development and understanding of Ulster-Scots might be aided by broadcasting, and broadcasting not just involving 'native speakers', as we learn to call those imbibing Ulster-Scots without pause from the cradle, but "revivalists"[4], and also, significantly, those wishing to learn some Ulster-Scots from the ground up. I would welcome approaches from bodies or individuals as to how a programme of language-learning[5] for Ulster-Scots might be achieved within a radio series and an associated website.

Following on from that initial series of four half-hour radio programmes in March 2002, the provision for broadcasting in Ulster-Scots has been thus: a further series of four *A Kist o Wurds* programmes across January and February 2003, and a current series of six programmes which end on 12 October 2003. The anecdotal evidence suggests that the programmes are well received, amongst native speakers, revivalists and even Anglophones and gaelgors. As I understand it, they represent a significant advance on any such provision BBC Scotland might have for programmes in Scots, and importantly demonstrate the "living" quality of Ulster-Scots, which can be heard in a non-formal setting – that is, not just in what has been offered heretofore, such as crafted poems or rhymes, or owersettings of passages from the Scriptures, or other holy books, but in day to day collogues, and again, not just wi aulder boadies taakin aboot auld times, but with younger folk forby, as this extract shows:

> *Conal Gillespie: Gif ye hear anyboadie alloo tha Ulster-Scots bes a leid fer auld-farrant an brok-moothed boadies lik me, hae a listen now tae Ian an Archie, twa lads o pairts frae fornenst Ballymoney, haein a collogue in their ain leein leid:*
> *Ian: An what aboot yersel Archie, ye're in Edinburgh airen't ye?*
> *Archie: Well, not at the minuite, like, but [laugh] aye, A hae been in Edinburgh, awright*

---

[3] Reference throughout to "the BBC" is a shorthand for BBC Northern Ireland, and its approach to the management of language matters, and by extension matters specifically Ulster-Scots.
[4] An interestingly evangelical term for those embracing Ulster-Scots as part of a re-born interest.
[5] "Dialect-learning" is the linguistically accurate term, of course, but to employ it just seems like bad English.

> *Ian: Right, well, ye see, whenever you first gaen ower there, did you fin that them fowk ower there – cud they unnerstan you awright?*
>
> *Archie: Well, it's funny ye should say that, like, 'cos, A mean, whenever A wes first there, A thought A'd be in Scotland, y'know, maist fowk'd be able tae unnerstaund me, but there's a brave wheen o Inglis fowk in Edinburgh y'know, an ye fin lik, ye'd fin yersel haein tae put on a – ye know, yer best Inglis – whenever you'd fell in wi a wheen o them, but whenever A hae a wheen o drinks oan me, A fin it gye haird not to lapse back intae Ulster-Scots anyway.[6]*

In spite of its critics amongst the Ulster-Scots lobby groups who demand increased programme provision, without thinking too closely what the content might be, or who and how many might be the contributors, for them the BBC considers that it *has* taken Ulster-Scots seriously, and points out that it is not working with infinite resources to apply to such broadcasting. Some television programmes have been broadcast over the years, notably *A Nicht o Ulster-Scotch / An Ulster-Scots' Night*[7] in January 2000, which was almost two hours of broadcasting including a gala concert, plus a documentary on the speech, and placed around these were specially filmed pieces with Ulster-Scots folk at home, at school, or at work, all talking the hamely tongue. This night of themed programming doubled the regular Saturday night viewing figures for BBC2 Northern Ireland, and there have been requests ever since for a similar broadcast.[8] Since that significant night, there have been other television programmes such as *The Ulster-Scots Italian Job*[9], chronicling a visit to carnivals in Italy and France by Ulster pipers, dancers and musicians.

There was also something of an Ulster-Scots presence, although not branded as such, within the former BBC Northern Ireland television series such as *Country Times*, *Sky High*, or *Hammond's Ireland*, which occasionally featured contributors from Ulster-Scots backgrounds; and on radio, in those perennial favourites of the piping clan, *A Touch of Tartan* and *Pipes and Drums*. At present [September/October 2003], *A Kist o Wurds* is on air, and, in the style of the pan-BBC Voices Project of earlier in the year, which was devised to give a platform to those voices not regularly heard within a community, an Ulster-Scots Voices will soon launch, with an accompanying dedicated website, so this facility will be constantly available to all with internet access. Furthermore, two of the individuals featured in the Ulster-Scots Voices have been filmed, and their stories will be screened later in the year, or early in 2004, as a thirty minute television documentary.

---

[6] Ian McClure and Richard 'Archie' Archibald, Ballymoney, *A Kist o Wurds*, BBC Radio Ulster, 7 September 2003. Ian is in his final year studying Spanish and French at Strathclyde; in 2003, Archie was awarded his Masters in Astrophysics from Edinburgh, a subject far removed from the turf moss.

[7] BBC2 Northern Ireland, 21.05h – 22.50h, 29 January 2000. The Radio Times billing read thus: *A Nicht o Ulster-Scotch [An Ulster-Scots' Night] Fair fa' ye tae a nicht o sang, stawrie, musack an pooetry, tha heel o Jennerwarry for tae mairk. At the end of January, Helen Mark welcomes you to a night of song, story, music and poetry with an Ulster-Scots' and Scottish flavour.*

[8] At time of writing, it is likely that a second Ulster-Scots Theme Night will be broadcast on BBC2 Northern Ireland television in January 2004.

[9] BBC1 Northern Ireland, 25 February, 2002.

So in a fairly rapid distillation, that is the present context with regard to BBC Northern Ireland and Ulster-Scots. It might be worth noting that the other public service broadcaster based here, Ulster Television, has not, as far as I am aware, been lobbied in the manner the BBC has, with regard to provision of Ulster-Scots programming. The expectation amongst the lobbyists is that any obligation to provide such programmes falls to the publicly funded broadcaster. In the space left to me, let us consider some, but not all of the questions posed by the directors of this symposium, and attempt to answer them with regard to the BBC and Ulster-Scots. I will take a backwards route, if I may. The answers offered here are of necessity succinct, owing to the time constraints imposed by the symposium.

Is the use of Ulster-Scots simply an educational issue? No, and at present it is perhaps not even that. This could surely be an area for future development.

How far does the use of Ulster-Scots express or substantiate culture, or is its use merely symbolic? As I outlined earlier, the thinking behind the radio series and any television I have produced has been to celebrate and promote the culture. The merely symbolic has never been a consideration.

What cross-current themes are being addressed? On the radio series, the themes are those of any similar topical magazine in any tongue – although they would often veer towards the cultural. There is little or no formal coordination between broadcasting and the press and the performing arts, although when performances of an Ulster-Scots nature are staged they will feature.[10] Theatre venues have made approaches to the BBC with regard to staging Scots-themed entertainments around the "Burns Season" in January. The local press receive weekly up-dates of the programme content of *A Kist o Wurds,* and they run the occasional feature. I am not aware of any plans for Ulster-Scots drama on radio, on television, or film.

What questions are being addressed, and does broadcasting co-ordinate with language policy? As before, the questions are seen to be topical, and of specific interest to the Ulster-Scots community. They could be to do with the provision of facilities in west Tyrone; discussing the absurdities of neologisms in the speech; focusing on the policies of the Ulster-Scots Agency, or the workings of the Heritage Council. In the absence of or agreement for a formal language development policy what does broadcasting do? There are several voluntary groups with enthusiastic amateurs working on aspects of Ulster-Scots speech, but their combined linguistic status is not of great academic strength, and so I feel personally that it is difficult to see how any policy towards the development of Ulster-Scots speech could be furthered without the input from professional linguistic and teaching expertise across all three levels of education, and from within Ulster.

Who is Ulster-Scots broadcasting for, and who decides this? I believe I have answered this for you earlier, when I alluded to the way in which the BBC determines its specialist programme output.

How does broadcasting contribute to minority language development, and to the development of its speakers? With regard to Ulster-Scots and BBC Northern

---

[10]   One such was the stage musical *Premonition.* Performed in St Anne's Cathedral in March 2002, as part of a Belfast Ulster-Scots Festival, it retold the story of the Siege of Derry, and the tragic love affair between Jane and Michael Browning.

Ireland I would submit that in comparison to other media and artistic outlets, including the regional press and our performing arts, and although with only an occasional series of programmes such as *A Kist o Wurds*, the BBC is making a significant and important contribution, which Ulster-Scots speakers genuinely appreciate. That is not to say we could not do more. Indeed we could, and with a properly constructed and implemented policy towards the development of Ulster-Scots speech, I am sure we will.

How far is the European Charter being implemented? What is the shortfall, and what is preventing any improvement to the current position? If we consider the various obligations of Article 11 of the Charter, at present here in the BBC we are certainly offering programmes in Ulster-Scots [Section 1, sub-section a iii], but also at present there is no sign of a dedicated radio or TV channel for the tongue.[11] Section 1, sub-section b ii, asks for radio programmes "on a regular basis". In the last broadcasting year, 2002-03, which follows more or less the financial year, i.e. April to March, two hours of Ulster-Scots radio were broadcast. The prospect for this current year, 2003-04, promises twelve hours, that is two series of six half hour magazines, repeated within the week, to make each programme count as an hour's airtime. I leave it to your judgement as to whether that amount of airtime, although a 600 per cent increase on the previous year, represents programmes on a "regular basis". The situation in television is similar, with programming being sporadic or rare, rather than regular. As any Ulster-Scot will tell you *"Aething's better nor naething"*, but with relative ease of achievement, there could be a further increase in the number of radio programmes, to offer a topical weekly presence. Outwith an editorial and strategic commitment to fulfil any obligation to broadcasting in Ulster-Scots, a commitment which has to come from senior management and be approved as one of its objectives, another major matter at issue is the financial cost of resources and staffing that this extra programming would entail. However, with the commitment from the BBC that the situation will improve somewhat with regard to extra broadcast hours for Ulster-Scots in 2004, there are nevertheless issues with regard to the inclusion of all the Ulster-Scots activist groups[12], who must feel that they can "buy in" to such an expansion of airtime, even though it would not fulfil all their aspirations.

Tantalisingly, I see in Article 11, Section 3, that cross-border broadcasting is considered a welcome thing. I would love to have programmes made here, not necessarily *A Kist o Wurds*, shared by listeners in Scotland, or the Irish Republic, when transmitted on their radio stations. Perhaps this is something for discussion with other broadcasters at a later date? In conclusion, I shall leave the last word to a contributor who came on the programme to make an important point, and one of which not everyone here might be aware. This is Liam, he comes from North Antrim, and as he points out, folk like him from the Roman Catholic tradition are as good Ulster-Scots speakers as any:

---

[11] Nor are there such channels broadcasting in the north of Ireland for the Irish language, nor are there dedicated television channels in Scotland for Scots or Gaelic. BBC Scotland has a Gaelic language radio service, Radio Nan Gaidheal, but no service in Scots.

[2] Including the Ulster-Scots Language Society and the Ulster-Scots Heritage Council, whose Director was very critical of the BBC and its Ulster-Scots policy at the Language and Law Symposium held in Belfast in February 2003.

What aboot Loughgiel, Magherhoney, Corkey, Garrydoo, Anticur? Maist, but not aa o them places, is what a boadie micht caa 'No vera Protestan'. Ah'm feared tha a lock o them Bilfawst yins, if they were nae weel edumicated, wud think that fowk fae D'loy an aa didnae speak the hamely tongue. We dae, in oor hearts, an in oor mooths.[13]

---

[13] Liam Logan, Dunloy, *A Kist o Wurds*, BBC Radio Ulster, 27 March 2002

Súil Eile

Seosamh Ó Cuaig

A chairde, tá an-áthas orm a bheith anseo i mBéal Feirste as ceartlár na craoltóireachta raidió agus teilifíse Gaeilge sa tír agus sa domhan, is é sin Gaeltacht Chonamara. I nGaeltacht Chonamara atá TG4, is ann atá na comhlachtaí scannánaíochta is forásaí sa nGaeilge, is ann atá Telegael, Cinegael agus go leor eile. Is ansin freisin atá an rud is mó ar fad a bhfuil bród agamsa as, Raidió na Gaeltachta.

Murach Conamara ní bheadh iriseoireacht na Gaeilge ar an raidió agus ar an teilifís mar atá inniu. Ach fuair muid cabhair as áiteacha eile, agus as an Tuaisceart freisin.

Bhí tionchar an Tuaiscirt orm féin nuair a thosaigh mé ag craoladh i 1968. Ní raibh duine ar bith eile is eol dom ag an NUJ sa nGaeltacht an uair sin. Fear as an Tuaisceart a chuir leis an gceird mé, Proinsias Ó Conluain, sárchraoltoir agus scríbhneoir agus iriseoir. Na daoine eile a thug lámh chúnta dom ag an am b'as an Tuaisceart iad féin ; Ciarán ó Nualláin (deartháir do Mhyles na gCopaleen), Tarlach Ó hUid agus Liam Mac Reachtain, beirt a chaith seal i bpríosún.

Nuair a chuir muid SaorRaidió Chonamara ar bun – pirate station – i Ros Muc is i nDoire Cholm Cille a fuair muid an múnla. Bhí Radió Free Derry ar an aer agus nuair a chuaigh muid síos abhaile shocraigh muid Radio Free Chonamara a chur le chéile. Arú anuraidh phléigh mé an scéal seo le Martin Mc Guinness agus, ar ndóigh, bhí cuimhne mhaith aige ar Radio Free Derry. Bhí sé páirteach ann – bhí Martin Mc Guinness páirteach in go leor rudaí i nDoire na blianta sin! B'údar áthais dó a chloisteáil go raibh an oiread sin tionchair ag Radio Free Derry ar ShaorRaidió Chonamara.

Tá mo shaol caite thiar agam ó shin ag plé le raidió, ag déanamh corrchlár teilifíse, ag plé le cúrsaí polaitíochta, agus ag meascadh na rudaí seo ar fad trína chéile agus "still getting away with it," mar deir an Béarla.

Ach scaití fiafraíonn tú díot féin an bhfuil tú ag déanamh aon mhaith nó an bhfuil daoine ag éisteacht? Is beag an rud a thugann ardú croí duit. Bhí mé istigh Tigh Mhaidhcó, pub I Ros Muc, oíche nuair a dúirt seanfhear liom gur thaithnigh mo chuid craoltóireachta leis. "Tugann tú sólás do na daoine," a dúirt sé. Is cosúil le caint as an mBíobla é. Nó Martin Hayes, an ceoltoir iontach as Co. an Chláir, cúpla mí ó shin nuair a bhí muid I Virginia ag caint faoi "Re-imagining Ireland" – tháinig sé chugam agus dúirt go mbíonn sé ag éisteacht go hanmhinic le Raidió na Gaeltachta ar an idirlíon i San Francisco. Nó aríst le linn dúinn a bheith i mBoston sa teach atá ag deartháir mo mhná céile, dúirt duine eicínt gur gearr go mbeadh nuacht an iarthair ar Raidió na Gaeltachta. Ár mac, Colm, nach raibh ach tri bliana déag, a fuair ar an idirlíon é agus cé a bheadh ag léamh na nuachta ach ár n-iníon Máire Áine!

Dá bhfeicfeá an bród a bhí ag an uncail astu. Is beag raidió a bhí i Roisín na Mainíoch nuair a d'fhág seisean é, gan trácht ar an teilifís.

Tá sampla beag eile agam a bhaineann leis an Tuaisceart: oíche a raibh muid i gCumann Chluain Aird bhí lead ann a raibh beagán aithne agam air. D'fhiafraigh mé de cén chaoi a raibh a athair. "Bhuel," a dúirt sé, "níl sé go maith. Tá sé sa Royal Victoria," a deir sé, "agus bheadh sé básaithe murach Raidió na Gaeltachta. Tá an raidió   lena thaobh ag an leaba aige agus is é atá á choinneáil beo na laethanta seo."

Níl ach dhá rud eile ar mhaith liom béim a leagan orthu inniu agus is iad sin an modh oibre ar a dtugann siad "Súil Eile" agus, ar ndóigh, an Ghaeilge féin. Murar "súil eile" a bheas ar an raidió agus ar an teilifís atá againn leáfaidh siad sa deireadh, sleamhnóidh siad agus imeoidh siad. Anois d'fhéadfaí an-argóint a thosú faoi céard é an "súil eile "seo. Ach tá a fhios againn go rí-mhaith céard nach é. Ní homogenisation é agus ní consumerism é agus ní ionsaí ar an Iaráic é. Ní impiriúlachas é, ní imeacht le sruth é agus ní babe-achas é. Is maith liomsa a bheith ag breathnú ar na babes mé féin ach nuair a fheicim duine acu ar tábhachtaí í a bheith dathúil ná inseacht dhúinn cén chaoi a mbeidh an aimsir amárach b'fhearr liom duine nach mbeadh leath chomh suntasach.

An babe-achas seo, an nua-aimsearachas seo … this is a fight between modernity and old ideas ... chomh maith agus go bhfuil chuile rud atá "modern" go maith agus chuile "old idea" go dona – caithfidh muid a bheith san airdeall air.

Rud eile a chaithfear a sheachaint; a bheith ag aistriú propaganda Mheiriceá go Gaeilge ó lá go lá. Bhí mé féin i Raidió na Gaeltachta an oíche sular "thit" Saigon. Tháinig tuairisc isteach,"there are fears in Saigon tonight that the city will fall before morning." Ba sheo é Raidió na Gaeltachta i dtír a throid in aghaidh Impireachta ar feadh na gcéadta bliain. Shuigh mé síos agus scríobh mé mar seo: "Tá an Viet Cong ag scuabadh ó dheas agus má leanann siad den scríb reatha seo beidh siad i Saigon roimh mhaidin. Tá Meiriceánaigh ag teicheadh lena n-anam. Ní fhéadfadh an DG glaoch orm agus a rá go raibh sé mícheart ach "súil eile" a bhí ann.

Anois an Ghaeilge. Mura mbeidh meas ar an nGaeilge féin sna cúrsaí seo ní fiú an tairbhe an trioblóid. Go minic is iad na foghlaimeoirí a bhíonn ag leagan síos an chaighdeáin, daoine a bhfuil an Ghaeilge foghlamtha go dona acu a bhíonn i gceannas. Ba cheart don dream a bhfuil an Ghaeilge chruthanta acu a bheith tréan leo seo agus iad a dhíbirt nuair is gá. Cinnte is ceart a bheith foighdeach leis an bhfoghlaimeoir ach nuair is daoine a d'fhoghlaim go dona í a bhíonn á múineadh tá sé in am labhairt. Chonaic muid ar chuid de na cláracha foghlama a rinne RTÉ é. An bhfuil aon dream sa domhan a bheadh ag iarraidh Fraincis a fhoghlaim a ghabhfadh ag caint le daoine a d'fhoghlaim go dona í iad féin?

Tarlaíonn rudaí mar seo in Albain freisin. Dhá bhliain ó shin bhí mé i Stornoway agus bhí beirt chailíní a bhí dathúil agus meabhrach ar an tsráid ag díol leabhra Gaidhlige. D'fhiafraigh mé díob ar chuala siad caint ar na "After Eights". D'fhreagair siad go bhfuil seacláidí ann a dtugtar "After Eights" orthu. Ní hea, a deirimse, chuala muid in Éirinn nuair a chuir Maggie Thatcher ocht milliún punt ar fáil le cláracha Gaidhlige a chui ai an tcilifís go raibh daoine nach raibh suim soip acu sa nGaidhlig tagtha lá arna mháireach agus fonn orthu a dhul ag déanamh na gcláracha. Tugadh na hAfter – Eights orthu.

Ní raibh sé cloiste acu, "We haven't heard it," a dúirt siad "but it is so true!" Bhreathnaigh mé i mo dhiaidh agus mé ag siúl uathu. Bhí siad ina seasamh i lár na sráide agus iad fós ag rachtaíl gháire.

Irish Language Broadcasting

Tomás Mac An Iomaire

Ó thaobh aon mheán, meán craolta nó meán clóite, is í an cheist thábhachtach ag deireadh an lae - an féidir déanamh á uireasa?

Cuirtear an cheist go minic an fiú é a bheith ann, bíodh sin ina stáisiún raidió, stáisiún teilifíse, nuachtán nó iris, agus i bhfurmhór na gcásanna faoi aon tseirbhís de chuid na meán is é an freagra 'Is fiú'. Ach nuair a chuirtear an cheist an féidir déanamh á uireasa, cuireann sin iachall orainn aird a thabhairt ar an gceist, scrúdú beag nó mór a dhéanamh orainn féin agus freagra a thabhairt a mbeidh muid sásta nó in ann seasamh air?

Más féidir déanamh á uireasa tá sé níos éasca an cheist a réiteach. Níl oiread de phian ag baint leis má ligtear an tseirbhís sin i léig nó má scaoiltear léi ar fad. Agus an teist mhór muna mbíonn ruaille buaille ón bpobal is féidir glacadh leis go minic nach bhfuil drochbheart déanta nó má tá níl sé chomh tábhachtach i súile an phobail go gcuireann sé as dóibh. Ach munar féidir déanamh á uireasa tuigeann muid ansin go bhfuil seirbhís agus meán den scoth againn, gur páirt dar saol laethúil é; go dtugann sé dúinn rud éicint nach bhfuil muid a fháil in aon áit eile agus gó mba bhoichte muid á uireasa.

Ag an bpoinnte sin tosnaíonn muid ag cur ceisteanna orainn féin agus ar ár gcairde: Céard atá ag an mean seo nach bhfuil muid in ann déanamh á uireasa; céard a thugann sé dúinn a dhéanann ár saol laethúil níos saibhre; cén fáth go gcasann muid air an meán raidió nó teilifíse nó an léann muid an nuachtán seo gach uile mhaidin nuair a éiríonn muid aniar sa leaba.

Is féidir a rá faoin Éireannach gur daoine muid a éisteann le cuid mhaith raidió, a bhreathnaíonn ar chuid mhaith teilifíse agus a léann cuid mhaith nuachtán.

Ach cén fáth go roghnaíonn muid go minic meán amháin agus a dtugann muid dílseacht dó thar aon mheán eile? Roghnaíonn muid nuachtán thar nuachtán eile, stáisiún raidió nó teilifíse thar chinn eile. An freagra atá ar an gceist sin ná go guireann an meán sin ar fáil dúinn na nithe atá ag teastáil uainn nó a thugann sásamh dúinn.

Déanfaidh mise tagairt do mheán amháin, an meán a bhfuil taithí agus cleachtadh agam air-Raidió na Gaeltachta. Craolann Raidió na Gaeltachta 24 uair sa ló, seacht lá na seachtaine ar fud na tíre. Tá fáil air freisin ar an idirlíon ar fud an domhain. Creidim gur fiú Raidió na Gaeltachta a bheith ann agus rachaidh mé chomh fada lena rá go bhfuil pobal mór amuigh ansin a déarfadh linn nach féidir déanamh á uireasa.

Creideann Raidió na Gaeltachta san obair atá ar bun aige—Creideann sé freisin san meán trína ndéanann sé a chuid oibre - meán na Gaeilge. Seirbhís iomlán tré mheán na Gaeilge é. Ní ghabhann sé aon leithscéal faoi sin. Is é an t-aon sheirbhís iomlán raidió nó teilifíse tré mheán na Gaeilge é in Éirinn. Ní áirím sin ach is é an t-aon sheirbhís raidió nó teilifíse é tré mheán mionteanga go hiomlán i measc na dtíortha Ceilteacha.

Agus cuireann tú ceist céard atá ar siúl ag Raidió na Gaeltachta a bhfuil muid chomh mórtasach sin as?

Séard é Raidió na Gaeltachta ná seirbhís phoiblí raidió tré mheán na Gaeilge, atá ar fáil saor in aisce ar fud na tíre agus a dheineann freastal ar phobal iomlán, pobal mionlaigh san áireamh. Deineann sé na trí (3) nithe is dual do sheirbhís phoiblí a dhéanamh - cuireann sé an pobal ar an eolas, cuireann sé oideachas ar an bpobal agus cuireann sé siamsaíocht ar fáil dóibh.

Sin na príomhábhair d'aon mheán - go gcoinneofaí an t-éisteoir ar an eolas faoina nithe sin a bhfuil suim aige nó aici iontu ar nós cúrsaí nuachta agus cúrsaí reatha-na cúrsaí sin atá ag tarlú thart air-ina phobal féin, ina thír féin agus ina dhomhan féin. Tá suim agus spéis ag an ngnáthéisteoir sa méid sin - a bheith coinnithe ar an eolas. Sin an fáth a bhfuil ag éirí le stáisiúin raidió áitiúla. Sin an fáth ar éirigh le blianta le nuachtáin áitiúla.

An difríocht mhór idir na stáisiúin áitiúla agus seirbhísí eile go bhfuil na seirbhísí áitiúla go hiomlán áitiúil agus go gcaithfidh tú triall áit éigin eile le do chuid fiosrachta a shásamh má tá spéis agat i nithe taobh amuigh de do phobal féin.

Agus tá spéis ag an bhfurmhór againn sa saol mór amuigh ansin. Tá spéis againn céard atá ag tarlú taobh amuigh dar gcontae féin, taobh amuigh dár gcúige féin agus taobh amuigh dar dtír féin. Sin an fáth go dteastaíonn seirbhís níos iomláine ná an tseirbhís áitiúil. Ag fanacht le Raidió na Gaeltacha cuireann sé oideachas ar an bpobal tréna chuid eolais, tréna chuid nuachta agus cúrsaí reatha agus tré mhalartú tuairimí.

Ní oideachas foirmealta é seo ach is oideachas é a shúnn muid isteach le fonn go laethúil   Agus mar shiamsaíocht faigheann muid ceol, amhráin, drámaíocht, spórt agus mar sin de. Cén bhaint atá aige seo le forbairt teangan, le forbairt mionteangacha, le cúrsaí oideachais, leis an eacnamaíocht?

Caithfidh an meán in aon mhionteanga féachaint ar fhorbairt na teangan sin. Caithfidh sé féachaint ar chúrsaí oideachais ach má fhanann an meán sin sáite taobh istigh de na gnéithe oifigiúla agus foirmeálta den obair i.e. forbairt teangan agus oidhreachta, tá an meán sin ag cur lámh ina bhás féin.

Ní shin le rá go gcaithfidh gach meán mionteangan a bheith ina chuile ní do chuile dhuine. Go deimhin ní féidir leis sin a dhéanamh ach caithfidh sé cúrsa a mharcáil amach dó féin, cúrsa atá sách leathan ach ag an am céanna cúrsa atá sé in ann a leanacht agus a chinntiú gur cúrsa den scoth a bheidh ann dóibh siúd ar a bhfuil sé ag freastal.

Níor leag Raidió na Gaeltachta amach ariamh aon phlean leis an nGaeilge a shábháil. Níor leag Raidió na Gaeltachta amach ariamh aon phlean leis an nGaeilge a fhorbairt ná níor leag sé amach ariamh aon phlean a dúirt go mbeadh níos mó daoine ag labhairt Gaeilge faoi cheann fiche bliain eile mar shampla.

Ní hé sin gnó na gnaithe na seirbhíse.

Tá eagrais eile atá ina bhun sin le blianta fada - Conradh na Gaeilge, Comhdháil Náisiunta na Gaeilge, Foras na Gaeilge, Cumann Lúthchleas Gael; b'féidir fiú Fianna Fáil.

Ach tá mé cinnte gur mó atá déanta ag Raidió na Gaeltachta i bhforbairt agus i gcur chun cinn na Gaeilge ná mar atá déanta ag go leor eagras cé nach shin é an ról a leagadh amach dó. Cinnte tá ról an-tábhachtach ag Raidió na Gaeltachta i bhforbairt na teangan. Ach tá sin aige ní mar phríomhról ach mar ról tánaisteach, ról a tharlaíonn go nádúrtha, ról nach bhfuil eagraithe ach a thagann go nádúrtha tréna chuid craoltóireachta.

Ta an fhorbairt chéanna déanta aige ar an gceol, ar an drámaíocht, ar an scríbhneoireacht, ar an amhránaíocht. Ach tá sin déanta aige ina ról mar chraoltóir toisc dar liom nach é ról Raidió na Gaeltachta, ná aon mheán chraolta eile go deimhin, a bheith ina chaomhnóir na ina eagras forbartha teangan. Ní ar bhealach oifigiúil ar aon nós.

Dá dtógfadh Raidió na Gaeltachta an bóthar éasca agus ceol le lirici Béarla a chraoladh ní bheadh an fhorbairt sin tagtha ar an gceol gaelach sa tír ná ar an amhránaíocht tré Ghaeilge. Agus níl mé ag caint ar amhránaíocht ar an sean nós amháin. Tá mé ag caint ar phopcheol, ar cheol tíre, ar bhailéid. Tá mé ag caint ar Chlannad, Altán, ar John Spillane, na hAncairí, Danú, Deirbhis, Dolores Keane, Mary Black, Mairéad agus Tríona Ní Dhomhnaill, Karen Casey, Cherish the Ladies, Solas agus cuid mhaith eile.

Murach go raibh meán ag na ceoltóirí seo lena gcuid ábhar a chraoladh air agus a chasadh ní bheadh an t-ábhar ann. Sin dar liom forbairt teangan. Dá rachadh Raidió na Gaeltachta an bóthar éasca - go deimhin déarfainn an bóthar leisciúil - agus an rud seo ar a dtugtar freastal ar an óige a dhéanamh tré neart popcheoil agus ceol eile i mBéarla a chasadh go rialta ní bheadh an fhorbairt atá anois ar ár gceol dúchasach agus ar an gceol nua tré Ghaeilge againn.

Mar a chéile le caighdean na Gaeilge ar an tseirbhís. Deirtear linn go minictog go réidh é nó caillfidh sibh na foghlaimeoirí. Tá sin cosúil le rá leis an mBBC labhair níos moille, ná bíodh do chuid Béarla chomh saibhir nó caillfidh sibh na foghlaimeoirí.

Níl Raidió na Gaeltachta ann le bheith ag múineadh na teangan ach is iontach an áis foghlamtha é. Is iontach an áis oideachais é cé nach mar áis oideachais a buníodh é ná a ghníomhaionn sé cés móide den uair a mbíonn sé ag plé le craolta oideachais. Mar chruthúnas air sin níl aon Ollscoil in Éirinn nach bhfuil cartlann de thaifead Raidió na Gaeltachta acu. Tá sí ag Ollscoil na hÉireann, Gaillimh go hoifigiúil ach tá a fhios agam go bhfuil sí ag na hOllscoileanna eile go neamhoifigiúil. Níl aon locht agamsa air sin. Go deimhin is breá linn é sin.

Cé nach ar an mac léinn atá craoladh Raidió na Gaeltachta dírithe - agus nár chóir gurb ea - tá sé ansin don fhoghlaimeoir ag gach leibhéal agus don scoláire freisin. Tá clár ar leith ar ndóigh atá an-tábhachtach i gcúrsaí forbartha teangan, Leagan Cainte, a phléann foclaíocht agus structúir teangan. Tarlaíonn sé seo ó am go chéile ar chláracha eile freisin ar nós an chláir as Maigh Eo 'I Measc na nDaoine'.

Is fiú a mheabhrú freisin go bhfuil an chartlann is mó in aon mhionteanga ar domhan ag Raidió na Gaeltachta. Tá mé cinnte nach amháin gur ábhar oideachais do mhic léinn na linne seo atá inti ach go mbeidh sé amhlaidh ar feadh blianta fada amach anseo.

Níor mhiste a lua ag an bpoinnte seo an ceangal atá ag Raidió na Gaeltachta le BBC Raidió Uladh agus le BBC Raidió nan Gaedhal le cláracha ar nós *Blas* agus *Sruth na Maoile*. Ba chóir gur scáthán ar an saol é aon mheán. Tá súil agam gur scáthán ar an saol é Raidió na Gaeltachta. Tá a chuid oibre dírithe ar an bpobal beo agus cé go gcuirtear inár leith gur chaitheamar an iomarca ama ag plé le seandaoine agus ag bailiú eolais uathu sin rud **a bhí le déanamh** ag seirbhis óg agus rud ar chóir dúinn a bheith bródúil as. Tá na daoine seo anois imithe ar shlí na fírinne agus murach gur tógadh an t-ábhar uathu nuair a deineadh ní bheadh an t-ábhar oideachais againn inniu ná ní bheadh an chartlann thábhachtach sin againn i ngach uile chanúint sa tír.

Ní amhlaidh go ndearnadh dearmad ar aon aoisghrúpa eile. Níor deineadh. Agus ní dhéanfar.

Bua mhór d'aon mheán a bheith neamhspleách. Neamhspleách ar bhrú polaitiúil agus ar bhru Rialtais, ar bhrú na heaglaise. Ach i gcás na meán mionteangacha tá neamhspleáchas eile tábhachtach. Is é sin neamhspleáchas ar na heagrais mionteangacha - na cinn oifigiúla agus na cinn neamhoifigiúla.

Ní aon mhasla é seo do na heagrais Ghaeilge, na Gàidhlice, na Breathnaise.

Ach ní ionann sin agus a rá nár chóir comhoibriú leis na heagrais seo. Ní shin atá i gceist. Séard atá i gceist go mbeadh gach meán in ann gníomhú ar a chlár oibre féin seachas a bheith ag gniomhú ar shaghas clár oibre aontaithe ar bhonn teangan. Ni bheadh sin ceart na folláin.

Ar an gcaoi chéanna is nach bhfuil sé ceart feachtas a bheith ar bun ag aon mheán i gcoinne aon cheann de na heagrais seo. Ach ag an am céanna caithfear a chinntiu go gcaitear leis na heagrais mionteanga mar a chaitear le gach eagras nó eagraíocht eile. Sin gnó na meán.

Mar fhocal scoir tá ról an-mhór agus an-tábhachtach ag na meáin i gcothú agus i bhforbairt teangan agus cultúir. Go minic siad na meáin, go háirithe an teilifís agus ansin an raidió, a chinneann bás nó beatha cultúir agus teangan. Sin an fáth a bhfuil sé chomh tábhachtach díospóireacht agus plé a dhéanamh ar ról na meán atá ag freastal ar mhionteangacha. Sin an fáth freisin go gcaithfear breathnú go fadthéarmach ar ról na meáan seo agus gan a bheith ag breathnú, mar a deintear go minic, ar céard atá "tábhachtach" inniu, nó cén freagra a oireann inniu.

Sinne ata ag obair sna meain agus a bhfuil an dualgas orainn treoir a thabhairt caithfidh muid a bheith san airdeal I gcónaí gur b'é an rud ceart a dheineann muid seachas an rud a bhfuil tóir air inniu nó mar a deirtear san mbearla an rud atá popular.

Irish Language Broadcasting

Mairead Ní Nuadhain

Tá réimse leathan pointí tagartha ag an siompóisiam seo - cuid acu a bhaineann leis an obair a bhíonn idir lámha agam agus cuid nach mbaineann. Towards Our Goals- a deir sé sa teideal agus ansin cuirtear roinnt ceisteanna faoin dul chun cinn a dhéanann teanga neamhfhorleathan i gcásanna áirithe; in mo chás-sa, an chraoltóireacht teilifíse. Cén aidhm atá agamsa mar Eagarthóir Comisiúnaithe na gClár Gaeilge in RTÉ? Déanfaidh mé tagairt do na ceisteanna a cheapaim a bhaineann liom agus déanfaidh mé neamhaird díobh siúd nach mbaineann.

Forbairt na teanga - an aidhm í sin no an dtarlaíonn sé mar thoradh ar an bpríomhobair? Breathnóimid air sin. *European Charter for Regional and Minority Languages* - ní bhaineann sé linn; An Bille Teangacha -ní bheidh baint dhíreach aige linn ach an oiread. "For whom are minority language outputs in broadcasting intended? Who decides?" Feicfimid.

Ar dtús, ní miste beagáinín cúlra a thabhairt fúm féin. Mo theideal iomlán anois le cúpla mí anuas, ó cuireadh atheagar ar Rannóg Gnó na Teilifíse in RTÉ ná: Eagarthóir Coimisiúnaithe na gClár Gaeilge, Oideachais agus Ilchultúir. Sular ceapadh mar eagarthóir Coimisiúnaithe mé trí bliana ó shin, bhí mé i mo léiritheoir teilifíse agus i rith an ama sin chuir mé tús leis an tsraith "Léargas,"clár atá ann i gcónaí.

Na dualgaisí i leith na Gaeilge atá ormsa faoi láthair ná cláracha Gaeilge a choimisiúnú do RTÉ féin agus 182.5 uair an chloig de chláracha Gaeilge a sholáthar gach bliain do TG4. Titeann an dualgas ormsa freisin féachaint chuige go n-úsáidtear an Ghaeilge ar ócáidí speisialta agus bíonn sé de phribhléid freisin agam labhairt le hiriseoirí ó am go chéile nuair a bhíonn ceisteanna acu faoi líon na gclár Gaeilge ar RTÉ.

Má dhírím m'aird ar na chéad ceisteanna anseo - an fhorbairt a tharlaíonn i measc cainteoirí na teanga neamhfhorleathan agus insan teanga féin....arís, b'fhearr liom an cheist a scrúdú trí phriosma mo chuid oibre féin.

D'fhéadfainn a rá go n-éiríonn thar cionn le craoltoirí a mbíonn an Ghaeilge acu - idir thuairisceoirí raidió agus teilifíse, lucht léirithe agus riaracháin. Ní gá ach féachaint ar an gceapachán is deireanaí do phost an ArdStiúrthóra in RTÉ féin - Cathal Goan, a chuir tús lena shaol craoltóireachta sa leabharlann fuaime agus a bhí ar dhuine de na léiritheoirí agus eagarthóirí ba mhó cáil i réimse na gclár Gaeilge. An Príomhstiúrthóir atá díreach eirithe as - Bob Collins, fear eile a raibh stádas ar leith aige i saol na Gaeilge agus a thapaigh gach deis í a labhairt. Cainteoir líofa freisin é an Stiúrthoir Raidió, Adrian Moynes.

Níl aon amhras ach go mba íontach an doras isteach i saol na craoltóireachta in RTÉ é i gcónaí an Ghaeilge- liosta le háireamh é an líon daoine a thosaigh le post réasúnta íseal agus a d'ardaigh iad féin ina dhiaidh sin ar an dréimire proifisiúnta. Agus anois, agus dream nach beag ag teacht amach san earnáil phríobháideach agus iad traenáilte go dtí an caighdeán is airde faoi scáth TG4 is léir go bhfuil domhan iontach nua oscailte do lucht labhartha na Gaeilge. Ní gá ach féachaint ar an liosta creidiúinti ag deireadh cláir nó fiú amháin scannáin, anois chun an fhianaise a fheiceáil.

Ceist eile ar fad í an bhfuil sé seo ag déanamh mórán maitheasa don teanga féin? Mar shampla, ba dheacair a dhéanamh amach cén fhorbairt a dhéanfaidh an Ghaeilge toisc go bhfuil triúr cúntóirí léirithe a bhíodh ag obair ar *Ros na Rún* anois ag obair ar *Fair City?*

An maitheas nó olc a dheanann sé gur traenáladh léiritheoirí in RTÉ le dul ag obair trí Ghaeilge agus go bhfuil siad anois ag obair ar an *Late, Late, Show*, ar *Would You Believe*, agus ins an earnáil phríobhaideach? Maitheas dóíbh féin cinnte.

Ach is fearr sampla a thabhairt b'fhéidir a léireoidh a bhfuil bainte amach le deich mbliana anuas - leis an gceist a chíoradh ó thaobh na Gaeilge féin.

Tá sraith 20 clár leathuair an chloig coimisiúnaithe agamsa i mbliana - sraith foghlama Gaeilge atá ann. Obair mhór í seo do na comhlachtaí léiriúcháin a fuair an coimisiún. Beidh mír ghearr i ngach clár a bheas cosúil le sobaldhráma réalaíoch. Idir cheithre agus cúig nóiméad in aghaidh an chláir a bheas ann - sin thart ar 90 nóiméad drámaíochta san iomlán don mhír áirithe sin.

Chaith mé tamall insan stiúideo sa Spidéal le gairid agus an dráma á thaifeadadh. B'iontach go deo an ócáid domsa í - bhí an dráma seo scríofa go háitiúil - scigathris ar "reality television" atá ann- agus é á léiriú go háitiúil ag an gcomhlacht a léiríonn "Ros na Rún."

Gaeilge ar fad a bhí á labhairt ar an láthair taifeadta: An stiúrthóir, an bainisteoir urláir, lucht ceamaraí, na haisteoirí, lucht smidithe, na siúinéirí agus na leictreoirí. Agus taifeadadh an tsraith iomlan in imeacht coicíse. Ní fhéadfadh sé seo tarlú deich mbliana ó shin. Ní hé nach mbíodh stiúrthóirí agus daoine eile taobh thiar de na ceamaraí in ann an Ghaeilge a labhairt, ach ni raibh riamh an oiread daoine le scileanna éagsúla ann chun "imshaoil" Ghaeilge mar sin a chruthú.

Agus fo-nóta leis an scigaithris áirithe sin- baineann sé le forbairt agus "inghlacthacht" teanga, is dóigh, nuair a fheileann sé do dhaoine a shamhlófá a bheadh ina coinne. Nuair a cuireadh amach beagáinín poiblíochta faoin mionsobal seo, léim an Daily Mirror ar an scéal agus dfhoilsigh é faoin gceannteideal "Dearthair Mór." (bhí an fotheideal "I'm a Gaeilgeoir - get me out of here" acu freisin ach ní bhacfaimid leis sin!

Cé air a ndírítear an t-ábhar Gaeilge teilifíse? Chun beagáinín solais a chaitheamh ar an gceist áirithe seo ní mor dom cúlra an scéil maidir le RTÉ agus a inchur i TG4 a thabhairt. "Who decides? a deir an nóta eolais agus "And with what success?"

Tabharfaidh mé figiúirí lucht féachana ó oifig thaighde lucht féachana RTÉ freisin é chun an cheist dheireanach a fhreagairt.

Ba é An tAcht Um Craolacháin 1960 a bhain le bunú na seirbhíse teilifíse agus bhi an méid seo ann maidir leis an nGaeilge :

> "Ag comhlíonadh a fheidhmeanna don údarás, coimeádfaidh sé i gcuimhne i gcónai na haidhmeanna náisiúnta atá ann an Ghaeilge a aisiriú agus an tsaíocht náisiúnta a chaomhnú agus a fhorbairt agus déanfaidh sé dícheall ag cabhrú leis na haidhmeanna sin a chur i gcrích."

Luadh an Ghaeilge arís i 1976 agus an tAcht á leasú....
"Beidh aird aige ar leasanna agus ar chúraimí an phobail uile, coimeádfaidh sé i gcuimhne a riachtanaí atá comhthuiscint agus síocháin ar fud oileán na hÉireann uile, cinnteoidh sé go léireoidh na cláir na haraíona éagsúla dá bhfuil saíocht phobal na hÉireann comhdhéanta, agus beidh cás ar leith aige do na haraíona a shainíonn an tsaíocht sin agus go háirithe don Ghaeilge."

Tiocfaimid ansin go dtí Tuarascáil an Fhóraim a foilsíodh sular chuir RTÉ isteach an dara iarratas i gcomhair ardú sa cheadúnas teilifíse anuraidh. Luadh ansin an tAcht um Craolachain 2001 agus (i mBéarla) dúradh

"that RTE should provide in its schedules a range of programmes *in both Irish and English* that....
- reflect the cultural diversity of the whole island of Ireland
- cover sporting, religious and cultural activities
- cater for the expectations of the community generally as well as members of the community with special or minority interests
- cover news, current affairs, including coverage of the houses of the Oireachtas, and the European Parliament
- facilitate or assist contemporary expression and encourage or promote innovation and experimentation in broadcasting"

Bhí an méid seo a leanas freisin sa tuarascáil:
Insan Achoimre:

33) The fulfilment by RTE of its obligations to Irish language broadcasting should be a key element of the Charter. This could include, for instance, more programmes of a bilingual character.
34. Programme aimed at learners of Irish, both adults and children, should be available at a variety of levels on RTE 1 or TG4.

Tá a fhios ag an saol mór go raibh deacrachtai móra airgid ag RTÉ sna blianta sular ceadaíodh an t-ardú sa cheadúnas. Mar sin féin bhí obair thaighde ar bun agamsa i leith sraith foghlama Gaeilge i rith an ama. Mar sin, nuair a luadh i dtuairisc an Fhóraim freisin go raibh faillí déanta i réimse na foghlama Gaeilge le blianta beaga anuas, thapaigh mé an deis chun cás a dhéanamh airgead a fháil ón ardú ceadúnais, má bhí a leitheid le bheith ann, chun sraith dá leitheid a dhéanamh.

Gheall mé freisin go bhféadfaí a leithéid a dhéanamh taobh istigh de bhliain agus sin é an fáth go bhfuil sruthán allais fágtha ina ndiaidh acu ag an gcomhlacht teilifíse agus an buíon léiriúcháin atá ar turas timpeall na tíre faoi láthair ag taifeadadh na bhfiche clár.

"Who decides," a deir an bhileog don siompóisiam? Bhuel, sa chás sin , ar nós Dev, d'fheach mise isteach i mo chroí, bhí Eagarthóir Coimisúnaithe i TG4 ag smaoineamh ar shraith dá chincál freisin ach is muide is túisce a fuair an t-airgead. Is ar an mbonn sin go minic a dhéantar cinní i saol na craoltóireachta.

Ar an gcaoi chéanna roinnt bhlianta ó shin agus mé im' léiritheoir, nuair a tugadh an cúram dom sraith Ghaeilge a dhéanamh agus áit sa sceideal aige ar RTÉ 1, chinn mé sraith clall clall clall clláracha fáisnéise leathuair an chloig a dhéanamh. Ag an am, is beag eile sraith leathuair an chloig a bhi ann ar RTÉ ná fiú ar TnaG . Ach measaim féin an cinneadh ba mhó a raibh toradh air ná fotheidil oscailte a chur ar an gclár. Arís de bharr an dul chun cinn sa saol tar éis bunú TnaG bhí na scileanna fotheidealaithe fairsingthe go mór agus ón gcéad lá bhí lucht féachana mór leathan ag an gclár.

Ag freagairt na ceiste cé air a mbíonn se dírithe? An freagra simplí ná ar an lucht féachana is mó is féidir a aimsiú ag an am sin den oíche.

Ni raibh sé riamh mar aidhm ag an gclár an Ghaeilge a athbheochan ná freastal go hiomlán ar lucht féachana Gaeltachta. Ach ní féidir le craoltóireacht Ghaeilge bheith beo gan an dream sin a bheith ann sa chéad áit. Bhíodh Breandán Ó hEithir go minic ag trácht ar an léitheoir i Muicineach idir Dhá Sháile ina chuid scríbhneoireachta. Bhíodh sé mar shlat tomhais agam féin i gcónaí go gcaithfinn freastal ar úineara na teilifíse sin i Muicineach agus mura mbeadh seisean in ann ciall agus taitneamh a bhaint as an gclár, níor cheart é a dhéanamh.

Obair shuibiachtúil atá ann sa mhéid sin - ní ábhar eolaíochta é an léiriú teilifíse. Má tá clár go maith, tá sé go maith toisc go raibh dúil mhór ag an léiritheoir sa scéal - biodh sé sin ina scéal faoi bhaint fheamainne nó sceal faoi dhaoine gan talamh sa Bhreasaíl.

Sular bunaíodh TnaG bhí reimse réasunta leathan cláracha Gaeilge ar RTÉ. An tsraith ba mhó cáil sna blianta sin "Cúrsaí" a théadh amach cúig oiche sa tseachtain ar Network a Dó, ba é Cathal Goan an t-eagarthóir air formhór na mblianta sin. Bhí cláracha ann do dhaoine óga freisin agus cláracha aonaracha fáisnéise agus siamsaíochta.

Nuair a scrúdaítear figiúirí féachana go minic déantar dearmad ar an ROGHA a bhíonn ar fáil ag daoine. Ní féidir, mar shampla, an líon daoine a bhíodh ag feachaint ar FÉACH (os cionn 600,000 duine) a chur i gcomparáid leis an líon daoine a fhéachann ar chlár Gaeilge anois. *Sula* dtabharfaidh mé aon fhigiuirí, seo cúpla blúire eolais maidir leis na hathruithe atá tarlaithe sa tír le tamall de bhlianta anuas:

Sa mbliain 1984 (an bhliain tar éis do Féach imeacht ón aer) - bhí fáil ag lucht féachana teilifíse in Éirinn ar na cainéil seo a leanas:

RTE1 - 100%, Network Two, 96%, BBC 1,BBC 2 UTV, HTV agus Channel 4 - *seacht gcinn ar fad.*

Deich mbliana ina dhiaidh sin, i 1994, bhi fáil (ag céatadán áirithe acu) ar *dheich gcinn* - iad sin thuas móide le S4C, Sky One agus Sky News.

I mbliana (2003), tá fáil ag os cionn 30% ar a laghad den lucht féachana ar *16 de chainéil (talún?)* agus tá fáil ag os cionn 25% *agus é ag fás* – ar na bealaí nua digiteacha (os cionn 100 b'fheidir) Bí ag caint ar chomórtas!

Ní raibh fotheidil ar chláracha Gaeilge i 1994. Sa mbliain 1995 chuir mise fotheidil oscailte ar chlár faoi féinmharú agus chonaic mé an difríocht shuntasach sna figiúiri agus b'fhacthas dhom ar an bpointe go raibh lucht féachana mór amuigh ansin a raibh faillí á dhéanamh orthu. Sin é an fáth go ndeirim go ndírítear ar an lucht féachana is mó is féidir a fháil.

Maidir le Cúrsaí, sa bhliain 1993 bhi TAM rating ar meán de 2 aigc agus lucht feachana de 64,000 duine. Bhi 51,000 duine fásta ann agus i measc feilméaraí bhi 8,000 ag féachaint air.

Maidir le "Léargas"(ar RTE 1 cuimhnigh), tógaimis an dá shéasúr atá díreach imithe thart:

Ó Mheán Fómhair go dtí Márta bhí meánsciar aige de 19%. Sin mean lucht féachana de 207,000 duine. Bhí níos mó daoine san aoisghrúpa os cionn 55 ag féachaint air ná aon aoisghrúpa eile, bhí sé cothrom ó thaobh aicmí sóisialta de agus bhí níos mó daoine ag féachaint air i So Mhumhan ná aon chúige eile (má thógtar BAC amach as).

An bhliain roimhe sin, bhí meánsciar de 23% aige agus 269,000 ar meán ag féachaint air. Bhí na céatadáin eile mar a bhí thuas.

Ar cheann de na sraitheanna a dhéanaimid a choimisiúnú do TG4 tá "An Tuath Nua" irischlár tuaithe agus mar is gnách anois, fotheidil oscailte air.

An séasúr seo caite bhí meánsciar de 1% aige agus lucht féachana de 16,000 agus mórán mór an rud céanna an bhliain roimhe sin.

Arís maidir le "who decides", seo cúlra an tsocraithe idir RTE agus TG4 maidir le soláthar na gclár: san Acht Um Craolachain 2001 Alt 47 deirtear go foirmeálta, rud a bhí neamhfhoirmeálta go dtí sin:

"The Authority shall provide to Teilifis na Gaeilge programme material in the Irish Language of such amounts and at such times as may be agreed between them, being such amounts and such times as, in their opinion will result in the equivalent of one hour of such programme material being provided by the Authority to Teilifis na Gaeilge."

Bristear sios an 365 uair an chloig sin idir nuacht agus cláracha - 182.5 uair an chloig nuachta agus 182.5 claracha, idir chlaracha nua agus abhar ceannaithe. I mbliana beidh RTÉ ag solathar sraith 26 clar uair an chloig "Ardán" - clár siamsaiochta beo ar an Satharn, 10 gclár uair an chloig siamsaiochta "Coinne le..." a taifeadadh i rith an tsamhraidh le foireann Léargas, 26 clár leathuair an chloig "An Tuath Nua" irischlár a théann ar fud na tire ag clúdach gnéscéalta agus scéalta reatha, 13 leathuair de"Bia agus Bóthar," clár bia agus taistil anseo agus thar lear, "36 uair an chlog de quizchlár "Cruinneas" le páistí a tháinig ó cheithre chearn na tíre chun a bheith páirteach ann, chomh maith leis an dá chluiche ceannais GAA, agus 76 uair an chloig d'ábhar ceannaithe isteach agus athghuthú Gaeilge orthu chomh maith le ábhar ón gcartlann. Bíonn plé idir TG4 agus RTÉ faoin ábhar a sholáthraítear gach bliain.

Anuraidh, idir an tseirbhís nuachta agus soláthar na gclár, móide costais eile, chaith RTE euro 8.578 milliún ar an soláthar sin agus costais eile.

Caithfidh sé nach fada ón bfírinne a bhí sa méid a dúrádh sa bPaipéar Glas um chúrsai Craolacháin a foilsiodh i 1995– inar dúradh go mbeadh RTÉ ar an léiritheoir is mó cláir Ghaeilge sa tir nuair a thiocfadh TnaG i réim.

Celtic Language Broadcasting

Pádhraic Ó Ciardha

"Now is the time for all good men and women to come to the aid of minority language and Celtic language broadcasting."

Is í seo tráth na cinniúna. Tá deis aonarach ann anois stáisiúin teilifíse na dteangacha Ceilteacha ar fad a leathadh ar fud an dá oileán seo. Tá a bhfuil mé rá ar fáil agus bunaithe sa Tuarascáil iontach seo atá eisithe inniu ag an Iontaobhas Ultach agus tá moladh mór ag dul don eagras sin agus do Don Anderson as a saothar. Molaim go láidir daoibh í a léamh agus smaoineamh ar na rudaí atá ráite ann.

Ar feadh na scórtha bliain, diúltaíodh craolachán sna teangacha Ceilteacha ar chúiseanna a bhí an – simplí: dúradh linn go raibh an speictream craolacháin teoranta, dúradh linn go raibh an craolachán costasach agus dúradh linn go raibh gá le rialáil ggéar a dhéanamh ar an gcraolachán. Fiú nuair a d'éirigh linn dul thar na laincisí sin, cuireadh teora tíreolaíoch le limistéir an tarchuir. Cuireadh teora tíreolaíoch nó ama leis an limistéir ina raibh cearta craolta againn d'aon ábhar a cheannaigh muid – "Tig leat, ar tháille, an scannán sin a thaispeáint sa Phoblacht ach ní sa Tuaisceart idir an dáta seo agus an dáta siúd".

Tá an ré sin caite agus deireadh leis na laincisí seo ar fad. Ceadaíonn an ré dhigiteach na céadta cainéal a chruthú. Cruthaíonn TG4 ar bhonn laethúil nach gá airgead mór le seirbhís ardchaighdeáin a rith. Tá an córas rialála náisiúnta agus idirnáisiúnta ag éirí níos scaoilte. Tig le satailít amháin a chomhartha a leathadh ar fud na hEorpa. Níl aon teora le cúrsaí craolacháin feasta.

Agus tá réabhlóid tarlaithe i gcúrsaí cearta freisin. Is ceart go leor den bhuíochas as seo a thabhairt do bheirt nach luaitear go minic le ceannródaíocht i gcraoladh na dteangacha Ceilteacha – Rupert Murdoch agus Greg Dyke. Fiú muna dtuigeann siad féin é, tá buíochas dlite don bheirt seo.

B'é Rupert Murdoch, bunaitheoir Sky Television agus BSkyB, a thionscnaigh an chéad réabhlóid mhór teilifíse nuair a tuigeadh dó go raibh ar chumas na satailíte comhartha a dháileadh chuig na milliún teaghlach i mórán tíortha, in éindí ach é incriptithe ionas go raibh an tomhaltóir i ngreim go deo agat -"Íoc an táille míosúil nó gearrfaidh muid an soláthar".

Le bunú an chórais Freesat – córas a bhunaigh an BBC i dtús an tSamhraidh 2003 – tá an dara réabhlóid tionscnaithe ag Greg Dyke, PríomhStiúrthóir an BBC. Is féidir anois gach seirbhís de chuid an BBC – raidió agus teilifís, náisiúnta agus áitiúil – a fháil i ngach áit ar an oileán seo agus ar an oileán thall, gan incriptiú, gan cíos míosúil ná táille bliantuil. Níl ort ach an trealamh a cheannacht agus sin a mbeidh len íoc agat go deo.

Den chéad uair riamh, b'fhéidir, tá an daonlathas curtha i bhfeidhm ar an gcóras craolacháin.

Faoin gcóras Freesat, is é atá déanta ag an BBC ná a dhearbhú gur gá dó dul ar an satailít le seirbhís a chinntiú do gach saoránach sa Ríocht Aontaithe. Admhaíonn an BBC go bhfágann sin go gclúdaíonn an comharatha satailíte Éirinn ar fad freisin ach deir siad nach bhfuil neart air.

Is é atá Tuarascáil an Iontaobhais a rá ná gur ceart agus gur féidir an loighic chéanna sin a úsáid le cás láidir a dhéanamh le gur féidir comhartha TG4 a sholáthar sa Tuaisceart – agus dá ndéarfainn é ar fud na Ríochta Aontaithe freisin.

Deir Comhaontú Bhéal Feirste gur ceart comhartha TG4 a leathadh ar fud an Tuaiscirt. Is féidir seo a dhéanamh ar thrí bhealach: tarchuradóir áitiúil a bhunú sa Tuaisceart nó dul ar BSkyB do chustaiméirí sa Tuaisceart freisin. Tá TG4 ag obair le go mbeadh muid ar fáil ar an dá dhóigh sin. Rogha eile dul suas ar Freesat ach níl seo an-fhurast mar go bhfuil an comhartha ar fáil ar fud an dá oileáin agus tá deacrachtaí cearta le socrú chuige sin.

Tá cearta teanga ag gach éinne. Tá cainteoirí Gaeilge Huddersfield agus Ghlaschú le tabhairt san áireamh anseo freisin agus is minic iad sin ligthe i ndearmad sna cainteanna seo ar fad. Chuirfeadh dáileadh ar Freesat TG4 ar fáil dóibh sin ar fad.

Ba mhaith liom focal nó dhó a rá faoi thaighde an lucht féachana, mar fhocal scoir. Caitheann craoltóirí na dteangacha Ceilteacha go leor airgid i mbun taighde ar ár lucht féachana – lucht na Gaeilge mar shampla. Ach is furast a dhearmad go bhfuil teanga eile ag na daoine seo freisin – Béarla. Is maith linn breathnú ar *Coronation Street* chomh maith le *Ros na Rún* ach ní i gcónaí a insíonn muid sin do lucht na taighde! Mo chomhairle d'aon dream a bheadh ag bunú seirbhíse i nGáidhlig – aimsigh an taighde ach ná dearmad go dtig le duine a rá leat gur mhaith leis clár Gaeilge faoi rud éigin gach oíche Chéadaoin ag 9pm ach nach ndéarfaidh sé leat go mbíonn sé féin ag cruinniú gach oíche Chéadaoin ag 9pm!

The State of Gaelic Broadcasting in Scotland: Critical Issues and Audience Concerns

Catherine Ann MacNeil

Background

Advancements in technology, the growth of new media and the implementation of a fresh legislative agenda have placed the communications industry worldwide in a state of metamorphosis. The changes taking place have already enhanced consumer choice in terms of when, how and what they access in the media. While technology is providing a means of breaking down traditional geographical barriers, it brings with it the threat of a homogenous globalised culture. Minority language broadcasters have always faced additional pressures in competing with the mainstream while still fulfilling the diverse and demanding expectations of their linguistic communities. The divergence between their broadcasting priorities and those of the mainstream are continuing to grow and the challenges faced in the wake of the broadcasting revolution are greater now than ever before.

One of the fundamental aims of the *European Charter for Regional or Minority Languages* is to act against complete homogenisation and protect the linguistic and cultural communities that are currently under threat. But how effective a safeguard is this charter likely to be in the light of such radical developments in the mass media? And what role will minority language broadcasting be able to play in language revitalisation as it competes to stay afloat in an increasingly commercial and competitive market. In seeking to answer such questions, it is necessary to explore the actuality. This paper will focus on the strengths and weaknesses of Gaelic Broadcasting in Scotland within the context of the European charter – or specifically within the context of three key areas of provision as adopted by the UK government – Paragraphs 1a(ii), 1b(ii) and 1c(ii) within Article 11:

> The Parties undertake, for the user s of the regional or minority languages within the territories in which those languages are spoken, according to the situation of each language, to the extent that the public authorities, directly or indirectly, are competent, have power or play a role in this field, and respecting the principle of the independence and autonomy of the media:
>
> a (ii) to the extent that radio and television carry out a public service mission: to encourage and/or facilitate the creation of at least one radio station and one television channel in the regional or minority languages …;
>
> b (ii) to encourage and/or facilitate the broadcasting of radio programmes in the regional or minority languages on a regular basis;
>
> c (ii) to encourage and/or facilitate the broadcasting of television programmes in the regional or minority languages on a regular basis.

Overview of Gaelic Broadcasting Provision in Scotland

December 2003 marks 80 years of Gaelic broadcasting in Scotland. In that time, the level and diversity of output has increased considerably as have the outlets for Gaelic programming. Radio nan Gàidheal now has its own bandwidth and provides approximately 65 hours of output per week, or over 3000 hours of programming annually. The use of cross media approaches has also been embraced and Radio nan Gàidheal's availability on digital satellite and via the internet effectively makes it a worldwide service.

Gaelic television programmes are available on both analogue and digital platforms. At present, viewers enjoy over 300 hours of output on analogue, around half of which is broadcast by the BBC and the remainder of which is transmitted by ITV's Regional Broadcasters Scottish Television and Grampian Television. Additional programming is also accessible on digital terrestrial television (Freeview), with TeleG on Channel 8 providing an hour of peak-time broadcasting each day of the year.

On the surface it may appear that Gaelic broadcasting is adapting well to the developments taking place in the industry and fulfilling the remit of the charter. There is a dedicated radio station broadcasting Gaelic programmes on a very regular basis. There are also established slots for television programmes, including peak-time provision every night on digital. But is this provision sufficient and perhaps more importantly, is it working? For answers to these questions, we must look to the core audience group – the Gaelic community of Scotland. Since 1993, data on the viewing choices and opinions of this user group have been collated on a weekly basis using an audience response panel, which is maintained by Lèirsinn Research Centre for Comataidh Craolaidh Gàidhlig (Gaelic Broadcasting Committee - the body with responsibility for administering Government funding for Gaelic programmes). The panel is designed to be representative of the Gaelic speaking population of Scotland as defined by the most recent Census, in terms of age, gender and geographical location. At any one time the panel consists of around 250 individuals, which represents approximately 1 in 200 Gaelic speakers.

Sustaining the Audience Base

On the surface, response to Gaelic broadcasting is extremely positive. Reach levels or market penetration for Radio nan Gàidheal and for analogue broadcasts are consistently high, highlighting the capacity of these services to attract and hold their audience base. This is illustrated in the graphs below.

Figure 1: Weekly Gaelic Television Reach: All Analogue Output from 2001 to 2003

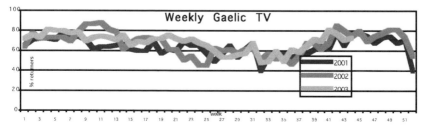

Figure 2: Weekly Reach for BBC Radio nan Gàidheal 2001 to 2003

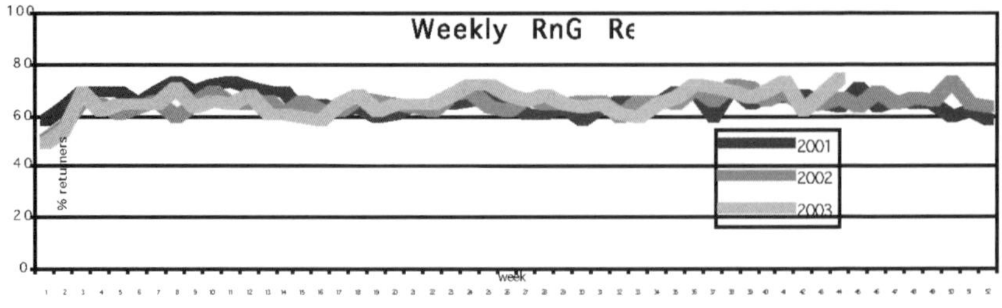

In addition, viewing within key timeslots has generally risen over the last couple of years, with those individuals that are tuning in, tending to do so more frequently over the course of any given week. This goes against the national mainstream trend of falling audience levels which one might almost inevitably expect given the increasingly competitive broadcasting market. The sustained loyalty of the Gaelic community is not due to programme content alone, but associated with the wider expectations that the audience have of Gaelic broadcasting. Research has consistently shown us that viewers and listeners are looking for considerably more than entertainment from their Gaelic media consumption. They look to radio and television programmes to:

Act as a standard bearer for the language;
Uphold moral values, particularly within provision for children;
Provide language support in the home for all age groups and categories of learner;
Provide access to an authentic Gaelic speech community, particularly idiomatic Gaelic;
Extend the use of Gaelic outwith classroom situations;
Promote Gaelic culture – both traditional and contemporary.

Gaelic programming has also been identified as a resource commonly used in Gaelic medium classrooms, with Gaelic television programmes in particular being praised for their effectiveness in engaging the attention of the children and for their use in differentiated teaching activities.

Structural Issues

While the role of broadcasting in language revitalisation is widely recognised, the effects can be diluted if appropriate structures and strategies are not in place. Radio nan Gàidheal is a strong, well-established radio service with a loyal audience base but arguably its greatest weakness and possibly the greatest threat to its long-term sustainability are its gaps in provision for children, young people and learners of the language. However, Radio nan Gàidheal is in the fortunate position of being able to address these issues and adapt accordingly. Gaelic television is in a less privileged position in that it has, at present, virtually no control over its destiny. It has no power over commissioning or scheduling.

Although viewing levels are being sustained, the audience have consistently expressed concern about the scheduling, quality and diversity of Gaelic programmes. Of those people who have multi-channel access, relatively few have subscribed to digital terrestrial, satellite being the preferred and more accessible platform for the vast majority as illustrated in the graph below. The result is that recorded viewing levels for programmes on TeleG (on Freeview) are extremely low.

Figure 3: Digital technology Available In Gaelic-speakl Households in Scotland (August 2003)

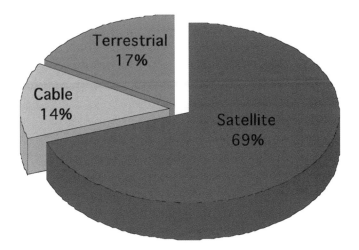

In terms of the Gaelic provision on analogue, regular slots have been established but the overall output is fragmented and the slots in use appeal more or are more easily accessed by older viewers. Research undertaken by Lèirsinn has shown that many of those who are unable to watch regularly have indicated that the timeslots are incompatible with their usual viewing. They want to be able to watch, but the slots don't always comply with their lifestyles and viewing habits.

At present [September 2003], there are relatively few viewing opportunities over the course of each week. Slots for a typical week's adult viewing might include:

A Sunday morning religious slot of an hour (eight in all over the year);

A half hour broadcast at approximately 6.00pm on Sunday evening on Scottish/Grampian Television;

Two hours of programming on Scottish/Grampian Television commencing at 11.30pm on Tuesday nights;

Two hours of programming (including 30-45 minutes of children's) between 6.00 and 8.00pm on Thursday evenings on BBC2.

At present viewing is determined more by slot than by content, with individuals watching when they can, irrespective of what is on. The use of strands on Tuesdays and Thursdays has helped to maximise audiences for follow-on programmes but on the whole, viewing opportunities are very restricted. Over the past two years, over a third of the total Gaelic output has been transmitted in late evening or post-midnight slots. If children's programmes are taken out of the equation then half of all adult provision is broadcast after midnight, with around 60 per cent being shown after 11.00 pm. In any week where peak-time broadcasts are dropped, weekly reach falls dramatically.

The situation isn't much better in considering programmes for children. Although over 40 per cent of the total Gaelic output is made up of provision for children, around 70 per cent of this is shown while children are at school. Obviously, pre-school children will still benefit, but the potential language impacts that these programmes could have on the target audience are strongly reliant on parents recording output.

Another issue of concern is that of continuity of output. Over the course of the year, viewers can enjoy an average of approximately six hours per week of Gaelic programming. However, as the graph below illustrates, this may range from one hour of output to 10 hours of output depending on the time of year. Programming is at its peak over the autumn and winter months, but there is very little output over the summer months. Regular and predictable slots are important for building audiences and continuity is also an important facet of learning. Yet again, the potential impacts of broadcasting are being diluted by ineffectual or indifferent scheduling strategies.

Figure 4: Fluctuations within Weekly Television Output 2001 to 2003

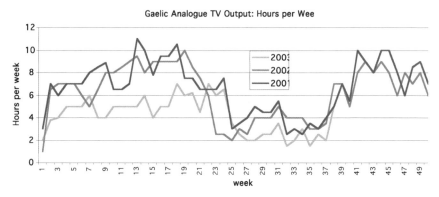

Lack of continuity is also evident within the slots attributed to programmes. The Sunday morning religious slot is sporadic and highly unpredictable. This year, Gaelic church services have been broadcast in weeks 4, 7, 18, 24, 31 and 34. The gaps between transmissions are rarely equidistant, leaving the viewers uncertain of where to expect the programme within schedules. Over 2002, Gaelic broadcasts were only available within the peak-time Thursday evening slot on BBC2 for two-thirds of the year. Frustratingly, the greatest degree of continuity is evident within the least accessible slots – those after midnight.

Figure 5: Lack of Continuity within Gaelic Television Output: Weekly Slots over 2002

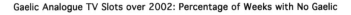

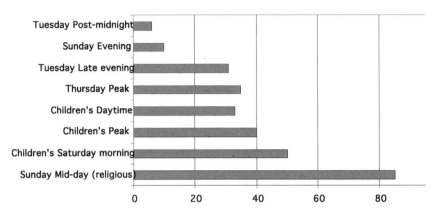

Gaelic Analogue TV Slots over 2002: Percentage of Weeks with No Gaelic

Conclusion

To secure the long-term sustainability of a Gaelic television service, programme planning needs to be more audience-centred. At the moment, the range of programmes broadcast is insufficient to appeal to the whole spectrum of viewers. Viewers want to see current output extended to take account of the gaps in provision, particularly that for teenagers and young people. They also want to see the wide and diverse interests of a bilingual and bicultural community catered for.

The impending Communications Act will provide commissioning powers, which will go some way to alleviating the problems being faced. However, control of scheduling will remain with the host broadcasters. Gaelic broadcasting has a vital role to play in language development, not least in adding to the critical mass of Gaelic available for consumption. But without audiences, there are no additional language benefits to be gained. The European charter lacks real substance and new legislation promises little change.

The Gaelic community of Scotland recognises the need for integrated strategies to ensure the survival of their language and culture. Broadcasting has a critical role to play within this, but it requires proper legislative control and resourcing. A Gaelic channel is seen as a means of preventing further marginalisation and providing real opportunity to engage audiences more effectively. In order to maximise the additional benefits – linguistic and otherwise – that a minority language channel can bring, the needs of the target audience must take priority. The fundamental issue is that without audiences, there can be no additional gains and current legislative provision is doing little to promote the development of a comprehensive and cohesive Gaelic broadcasting service, which is able to respond to the multi-faceted needs of its core user group.

References

Comataidh Craolaidh Gàidhlig Weekly and Occasional Reports 1993–2003.

MacNeil, M.M., (1996), *Use of Gaelic Television Programmes in Gaelic Medium Classrooms,* Lèirsinn Research Centre for Comataidh Craolaidh Gàidhlig.

Stradling, R.N. and MacNeil, M.M., (1996), *Gaelic Medium Education: The Critical Skills,* Lèirsinn Research Centre for the Inter-Authority Standing Group for Gaelic.

MacNeil, M.M. and MacDonald, B.K, (1997), *Gaelic Television Programmes as a Resource for Language Learning,* Lèirsinn Research Centre for Comataidh Craolaidh Gàidhlig.

MacNeil, Catherine A., (2003), *BBC Radio nan Gàidheal: Response to Service Developments*, Lèirsinn Research Centre for BBC Alba.

BBC Craoladh nan Gaidheal: Co sinn?

Ishbel MacLennan

Tòisichidh mi le bhi a dèanamh dealbh air BBC Craoladh nan Gaidheal , roinn Gàidhlig a BhBC. Mar is docha a bhios fios agaibh tha freumhaichean na roinne domhainn , is am BBC air a bhi sàs gu ire a choireigin ann an craoladh Gàidhlig bho chionn còir is ceithir fichead bliadhna. An diugh tha cuisean gu math eadar-dhealaichte, is a' roinn a' nise a' craoladh sa bhitheantas tri fichead sa còig uair an uaireadair air an aona seirbhis rèidio Gàidhlig nàiseanta san dùthaich , ceud gu leth uair air telebhisean eadar BBC a h-aon is a dha Alba, agus a' frithealadh seirbhis eadar-lion. Is sinn an aona chraoladair ann an Alba a tha a tabhann seirbhis thar na tri meadhanan.

Tha sinn a-sàs anns gach gnè prògram eadar na seirbheisean sin ri linn is gum bheil a luchd-cleachdaidh againn ioma-fhillte nan iarrtasan dìreach mar luchd-cleachdaidh sam bith eile. Mar sin chithear is cluinnear is faodar tadhal air programan is duilleagan eadar-lion airson òig is aois is meadhan-la a' dèiligeadh ri naidheachdan, cuspairean a' la, dòigh-beatha, cultair, cànan, creideamh, cèol, fòghlam, cur-seachad. Bhon ire is òige – fo aois sgoile chun fheadhainn is sinne tha sinn ag amas air stuth a' chruthachadh leinn fhèin is ann a co-bhuinn le companaidhean riochdachaidh neo-eisimeileach agus le taic bho Comataidh Craolaidh Gàidhlig a fhreagras air iarrtasan gach buidheann fa leth.

De a tha dhith fhathast / co dha a tha e?

Mar a tha sinn air a bhi a' cluinntinn tha seirbhis cunbhalach air telebhisean agus ionmhas a chumas taic ri amasan a luchd-cleachdaidh fhathast a dhith. Tha am BBC air a bhi a-sàs anns a bhuidheann co-obrachaidh a steidhicheadh leis a' riaghaltas mar thoradh air gluasad bile a' chraolaidh gu Achd craolaidh agus bi riochdaire air Seirbhis na Meadhanan Gàidhlig. Tha àite agus eòlas àraidh aig a BhBC ann a bhi a' frithealadh luchd na Gàidhlig agus bhitheamaid an dùil a' leantainn a' cleachdadh iad sin gu buannachd coimhearsnachd na Gàidhlig.

Se glè bheag de dh'fheum a nith an Achd mar a bith goireasan ga rèir. Tha a luchd-cleachdaidh a dùileachadh seirbhis dìreach cho farsainn ri luchd-cleachdaidh chànanan eile – is carson nach biodh. Tha a' Ghàidhlig dhar ceangal ach chan eil sin ag ràdh gur e aona bhuidheann slàn a th'unnainn. Co a tha dearbhadh co iad an luchd-cleachdaidh , tha iad fhèin. Na bitheamaid air ar mealladh tha na làithean far am biodh dìlseachd aig daoine do phrògram dìreach bhon is ann as a Ghàidhlig a tha e , gus a bhi seachad. Agus taobh eile na cùise tha luchd-clcachdaidh gum Ghàidhlig a roghnachadh a bhi air an àireamh cuidcachd , ri linn is le taic le fo-thiotalan gum bheil iad a' faicinn gum bheil rud ann dhaibh-san. Is docha gum bheil am prògram Eòrpa na dheagh eisimpleir air a sin, a' dèiligeadh bho sheachdain gu seachdain ri sgeulachdan a tha a' beantainn ri beatha dhaoine air feadh na roinn Eòrpa bi e toradh a chogaidh san t-seann Iugoslavia neo buaidh na dibhe air coimhearsnachdan Eileanan Siar na h-Alba.

Sreath a th'air a bhi dol a' nise le taic bho CCG airson coir is deich bliadhna a th'air duaisean a bhuannachd agus air am bheileas a' bruidhinn ann a lethid paipear naidheachd nàiseanta anns an dòigh seo:-

Sunday Herald; 'Bithidh *Eòrpa* a' ruigsinn nan raointean far nach tig prògraman eile a tha stèidhichte air Rathad na Banrighrinn Maighrearad ann an Glaschu'. – agus sin bho fhear a bh'ann is a chunnaic, Tom Shields!

Is ged a' thigeadh na cothroman agus na goireasan feumaidh co-ordanachadh a bhi ann, feumaidh strategy a bhi ann gus am feum is fheàrr is urrain a thoirt as gach rud. Tha co-obrachadh feumail air a bhi ann chun a seo ach feumar gluasad nas fhaide buileach le sin – ged a tha an àite fhèin aig structairean, obair cruthachaidh cosnadh, trèanadh is eile ; se an luchd-cleachdaidh is cudthromaiche buileach. Mur a bheil ar h-aire orrasan as gach ceum a tha sinn a' gabhail chan eil a gu bhi as na nithean eile ach rud a thig leis a ghaoith. Is mar Leòdhasach, tha deagh fhios agam a rud a thig leis a ghaoith, falbhaidh e leis a ghaoith.

Innsidh luchd-rannsachaidh dhuinn na h-uibhir mu cho math is a tha a' dol dhuinn na ar h-amasan agus chan eil teagamh ann ach gum bheil e duilich cuid a bhuidheann a thàladh – de cho tric is a tha sinn a' cluinntinn gu feum a' Ghàidhlig a bhi 'cool' mas blais an òigridh air agus gum bheil iad sin a tha eadar 25 is 45 buailteach a bhi a' meas gum bheil craoladh Gàidhlig cudthromach ach gum bheil e do dhaoine 'nas sinne na tha iad fhèin'. Gu math tric chan e idir a rud a tha thu a' dèanamh a tha a' cunntadh ach de a tha daoine a' smaoineachadh a tha thu a' dèanamh. Mar sin tha dùbhlan ga thoirt dhuinne a tha a-sàs ann an craoladh Gàidhlig , sinn foillseachadh fhaighinn dhan bheartas a tha mar tha - agus a tha sinn an dòchas a bhios fhathast a' lùib na seirbheisean againn , ach air taobh a-muigh na seirbheisean sin. Feumaidh sinn faighinn gu na daoine nach eil a cleachdadh na seirbheisean againn an dràsda.

Leasachadh cànan

Chan eil ceist ach gum bheil àite cudthromach aig craoladh ann a bhi a' leasachadh cànan. Ged is ann a Leòdhas a tha mise le dual-chainnt ga-rèir, cluinnear blas ioma sgìre eile nam Ghàidhlig. Ciamar , tha gun thogadh mi ag èisteachd ri rèidio Gàidhlig agus gum bheil mi air earrainn mhath de mo bheatha a chuir seachad ag obair anns a mheadhan sin. Mar a thuirt tè-sgrùdaidh phrògraman am pàipeir-naidheachd a Scotsman bho chionn ghoirid:-

"tha Radio nan Gaidheal mar choimhearsnachd agus luchd nam prògraman mar eòlaichean a' tighinn air cheilidh dhan dachaigh, a' tighinn mar a thig nàbaidhean – cuid le naidheachdan, cuid le fiosrachadh, cuid le brosnachadh, cuid le dibhearsain agus cuid a chuireas fearg oirnn bho àm gu àm …" Criosaidh Dick (*The Scotsman*)

Agus a rud nach tuirt i sin gach aon a' tighinn len dual-chainnt fhèin. Tha craoladh Gàidhlig air luchd-labhairt na Gàldhlig a' tharraing nas dlùithe ri chèile, agus tuigse a thoirt dhuinn air dòighean-labhairt càch a chèile agus nach math sin.

Tha an ùine team ach bheir mi dhuibh dha neo trì eisimpleirean air na nithean anns am bheil sinne a-sàs co-cheangailte ri leasachadh cànan:

• Litir do luchd-ionnsachaidh - co-obrachadh eadar am BBC, CCG, eòlaiche cànan a tha cuideachd na chraoladair Ruaraidh Macilleathain agus difir phàipeir naidheachd gus cothrom èisteachd is leughaidh

Gàidhlig a thoirt do dh'fheadhainn a tha ag ionnsachadh a chànan ann an Alba ach cuideachd air feadh an t-saoghail troimh'n eadar-lion.

- Prògram leasachaidh cànan do luchd-obrach taobh a-stigh na roinne againn fhèin – is sinn a' tuigsinn an ìre gu neartaich neo gu lughdaich na tha sinne ag ràdh air an aer beartas na Gàidhlig sa choimhearsnachd.
- Prògraman fòghlam do sgoiltean, a' cleachdadh eòlas a BhBC sa roinn seo, amasan na poileasaidhean fòghlam nàiseanta agus taic a CCG gus na goireasan a th'ann do sgoileirean Gàidhlig a' leudachadh. Is sin an còmhnaidh a' feuchainn ri na prògraman sin a dhèanamh taitneach dhan a luchd-cleachdaidh – tha sinn an drasda ag obair air sreath Snas, anns am bheil còmhlan-ciùil leis an t-ainm sin agus tha mi cinnteach a chuireas gach smuain air S Club 7 a-mach a inntinn na cloinne nuair a chi iad iad. Tha iad dìreach snasail!
- Luchd-obrach a-sàs ann am buidheann-obrach lethid *Faclair na Pàrlamaid* agus am faclair sin an uairsin ga chleachdadh leis a roinn.

Chan urrainn agus chan iarradh sinn an uallach airson a' Ghàidhlig mar chànan a' leasachadh a chuir bhuainn. Mar a luchd-cleachdaidh feumaidh sin a bhi aig cridhe gach nith a tha sinn a' dèanamh, agus tha iarrtas mòr ann fhathast bho luchd-ionnsachaidh na Gàidhlig nach eil ga choilionadh. Is leanaidh sinn a strì ris a sin.

Dearbhadh oirnn mar Ghàidheil

Chan eil mi idir a meas gun do dhèilig mi ris gach ceist a chaidh a chuir romham ach lùiginn crìochnachadh le smuain neo dha air buaidh na meadhanan oirnne a tha nar Gaidheil. Tha caraidean agamsa a tha beagan nas òige na mi. Nuair a chaidh iadsan dhan bhun-sgoil ann a Leòdhas bha an dealbh air aghaidh aon de phàipearan naidheachd nàiseanta a la. Carson, uill bha iad a' dèanamh inneas air a chlann seo a bha a' dol dhan sgoil is gun facal Beurla aige. An diugh is gann gum bheil facal Gàidhlig aca. Se pàirt dhen aobhar airson sin nach robh iad a' faicinn a' Ghàidhlig ann a suidheachadh sam bith eile ach mar chànan na dachaidh agus corra chlas anns a' sgoil, eu-coltach ris a Bheurla a bha mu chuairt oir agus air telebhisean is rèidio. An diugh tha clann, daoine òga, daoine na meadhan-aois agus seann daoine a' faicinn agus a' cluinntinn a' lethid fhèin air telebhisean is rèidio gach là. Agus sin – an diugh gun mhothachadh dhuinn – a' dearbhadh dhuinn gum buin sinn dhan t-saoghal anns am bheil sinn a' tighinn beò, nach eil sinn mar choigrich.

Chan eil teagamh agam ach gum bheil na meadhanan air leth-cudthromach airson na mion-chànanan. Is urrain dhuinn an inbhe agus an cumhachd a chleachdadh gu maith cànanan is cultaran mion-shluaigh na h-Eòrpa, a' cuimhneachadh gur iad na meadhanan na seirbhaillitan is chan e na maighstirean.

Overview

BBC Craoladh nan Gaidheal is the BBC's Gaelic Service. As you perhaps know the links between the BBC and Gaelic date back almost to the beginning of the Corporation itself, over 80 years ago. From those small beginnings have come today's much expanded service. We broadcast an average of 65 hours of Gaelic programming per week on radio, providing the only national Gaelic radio service in Scotland. On television we have c.150 hours annually on BBC 1 and BBC 2 Scotland and we provide an on-line service. We are the only provider of a multi-media service in the language in Scotland.

The service targets a diverse range of audiences from pre-school to the 'more mature viewer' (!) and incorporates all genres of programming including news, current-affairs, life-style, culture, language, religion, music, education and entertainment. We aim to produce in-house and jointly with independent producers and the CCG programmes which serve the many and varied interests of our diverse audience.

What do we still need? / Who are the services for?

As we've heard a Gaelic television channel has still to be delivered as well as the resources to support the comprehensive service the audience wants. The BBC has been part of the working group set up by the government as the Broadcasting Bill went through it's various stages and the BBC will have membership of the new Gaelic Media Service. The BBC has a commitment to the language and a wealth of experience which we hope will continue to the benefit of the Gaelic community.

The provisions in the new Act will not even begin to transform the world of the Gaelic viewer and listener unless sufficient resources follow. The Gaelic audience have similar expectations to other audiences and why not? Yes they have the language in common, but that does not make them a homogenous mass. Who are the audience – who decides? I would suggest that the audience decides. Let's not kid ourselves the days when people would watch or listen to any programme just because it was 'Gaelic' are virtually gone. The other side of the coin is that of the non-Gaelic speakers who are choosing (with the help of sub-titles) to join the Gaelic audience. If I might take for an example our long-running European affairs series Eorpa. This award-winning series produced by BBC Craoladh nan Gaidheal and funded by CCG has for over 10 years brought real people and real stories from across Europe, to the audience. It was described in one national newspaper, in the following terms:-

> '*Eòrpa* reaches the parts that other programmes from Queen Margaret Drive (BBC Scotland Headquarters) don't reach.' (Tom Shields, in *The Sunday Herald*)

Once you have the opportunities and the resources you also need coordination and a strategy to ensure the greatest return for the audience. We've had valuable cooperation in Scotland but much more will be needed in the future. Structures, economic development, training etc are all important without a doubt; however the audience is of paramount importance. If we lose sight of them the other elements will prove transitory.

Researchers can tell us a great deal about the audience and how we're performing in relation to them. It's clear that it's difficult to attract certain groups – how often do we hear the refrain that we need to make Gaelic 'cool' to attract young people and that the 25–45 age group consider Gaelic broadcasting to be 'important' but that they view it as something for 'people who are older than themselves'. The audiences' perception of what you do is often as important as what you actually do. The challenge for us as Gaelic broadcasters and programme-makers lies in reaching the non-listeners/viewers/users outside of our existing services. For instance if they're not listening to BBC Radio nan Gaidheal it doesn't matter how often we use that very same service to promote what we're doing for them, they're not going to hear it!

Language development

There is no doubt that the media has an important role to play in the development of minority languages. I come from Lewis and speak what is known as Lewis Gaelic. However my Gaelic also has a strong flavour of Gaelic as it is found in other communities. Why? Well I grew up listening to gaelic radio, I've spent a large part of my life working in Gaelic radio and I've picked up these flavours as I've gone along. One radio critic recently described the BBC Radio nan Gaidheal service in these terms in the Scotsman newspaper:-

> 'Radio nan Gaidheal is like a community and it's presenters and programme- makers are like neighbours who pop in to visit you at home – some with news, some with information, some to encourage, some to entertain and some to infuriate you from time to time.'
> (Chrissie Dick, in *The Scotsman*)

and what she didn't say , each with their own 'Gaelic'. Gaelic broadcasting has drawn the Gaelic community closer together, helping us literally to understand one another. I'll give you a few examples of areas in which we are involved in language development:

- Litir do luchd ionnsachaidh – a co-production between the BBC, CCG a language learning expert & journalist Roddy Maclean and various newspapers which gives learners of Gaelic both in Scotland and wider afield (via the internet) the opportunity to develop their comprehension skills.
- An on-going language skills development programme for staff – recognising the influence the language that we use on-air can have on the language that listeners/viewers use
- Education programmes for schools, utilising the BBC's expertise in this field, national education policies and CCG support to expand the range of resources available to Gaelic students and teachers.
- Staff contributing to consultative groups i.e. Faclair na Parlamaid, and it's adoption within the department.

We can't and would not wish to divest ourselves of our responsibilities in relation to Gaelic language development. Like the audience, the language must be at the heart of all that we do. We are aware of a great demand for more programming from learners of Gaelic and we continue to address that.

Personal development ?

I'll like to finish with a few thoughts about the impact of the media on how we see our selves as Gaels. I have friends who are a few years younger than me. When they went to primary school in Lewis they found themselves on the front page of one of the national newspapers of the day. Why? Simply because they were Gaelic speakers, going to school without a knowledge of English. Today they hardly speak a word of Gaelic – and their story is not unusual. Why? Well the usual well-documented one, the only place where they heard Gaelic was at home and in occasional classes in school, everywhere else English. Today, children, young, middle-aged and elderly people see and hear people like themselves speaking Gaelic on TV and radio every day. It's probably not even something we're conscious of anymore, but it helps us to see ourselves as people that belong to this society rather than as strangers in a strange land. We've still got a way to go but we have made a great deal of progress.

I firmly believe that the media is of crucial importance to minority languages. We can use it to the benefit of the minority culture of Europe, remembering that the medium is the servant not the master.

Gaelic-medium Broadcasting: Reflections on the Legal Framework from a Sociolinguistic Perspective

Robert Dunbar

On my first trip to Belfast, in March 1998, I gave a paper in which I made a number of comments about Gaelic-medium broadcasting. Although much has changed over the last five and one half years with respect to Gaelic-medium broadcasting, and much else in the Gaelic world, the overall picture is broadly similar. In the short time available, I shall explore a few of the themes I explored on that first trip to Belfast, setting them in the context of the new environment created by the *Communications Act 2003*.

The provisions in the *Communications Act 2003* with respect to Gaelic-medium broadcasting represent the culmination of a protracted campaign waged by Gaelic organisations and activists for a stand-alone Gaelic television channel. The significant limitations of the present structure, in which the Gaelic Broadcasting Committee (the Comataidh Craolaidh Gàidhlig, or the "CCG") is provided with a fund of £8.5 million out of which it can fund the production of Gaelic radio and television programmes, but in which the programmes are commissioned and broadcast by others – BBC Scotland, and Channel 3 licenseholders in Scotland such as Grampian and Scottish Television – have been thoroughly canvassed elsewhere, including by the Gaelic Broadcasting Task Force, chaired by the former Director-General of the BBC, Alasdair Milne,[1] and, indeed, in another of the papers presented at this symposium.[2]

The main response of the Gaelic Broadcasting Task Force to the present inadequate state of affairs was the recommendation of the establishment of a Gaelic Broadcasting Authority to, amongst other things, oversee the establishment of a Gaelic Service. This Gaelic Service was to be a public service, available "free to air" on all digital platforms, which would broadcast three hours of original Gaelic television programmes per day in peak time, and which would be financed by a legislatively-based funding formula producing an annual subsidy of £44 million at 2000 prices, indexed-linked to protect against the effects of price inflation. In the end, the *Communications Act 2003* did not provide for the creation of such a Gaelic Service nor, of course, for the funding formula to support such a service. The Act did, however, provide for a new body, the Gaelic Media Service ("Seirbhis nam Meadhanan Gàidhlig" or the "SMG"), which is to replace the CCG and which will have somewhat expanded statutory powers, and advocates of a stand-alone Gaelic channel are hopeful that these expanded powers will at least potentially allow for the development of a service similar to that envisioned by the Gaelic Broadcasting Task Force. In the meantime, however, it is likely that the present situation will, broadly speaking, continue under the new body.

A letter which recently appeared in the pages of *The Scotsman*, the Edinburgh-based broadsheet, and in which the writer was bold enough to touch on questions of the value of particular Gaelic programmes, provides a useful place from which

---

[1] *Gaelic Broadcasting Task Force Report*, available at: http: //www.scotland. gov.uk/ library3/heritage/gbtf-00.asp.
[2] See Catherine Anne MacNeil's contribution to this volume.

to consider some of the themes which have been central to an ongoing debate of which the recent efforts in the context of the *Communications Act 2003* form only a part. This is the letter in its entirety:

> I listened with interest to BBC Radio Scotland's timely programme on the future of Gaelic, in the light of the debate in Gaelic circles on how to make the language "sexy".
>
> The BBC, to its credit, has responded positively with projects such as an excellent interactive website and more modern and "youth-centred" radio, such as the *Rapal* programme.
>
> The other side of the coin is the *Eadar Seo agus Ceann a' Bhliadhna* series on ITV. Here we have yet another "music programme" where people sing the same old, mostly "spiritual" songs, few of which have been composed in the last three or four decades.
>
> This does not portray a healthy living language. Young Gaels must have the chance to create a vibrant, modern culture which exists outside the classroom.[3]

Rapal is a radio programme which is aired weeknights from Monday to Thursday on BBC Radio nan Gàidheal. Featuring a young presenter and young contributors – often secondary and university students – *Rapal* plays contemporary music, and it seems to have a pretty eclectic and reasonably cutting-edge mix which would, I think – though I am no longer an expert on such matters! – compare well with similar English-medium output. Of course, aside from the chatter between songs, the musical content is largely "English-medium", and this raises all sorts of interesting issues with respect to minority language broadcasting in general, and space does not permit a closer examination of these issues in this short article. *Eadar Seo is Ceann A' Bhliadhna* is a short series of half-hour television programmes that was broadcast every Sunday, in the late afternoon in the late summer of 2003. There is, in fact, considerably more to this series – and, I would argue, more to recommend it – than the letter-writer admits. But it is certainly programming that is based on Gaelic traditional culture, rather than on modern, English-medium, capitalist, market-driven youth culture. It is also likely that it is aimed at an older demographic, although the fact that many of the singers of these "old", "mostly spiritual" songs are, in fact, young Gaels is something worth considering – indeed, the idea that young Gaels can live in and draw ideas from both "the new" and "the old", and that a simple "new = good" and "old = bad" dichotomy exists are both issues which deserve deeper reflection, although, once again, space does not permit me to do so here.

The letter is, however, an interesting one for a number of other reasons. In particular, it raises three issues which are, in my view, of crucial importance to any minority language broadcasting endeavour, namely: who is the broadcasting for; what is the broadcasting for; and, a question related to the first two, who "owns" the broadcasting initiative? I will take a closer look at how the letter addresses these issues, and then set these responses against the broader framework which is created by the present legislative rules.

First, who is Gaelic-medium broadcasting for? The letter shows how dreadfully difficult programme development must be. The audience, even the

---

[3]   S. Adams, Allanfield, Edinburgh, in *The Scotsman*, "Letters", 10 September 2003, p. 19.

small one for broadcasting in a minority language like Gaelic, is diverse; and like the writer of the letter just quoted, everyone has a strong opinion about what is "good" quality programming and what is "bad". Gaelic broadcasters must try to read this audience, and create programming which caters to various tastes and preferences. They must please the audience. But which audience? The letter-writer seems to be implying that, of the various components of the audience for Gaelic-medium programming – or should we say the various *audiences* for such programming – it is young people who matter most. The underlying logic seems to be that young people are the future of the language and, therefore, Gaelic-medium programming should be directed at pleasing and attracting *this* audience. But there are other possible answers to the question of who Gaelic broadcasting is for. It is possible to argue that, if the service is meant primarily to *please* the audience, Gaelic-medium broadcasters must accept and respond to the reality that middle-aged to older viewers make up a majority of the Gaelic speech community, and that the broadcasters should therefore focus more closely on these viewers. But there are other possibilities. A significant percentage of Gaelic-medium programmes are commissioned and broadcast by commercial broadcasters, and these broadcasters may argue that Gaelic programming, like other programming, should aim to get the biggest market share possible, and that through the use of subtitles, this market share may include significant numbers of non-Gaelic speakers. Indeed, even the public service broadcaster is not indifferent to viewer figures, and subtitling has, without a doubt, created a non-Gaelic speaking audience for Gaelic-medium programmes which may, at times, outnumber the Gaelic-speaking audience. And it should also be remembered that least some Gaelic-medium programming has been sold abroad, sometimes to be re-broadcast in another Celtic language. Thus, it may be necessary – and, in a broadcasting world in which commercial pressures are an ever-increasing reality, it may even be inevitable – to look beyond the needs and interests of the Gaelic-speaking audience for Gaelic medium programming.

The legislative framework for Gaelic-medium broadcasting provides very little guidance as to who Gaelic-medium broadcasting is meant to be for. As we shall see shortly, the *Broadcasting Act 1990*, as amended by the *Broadcasting Act 1996*, simply required that the CCG use the Gaelic Broadcasting Fund to finance the making of television and sound programmes in Gaelic primarily with a view to the broadcasting of such programmes for reception in Scotland[4], and more generally simply required that the CCG perform its grant-making function in such manner as they consider will secure that a wide range of high quality television programmes in Gaelic are broadcast for reception in Scotland and will widen the range and improve the quality of sound programmes in Gaelic that are broadcast for reception in Scotland.[5] As reference is made to reception of programmes primarily in Scotland, the potential audience are, by implication, primarily persons in Scotland. The statutory framework told us little more than that about the potential audience for Gaelic-medium programming. The duties of the new SMG,

---

[4] Section 183(4)(a)(i), *Broadcasting Act 1990*, as amended by section 95(5), *Broadcasting Act 1996*.

[5] Section 183(6), *Broadcasting Act 1990*, as amended by section 95(6)(b), *Broadcasting Act 1996*.

while somewhat different, as we shall see in a moment, are drawn by reference to essentially the same primary potential audience: the *Communications Act 2003* makes reference to programmes which are broadcast or otherwise transmitted so as to be available to "persons in Scotland", although this term is defined in this legislation to including both persons in Scotland and others.[6]

The *Communications Act 2003* does go on to provide that the SMG may finance or engage in research into the types of programmes in Gaelic that members of the "Gaelic-speaking community" would like to be broadcast or otherwise transmitted[7], thereby implying that Gaelic-medium broadcasting may be for this Gaelic-speaking community. Unfortunately, the act does not define this concept of the "Gaelic-speaking community", and precisely how it should be interpreted is unclear. The reference to "Gaelic-speaking" suggests that a person must have competence in spoken Gaelic to be a member of this community; it does not, however, seem to require that a person be a native speaker of the language, meaning that learners may form part of the group of people for whom Gaelic-medium broadcasting is made, although what level of competence in spoken Gaelic is necessary is uncertain. The reference to a "community" is also problemmatic. The word suggests a degree of social integration which goes beyond merely the ability to speak Gaelic, but it does not indicate the bases upon which community membership should be determined. Presumably, the contours of communal identity would have an objective and a subjective component, but it is difficult to determine what these are or should be. Thus, the new SMG, in conjunction with the broadcasters themselves, will have a very wide statutory scope, at least, for determining who is the audience for Gaelic-medium programming, and it would be surprising, given the general structure of Gaelic-medium broadcasting, outlined below, whether any radical redefinition of the audience will take place, at least in the short term.

The first question, who is Gaelic-medium broadcasting for, is related to the second one implied in the letter with which I began, what is Gaelic-medium broadcasting for? This is a question that is particularly difficult, because it has layers which majority language broadcasters generally do not need to consider. For majority language broadcasters, the answer will depend to a certain degree on whether you are a commercial or a public service broadcaster. A commercial broadcaster may argue that broadcasting is primarily for attracting audiences, thereby generating greater advertising revenues, thereby increasing shareholder profits. The profit-motive does not necessarily mean that such broadcasters are indifferent to other values and concerns, but the demands of the consumer are crucial. Public service broadcasters cannot be indifferent to "the consumer", but their very existence has generally been justified by other considerations. In addition to the classic objectives of informing, educating and entertaining the audience,[8] public service broadcasters such as the BBC will also seek to provide a broader reflection of the diversity of the societies in which they operate, but may

---

[6] Section 208, *Communications Act 2003*.

[7] Subsection 208(3), *Communications Act 2003*, which amends section 183 of the *Broadcasting Act 1990* through the creation of this provision, a new paragraph 183(4A)(c), along with other provisions, some of which will be described below.

[8] The *Gaelic Media Taskforce Report*, *supra*, at para. 34.

also seek, either explicitly or otherwise, to strengthen social cohesion by building and protecting a national culture and identity.

Since Gaelic-medium output is delivered by both the BBC Scotland, perhaps the classic public service broadcaster, and commercial broadcasters such as Scottish Television, all of these considerations will be brought to bear on Gaelic-medium broadcasting. But for minority language-medium broadcasters, there is arguably an added dimension: the role of the broadcaster in the effort to preserve and reinvigorate and expand the threatened linguistic minority. This theme also emerges in the letter quoted at the beginning of this article. For the letter writer, the overarching concern is language revival, and language revival is best accomplished by making the language "sexy" or attractive to young people, thereby convincing young non-speakers of the social attractiveness of learning the language while simultaneously reinforcing the loyalty of young people who are speakers of the language, by assuring them that their language fits with their experience as young people in the modern world. The older native speaker, assumed to be well past the age at which he or she can contribute meaningfully to the production of new speakers (an assumption that may not be true, given, for example, the role that a Gaelic-speaking grandparent can play in the linguistic development of grandchildren) is by implication less important, at least according to this way of thinking.

The idea that minority language broadcasting should not merely aim at pleasing audiences, but should play a role in the maintenance of the linguistic community, raises a very large number of pertinent considerations which go well beyond those suggested by the letter-writer, however. Making the language "cool", even if a legitimate goal from a language maintenance perspective, is only one of many strategies which must be deployed. Broadcasting can, for example, play an important ideological role, by helping to define the minority language community's identity and by helping to define and reinforce its core values. Given the emphasis which theorists of language revival place on such ideological issues in the process of language maintenance in general – the importance of social boundary delineation and maintenance runs like a golden thread through the work of theorists such as Joshua Fishman – considerably more attention needs to be played to the role of broadcasting in this ideological struggle. In this context, any attempt to use minority language broadcasting to make the minority language "sexy" or "cool" must be treated with a considerable amount of care, because such concepts are generally defined by and through the majority language mass culture, especially where teenagers and young adults are concerned.

If one accepts the letter-writer's premise that minority language broadcasters should concern themselves with the role of broadcasting in minority language maintenance and revival – and I would accept this premise, without reservation – a large number of other contentious language planning issues are, however, raised, above and beyond the question of the ideological role of minority-language broadcasting. It would, for example, be important to consider the role of broadcasting in strengthening Gaelic-speaking communities in even more tangible ways – by, for example, bringing employment to Gaelic-speaking areas, and so forth. The job-creating potential of Gaelic-medium broadcasting is significant – the Gaelic Broadcasting Task Force had estimated that about 316 full-time equivalent jobs were being sustained by Gaelic media at the time of its report and that this number would rise to 802 if their Gaelic Service were to be created.[9] But where, from a language maintenance perspective, should these jobs best be created? From a language planning perspective, would such jobs be better placed in Lewis or in Glasgow? To what extent does the answer depend on how we define "the Gaelic community"? And we must consider whether jobs in Gaelic media necessarily implies that the job-holder is a Gaelic-speaker, for it is a reality that a significant number of jobs in Gaelic broadcasting – particularly off-screen technical jobs – are not filled by Gaelic speakers at all. So, even if we were to conclude that, based on language policy grounds, the Gaelic media jobs should be based in Lewis (a conclusion which some activists would contest!), a great deal of care would have to be taken to ensure that any linguistic benefits which could come by virtue of those jobs would not be diluted, or even offset, by a significant influx of non-Gaelic-speakers to fill them.

Once again, the legislative framework gives only limited guidance with respect to this second question, what is Gaelic broadcasting for? Under the *Broadcasting Act 1990*, as amended by the *Broadcasting Act 1996*, the CCG was, as noted above, required to perform their functions in such manner as they consider will secure that a *wide range* of *high quality* television programmes in Gaelic are broadcast and will *widen the range* and *improve the quality* of sound programmes in Gaelic.[10] Thus, the focus is on the programming itself – particularly its range and quality – rather than on any other consideration. The legislative framework made no reference to the role of Gaelic broadcasting in the maintenance and revival of the language community, and strictly speaking, the CCG did not seem to have any statutory basis for the consideration of language planning issues in their work, although it is clear that the CCG has often sought to bring such considerations to bear. Significantly, the *Communications Act 2003* introduced no real changes, at least in this regard. The functions of the new SMG will still be directed to the programming itself: the SMG is to secure that a *wide and diverse range* of *high quality programmes* in Gaelic are broadcast or otherwise transmitted so as to be available to persons in Scotland.[11]

The difficulty, however, is that giving primacy to the production of a wide range of high quality programmes may not, in all cases, be consistent with language planning goals. All things being equal, of course, production values are certainly important, from the perspective of language planning and maintenance – viewers of Gaelic-medium programming should be entitled to expect the same quality as the majority population, and if Gaelic programmes are considered to be of poorer quality or of limited scope, they will be less attractive to the Gaelic audience and may contribute to the idea that Gaelic-medium is inferior, a dangerous idea from a language planning perspective.[12] Given the limited resources available to Gaelic-medium broadcasting, though, there is a

---

[9] *Gaelic Media Task Force, supra*, Appendix C.

[10] Section 183(6), *Broadcasting Act 1990*, as amended by section 95(6), *Broadcasting Act 1996*.

[11] Section 208, *Communications Act 2003*, which creates a new section 183(3B) in the *Broadcasting Act 1990*.

[12] Once again, points made in the contribution of Catherine Anne MacNeil to this volume concerning the range of Gaelic output, for example, nicely illustrate this problem.

considerable dependence, particularly with respect to television programming, on non-Gaelic speaking production staff. Until this problem is addressed through training policies – and it must be acknowledged that the CCG, together with the Sabhal Mòr Ostaig (the Gaelic college on Skye), has been working hard to address such skills shortages – a significant expansion of production activities in Gaelic-speaking areas such as Lewis may, ironically, result in the significant expansion of a non-Gaelic speaking presence, with a potentially negative impact on language planning activities in the locality. Such issues can be addressed through proper planning, but in order to do so, language planning considerations must be recognised, and at present, such considerations are not recognised in the statutory framework, at least. It is notable that even in the otherwise excellent Gaelic Broadcasting Task Force Report, more detailed language planning considerations were not considered. The Report did recognise the overall importance of broadcasting to minority language maintenance and revival, but while sociolinguists would accept that broadcasting is now very important in any minority language maintenance and revival effort, a wide range of difficult issues, from a language planning perspective, are also raised and must be carefully considered.

This brings us to the third and final of the questions raised by the letter quoted at the outset, who owns the minority language broadcasting initiative? The letter writer did not address this question, but in directing his comments at the BBC and Scottish Television, he acknowledges the present reality, which is that in a very important sense, the programming, whoever it is *for*, is in the hands of and, therefore, is in an important sense owned by the broadcasters. This essential truth has been acknowledged by virtually everyone who has commented on Gaelic-medium broadcasting, and was, as already noted, a central criticism of the status quo in the Gaelic Broadcasting Task Force Report. The only body that could be said to represent the Gaelic community – and I have already adverted to the increasingly contested nature of the concept of a single homogeneous "Gaelic community" – is the CCG (although how truly representative the CCG, or its successor the SMG, is will be considered, below). Yet, under the *Broadcasting Act 1990*, as amended by the *Broadcasting Act 1996*, the CCG had only the most limited of statutory powers. The CCG was simply a funding agency which was charged with managing the Gaelic Broadcasting Fund, a relatively small fund of £8.5 million, the nominal value of which is at the same levels it was at when it was first created, and real value of which has been eroded by almost 50% by inflation.[13] The CCG could only *finance* the making of television and radio programmes and *finance* the training of personnel; it could not itself actually engage in the making of programmes or, certainly, the broadcasting of programmes, and also could not, strictly speaking, train personnel itself. In reality, it was forced to try to coax

---

[13] Comataidh Craolaidh Gàidhlig, *Aithisg Bhliadhnail & Cunntasan/Annual Report & Accounts, 2002-03*, 22 May, 2003, "Aithisg a' Chathraiche / Chairman's Report", p. 4. As the Chairman noted, current funding levels "make innovation, far less expansion, impossible. The mantra expressed consistently by the Committee and by the Gaelic community may be tedious, but it's true: the current provision is deficient and untenable." The fund was originally intended to fund the creation of 200 hours of original programming per year, and it presently funds considerably fewer hours.

broadcasters with a funding carrot, and in this way to try to influence programme content and broadcasting strategies; in practice, the CCG has always been highly dependent on the good will of the broadcasters themselves, who ultimately wielded decisive power.

The *Communications Act 2003* has created at least a window of opportunity for the new SMG, the body which will replace the CCG. In particular, the SMG is not only able to finance, but may also *engage in* (a) the making of programmes in Gaelic with a view to their being broadcast or otherwise transmitted so as to be available to persons in Scotland (defined, as noted above, to include persons in Scotland and others), (b) the provision of training for persons employed or to be employed in connection with the making of programmes in Gaelic, and (c) research into the types of programmes in Gaelic that members of the Gaelic-speaking community would like to be broadcast or otherwise transmitted.[14] By statutorily empowering the SMG to not only fund programmes and other activities, but to engage in the making of such programmes with a view to their transmission, it is argued that the new body has considerably expanded powers. However, there remain both practical and legal barriers to the SMG moving towards being the sort of institution envisioned in the Gaelic Broadcasting Task Force Report. On a practical level, the power to engage in the making of programmes and the provision of training is hampered by the fact that the *Communications Act 2003* made no provisions with respect to the financing of the SMG. Thus, it is likely that the new body will have to be contented with roughly the same level of funding currently enjoyed by the CCG. On a legal level, the SMG was not conferred the power to actually broadcast programmes itself, but only to engage in the making of programmes with a view to their being broadcast or otherwise transmitted. Thus, even if the SMG decided to make a programme itself, it would appear to be dependent on broadcasters, in much the same way that the CCG is. So, while the SMG looks to have a somewhat greater scope of powers on paper, control, and therefore ownership, still lies firmly in the hands of the broadcasters.

And even if the SMG did have the powers and the purse to claim ownership of Gaelic medium broadcasting, who controls the SMG? In particular, can the Gaelic community be said to own this new institution? The CCG, the predecessor to the SMG, was in no real sense owned by or even representative of the Gaelic community. Under the *Broadcasting Act 1990*, as amended by the *Broadcasting Act 1996*, the CCG consisted of a Chairman, appointed by the main broadcasting regulatory agency, the London-based Independent Television Commission (the "ITC"), and between four and eight other members, also appointed by the ITC.[15] In making its appointments, the ITC was required to ensure that a majority of the members of the CCG were people who appeared to the ITC to represent the Gaelic-speaking community.[16] How the London-based ITC would make such a

---

[14] Section 208, the *Communications Act 2003*, which created a new section 184(4A) in the *Broadcasting Act 1990*.

[15] Section 183(3), the *Broadcasting Act 1990*; as the powers of the CCG were widened under the *Broadcasting Act 1996* to include the funding of radio programming, the ITC was required under that later act to consult the radio regulator, the Radio Authority, before making any appointments to the CCG: section 95(4), the *Broadcasting Act 1996*.

[16] Section 183(7), the *Broadcasting Act 1990*.

decision is unclear, but this statutory formula hardly guarantees that the membership of the CCG was in any real sense representative of the Gaelic community. As they were appointed by the ITC, not selected by the Gaelic community, the members of the CCG would clearly be responsible to the ITC, rather than to the Gaelic community.

The new SMG will be no closer to the Gaelic community. Under the *Communications Act 2003*, the SMG will have not more than twelve members, including one chairman, all of whom shall be appointed by the new regulatory agency, OFCOM, with the approval of the Secretary of State.[17] However, one of the members appointed by OFCOM must be nominated by the BBC, one must be nominated by Highlands and Islands Enterprise ("HIE"), and one must be nominated by the new Gaelic Development Agency, Bòrd Gàidhlig na h-Alba (the "Bòrd") (the membership of which is itself appointed by the Scottish Executive). In making its appointments, OFCOM must also secure, so far as it is practicable, that the interests of four different constituencies are represented on the SMG: first are the holders of licenses to provide regional Channel 3 services for areas wholly in Scotland (this would be Scottish Television); second are the holders of licences to provide regional Channel 3 services in respect of areas the greater part of which are in Scotland; third are the independent television and radio production industries in Scotland; and fourth are "other persons and bodies concerned with the promotion and use of the Gaelic language, including those concerned with education in Gaelic and in Gaelic culture".[18] It is only really this very last category which could be said to be at least in some way representative of the Gaelic community, but the power to determine which persons or bodies qualify remain with the London-based regulator OFCOM. Finally, OFCOM is under an overriding obligation to have regard, in making its appointments to the SMG, to the desirability of having members of the SMG who are proficient in written and spoken Gaelic[19]; thus, it is entirely possible that non-Gaelic speakers may qualify for membership on the SMG.

The structure of the SMG raises many significant and troubling issues, not the least of which is the apparent institutionalised conflicts of interest which have been created, for the SMG will almost certainly be negotiating with and entering into funding arrangements with several bodies who will be represented on the board of the SMG, including the broadcasters such as the BBC and Channel 3 providers (Scottish Television), and independent producers. Given that the Bòrd will have a significant role in the language planning process for Scottish Gaelic, it is encouraging that it will be represented, and it is hoped that its representative may be able to bring broader language planning considerations to bear, and may be able to help tie initiatives with respect to Gaelic-medium broadcasting in more effectively with other initiatives for the language and with an overall strategy for the language. But it is not at all clear why HIE should be represented on the board

---

[17] Section 209, the *Communications Act 2003*, which creates an amended section 183A in the *Broadcasting Act 1990*, of which these provisions are contained in section 183A(1)-(3).
[18] Section 209, the *Communications Act 2003*, which creates an amended section 183A in the *Broadcasting Act 1990*, of which these provisions are contained in section 183A(7).
[19] Section 209, the *Communications Act 2003*, which creates an amended section 183A in the *Broadcasting Act 1990*, of which these provisions are contained in section 183A(6).

of the SMG. HIE has financially supported Comunn na Gàidlig ("CNAG"), which was, until the Bòrd's appearance, the main Gaelic language development agency. But HIE is primarily an economic development agency which has not shown any particular expertise in language planning or, for that matter, broadcasting; the inclusion of HIE seems to imply that Gaelic broadcasting is partly a matter of economic development for the Highlands and Islands, and this is troubling. First, it is not clear that economic development and minority language development are necessarily mutually reinforcing propositions. Second, the notion that broadcasting should contribute especially to the Highlands and Islands economy is something that would also be contested by many Gaelic activists, who point out that almost half of all Gaelic speakers in Scotland now live outwith the Highlands and Islands. And, of course, the method of appointment of the SMG does not guarantee that the body will be representative of the Gaelic community, and ensures that it is certainly not accountable in any way to that community. As noted earlier, the SMG will have the power to research the types of programming in Gaelic that members of the Gaelic-speaking community would like to be broadcast or otherwise transmitted. Thus, the SMG can (though does not necessarily have to) conduct market surveys amongst Gaelic-speakers. But, of course, no one would equate market research with democratic accountability. So, someone may be asking us what we would like to see, but the real decision making power with respect to Gaelic broadcasting remains fairly well removed from the Gaelic community.

Programming for Gaelic Digital Television: Problems and Possibilities[1]

Mike Cormack

Recent years have seen a vigorous campaign in Scotland for a Gaelic digital television channel to replace the established Gaelic television arrangement. Currently the Comataidh Craolaidh Gàidhlig (CCG) funds much of Gaelic programming, amounting to 146 hours of new programmes in the year 2002-03 (CCG 2003a: 4), which is broadcast across BBC1, BBC2, Scottish and Grampian. This campaign has raised a number of issues, not least where the finance for a digital channel is going to come from. My concern here, however, is not with the financial problem, nor with questions to do with how the channel should be run (both of which are clearly vital issues), but rather about programming. What kind of programming should there be on a Gaelic digital television channel? What are the problems which are likely to arise in relation to programming for such a channel? What aims should direct programming decisions?

First, some information about the current situation will be appropriate. Following an energetic campaign for a digital channel, led by the CCG, the Communications Act, given the Royal Assent in July 2003, has changed the CCG to a new organisation, Seirbheis nam Meadhanan Gàidhlig (Gaelic Media Services), which takes over in January 2004. The head of this new organisation is Neil Fraser, who has had a distinguished career in Gaelic broadcasting at the BBC and was author of the 1998 report (commissioned by Brian Wilson, then at the Scottish Office) that first laid out the possibilities for Gaelic digital television. The function of the new organisation is much the same as that of the CCG, but with a remit broadened beyond conventional broadcasting (hence the rather uninspiring name). Although the government has shown a willingness to consider the possibility of a digital channel for Gaelic, there has so far been no word as to where the finance might come from. The cost was being quoted at £44 million per annum in 2001, but has no doubt gone up by now. This is a major increase on what is currently given to Gaelic broadcasting (in 2002-03 it was £8.5m) and, assuming that the costs will have increased somewhat by the time such a channel appears, is not too far off £1,000 per Gaelic speaker. However a comparison can be made with other broadcast costs. According to a recent report in *The Guardian* the digital channel BBC3 (formerly BBC Choice), which broadcasts only from 7.00 pm in the evening, is currently costing £97m, but is only getting 0.53% of the digital TV audience (*The Guardian* 14.11.03). This money is of course coming from the licence fee which all television owners must pay, regardless of whether or not they get digital television.

In fact, Gaelic is already established on digital television. Since November 1999 TeleG (see their website at: www.teleg.co.uk) has been broadcasting on the S4C multiplex, but only for one hour each day (6.00–7.00 pm). It is only allowed at this stage to use material already broadcast on traditional analogue television.

---

[1] This paper was first presented at a conference on Language and the Media in Scotland, 15 November 2003, Stirling, arranged by the Association for Scottish Literary Studies, and is included in the present volume because of its intrinsic relevance.

The current TeleG schedules include repeats of well-known recent Gaelic programmes ("Dè a-nis?", "Sin Thu Fhein", "Eòrpa", "Obair-Là") along with the Irish language soap opera "Ros na Run" dubbed into Scottish Gaelic. It is, however, very difficult to find anyone who has actually seen it. As Morag MacNeil has carefully put it: "As yet, however, there has been very little engagement with the opportunity to access programmes on this Gaelic channel" (NicNeil 2001: 101). This is not surprising since it is only available on terrestrial digital, but people in the highlands and islands are probably more likely to get satellite digital, given the inherent problems of reception in many parts of the area.

The current plans for a full digital channel are for up to about three hours of new programming each day (part of which would be news and current affairs), along with repeats, and possibly using Gaelic radio when television programmes are not being broadcast. John Angus MacKay (Director of the CCG) has described one possible version in an "indicative weekly schedule" (attributed to Scott Ferguson) for a Gaelic digital channel (MacKay 2002: Appendix 8). This schedule operates from 9.00 am to midnight, but includes Gaelic music and/or radio in the first three hours. The remaining twelve hours are split between news-related programmes, children's programmes, repeats of material already broadcast, new programming which is not news-related or for children, and English language programmes. Outside of news programmes and children's programmes there is just 30 minutes of new Gaelic programming each day, and the English programming covers seven of the twelve hours. This of course is just a first sketch of one possibility of digital television programming and no doubt there will be much difference of detail if and when such a channel finally appears. However there is no reason to believe that it does not indicate the most likely pattern of the balance between the different categories mentioned above. It may at first seem odd that there is so much English language programming here but there are, in fact, precedents for this. It is like a slimmed-down version of S4C's programming. The Welsh Channel 4 broadcaster does not broadcast a full schedule in Welsh on its analogue channel, but rather mixes it with English language Channel 4 programmes (see its website at: www.s4c.co.uk). Having said that, the situation is different on S4C's digital channel which was launched in November 1998. This gives over 80 hours a week of Welsh programming, broadcasting from noon to late evening each day, and includes no English language programmes at all. In 2000 the funding for S4C was just over £78m. The Irish language channel, TG4, broadcasts from 7am to 2am each day and also includes English language programming. As its website says (www.tg4.ie), it provides "over seven hours of innovative quality programming in Irish supported by a wide range of material in other languages". It is not available as a digital channel as there is currently no terrestrial digital television broadcasting in Ireland.

A Gaelic digital television channel would create a situation very different from the present one. There would be access to a larger audience, such as Gaels living outside Scotland. John Angus MacKay's research included investigating what Gaelic speakers in London want from such a channel. This might well complicate matters as far as programming is concerned. There may be differences between the kinds of programmes desired by Gaels in London and Gaels living in the Gaidhealtachd (as in fact MacKay's research showed to some extent). There would also be increased competition from other channels. Many Gaelic speakers have indicated they are more likely to go digital if there was a Gaelic channel, but of course that means that they would also have many other channels available. The free-to-air terrestrial digital channels provided by Freeview consists of 30 television and radio channels (including eight television channels from the BBC – BBC1, BBC2, BBC3, BBC4, CBBC, CBeebies, BBC Parliament, BBC News 24 – along with ITV1, ITV2, Channel 4, Channel 5, Sky News and a clutch of others). A digital channel automatically means greater competition for that channel than is currently provided by the five terrestrial analogue channels.

This means that the actual content of such a channel will be critical. There will be a core audience of committed Gaelic speakers who will watch it whatever the circumstances and whatever the variations in content, but the larger audience of not-so-committed Gaels and learners (at various stages of proficiency) will also be important. This channel will have to show its worth. It will have to have a decent audience (relative of course to the size of the Gaelic population) if public money is to be put into it year after year. And the more money that goes in, the more it will have to prove itself, and that proof will be seen primarily in terms of audience numbers. More important measures (how the channel helps the survival of Gaelic) will only become apparent gradually as the years pass. The bottom line is that it does not matter how good the programmes are and how many prizes they win. If they do not get the audiences, the channel will be seen as a failure. This is not just economic and political reality. If this channel is to help the language, it has to maximise the audience. However, going in the opposite direction and aiming for the lowest common denominator is also not a sensible option since the most obvious way of doing this – simply repeating the familar formats of popular television – is unlikely to retain the audience. Viewers can get this kind of programming elsewhere on television, and usually made with more money than would be available for the Gaelic versions. Gaelic programming has to be different, it has to be meaningful for a Gaelic audience, and it has to attract that audience if it is to help the language.

Yet there is disagreement amongst language experts concerning the value of television in relation to minority languages. Most famously Joshua Fishman has expressed scepticism. When, in his book *Reversing Language Shift*, he discussed intergenerational language loss and the ways in which this might be prevented, the usefulness of the media was put not only well behind the use of language in the home and community, but also behind such elements as education and the workplace (Fishman 1991: 395). In his more recent writing he has noted that the media are more likely to interfere with mother-tongue transmission than support it, simply because there will always be a greater quantity of media output in the dominant, majority language (Fishman 2001: 473). He has even referred to "the mass-media 'fetish' of some minority language activists" (Fishman 2001: 482), noting how unrealistic their expectations of the media can be. Perhaps there are few people working in minority language media who would agree with this assessment, but, at the very least, it should make us wary of overestimating what can actually be achieved by a digital television channel. It might even suggest that far from being a necessary condition for the survival of Gaelic in the 21st century, putting large amounts of money into a digital television channel is actually a high-risk strategy.

Related to this uncertainty is the question of exactly what such a channel should be aiming for and how its success or failure should be judged. There are various aims which a minority language television channel might have or which it might have to prioritise (particularly when resources are scarce). Consider the following possible aims (a slightly different version of this is given in Cormack 1999): (1) maintaining the current number of language speakers; (2) increasing the number of language speakers; (3) defending and/or promoting the language's culture; (4) giving viewers popular programmes in their native language. These aims can quite easily give rise to programming conflicts. Programmes aimed simply at maintaining the language will be aimed at fluent speakers. Programmes aimed at increasing the language will be aimed at various levels of learners. Programmes concerned with Gaelic culture might well have a very different content from programmes which are simply concerned with maximising the audience. A programme might be a popular success but contribute nothing to a native speaker's will to continue speaking his or her language. The Broadcasting Act of 1990, which first set up the Comataidh Telebhisein Gàidhlig (the predecessor of the CCG), talked only of providing a range of quality programming (and of course does not offer any definition of what this might mean). The Communications Act of 2003 follows suit. The point of all this is that while such different aims might be of little practical consequence to a well-funded 24 hours-a-day channel which would thereby have the resources to satisfy all of these aims, they become an urgent problem when we are faced with an under-resourced channel, with possibly as little as 30 minutes a day of non-news and current affairs programming for adults.

The CCG has recently attempted to deal with such questions. In a booklet issued to celebrate its first ten years, a set of five "primary objectives" was given (CCG 2003b). These were: (1) "to meet the requirements of the Gaelic community and viewers throughout Scotland for a comprehensive, high quality and attractive Gaelic television service available at appropriate viewing times"; (2) "to extend the range and improve the quality of sound programmes broadcast in Gaelic"; (3) "to promote Gaelic broadcasting as a distinct but integral element in the development of the Gaelic language and culture"; (4) "to ensure that Gaelic broadcasting is not only relevant to the community it serves but is also rooted in the culture and values of that community"; (5) "to recruit, train, nurture and retain well-qualified and dedicated staff who care for the customer." (Even this last is relevant to programming issues since one way of retaining staff is giving them interesting and challenging programmes to work on.) These objectives do begin to suggest certain key elements, once we get beyond the standard invocations of quality and range. However, problems are not difficult to find. How is "the Gaelic community" to be defined? Is it just those communities in which Gaelic is still part of everyday life? Does it include those areas where native speakers are living but Gaelic is no longer the preferred language of public interaction? Does the addition of "viewers throughout Scotland" imply that Gaelic speakers living in, for example, Glasgow are not part of anything that might be called "the Gaelic community"? Does it, indeed, make any sense to talk about the Gaelic community as a singular entity, rather than referring to Gaelic communities? The point about relevance in item 4 is certainly important, but how are we to identify the values of the Gaelic community? Like any other community, that of the Gaels (however it is defined) has its divisions. It is not at all clear that a set of values could be suggested which all Gaels – or even a significant majority of them – would accept without question.

Despite these problems, I want to argue that questions of community and identity must be central to digital television programming. If programming does not deal with these issues, then it is difficult to see how it will be any different from much of the rest of television output, apart from the fact that it is in Gaelic. It is only by strengthening the community that Gaelic will survive, and identity – how Gaels think of themselves – is central to that. But a broad view must be taken here. The Gaelic community, like any other language community, is a wide one. It is found not just places like Ness, Staffin or Barra. And Gaelic identity must be defined in a way which opens up possibilities rather than limits them.

How, then, is this to be achieved by digital television programming? It must be popular but, as already argued, there is little point in simply replicating standard formats. The culture and community shown is vitally important but it needs to be a contemporary view (even if closely related to and developing out of traditional Gaelic culture and society), not just a historical one. Cultures and societies (particularly in the 21st century) are best seen as changing entities, continually developing, rather than being static monoliths. There are different audiences to be catered for, and this brings a concomitant need for a wide range of representation and of political and social opinion. Also implicit in such an approach is a need for community involvement – something that broadcasters in general are good at talking about but not so good at carrying out in anything beyond the most elementary ways.

This is a difficult line on which to balance – a channel which relates to contemporary Gaels, recognising the importance of those communities in which Gaelic is still part of everyday life, but keeping the broader sense of community in view. The major problems of limited finance and a limited pool of programme-makers add to the difficulties. But there will not be another chance. If, at the next census, the number of Gaels continues in its decline, then governments of whatever persuasion are likely to give up not just on a Gaelic digital channel but on the language itself.

References

Comataidh Craolaidh Gàidhlig. 2003a *Annual Report and Accounts, 2002-03.* Stornoway: CCG.

Comataidh Craolaidh Gàidhlig. 2003b. *At 10 / Aig 10.* Stornoway: CCG.

Cormack, M. 1999. "Minority Languages and Television Programming Policy." *International Journal of Cultural Policy* 5: 1-21

Fishman, J. 1991. *Reversing Language Shift.* Clevedon: Multilingual Matters.

Fishman, J. ed. 2001. *Can Threatened Languages Be Saved?* Clevedon: Multilingual Matters.

Fraser, N. 1998. *A Review of Aspects of Gaelic Broadcasting.* Glasgow: Fraser Production and Consultancy for The Scottish Office, Education and Industry Department, Arts and Cultural Heritage Division.

MacKay, J.A. 2002. *A Gaelic Digital Television Channel: Survey of Potential Audience Requirements.* Unpublished MSc thesis, Stirling University.

NicNeill, M. 2001. "Gaelic Broadcasting: On the Threshold of a New Era." *Mercator Media Forum* 5: 99-106

BBC Radio Scotland and Scots

Maggie Cunningham

Radio Scotland has a complex role in broadcasting to the whole of Scotland, which has a widely changing demographic. As the number of Scots decrease and there is a greater inward migration, the task of reflecting the country to itself and of reflecting the world from a Scottish perspective becomes increasingly more challenging. However, on a positive note more than 1 million people listen to the station every week and evidence is that they enjoy what they hear.

Radio was almost written off towards the end of the last century with the advent of personal computers, and an increased offering from television in the form of a greater number of channels. However, I am pleased to say that radio's demise has been exaggerated and that the number of overall listeners to the oldest service is holding steady, if not increasing. All of the major technological innovations have helped radio - you can listen online, and we have listeners all over the world who do, on television and soon possibly on your mobile phone.

In this context how does Radio Scotland deliver a service. As the nation's only national broadcaster, we have a public service duty to provide a wide range of programmes and that is done effectively through a spine of news, current affairs and sport. Some people may question the air-time we give to football, but there is no doubt that there is a big appetite for the game across the country and that is an important part of our culture which is verified by the number of people who tune in to us.

I believe our confidence as a station is reflected by the tone we use and by how comfortable we are within our skins. Over the past two years, I have encouraged our presenters to use language and words that they are comfortable with and have authority in using.

This is especially true of Scots, and we created a small lexicon for them as examples of ways in which they could develop their use of Scots. This lexicon comprises the following 70 words:

Sayins/saws: *facts are chiels that winna ding, a stout hert for a stey brae, a gaun fuit is aye gettin, ne'er cast a cloot till Mey's oot*;

Wather: *haar, dreich*, also *gey dreich, drookit, stoatin, smir o rain,* ('drizzle'), also *drowe* ('drizzle'), *smoored wi snaw/fog/haar* ('smothered covered with'), *chitterin cauld*, also *fooneran cauld, braw, bonnie, the gloamin, a snell wind, waterdaw* ('a fading rainbow'), *feechie* (North East, literally 'dirty', worse than *dreich*);

Fitba: *sclaff, blooter, stoat, jouk past, caw the feet fae*;

General: *tae airt* ('direct'), *airt* ('place'), *antrin* ('odd', 'occasional'), *bachle, chancer, cloot, clarty, clype, coorse, couthie, crabbit, tae chave* ('to work'), also *chavin* ('working'), *darg* ('work', 'task') e.g. *a sair darg, a day's darg, doolally, doited* ('stupid'), *dicht* ('wipe'), *frichtsome, gowpin* ('throbbing'), *gomeril, gowk,* haliket ('big and clumsy'), *jalouse* ('surmise', 'guess'), *hame knitted, hunkers, hunkerin doon, kenspeckle* ('conspicuous', 'eminent'), *mingin* ('smelly'), *bowfin* ('smelly'), *orra*, also *orrie* ('occasional', 'coorse'), *rammy, sair* ('sore') e.g. *a sair* *fecht* ('a struggle'), *scheme*, also *schemie, scunnert*, also *scunnersome* ('sickened') e.g. *to tae tak a scunner at* ... , *sonsy* ('buxom'), *tae speir* ('to ask', 'to question'), *speirin* ('inquisitive') e.g. *a nebby speirin kinna bodie, tae sprachle* ('to climb awkwardly'), *stound* ('pain', 'shock'), *sweirt* ('reluctant'), *tae tak a grue at* ('sickened') e.g. *it garred ye grue, taiglet* ('delayed'), *tae thole* ('to bear', 'to ensure'), *thrawn* ('stubborn'), *tae threap* ('to assert', 'to contend', to argue'), *wabbit*, also *puggled* ('tired'), *wersh*, also *wersht* ('bitter') e.g. *gey wersh.*

We decided to follow down a main stream route with Scots in encouraging presenters to use the language and this is true in areas such as Off the Ball, our football fanzine in which Tam Cowan from Lanarkshire uses a great deal of contemporary Scots vocabulary in an entirely natural way. Lesley Riddoch, although not grown up with the language is beginning to employ a number of words and idioms within her daily news and phone in programme and this is something which I encourage. Robbie Shephard is a Doric speaker who uses his language regularly on his weekly shows and our gardening programme is a treasure trove of good Scots idiom.

We also encourage some of our key programme makers to use Scots within their scripting. Billy Kay is a prime example of this. His series, *Scotland's Black History*, is the most recent example of this but there are other examples. *Street Kids* was an exploration of the poverty of street children in Brazil and the combination of language in this programme was a joy to hear. All of Billy's series are presented in Scots, with the richest seam being his *People's History* series which runs every year.

There are many more examples which I could offer, but I do understand that our particular direction will not please all advocates of the language. However, our experience is that we should not ghettoise programmes and that all of Scotland's diversity should sit within the mainstream of the schedule. Over recent years, we abandoned our ethnic programme which was broadcast on Sundays at 9.00 pm because it was clear that it was a ghetto slot and not attracting the listeners for which it was intended. We have since incorporated the features of this programme within our mainstream schedule, both speech and music.

I believe this is the best way forward for Scots as well. It is also an evolutionary process. Radio listening is very habitual and presenters, content and listeners grow together. We will continue our commitment to Scots and will do feature programmes and regular series which looks at the development of the language as well as debate this within our daily strands. For national poetry day, we commission and broadcast six contemporary poets, many of these are in the Scots language and we will continue to do this. There are many initiatives such as these that we will continue to develop on a regular basis, but I do believe that placing programmes and content within our mainstream schedule is the future, both for building confidence among speakers who may also be listeners, but also to create greater awareness of Scots among those who do not know about its richness and diversity.

[Editorial note: Billy Kay (personal communication) has informed us, and Maggie Cunningham's office has confirmed, that it was he who provided BBC Scotland with this list as examples of commonly used Scots words.]

Broadcasting and Scots

Stuart McHardy

In Jamieson's *Dictionary of the Scottish Language* he gies the defintion o leid as meanin baith tung an culture. This arises the pynt that nae language ivver exists in a vacuum, een tho linguists aften attempt tae tak an objective view. The practicalities o language politics mean we cannae afford tae tak sic an approach the problems anent Scots in eethir Scotland or Northern Ireland. Ane o thir chief problems is that o representatio,n an it is ane that haes seen a rowth o discussion for a fell lang time. Gin we speak for Scots, wha dae we think we're speakin on behauf o? Answers tae this in the past hae aye been restrictit by notions o the defineetion o the leid itsel, an hou braid a spectrum o speakers athin the Scots tae Scottish English leid spectrum cin be includit. The verra quaistion pits me in mind o an auld chestnut that is seyed tae hae its origins somewhaur athin Ireland. A mannie asks anither hou tae get tae a certain place an is gien the answer – "Gin A wis gangin there A widnae stairt fae here."

Whit A pit forrit is that we demand that a leid policy is developt that disnae jist gie Scots its place, as it exists the day in the places it is spoke, an ther's a wheen o argiein te be done anent that forbye,. This means respectin the leid fowk actually speak an haein professionals in braidcastin wha refleck the reality o sic speak. Nou the BBC haes tae be seen as pairt o the problem for nae mair reason than its oors – we pey for it. Bit whit dae we get for oor licence fee? While A walcum the braidcastin o *A Kist o Wurds* in Northern Ireland an commend the BBC NI for pittin it oot, whit is ther at aw like it in Scotladnd itsel? Here aw we get is the occasional presenter wha uises Scots, an the list disnae gang muckle further nor Lesley Riddoch, Rabbie Shepherd, Tam Cowan an occasional ither voices, wi the odd haill programme in Scots bi the likes o Billy Kay. Nou BBC Scotland haes its ain set o problems as the stramash ower the norie o oor aine news programmin at six o'clock showed a wee whilie back. Thoi this waes aw aboot televeesion programmin it showed up a raft o problems. Ilka day we hear a caw sign that claims BBC Scotland tae be Scotland's National Radio! It is nae sic thing. As far as the BBC itsel is concernt, an the heid o the baist bides in London, Scotland is a region an in terms o programmin, policy an payment it is only ane o the BBC's regions Because o the ignorance o oor leids in the cultural sense, ther's nae problem wi Gaelic for the deceesion makkin fowk, wi aw their metrovincial assumptions an blin ignorance o Scottish culture. Thay unnerstaun the difference atween Gaelic an English alang the lines o "what on earth are they going on about, with this Scots stuff?". Thay dinnae ken that Scots is a distinct leid an A'm fell siccar thay widnae care muckle gin thay did. Altho we hae seen a gradual improvement in the amount o Scots on baith BBC radio an the television it still disnae refleck the reality that mair nor a third o oor population speak it as their first, an aften only, tung. The seetuation re the commercial stations is waur, tho nou an agin ye get a presenter wha speaks in a natural Scots vyce, but that's tae dae wi thair personality an professionalism, no policy.

The thing that maks this plain is phone-ins – ye hear the haill reenge o Scots vyces there! . Muckle o Scottish culture – an no jist the tradeetional kin, uises the auld leid bit ye widnae ken ither nor wee bits o folk music an the Robbie Shepherd coverage o the Scots dancing scene. An that's aboot hou Robbie daes things an nae oniethin really tae dae wi clear management policy. There are problems wi representin onie level o tradeetional culture in Britian – the problems o heich an low art an muckle o the consequent lack o clarity comes fae the hidebound limitations o thinkin that arise fae the English class system that sits a bit uneasy in SCOTLAND, but haes sic an effect, particulary athin education. An American education academic, on BBC Radio Scotland raicently seyed he waes astoundit bi the fack that in awthin he had read concernin education, in baith England an Scotland, there had been nae mention o class. It taks an affcomer tae pynt oot the truth. There's a blin fear o dealin wi sic kins o reality an aw levels o publick seetuations in the UK an we cannae sey the BBC are waur nor oniebodie else.

Nou a couple o year syne at the Association of Smallscale Scottish Broadcasters (nou defunct) we lookit at the quaistion o leids in general. At a conference in Embra in1999 that waes attendit bi local Gaelic braidcasters and a wheen o fowk fae non-indigenous minority groups athin oor society, we had tae tak tent o mair nor jist the problems o Scots an/or Gaelic. The conference came thegither around the norie that ae wey forrit wuid be for the BBC or the government itsel tae support a languages channel – that wuid allow baith the expressin o cultural an linguistic identity, an the discussion o language development tae be pitten oot on a permanent basis. Whither or no the Gaelic media fowk wuid be interestit in this is no ma concern – A think that it cuid be a wey o keepin up braidcastin tae the Gaelic-speakin population wha arenae the same as the Gaelic media fraternity - despite whit some micht think! A pit forrit this norie as a wey o getting the lack o clear language policy addresst an gin the ASSB had survived an no been divertit intae ither areas it micht hae happent! Nae leid is o onie mair warth nor anither an tae act gin it is, is tae insult fowk wha dinnae speak the dominant, or acceptit leid or leids, oniewhaur, onietime. Forbye that, it is a manifest breach o a wheen o international treaties regairdin discreemination that the UK government haes signed up til.

As regairds Scots in general whit is needit nou,is the implementatin o Pairt Three o the Chairter – an in terms o the media the BBC in Scotland cuid gie a lead tae this. We aw ken fine that policy is decidit by fowk wha suffer fae metrovincialism – sittin doun in London thinkin that is the centre o aw that's meaninfu – politically, economically an culturally – thay're wrang bit that winnae cheenge thair wey o seein things. We maun tlk this on board. The American academic mentiont abune, Richard Majors, comes fae outside o the British Isles an sees things clearly that politeecians an ceevil servants here canne, or willnae, see whan he brings up the problems o class. The truth is that maist Scots is spoken by fowk wha arenae middle class an the media, like aw o our institutions, is rin by fowk wha are maistlike middle class. In education this cin be seen as partícklarly pernicious – aw the intiatives addressin the needs o communities in areas o multuple deprivation in Scotland – maist o the inhabitants o which, speak naethin but Scots – are aye prentit in English, the leid o the professional educators an linguists and politeecians.

We aw ken fine that lip service haes lang been peyed tae the norie o respectin the language bairns bring tae schuil but whan push comes tae shove, hou can ye expeck teachers tae deal wi Scots whan thay nivver get onie trainin in the leid an ower monie o thaim hae had thair own Scots wheedlit oot o thaim?

Whit is needit is baith radio an televeesion shows that refleck the variety o speech that exists – this lets speakers realise that thair ain leid is a leid, an no continue tae haud ontae the class-driven an patronisin havers that Scots is jist some kin o bastardised Inglis!

In terms o the day to day braidcastin situation ther is a problem wi the advertisin culture that haes een got the BBC carin mair aboot ratins nor quality, an certainly mair nor thair statit aims o "to inform, educate and entertain" – Lord Reith maun be birlin i the mools as A write this. Houaniver it is athin this precise area that howp lees – niche marketing is aw the thing in braidcastin as the plethora o different platforms keeps on increasinn. A waes performin a show in the last Embra Festival Fringe an it waes bein braidcast straicht tae the Web wi a set-up that cost nae mair nor fifteen thousan punds. In braidcastin terms yon's peanuts, an means that for verra little siller -, it'll likely be cheaper neist year - we cuid be coverin aw kins o cultural events on ane or mair o the BBC stations. Gin we get the leid on the air, aw levels o language development get a heeze as baith the population an the politeecians wakken up up tae whit reality is, in terms o Scots.

Televeesion shows like Chewin the Fat an Still Game show whit cin be done – an like the rather less PC acceptable Rab Nesbitt shows these are programmes that even the English can follae maist o – sae whaur's the problem? Lack o confidence, lack o power mean lack o siller an thus we cin be fobbit aff aw the time.

There's a wheen o problems anent Scots in education that wuid be gien a guid haun bi the simple o expedient o jist letting bairns hear mair o thair ain tung, an no jist on vox pop shows. Hou cin we no hae politics in Scots? Economics in Scots? International news in Scots? A ken fine ther arenae monie fowk warkin in journalism, prent or braidcast that are shair o hou tae speak in Scots but gin we arenae alloued tae mak mistakes we nivver learn. Gaelic tv braidcastin cam about thro bein supportit wi siller, fae a base level o whit? Naethin! But ther waes political will. C4 in Wales waes forced intae be bein bi a hunger strike! Mebbe it's jist time tae up the ante – we keep winnin the argiements an getting nae place sae we need tae think on hou serious we are an stop bein sae bluidy polite!

Lá: A Daily Newspaper in Irish

Ciaran Ó Pronntaigh

Mar an gcéanna le cuid mhaith coincheap, go minic bíonn sé doiligh an coincheap simplí a mhíniú. Cé go raibh Lá ag teacht amach go laethúil ar feadh roinnt blianta roimhe seo, is é seo an chéad uair a bhí an oiread acmhainní ag an nuachtán agus atá aige faoi láthair. Is leis an ghrúpa nuachtán, 'Nuachtáin', Lá anois agus tá idir chabhair bhainisteoireachta agus chlódóireachta ar fáil, mar aon le hoifigí a bheith aige. Cuireann sé le héifeachtúlacht an nuachtáin chomh maith go bhfuil sé mar chuid de ghrúpa níos mó, ó thaobh scéalta agus taithí de.

An Coincheap

Tá thart ar 35 nuachtán laethúil ag mionteangacha ar fud na hEorpa, cé go mbaineann an chuid is mó acu le mionteanga ar mórtheanga i dtír eile í. Is é Berria, an nuachtán Bascaise an sampla is gaire do staid na foilsitheoireachta nuachtáin laethúil i mionteanga arb í teanga na tíre í chomh maith. Go bunúsach is é atá i gceist le nuachtán laethúil i mionteanga go mbeadh an focal scríofa 'de dhíth' chun eolas a chur ar fáil don phobal. Tugann sé seo an teanga go dtí leibhéal níos airde ná nuachtán seachtainiúil. An fhadhb a chonaic muid le nuachtán seachtainiúil gur mó d'uirlis chultúrtha é an nó is lú a mbítear ag brath air chun eolas a chur ar fáil.

Ar ndóigh, is í an bhearna eolais an gad is gaire do mhionteanga, go háirithe má tá sí le bheith ina huirlis chumarsáide a mbeadh aon tábhacht léi.

Maoiniú

Cé gur fiontar tráchtála é Lá, faigheann sé deontas measartha mór ó Fhoras na Gaeilge (thart ar £160,000 in aghaidh na bliana) agus faigheann sé deontas beag ón Chomhairle Ealaíon. Tá deontas fostaíochta gearrthréimhseach ar fáil don oifig i gConamara. Taobh amuigh de mhaoiniú stáit is as fógraí a thagann an chuid is mó de mhaoiniú an nuachtáin, agus ar ndóigh, an méid a fhaightear as díol an nuachtáin féin.

Bailíodh £50,000 chomh maith trí scaireisiúint do ghrúpaí Gaeilge agus daoine aonair. Bhí dhá chúis leis sin, an chéad rud chun airgead caiptil a thógáil agus an dara rud chun úinéireacht a thabhairt do phobal na Gaeilge.

Scaipeachán

Ceann de na dúshláin is mó a bhí romhainn agus muid ag pleanáil an nuachtáin laethúil córas iontaofa scaipeacháin. Bhí a fhios againn ónar dtaithí féin ar nuachtán seachtainiúil gur bheag an aird a tugadh do nuachtán beag, fiú dá mbeadh sé á scaipeadh ar fud na tíre. Chomh maith leis an chóras scaipeacháin, bheartaigh muid córas nua síntiúis. Is gnách go bhfaigheann síntiúsóir cóip den iris nó nuachtán tríd an phost, slí a oibríonn go maith más seachtanán nó tréimhseachán atá ann ach níl an córas poist ag an leibhéal sin, áit ar bith in Éirinn, chun go bhfaighfí an nuachtán an lá dár gcionn.

An córas a thionscain muid go dtiocfadh le síntiúsóir a chóip a ordú agus í a bhailiú sa siopa ar lá a fhoilsithe, ar phraghas níos ísle agus gan aon airgead a íoc leis an siopadóir. Is é seo an dóigh ar fearr linn déileáil le síntiúsóirí nua.

Oifigí

Shocraigh muid go mbeadh trí oifig ann ar fad, ceann i nGaillimh, áit a bhfuil ceanncheathrú na meán Gaeilge uile, mar atá Raidió na Gaeltachta, an tseirbhís teilifíse, TG4, agus an nuachtán seachtainiúil, Foinse. Is í an oifig sin is mó a phléann cúrsaí Gaeltachta. Tá oifig eile i mBaile Átha Cliath agus tugann sí a haghaidh cuid mhaith ar cheisteanna náisiúnta, go háirithe polaitíocht agus an Dáil. Is san oifig i mBéal Feirste a dhéantar an eagarthóireacht agus an leagan amach agus is ansin fosta a chuirtear cló ar an nuachtán.

Scéalta

Is é a chuir muid romhainn scéalta a bhain leis an Ghaeilge, le pobal na Gaeilge, scéalta náisiúnta agus scéalta idirnáisiúnta a chur ar fáil. Le cur leis an choincheap gur chóir go mbeadh an nuachtán ag líonadh bearna eolais cuireann muid isteach rudaí cosúil leis an sceideal teilifíse agus scéalta báis i bpobal na Gaeilge.

Cur agus Cúiteamh

Le linn na cainte, cuireadh an cheist faoi neamhspleáchas agus bheith ag fáil deontais, go háirithe ó Fhoras na Gaeilge, an t-eagras uile-Éireann a phléann le forbairt na teanga. Is ar bhonn conradh trí bliana a thugtar amach na deontais, rud a fhágann nach mbeadh an oiread tionchair á imirt agus a d'fhéadfadh tarlú dá mbeadh conradh níos giorra i gceist. Ceist eile a tógadh an méid scéalta faoi chúrsaí Gaeilge a bheadh ar an nuachtán. Dúirt roinnt daoine gur nós é ag nuachtáin Ghaeilge barraíocht béime a chur ar chúrsaí na Gaeilge agus cúrsaí teanga.

Resumé

This presentation deals mainly with the philosophy behind a daily newspaper in a minority language (*Lá*), how this is financed, some of the editorial questions which arise, and a look at how this can be organised. It is a summary of the first six months of the newspaper going daily and some of the preparations involved.

The Case for a Weekly Gaelic Newspaper in Scotland

Mike Cormack

Why should we bother with a Gaelic-language press in Scotland? In these days when television and radio take centre stage, for Gaelic as much as for other languages, and the Internet seems able to provide a wide range of up-to-the-minute information, why bother with the need for a Gaelic newspaper? When a Gaelic digital television channel is going to cost so much more than current Gaelic media, why argue for putting some money into developing the Gaelic press, particularly when such an enterprise is almost certain to be loss-making? I want to argue that there <u>is</u> a case for establishing a weekly Gaelic newspaper and – despite the inherent problems (not the least of which is funding) – we should not simply abandon the idea, with the assumption of a purely electronic media future.

To begin with, it is perhaps worth reminding ourselves about the current situation with regard to Gaelic in Scottish newspapers. There is no regular 'hard' news in Gaelic, just weekly columns in several newspapers, and these columns are seldom concerned with political and related issues. *The West Highland Free Press* and the *Stornoway Gazette* do have occasional news items in Gaelic, but only ones that are directly to do with the language itself. I have argued elsewhere (Cormack 1995) that much of the use of Gaelic in these newspapers can be seen as a kind of 'language display' in which the newspaper concerned uses a token amount of Gaelic to make a claim about its identity, while not using enough to alienate the non-Gaelic reader. The notion of language display was developed by Eastman and Stein in a 1993 article. They noted the how use of language can be an indicator of identity, when a specific language is used "to lay claims to cultural attributes" (Eastman and Stein 1993: 188) which are presumed to belong to the group whose language it is. They argued that language display is used to negotiate an identity in order to establish a broader conception of self in society" (Eastman and Stein 1993: 200). It is thus, as they put it, "symbolic rather than structural or semantic expression" (Eastman and Stein 1993: 200). Such displays may consist of only a few words of another language.

In order to be effective as display, however, certain conditions must apply. Eastman and Stein argue that "language display requires a context in which people share beliefs about desirable foreign attributes and recognise associated languages as symbolic expressions of social identity" (Eastman and Stein 1993: 189). Where disagreement exists over the interpretation of such language uses, the prevailing interpretation will be that of the more powerful group. Not surprisingly, they note that "language display is often most effective where there is minimal contact with keepers of a standard, with those in a position to judge" (Eastman and Stein 1993: 189). Use of the odd phrase from a different language is most effective among those who have least knowledge of that language.

One typical use of language display is to make a claim about ethnic identity, with ethnicity being maintained or reclaimed by the use of language. In the Scottish context, Gaelic is frequently used in such displays to indicate a putative 'real' Scottishness, even by speakers who know virtually nothing of the language other than a mangled pronunciation of 'slàinte mhath'. Gaelic is also used to indicate identity and sympathy with the remaining community of Gaelic speakers. This notion of language display is particularly relevant when dealing with newspapers' use of Gaelic. All of the Scottish newspapers which have occasional Gaelic items can be seen in this light. There is little attempt at providing a news service in Gaelic. Instead the language is used to bolster the newspaper's cultural credentials or to declare an identity with some of its readers. Although *The West Highland Free Press* does well by Gaelic in relation to other local papers in the highlands and islands, it is also the most blatant in its use of Gaelic as display, with the different sections of the paper labelled in Gaelic as well as English, even when there are no Gaelic items on the page concerned.

The one regular Gaelic publication in newspaper format is *An Gàidheal Ur* but this free (and therefore heavily subsidised) publication is monthly and largely concerned with matters to do with Gaelic language and culture. Indeed its monthly publication makes any attempt at dealing with what might be seen as more conventional news very difficult. In most issues there are only a few items dealing with more general highlands and islands news. In a recent issue (September 2003), for example, there were 26 items in the 12 pages (which includes four pages of adverts). Of these 26 items, 17 might be said to be news items (as opposed to regular features such as opinion columns, special features and items for children). Of these 17, 11 are about some aspect of Gaelic, and the other six are about current news stories relevant to the highlands and islands. This issue is slightly untypical in having a few more items about non-Gaelic matters than most issues.

I should emphasise here that I am not intending this to be seen as a downgrading of the importance of *An Gàidheal Ur*, merely to point out that its monthly frequency (and, presumably, the prohibitive cost of a full editorial staff) means that it is not able to perform the functions that we normally think of when we think of a newspaper. *An Gàidheal Ur* performs a very useful and important function, but it needs further development if it is to take on the role of a Gaelic newspaper, in the full sense of that term. It cannot at present perform the role of the weekly Irish-language newspapers *Là* (published in Belfast) and *Foinse* (published in Galway).

What is lacking, then, is a Gaelic newspaper which has a general news function, rather than being something which is primarily about the language, and I want now to argue for the political, cultural and linguistic importance of a more regular Gaelic press, ideally a weekly newspaper. Politically, a newspaper press can have great significance. Public debate can have a depth of detail in the press which is simply not available in broadcasting. Compare, for example, the 1200 or so words that Angus Peter Campbell is able to write each month in *An Gàidheal Ur*, and even the 600-700 words in the Gaelic opinion column in *The West Highland Free Press* (currently written by Peter MacAulay), with the three minute opinion slot that there used to be on the weekly edition of the television news programme *Telefios* (and now even that has gone). The newspaper format gives space for stories to be explained at length, for a greater range of stories, and for a greater range of views and opinions.

And let us not forget the other advantages of print. There is the accessibility and portability of the newspaper. It is a medium which allows us, the readers, to choose where and when we wish to use it. There is also a permanence to the printed word which broadcasting has never matched. It is easier to find library copies of hundred-year-old newspapers than it is to find tapes of Gaelic broadcasting from even a few years ago. The newspaper and periodical press have, of course, played an important part in the development of a written Gaelic culture in the past, from 'Caraid nan Gaidheal' in the nineteenth century through the 'Litir a Beàrnaraidh' in the *Stornoway Gazette* in the mid-twentieth century, up to Angus Peter Campbell's contemporary writings in *An Gàidheal Ur*. Indeed Donald Meek has noted how important nineteenth-century newspapers were for Gaelic poetry. They now form an archive of material, most of which would otherwise have been lost. "The newshounds and newspapers editors, in their desire to present hot news, had become collectors of what we now appreciate as a significant treasury of Gaelic songs" (Meek 1995: 13). Important in this was the way in which these newspapers (particularly *The Oban Times*) provided a platform for poets to make political comment. In doing this, as Meek notes, "the newspapers were recognising the time-honoured role of the poets as commentators on events of relevance to their own communities" (Meek 1995: 12). This all suggests that newspapers can play a significant cultural role and there is no reason to suppose that the development of the Internet and digital broadcasting is going to completely change things. Predictions of the imminent demise of the newspaper have been around for more than two decades, but newspapers still have an important function. If the Gaelic world gives up on the idea of a weekly Gaelic newspaper, then it is giving up something of great potential.

The significance of the newspaper can also be seen by considering its relationship with its readers, in comparison with the relationship between broadcasting and its audiences. We tend to identify with our daily newspaper in a way that is unusual in broadcasting. The *Guardian* reader, the *Times* reader, the *Sun* reader, the *Scotsman* reader – we have a sense of what these terms mean, however vague or (at times) inaccurate they may prove to be. We don't usually describe ourselves as BBC1 viewers or Channel Five viewers. And even although most people are still fairly regular in their radio listening habits, the strong identification that newspapers tend to produce is not there. The more active involvement that we need when reading, as opposed to watching or listening, no doubt contributes to this, along with the fact that we choose our newspapers to match our own outlook in a way that is seldom true of the audience for broadcast news.

If you are tempted to think that the future of news provision lies with the Internet, then it is worth considering these various points in relation to internet news sites, whether created by newspapers or by newer media organisations, and it will be clear that even the Internet is not likely to bulldoze the newspaper out of existence – at least not in the immediate future. A paper copy still has advantages of accessibility and portability. There is also the question of the public nature of the newspaper. The readership of a newspaper is a rather more publicly identifiable group (think how many people carefully brandish their newspaper as a sign of their political, national or regional identity, and of the significance of publicly buying or ordering a newspaper) than the fragmented and isolated internet audience. In other words, people can and do use their newspaper allegiance as a public sign of their general political and social stance. And of course, although web sites may have the capacity for constant updating, and can certainly act as very effective links across different access points, they are still usually much more limited in the length of individual news items than the larger newspapers are. And I haven't even mentioned yet the more obvious point that Internet access in the home is still far from being a universal capability.

These are not the only reasons in favour of a Gaelic press (although they might well be seen as sufficient). A Gaelic newspaper can play an important role in the development of the Gaelic community's sense of itself (however we define the notion of community). Precisely because of the reasons already mentioned, a newspaper is able to contribute to building an identity. This is not done by creating an artificially monolithic view of that community (and I know of no evidence that the Gaelic community does not have as many divisions within it as does every other community in Britain). Indeed it is precisely because it has room for varying views that a newspaper is able to reflect a community more convincingly than broadcasting. The letters page illustrates this, with debates being conducted through printed letters in a newspaper, often vigorously argued, but still written from within a more general community point of view which can encompass both sides of the argument. The *West Highland Free Press*, with the frequently robust debates which appear on its letters page, along with highly politicised editorialising, and strongly expressed opinion columns, shows how a newspaper can adopt a distinctive point of view, include strongly disagreeing contributions, but yet successfully appeal to a particular community.

This links to the notion that newspapers provide a closer reflection of the community of their readers than do other media. The community sees itself in its newspaper and to some extent has some control over that through its involvement in the newspaper (even if that involvement is at the minimal economic level of choosing whether or not to buy it). Thus part of what is at issue here is self-representation and the community's need to have some control over that. For centuries the Gaelic community has suffered from being represented by outsiders, whether literary tourists in the eighteenth century, novelists and landscape painters in the nineteenth or film and television producers in the twentieth. Just as the creation of the Comataidh Telebhisein Gàidhlig in the early 1990s was a major step forward in reclaiming the power of self-representation, so the establishment of a weekly Gaelic newspaper could contribute to this in a very important way.

The value of a Gaelic newspaper can also been seen by comparing it with broadcasting and by considering the image of the Gaelic community which the different media suggest. The listener to *Radio nan Gàidheal* will receive an image of a fairly lively and confident community. A variety of programming including regular news broadcasts, phone-ins, topical discussions, music request programmes (often emphasising traditional or traditionally-based forms of Gaelic music) and documentaries, paints a colourful picture, with lively presenters and much evidence of audience involvement. On Gaelic television, the image is rather different, with an overall image of the community more obviously modernized and youth-oriented than on radio, and less direct involvement from the audience. The representation of the Gaelic community is still fairly lively, although (perhaps inevitably) lacking the immediacy of radio.

When we come to newspapers, however, a very different view of the Gaelic community appears. The emphasis on rather serious cultural matters combined with the weight of topical comment in the opinion columns does not serve to suggest a lively community. And when this is combined with an obvious lack of confidence in the language in the newspapers' refusal to use Gaelic for news stories, the image appears of a community under threat, in which the language is becoming more a topic for academic and nostalgic interest, rather than the life-blood of a flourishing culture. Only in *An Gàidheal Ur* is a more confident and lively view of the Gaelic community apparent.

But if all this – or even part of it – is agreed, it still leaves the major question. How is a weekly Gaelic press to be established in Scotland? The standard mixture of subscription, advertising, and subsidy would undoubtedly leave the last of these as the major contributor. And, of course, it would be unrealistic to expect that it would be an immediate success. Any newspaper or journal needs time to establish itself, and there is no obvious reason why this would not be true of a Gaelic newspaper as well. The maximum readership for a popular Gaelic newspaper was once estimated by Derick Thomson as being about a quarter of the number of Gaelic speakers who could also read the language (Thomson 1984: 263). Using the most recent Census figures, this would lead to a figure well below 10,000, and that would be for a generally popular newspaper, not one which only appealed to language activists and those interested in Gaelic culture. But yet the benefits of establishing a weekly paper are clear. Perhaps the recently created Bòrd Gàidhlig na h-Alba and the soon to be created Seirbheis nam Meadhanan Gàidhlig might together look at this and see whether help might be given to allow *An Gàidheal Ur* to move to a weekly existence, and to expand its remit to provide the print journalism which the Gaelic world will continue to need, even after the brave new world of digital television and the internet is upon us.

References

Cormack, M. 1995. "The Use of Gaelic in Scottish Newspapers." *Journal of Multilingual and Multicultural Development* 16: 269-80

Eastman, C.M. and Stein, R.F. 1993. "Language Display: Authenticating Claims to Social Identity." *Journal of Multilingual and Multicultural Development* 14: 187-202

Meek, D., ed. 1995. *Tuath is Tighearna: An Anthology of Gaelic Poetry of Social and Political Protest from the Clearances to the Land Agitation (1800-1890).* Edinburgh: Scottish Academic Press for the Scottish Gaelic Texts Society.

Thomson, D. 1984. "Publishing in Gaelic." *Journal of Multilingual and Multicultural Development* 5: 259-65.

The Symbolic Value of Gàidhlig in the Scottish Sunday Newspapers

Chas Mac Donald

I would like to take a look at the symbolic value of our minority languages in two of our most important national Sunday papers in Scotland – the *Sunday Herald* and the *Scotland on Sunday*. I choose these titles because they are generally little considered in relation to language politics, although their combined readership is high,[1] and they represent a large element of the central Scotland press. The Central Belt press is important as this is the area of the country which has primary control of the money and largely sets the agenda for Gàidhlig – not the day to day agenda, but the structurally much more important financial one.

I reviewed most of the Gàidhlig related stories in these papers and the *Sunday Times* from the end of 2002 to September 2003. It is interesting to note that one of the most prevalent items to emerge while conducting the review was the face of Stuart Cosgrove – of which more later. The items in, or relating to Gàidhlig numbered just 32 with the proviso that there are some weeks missing and that I have not always collected the articles of Murchadh Mac Leòid which make up a little under 50 per cent of my sample – thus leaving only 15 as general interest. The period covered is one where media interest in Gàidhlig has been 'normal'. That is to say, after a flurry of activity earlier in 2002 with the debate over Bòrd na Gàidhlig and the Mike Russell Gàidhlig Bill creating a substantial acreage, if one uses the term loosely, dedicated to Gàidhlig. But in this period, Gàidhlig has no major events deemed newsworthy.

Mike Cormack (1995) and others have talked better than I about the symbolic nature of newspaper use of Gàidhlig. While I agree with a lot of what these writers have said, I would urge a sense of proportion. Until a substantial proportion of the country is able to use Gàidhlig, any Gàidhlig language daily or weekly will be symbolic in and of itself. 'Minorityhood' attracts such rhetorics as symbolism like Scotland attracts rain, and it is not always helpful. The 'symbolic' argument is important to note and understand, but rather less useful to get hung up on.

So, the Sundays. If we take the Murchadh Mac Leòid column out of the equation for a moment, we are left with some astonishingly low figures which I have broken down into two categories, as in Table 1: Gàidhlig-related articles which touch upon the culture which surrounds Gàidhlig, and articles which are specifically about the language.

Some underlying traits emerge. Firstly, Gàidhlig is generally a news item. By this I mean that it is an item which newspapers communicate information on (if not in). Such treatment equates the language to other items in the news. That is to say, they are of a 'foreign' nature to the reader – something of which they must be informed, something which does not and quite probably will never touch them. And by 'foreign' I do not mean something from furth of the parish. It is well to remember that a very large proportion of the public feel quite alien to our over scrutinised political events, events which will have definite effects on their lives.

---

[1] Total circulation – 144,163: *Scotland on Sunday* 84,422; *Sunday Herald* 59,741; Source: ABC Primary Figure, ABC Website - http://www.abc.org.uk accessed on 06.10.03

Table 1: Gàidhlig-related and Gàidhlig-specific articles in the Scottish Sunday Press

	Gàidhlig-related articles	Gàidhlig-specific articles	Total
Scotland on Sunday	1	3	4
Sunday Herald	4	3	7
Sunday Times Scotland	2	2	4
Total	7	8	15

In this manner of the alien, of the almost ethnic, we are disconnected ever more surgically from the Gàidhlig language as a meaningful element in our national, community and personal lives.

Secondly, the ubiquitous Mr Cosgrove. He regularly appears in the *Sunday Herald* whose first constituency is Glasgow where the media is an important economic player. Cosgrove fulfils a role as a sort of totem for the Scottish media fraternity which it can hold up to the consuming public. His peculiar status mix as a maverick, as a power and influence holder, earthily articulate commentator, football supporter, pundit and lost cause chaser, and a voice that does not forget its roots, brings a breadth to the man which suits the Scottish psyche well. He is something of a reflection of the nation, or at least that part of it which is most populous. He embodies the national myth of a people who can do well given the chance, but not forget their background, what made them what they are, and the tonalities of their nation. All nations need their heroes and Cosgrove fits the bill.

But there is a double edged sword to this hero status. Cosgrove is symbolic of the media. And the attention paid to the media industry in Scotland, even in the *Sunday Herald*, is much more ambivalent than perhaps it ought to be. There is a frequent sneering at any successes; more sneering at any pretensions to make a big film, or, heaven help us, a soap; and as for the notion that Scotland has, or could have, a viable media industry with bankable players is rarely accorded much credence – this despite the existence of a historically long list of successful film and media Scots. Such ambiguity could find Cosgrove on the outside as firmly as he is on the inside if the fickle tide of media fashion turns agin him.

What is the connection to Gàidhlig here? Well, pictures of Stuart Cosgrove, Ewan MacGregor, Peter Mullan and the like underline the need for a face in modern media. This is truer in the *Herald*, a palpably more visual paper than the *Scotland on Sunday*. Its use of arresting and articulate imagery closely resembles the *Independent*. Gàidhlig, however, has no face. It is not human and cannot be shown, except perhaps through an image of a Gàidhlig speaking television personality who becomes instantly symbolic, but never in the all encompassing totemic, magical, mythical fashion necessary and found in Stuart Cosgrove. This innate inability to muscle its way into popular culture is yet another structural way in which the language is pushed out to the margins.

The shallow fashion approach is clearly a dangerous one and should largely be avoided, although constant reference to a language's depth of meaning to the soul can grate. But, if Gàidhlig were to be featured in the *Sunday Herald*, in what we might somewhat obliquely refer to as a culturally useful fashion, the profile of the language *might* be enhanced, and brought to the attention of those who regard themselves as 'the sexy'. In other words it might become relevant to the general populace. It might find a niche in popular culture from which it could expand. It might actually end up having resonance and meaning, just like the afore-said Channels 4's Head of Nations and Regions.[2]

Which seems to be where Murchadh Mac Leòid comes in. Where, apart from dry peer review journals, did we last hear about the effects of text messaging on Gàidhlig, or Gàidhlig's use in that very 'now' domain. Mac Leòid discussed this in his *Scotland on Sunday* article on the 13 April 2003. Painful as it is to concede anything to the Neil era *Scotsman*, we have to be thankful that at least his paper is giving space to a subject (Gàidhlig, not text messaging) dear to our hearts. That said, it is worth considering the relevance of the language in relation to the falling circulation of the *Scotland on Sunday* or *Scotsman* and what this says about the language and Edinburgh's slipping grip. Furthermore, it is redolent of the "deep irony" which Tom Devine describes in the Lowlanders appropriation of things for which they had "contempt". (Devine, 1999: 233)

However, keeping Edinburgh in mind, I would like to recall that there are historic parallels here between the fortunes of Gàidhlig and the kilt, that other symbol of what is somewhat questionably called 'Gàidhlig culture'. The kilt was proscribed after the '45 as we know, and the language had been under positive attack since the early 1700s (Devine, 1999: 95). The language went stubbornly on, as we know, but the kilt took rather ambiguously momentous turns thanks to exiled chieftains, a Bannockburn weaver, a band of brothers, and some dubious design and classification ethics. Finally, Sir Walter Scott convinced King George IV to sport tartan on a visit to Edinburgh in 1822. As David McCrone has pointed out in *Scotland The Brand* (McCrone, 1995: 50), the south and east of Scotland appropriated to themselves the kilt, along with other symbolic items of Highlandism, to which they had no right, in an attempt to differentiate themselves from their English colleagues. (see also Devine, 1999: 292)

The unhelpfully divisive issue of rights aside, it is instructive that something similar should appear to be happening with Gàidhlig in our modern media. The east and south of the country where the retreat of Gàidhlig began is once again the place where (in the non-Highland print media at least) the language is being accorded most significance. The efforts of Magnus Linklater go a long way to redressing the balance on that score.[3]

---

[2] It is interesting to note that Cosgrove, unlike his BBC opposite, Aled Eírug, does not make many appearances at minority language media events such as this. He did appear at the Celtic Film and Television Festival in Belfast in 2003, in a conversation spot dedicated to English language comedy from the Celtic nations.

[3] "**As We Struggle to conserve a Dying Language Other Parts of Our Culture are Being Starved.** Has the plight of Gaelic reached the point where it can only be rescued by legislation. ... I regard this [free music tuition for all school pupils] as a far more important investment, with far greater potential for more of our people, than continuing the expensive and losing battle for Gaelic. ... However, unless substantial extra funds are produced for the arts, a brave minister will have to stand up sooner or later and pronounce the following verdict: "I am sorry, but the game is no longer worth the candle. Too many other good causes are losing out in the effort to protect the interests of a dying minority. The time has come for the haemorrhage to stop. I am therefore going to pull the plug." Magnus Linklater, *Scotland on Sunday* 17.11.02 (Extract)

To address some of the other questions to which the symposium addresses itself I would make the following comments. In relation to the economy there are clearly three major sectors of interest to Gàidhlig: education, tourism and the media. Education provides a limited number of jobs which are extremely useful and can inculcate a positive attitude towards the language. But even in this sector there is a constant demand for self-justification – '*what use is Gàidhlig?*', '*where can you use it*', '*why not spend the money on a better bus service to the bingo?*' The tourist industry, of vital importance to the Highland economy, is only now waking up to the potential of the language in its endeavours. Caution is necessary here too, where the unreality of the heritage industry ought to sound large warning bells to those interested in the long term survival of the language with its purely symbolic (ab)use in demand-led situations such as satisfying the in-built preformed misconceptions of the tourist.

Gàidhlig in the media suffers equally, if in more complicated ways. '*Why is that on the TV when I want to be watching snooker?*' The priority the CCG feels the need to put on the effect of its grants on the economy (CCG, 2003) is just another way in which those who use the language feel the need to justify themselves.

Colin Williams has been making the point of the importance of linguo-economic integration for a long time now.[4] Recent research by Douglas Chalmers of Glasgow Caledonian University[5] also testifies to the impact of the Gàidhlig language in general on the Highland economy. In the Gàidhlig context where a large proportion of speakers are scattered over a huge geographic area, economic significance cannot be underestimated in the integration of the language into these economies. For this reason, I would be averse to moving the CCG off Lewis. It would certainly make more sense to have it in Inverness.

As for the usefulness of the screen media to Gàidhlig, while it has a normativising effect, we should not delude ourselves into thinking that broadcasting (or even the press) is going to have a huge impact unless efforts are increased significantly. A recent *Sunday Herald* article reports a survey carried out by the Office for National Statistics which shows that a higher proportion of Scots than English prefer to stay at home and watch the television than to go out and socialise. It might seem at first glance that this is a golden opportunity for Gàidhlig screen media. But it does almost nothing to get the language spoken, and a language which is only listened to is no language at all.

One of the most fascinating aspects of this symposium is the question of media and language policy co-ordination. Here, I get anxious. When people start deciding upon the form of a language, all sorts of horrible demons appear. Accent is one place where we can lose contact with good sense and reality. But dialect, with its inevitable lexical differences, provides opportunities for linguistic fascism beyond compare. Indeed spelling, bound to be a more prominent consideration with the rise of web-based media, is another area of contention. Consider the adverse responses to the spelling of *Gàidhlig* which I use when writing in English.

---

[4] Colin Williams, Presentation to the Comhairle na Gàidhlig Còmhdail, Nairn, October 2002.

[5] Chalmers, Douglas. *The Economic Impact of Gaelic Arts and Culture.* Unpublished PhD thesis (2003), Glasgow Caledonian University. See also Douglas Chalmers in this volume.

Early indications of my research show that people are often very dedicated to their own idea of what the language should be and who (or rather who and with what abilities) ought to be representing it. Some would not allow a learner near a microphone – ever, not even supposing they were fluent. *Blas Beurla* – an English flavour – is not well tolerated and can elicit some strong opinions. In fact, I can see the need for some language co-ordination being used in the media. But this should be of the lightest of touches.

That said, the idea of a 'mid-Minch Gàidhlig', so derisorily referred to, is actually not so unhelpful an idea as it might seem. There has been a wealth of work published by linguists which attests to the manner in which speakers accommodate to each other in conversations – without realising that they are doing it. It baffles me why we should get so hung up on 'mid-Minch'[6] as a principle. If we want to communicate, we need to make ourselves understood. Broadcast media have obvious difficulties here, because they have no real idea of the actual audience and, at any rate, that audience is likely to be formed from the whole gamut of possibilities anyway. But from this difficulty, broadcast media, and radio in particular, has probably allowed speakers to learn and appreciate difference, accommodating to it rather than forging themselves into some standard which has few of the essential identity differentials which we are so vital to us.

But as indicated above, any level of language policy ought to be as light as possible. Nothing is so democratic as language, and it ought to remain that way. Inserting needless rules and making needless changes only irritates people, divides them and allows space for discord. Discord is not always a bad thing of course, but when you are so perilously close to the edge as Gàidhlig is in Scotland, we need to ca' canny with it.

And finally, relative to the *Sunday Herald* and the *Scotland on Sunday*, to answer the question 'is the media symbolic, expressive or substantiative of culture?' The answer is surely symbolic. And symbolism is a very weak, if not malign, basis for the personal development of the speakers of a language. It increases the oddity value, and encourages us to put the language away in places where it cannot attract opprobrium. Even the Murchadh Mac Leòid column falls into the symbolic category. What do we think would happen if he were not at the *Scotsman*?

In less prosaic phraseology, these print media couldn't give two hoots, mon.

References

CCG, 2003, *CCG aig 10*, Comataidh Croalaidh Gàidhlig, Stornoway.
Cormack, M., 1995, 'The Use of Gaelic in Scottish Newspapers', in *Journal of Multilingual and Multicultural Development*, 16.4, 269-280.
Devine, T., (1999), *The Scottish Nation, 1700-2000*, London: Allen Lane.
McCrone, D. et al, 1995, *Scotland the Brand - The Making of Scottish Heritage*, Edinburgh: Polygon.

Language and the Press in Scotland

Alex Law

I remember being ashamed of my father when he whispered the words out loud reading the newspaper.　　　　　　　　　Tom Leonard, *Fathers and Sons*

By outwardly vocalising words from his newspaper, Tom Leonard's father transgressed a primary cultural code: that of maintaining an inner voice for absorbing the written word. Leonard's embarrassment at his father's failure to contain the printed word within the shell of his own skull speaks to the peculiar nature of newspaper communication. Newspapers communicate on a daily basis but they rarely use the language spoken in everyday life. In tracing the sounds of the newspaper words, Leonard's father may have been doing a number of things: he might have been trying to hear what the authoritative reporting voice sounds like; or he may have been comparing the Standard English of the written word with the vernacular Scots of his own voice. Moreover, Leonard himself uses Standard English poetically here instead of the phonetic use of the Glasgow dialect that he is better known for.

Registering the gap between the reporting voice and everyday speech can be disconcerting. The daily success of newsprint relies on forgetting about this gap and switching effortlessly between the spoken and the printed sign. Everyday auto-switching becomes a banal operation, a 'second nature' built on the 'first nature' of native speech. It is only in assimilating their native language through verbal communication that children first reach consciousness, notes Volosinov (1973: 81), and only through the simultaneous learning of their first written language does it acquire the status of second nature. In Scotland, this second nature print language is overwhelmingly Standard English. However, newspapers do not simply reproduce the formal elements of standard language without modifying them into more colloquial forms, precisely in order "to narrow the gap between spoken and written language" (Cormack, 2000: 7).

Benedict Anderson (1991: 134-5) argues that while print language invents nationalism, language and nation are separable and that "nations can now be imagined without linguistic communality". Neville Alexander (1989: 9), the South African language policy theorist and activist, criticised the essentialist assumptions of linguistic nationalism:

> To be a nation, the individuals who make up that nation have got to be able, among other things, to communicate with one another. They need not, however, do so in any specific language. *All that is necessary* is that they be able to switch to the most appropriate language demanded by a particular situation. (my emphasis)

All nations are multi-voiced bodies. In order to exist, nations do not need a particular language *per se* since "in principle anyone can learn any language" (Anderson, 1991: 135). Perhaps. But it is what happens in everyday practice in the press and in other key institutions like education that matters. Newsprint language can indeed be an instrument of exclusion and cultural inferiority. In daily practice, some ways of speaking and writing are valued and others disparaged or completely excluded from public discourse carried on in newsprint. Nevertheless, this is not intrinsically bound-up with what constitutes a nation.

What are the implications of the separation of language and nation for print media in Scotland? It seems to me that what is important here are the conditions for creating a democratic 'empowering proficiency' in the hegemonic language of a national press while at the same time valuing and undergirding local and regional idioms. This paper analyses some of the ideological gaps in the use of language in the press in Scotland. It does so by considering the problem of the absence of Scots as a national print language and the role of English as a *lingua franca*. If, as Tom Leonard (1995: 51) claims, "*democracy is daily dialogue*, and *true democracy lies in the equality and equal power of all parties to that dialogue*", then the obstacles to democratic proficiency are not primarily national ones as linguistic nationalists claim. To support this claim the linguistic positioning by the best-selling newspaper in Scotland, the *Daily Record*, will be shown to constantly construct its readers as fellow nationals. Nation is the basic frame of reference for the daily ordering of the world for newspaper readers. National frames in newspapers switch between Scottish and British national identity as the context demands, for instance, whether the story concerns issues of government and statehood or issues of culture and sport.

Spoken Scots and Print-English

Scotland is a polyglot society. Some people in Scotland speak Gaelic, some Urdu, some Chinese, and some English. Most people speak some version of Scots and are able to switch registers with agile facility between different kinds of Scots in different contexts. Scots is not some unchanging monolithic national language, preserved in its purity by 'real Scots' from anglicising corrupters. In its concrete daily use it is a highly malleable, flexible, living language, forever taking on novel influences and unanticipated directions. Contemporary Scots ranges from 'Broad Scots' to Scottish Standard English, with the former often regarded as the more traditional, dense rural variety and the latter as the mixing by the educated middle classes of Standard English with 'Scotticisms' (Corbett, et al, 2003). Urban Scots is marked out as an inferior variety of Scots, too corrupted, elemental, restrictive and proletarian to serve as the basis for an elevated national language. Attempts to invent a distinct 'literary Scots' as a 'prestige' national language, reviving long-forgotten archaic rural words and phrases, have failed to translate beyond small coteries of cultural activists.

In newsprint, Standard English functions as the *lingua franca* for mediating between different speech communities. Occasionally, overt Scotticisms are deployed in a Scottish Standard English narrative while a slightly denser use of Urban Scots is sometimes given in reported speech (Corbett, 1997: 17). For some language policy campaigners, such as the Cross-Party Group on the Scots Language (CPGSL), an indigenous national language ought to be increasingly the medium for written intercourse to reverse the current situation of the highly restricted use of Scots in the communications media. By placing Scots on a low point in a putative hierarchy of cultural forms media producers limit the use of Scots to vocal forms in broadcast comedy, music or oral history. As a written form Scots barely exists in mass communications like newspapers. "In the print media, sic as newspapers an journals, Scots is haurlie seen at aw" (CPGSL 2003: 12). A more positive, wider cultural embrace of Scots and "the language wid suin tak its naitural place in the communications media" (CPGSL 2003: 12). The Scots Language Society (SLS) complains that Scots journalism only began to disappear when "outside interests (mainly English) took over papers in Scotland" (SLS, 2002). They go on to argue:

> Combined with hostile schools the media has done more than any agency in the 20th century to keep Scots in a provincial ghetto, discriminating against its speakers, and demolishing its foundations. It shouldn't matter if the media uses English or not but it does matter when broadcasting and the press are so biased; if Scots speakers saw and heard Scots being used in the media it would make a more balanced society, less anglicised and more Scottish in culture. Presently, Scots speakers are kept deaf and dumb.

Linguistic nationalism protests at the biases imposed from without and cherishes a national language as intrinsically worthwhile since it is perceived as being cultivated wholly from within. It wishes to expunge what it sees as the 'alien word' from the native lexicon.[1] Linguistic nationalism places the corrosion of an 'authentic' national voice squarely on the shoulders of outsiders who constrict the speech of Scottish insiders and ensure that Scots speakers are made to feel inferior. Language activists therefore demand that social life be even "more Scottish" (whatever that means), "balanced" and "less anglicised" than it is currently assumed to be. Linguistic nationalism yearns for the fullest correspondence of a discrete national culture and linguistic community. In so doing, a traditional hierarchy of cultural forms is invoked. The vocal and the comedic are relegated beneath the sonorous tones of the editorial column and the opinion pages. Notwithstanding the fact that humour, music and oral culture are weapons in the hands of the weak, the mass newspaper is seen to be a more prestigious cultural form in the hierarchy of pan-national communication. Linguistic nationalists therefore demand newspapers exchange print-English for print-Scots.

But any wide diffusion of standardised Scots in the press faces a number of serious difficulties (McClure, 2001: ch. 2). First, Scots has not achieved a canonical standard written form. Second, spoken Scots is regionally diverse. Third, even speakers with the closest relationship to Scots, monolingual English-speakers, find written Scots sometimes difficult to comprehend. Fourth, English is *the* medium for written communication for practical, informational and, to a lesser extent, literary purposes in Scotland. It is also now established as the unrivalled medium of the global market. Moreover, the very nature of the daily newspaper as a transitory cultural object rests on a time economy organised around the conservation of narrative energies, a technique perfected by tabloid narrative efficiency, and the psychological efficiency of auto-switching. In the teeth of such obstacles, Scots has not established an enduring presence in newsprint for over a century, still less has it become the hegemonic national print language.

---

[1] See the discussion of linguistic 'crossing' in the formation of historical cultures (and in linguistics itself) by Volosinov (1973: 74-81). He quotes Marr on the impossibility of autarchic national languages: 'In short, the approach to this or that language in terms of so-called national culture, as the mass, native language of an entire population, is unscientific and unrealistic; the ecumenical, classless national language remains a fiction' (1973: 76).

Standard English in newspapers generally reflects the British context of the emergence of mass literacy and mass newspapers, notwithstanding localised efforts to publish newspaper columns or comic strips in Scots or the use of the vernacular. In Victorian Scotland, as William Donaldson (1986) has shown, vernacular prose was deployed extensively by the popular press in a way unprecedented before or since. Papers like the Dundee-based *People's Journal* experimented with an orthography of written Scots responsive to local speech. Such a development reflected a unique constellation of conditions around distinct local prose traditions, strong local identities (and even radical politics) finding expression in a responsive local press. This was further stimulated by the wider development within journalism of verbatim reporting techniques.

While this vernacular upsurge reflected regional and local diversity, written Scots failed to become standardised nationally. At the turn of the twentieth century, as the newspaper industry became concentrated and centralised, the success of mass circulation titles depended on a more homogenous form of copy delivered in a standardised style. Since newspapers in Scotland are in fierce daily competition with each other it cannot be envisaged that they will risk experimenting with unfamiliar written styles where such a demand plainly does not exist among their consumers. Linguistic nationalists in Scotland see 'authentic' Scots in the print media as merely taking "its naitural place". Yet there is nothing 'natural' about any print language, in the sense that it might somehow represent an organic, unmediated, faithful expression of spoken language. Formal written language imposes a freeze on the creative inventiveness of and lags behind spoken language. Any system of standardising a language on behalf of a national community will inevitably be selective and exclusionary.

Linguistic Apartheid

But just how exclusionary is the press in Scotland? The failure to recognise the gap between nationhood and language in Scotland has led some to compare the lack of language rights to Scots speakers to a form of "linguistic apartheid" (Horsbroch, 2002). Under the apartheid regime in South Africa, linguistic separatism provided the premise for racialising and physically segregating the population. Afrikaner nationalism ideologically justified apartheid by codifying the separate development of Bantu 'nations' based on supposedly 'independent languages' (Afrikaans, Zulu, Xhosa, Tswana) (NoSizwe, 1979). Resisting apartheid therefore meant opposing language 'tribalism'. Under the influence of Stalin's theory of ethno-linguistic nationalism, the South African Communist Party advocated a unifying 'common language' after 1948. In contrast, the African National Congress and the Pan African Congress rejected linguistic nationalism and saw different language groups as sub-national communities coming under the unifying project of an Azanian nation. This effectively meant the universalisation of English.[2] Here the problem was, and is, that English is the preserve of middle class elites, including the progressive black political leadership. Post-apartheid, the urban and rural black working class are *de facto* disenfranchised even while the constitution formally guarantees multilingualism due to the absence of a shared democratic language. Neville Alexander (1989, 1997, 2000, 2001) thus advocates a policy of multilingualism in tandem with the promotion of English as the *lingua franca* for the whole nation.[3] Practical exclusion of the black working class from the national language of newsprint and public discourse, and the reification of discrete ethno-national cultures in formal multilingual policies runs the terrible risk of Balkanisation through the political mobilisation of racialised language communities. Archbishop Tutu's notion of a 'rainbow nation' is, for Alexander (2001: 150), an "illusion of coherence and unity" that "dissipates at the first touch of the bitter reality of racial, class and caste divisions". Language planning thus goes to the heart of what democracy, justice and nationhood means in post-apartheid South Africa.

Contemporary Scotland is plainly not apartheid South Africa. Contrary to some febrile accounts that see Scotland as akin to a colonised nation which has had its language long suppressed by outside forces, all classes in Scotland are proficient in the same dominant written language, Standard English. Unlike post-apartheid South Africa, in post-devolution Scotland neither Gaelic, regional dialects nor Urdu are likely to ossify around a reactionary language mobilisation. Indeed, the English used by the press permits entry to diverse speakers into the very public discourses of national identity that some linguistic nationalists want to restrict to a written form not widely comprehensible even to the people who might speak the language upon which it is based. So long as there is no difficulty switching between the spoken and the written for participating in the public discourse mediated by newsprint, there is no democratic basis for anything other than English to remain the *lingua franca* for the Scottish nation.

Class, Language and Newspapers

To the extent that readers and writers can readily switch to Standard English to communicate within and beyond the national community, a situation of democratic proficiency exists for newsprint in Scotland. There may, however, be some other case to be made for challenging print-English as the daily language of newspapers. Where the omissions and silences of newsprint in Scotland are patently undemocratic is related to issues around social class. For Volosinov (1973: 23), the language community and social class do not correspond to each other. The sign is "multi-accentual", forever shot through with social inflections, tensions, antagonisms and struggles.

Class does not coincide with the sign community, i.e., with the community which is the totality of users of the same set of signs for ideological communication. Thus various different classes will use one and the same language. As a result, differently oriented accents intersect in the ideological sign. Sign becomes an arena of class struggle.

---

[2] In finding a hegemonic language, the hated Afrikaans could not possibly unite the oppressed black masses. The Black Consciousness Movement emerged in the Soweto revolt in 1976 against learning Afrikaans, 'the language of the oppressor'. 'For the first time, the working people, spurred on by their children, took the language question into their own hands and began solving it in their own interests, as they understood them in 1976. The chilling slogan, **Kill Afrikaans!**, showed once and for all that the language question had to be taken very seriously.' (Alexander, 1989: 38)

[3] Neville Alexander can speak with some authority about the operation of actual linguistic apartheid. As a black militant, he was imprisoned for ten years on Roben Island in 1964 alongside Nelson Mandela, an unlikely prospect for any Scots language campaigners.

But although such multi-accentuality gives the sign a distorting and refracting facility a "closed system of value" operates to reify linguistic codes. As Tom Leonard (1995: 41) argues, "That reification will always contain as part of its mechanics the device to maintain the illusion that social conflict does not exist, or that such conflict as exists can be meaningfully recreated and resolved within its own perimeter". Newspapers nevertheless may well report and comment on social conflict but do so through a uniaccentual appeal to the nation as the ideological frame of reference shared by all its readers. National frames impart "a supra-class, eternal character" to the ideological sign, "to extinguish or drive inward the struggle between social value judgements which occurs in it, to make the sign uniaccentual" (Volosinov, 1973: 23). Alongside their second nature induction into written language, children are simultaneously enrolled ideologically into the taken-for-granted, mundane character of the nation. Where any ideology of nationhood functions successfully, it does so through "the naturalisation of its own arbitrariness" (Bourdieu, 1977: 164). In its full unremarked obviousness, co-nationals securely and spontaneously recognise their place within a world split into other nations (Billig, 1995).

Newspapers form what Volosinov (1973: 95) called "verbal performances in print ... calculated for active perception, involving attentive reading and inner responsiveness, and for organized, *printed* reaction". As a printed 'verbal performance', the mass newspaper anticipates and is constituted by pre-existing dialogue: "the printed verbal performance engages, as it were, in ideological colloquy of large scale: it responds to something, objects to something, affirms something, anticipates possible responses and objections, seeks support, and so on." (ibid.) Newspapers address their individual readers in an imaginary ideological relationship of authoritative speech about the world, from the word in the columns on its pages through to the internal cognitive processing of the sign by the anonymous reader. In other words, the 'inner speech' of newspaper reading is a continuous, active process to which the 'outer speech' of printed verbal communication is intricately connected and oriented towards. Within newsprint, centripetal tendencies press-in to demand unanimity and monological domination, while counteracting centrifugal tendencies pull away in resistance and heteroglossia. Newspaper reading is not a passive process but one where language is both repressive and expressive, and both at the same time. As such, all utterances carry an evaluative accent. Readers do not simply say or hear words, such as 'Irish', 'British' or 'Scottish', so much as say or hear the meaning, significance and truth-content that the word has for them (Volosinov, 1973: 70).

In Scotland, readers encounter print-English as their second nature habitus even though it departs in significant ways from the various ways that they speak. But different classes intersect around newsprint language and its national framing in different ways. Working class readers register a greater gap between spoken and written language. Nevertheless, in their everyday newspaper reading habits auto-switching between first and second nature continues in unmindful ways. More mindful are elite groups, some of whom feel that they are not fully accepted as part of the Scottish nation because they were socialised into Received Pronunciation at home and public school, even though they might strongly identify themselves as Scottish (Bechhofer, et al, 1999: 530, n.19). When such elites open their mouths to speak, their anglicised idioms mark them out culturally as not only upper class but as non-Scots or 'lesser Scots'. This is a salient factor in reverse of 'differently oriented accents intersecting in the ideological sign'. Such elites may be more accepted as Scottish when penning editorial or comment columns in the press than when speaking. Since all nations are cross-class constructs, paradoxically, the extra-verbal nation that exists in print (or image) is more fully Scottish than the one encountered in face-to-face spoken interaction. By being more inclusive, a newspaper written in English might in fact prove 'more' fully Scottish and more fully national in its empowering proficiency than the written Scots that language activists would have Scottish newspapers adopt.

Chronotopes of National Deixis

None of this resolves the problem of accounting for the translation of the quotidian ordinariness of the nation onto the pages of newspapers. Volosinov's associate, Mikhail Bakhtin, developed the notion of the 'chronotope' to help situate literary texts in an open-ended way within the contextual shifts of spatial location and temporal moments. All time-space co-ordinates operate through their utter inter-relatedness; space is at once temporal and time is at once spatial. As Bakhtin (1981: 99) put it, "the contingency that governs events is inseparably tied up with space, measured primarily by *distance* on the one hand and by *proximity* on the other". Newspaper stories do not typically work through linear chronological sequences but reconstruct significant fragments of an event. If this is done productively the reader gets the central meaning of the story with the least narrative energy expended and the time-space of the event reconstruction by the press goes unnoticed. Newspapers construct chronotopes of national time-space as its organising centre but in ways that reconstruct time-space as highly variable in a double sense: on the one hand, from narrative positioning *inside* the reconstructed event itself and, on the other, from contextual positioning *outside* the narrative. This double positioning produces a dynamic dialectic of reader and text:

> the event that is narrated in the work and the event of narration itself (we ourselves participate in the latter, as listeners or readers); these events take place at different times [...] and in different places, but at the same time these two events are indissolubly united in a single but complex event that we night call the totality of all its events. (Bakhtin, 1981: 255).

Newspaper readers are positioned by the time-space dialectic as fellow nationals both by direct address and by more sneakily indirect ways. One of these is the repetitively familiar, thus largely unnoticed, use of deixis. Deixis helps 'anchor' language in the world by 'pointing' to the contextual relationship to space and time (Nunberg, 1993). It does so by explicitly indicating some aspect of the context of an utterance; that is, it helps make the utterance concrete, specific and intrinsic to *this* time and place. Deictic centring establishes the zero-point for all other spatio-temporal coordinates, a veritable *axis mundi* for centring readers within a social world. As such, newspaper readers are organised in a relationship of proximity and distance to an assumed centre, here the Scottish nation (Law, 2001). In contrast, a specifically working class location is never the assumed deictic centre of newspaper personal address. Deixis operates in three dimensions: social or person deixis, spatial deixis and temporal deixis (Corbett, 1997: 133-7). National identity tends to be invoked by deixis in the routine employment of the 'wee words of nationalism', *us, our, we, here*, this versus *them, they, their, there, that*. When deixis works successfully newspaper readers barely notice when they are being arranged in social time-space by such words.

Figure 1: Dimensions of Deictic Speech (Standard English)

	Centred	Proximate	Distant
Social/Person	*I, me, myself, mine, we, our, us*	*You, yours yourself, him/her,*	*He/she, them, they, theirs, themselves*
Spatial	*Here, this, these*	*Near, intimate, close, around*	*There, that, those, away*
Temporal	*Now, today, immediate*	*Soon, tomorrow, , yesterday, after later*	*Ages, years, future, past, death, ending*

Systematic analysis of this kind of linguistic relationship between the press and national identity is currently being carried out by 'The Role of the Media Study Group' (RMSG) as part of Edinburgh-based research into constitutional change in Britain. This work promises to go beyond analytical illustrations of national deixis previously carried out by Billig (1995) and Law (2001) (cf. the claims in Rosie, 2003). Their research has added up the frequency of newspaper uses of 67 markers of national identity, including place names, institutions and 'national' nouns and adjectives, from 1140 articles in Scotland. Initial results show a high incidence for the explicit use of the noun *Scotland* and the adjective *Scottish* in an "unequivocally positive and newsworthy" context (Rosie, 2003: 7). In criticising the work of Billig (1995) on the deixis of British nationalism, the RMSG have also undertaken closer textual analysis. They report a "remarkable complexity" in the shifting context of deictic pointing words. Attention to shifting context, not least the political context, is something that Billig (1995) and others have argued previously. As Law (2001: 314) puts it: "While the generic idea of nation remains banal enough, each national identity must be generated daily with particular, though mutable, semiotic material". RMSG unnecessarily restrict the sense of deixis to the first person plural personal and possessive pronouns, *we* and *us*, and conclude that "our findings suggest that a simple model of a national press is simplistic (sic)" since there is "a wide range of potential '*we*'s to choose from" (Rosie, 2003: 11). A kind of 'wandering *we*' in the articles analysed reveals an ambiguous relationship between Scottish and British identities, which are arbitrarily labelled 'national and state categories' respectively.[4] However, analysis of newsprint language needs to extend the meaning of deixis well beyond the isolation of nouns, adjectives and personal pronouns, vitally significant though they are, to spatial demonstratives (not just the named or assumed location of institutions) and the tenses of temporal deixis. Analysis of some front pages from Scotland's biggest selling tabloid paper, the *Daily Record*, will further illustrate something of the deictic depth of the nation as the zero-point for contextualising newspaper stories.

Illustrating Deixis in the *Daily Record*

The *Daily Record* has historically reserved for itself the right to speak on behalf of all the varied interests contained within the Scottish nation, what its publicity campaign called 'Real Scots', even though its readership tends to be concentrated in west-central Scotland. Tabloids like the *Daily Record* typically blur public and private events and relegate the politics of nation states under the symbolic world of celebrity, sport and showbusiness (Kress and van Leeuwan, 1996). This process of de-emphasising political issues has been accompanied by the increasing subsumption of the linguistic means of communication by the visual layout of large headline blocks and graphics. The tabloid emphasis on the visual and symbolic does not mean that the idea of the nation is communicated any less to readers. Even where newspaper front pages highlight celebrity stories and images, these are oriented to the context of a world of readerships divided into nations. Whatever language it uses, newspaper text is always intimately related to national context as the established common sense for categorising entire populations (Billig, 1995).

Newspaper mastheads – that bit of the paper that is barely noticed because it seems so familiar – functions as the daily zero-point of the national newspaper. For over a century the *Daily Record* has claimed to be Scotland's mass-based national newspaper. Its masthead remained identical for decades at a time, though it has been changed more frequently in recent years. More usually, the only disruption of the masthead is to commemorate or celebrate nationally-significant events such as: *Jubilee Record*, headlined "25 Years … And Here's a Welcome From the People of Scotland" (17 May 1977); *Scotland In Mourning*, following the killings at Dunblane Primary School (16 March 1996); or the 1997 New Labour election, *Victory Edition* (2 May 1997). Masthead centring is typically reinforced by more explicit pointers to the national context of the masthead (see Figure 2). Below the masthead, front page stories repeatedly use the wee deictic words of national identity. These help to fix readers to the simultaneity of national time-space. I will analyse three front pages covering stories about sport and culture to show that the *Record* as a matter of routine deploys the wee deictic words of nation.

Figure 2: *Daily Record* Masthead By-Lines in the Twentieth Century

1900-09	"Largest sale of any morning or evening paper in Scotland"
1910-24	"The All-Scotland Newspaper"
1929-40	"Scotland's National Newspaper"
1954-69	"Scotland's National Newspaper"
1973-83	"Scotland's Biggest Daily Sale"
1984-91	"Forward With Scotland"
1992-94	"Your Paper – Made in Scotland"
1995-99	"Scotland's Champion"

---

[4] Though there is no logical reason why some Scots might not also possess a British national identity rather than something called a 'state category' (see Davidson, 2000).

When the Scottish national football team got a poor result at the 1978 World Cup in Argentina, Scottish newspapers talked about it as a humiliation for "us", that is to say, for the whole nation. On its front page the *Daily Record* of 8 June 1978 gave its 'Page One Opinion': "Cry for *us* Argentina" (see Figure 3).

Figure 3: 'Fans storm team bus: Cry for us Argentina', *Daily Record*, 8 June 1978.

The songs of Scotland died in our throats last night.
Barring a miracle, our team is out of the World Cup in a way no fan imagined possible.
Shamed. Humiliated. And shown to be fourth rate in front of the whole world.
In two million Scottish homes last night families sat stunned, silent and saddened as they watched an unbelievably bad Scotland team stumble to a 1-1 draw with Iran.
Ally MacLeod will take a lot of stick, and he deserves his share of it. But he can't be blamed for the gutless display of many of the players.
WE CHEERED the team that didn't qualify in the last World Cup because they fought and played and gave everything they had and made us feel proud.
WE CHEERED the present squad when they lost to England at Hampden because they played their hearts out and made us feel proud.
Today there is only emptiness and anger.
Cry for us, Argentina. For last night was the bitter end.

The dominant shift in context points outwards, from the deictic centre of the Scottish nation to the social, temporal and spatial distances of sporting failure. National centring occurs in the plural possessive pronoun of "our throats" and "our team" and the repeated plural personal pronoun "we cheered", bolsetered by the social and spatial centring of "families" in "Scottish homes", who were variously "shamed", "humiliated", "fourth rate". This works to reinforce the unnoticed temporal centring in the masthead dating of the copy. Having established the national centre as simultaneously personal, social, spatial and temporal, proximity is pointed to in the temporal closeness of "last night", the social closeness of "Ally MacLeod", "he", "his", "they", "their", "the players", and the assumed spatial nearness of Hampden football stadium in Glasgow. From inside the social, spatial and temporal centre and proximity of the nation the article points outwards to indicate how remote the nation is from its own sporting self-image. Expressions of extreme closure begin and end the article. A feeling of temporal and spatial finality is conveyed by "died" and "out" in the opening lines, which is mirrored in the final two lines in the sense of temporal finality of a "bitter end" and the extreme spatial distance of "only emptiness". All this shifting deictic pointing outwards from the inclusive centre to the dying, empty distances turns public anguish into the personal troubles of each individual member of the nation. The wee words of nationalism simply assume that writer and reader occupy a shared position as fellow nationals suffering from the same sporting malady.

Towards the end of the century, front-page layout had arrived at an advanced stage of tabloid minimalism. When Scotland were beaten 3-0 by Morocco in the 1998 World Cup, two-thirds of the front page was given over to a picture of an unhappy-looking Scottish goalkeeper, with the ball clearly visible behind him in the Scottish goal. As if to mock the performance of the Scottish team further the *Record* masthead also appeared behind the goalie containing the legend, "Scotland's Champion", implying that the reader could only rely on it to defend the Scottish nation. The bottom third of the page was dominated by a huge headline (or rather underline) "**OUT**", to which the only column of written text functioned visually as an exclamation mark. The earlier relationship between written and visual text was now completely reversed. Instead of the visual image acting as a supporting device to illustrate the written story, the message was conveyed instead by the interplay of the image and the underline, "**OUT**" (see Figure 4).

Figure 4: 'OUT', *Daily Record*, 24 June 1998.

The nation's heart was broken last night as Scotland's World Cup dream was destroyed in St Etienne.
A day of destiny which had promised so much ended in disappointment when we were beaten 3–0 by Morocco.
Two goals by striker Bassir and another from Hadda shattered the prospect of a second round clash with three-times world champions Italy in Marseille on Saturday.
To rub salt into the wounds, Craig Burley – a goal hero against Norway – was sent off in the second half.
But in the end, the result was rendered academic by Norway's 2–1 victory over world champions Brazil in Marseille. Brazil and Norway will now progress.

Written text now merely served to elaborate on the preferred meaning already established visually. Nevertheless, linguistic elaboration consolidated the national context of the story. Thus, "the nation's heart was broken … when we were beaten". "We" includes all of "us" who endure regular sporting failure as part of the national body. The dominant shift in context points out from the social centre, Scotland, to the temporal finality of an end to national representation in the competition combined with a social and spatial distance in the national remoteness from teams still in France, who will "now progress" and who could still become "world champions", which Scotland, it seems, can never be. A colloquial cliché, "rub salt into the wounds", is enlisted to reinforce the mounting sense of national tragedy. From "we", "the nation", the article points again, as in 1978, to extreme social distances, in naming opposition players, Bassir, Hadda, whose goals defeated the national team. A sense of "destiny" being "ended" is rendered in physical terms, national hearts "broken", dreams "destroyed" and prospects "shattered". Here the metaphorical extremity of sporting defeat expresses the most remote time-place imaginable to the national community.

Such sport stories regularly assume a masculine basis to Scottish identity, where the national fellowship of *our* and *us* slips easily into *he*, *him* and *his*. Other stories also reveal such assumptions. When the statistical agency Eurostat asked garment manufacturers to classify kilt production as "womenswear" the *Daily Record*'s front page, "Euro Insult: Kilts are for girls", 10 November 2003, positioned its readers proximally as sharing its deepest assumptions about gender, costume and national identity. Indeed, the *Record*'s splenetic attempt to secure the ideological trinity of national costume, masculinity and heterosexuality reveals a deep-seated neurosis about the nation. At the same time the *Record* distanced itself categorically from the outsiders of the European Commission, whom the *Record* termed "Eurocrats" led by a "Spaniard", Pedro Solbes, Commissioner for Economics and Monetary Affairs. Place, time and person deixis is deployed to engender, sexualise and nationalise the kilt. Celebrity Scots like Sean Connery and Hollywood stars like Samuel L. Jackson, ("a whole sort of Gladiator thing going on"), are used to help stabilise the meaning of the kilt as male, heterosexual and Scottish. Connery is quoted as saying "I am very proud to wear a kilt. It is certainly not women's wear. It is an important part of Scots tradition". The kilt's proximity to celebrity functions to legitimise the manliness of the national costume. Kilt manufacturer, and "dad of three", Patrick McGroarty lends authenticity claims to the *Record*'s "Euro Insult" headline. He is quoted as saying:

> *They* told *me* just to fill in the number of kilts *I* had sold in the space *they* had provided for women's skirts. But *we* don't make skirts and if *they* wanted figures for a women's apparel company, *they* should have gone to one.

A social distancing usage of "they", the "Eurocrats", is used eight times in the article to point to how far removed they are from the social centre of "our" cherished national tradition, as in *"They* are ignorant to *our* traditions and background". Spatial deixis can also be deployed in reverse to show how the kilt tradition helps maintain a sense of national identity for Scots living abroad: "The Perthshire firm also supply kilts to expat customers in far-flung places like Vietnam and Nigeria". The *Record* points outwards from the spatial centre, "Perthshire", to socially (if not spatially) proximate "expat customers" through to spatially distant "far-flung places", Vietnam and Nigeria. Frequent use is made of the male-female dichotomy around a kilt/skirt binary to establish that it is a national dress for men, as in "not women's wear" or "kilts are not for ladies". If male celebrities such as Jackson, Connery and "screen hunk" Vin Diesel wear the kilt then there can be "no gender confusion". To reinforce the gender of the kilt, male Scottish politician, Frank McAveety is quoted as saying that "If Vin Diesel can wear a kilt and not feel any less of a man, that is good enough for me". A deictically-centred man points towards a remote celebrity to establish the heterosexual nature of the kilt. An implicit binary of heterosexual patriot/deviant foreigner is mobilised when readers are further informed that "dad of three Patrick" found offensive the EU's "branding [of] kiltwearing Scotsmen transvestites". A day later the *Record* reported a "grovelling U-turn" by the EU under the byline "Kilties are not Girlies" (11 November 2003).

They apologised for classifying our national dress as 'womenswear' on official forms and gave the kilt a special category of its own after the *Daily Record* stepped in

A spokesman for EU statistics department Eurostat said: 'We regret this unfortunate error. There was no malice intended'.

In turning a simple administrative EU function into a principled defence of the sacred fabric of the nation, the *Daily Record* unwittingly exposed the fragile basis of the masculine heterosexual aspects of Scottish identity, something so banal and firmly secure in the arbitrariness of its own assumptions that it is ordinarily paraded with complete self-assurance.

Conclusion

The analysis of media and nationalism requires us to look at newspaper text in historical context. A sense of historical shifts and continuities can be gleaned from analysing the way that front pages of national newspapers attempt to communicate with a mass readership. The case of the *Daily Record* is significant in a Scottish context because it consistently claims for itself the right to speak on behalf of the Scottish nation, performing a continual balancing act poised between British and Scottish identities. As the *Daily Record* example amply illustrates, and the Edinburgh study exhaustively demonstrates, nations do not need a native print-language such as Scots to exist *qua* nationhood. An ability to auto-switch between spoken Scots and print English means that there is no principle of democratic proficiency at stake in the language used by the press in Scotland. In this sense, there is no 'linguistic apartheid', of a forced separation of language communities from the hegemonic print language even remotely comparable to the paradigmatic case of South Africa. All language, including print-language, is subject to intersecting social accents. Newspapers are not simply unilateral textual structures, repetitiously imparting national identity by means of encoded devices. Rather, they are better understood as 'dialogical performances in print', engaged in an open-ended time-space/insider-outsider dialectic. Newspapers are always subject to the dynamic evaluative judgements of social milieu and are entangled in wider socio-economic structures and conflicts. Social milieu is routinely inscribed by the spatial, temporal and social wee words of nationalism. Everyday life is unmindfully organised from the zero-point of the nation. Only by paying attention to shifts in the concrete utterance in its concrete context can the depths be plumbed of the banal routinisation of national affinity in the daily press.

References

Alexander, N. 1989. *Language Policy and National Unity in South Africa/Azania.* Cape Town: Buchu Books.

Alexander, N. 1997. "Language Policy and Planning in the New South Africa". *African Sociological Review/Revue Africaine de Sociologie* 1.1: 82-92.

Alexander, N. 2000. "Language and the National Question". In ed. G. Maharaj. *Between Unity and Diversity: Essays on Nation-Building in Post-Apartheid South Africa.* Cape Town: Idasa and David Philip Publishers.

Alexander, N. 2001. "Language Politics in South Africa". In ed. S. Bekker, M. Dodds and M.K. Khosa. *Identity? Theory, Politics, History. Volume II: Shifting African Identities.* Pretoria: Human Sciences Research Council.

Anderson, B. 1991. *Imagined Communities: Reflections on the Origins and Spread of Nationalism.* London: Verso.

Bakhtin, M.M. 1981. *The Dialogical Imagination.* Ed. M. Holquist. Austin, Texas: University of Texas Press.

Bechhofer, F., McCrone, D., Kiely, R., and R. Stewart. 1999. "Constructing National Identity: Arts and Landed Elites in Scotland". *Sociology* 33: 515-34.

Billig, M. 1995. *Banal Nationalism.* London: Sage.

Bourdieu, P. 1977. *Outline of a Theory of Practice.* Cambridge: Cambridge University Press.

Corbett, J. 1997. *Language and Scottish Literature*. Edinburgh: Edinburgh University Press.

Corbett, J., McClure, J.D., and J. Stuart-Smith eds. 2003. *The Edinburgh Companion to Scots*. Edinburgh: Edinburgh University Press.

Cormack. M. (2000) "Minority language media in a global age", *Mercator Media Forum*. 4: 3-15.

The Scots Pairlament Cross Pairty Group on the Scots Language (CPGSL). 2003. *Scots A Statement of Principles: A Road Forrit for the Scots Language in a Multilingual Scotland*. http://www.scottish.parliament.uk/crossparty/cpgscots.htm. (Accessed 2 November 2003).

Davidson, N. 2000. *The Origins of Scottish Nationhood*. London: Pluto Press.

Donaldson, W. 1986. *Popular Literature in Victorian Scotland*. Aberdeen: Aberdeen University Press.

Horsbroch, D. 2002. "The Executive o Scotland's Language Apartheid". In J.M. Kirk and D.P. Ó Baoill. *Language Planning and Education: Linguistic Issues in Northern Ireland, the Republic of Ireland, and Scotland*. Belfast: Cló Ollscoil na Banríona.

Kress, G. and T. van Leeuwan. 1996. *Reading Images: The Grammar of Visual Text*, London: Routledge.

Law, A. 2001. "Near and far: banal national identity and the press in Scotland". *Media, Culture & Society* 23.3: 299-317.

Leonard, T. 1995. *Reports From the Present: Selected Work 1982-94*. London: Jonathan Cape.

McClure, J.D. 2001. *Language, Poetry and Nationhood: Scots as a Poetic Language From 1878 to the Present*. Phantassie, East Linton: Tuckwell Press.

NoSizwe. 1979. *One Azania One Nation. The National Question in South Africa*. London: Zed Press.

Nunberg, G. 1993. "Indexicality and deixis", *Linguistics and Philosophy*, 16: 1-43

Rosie, M. 2003. "Who are 'we'? National Identities in the UK Press". Paper for the Fifth International Symposium on Ethnic Identities in the Post-Cold War World, Xanthi, July.

Scots Language Society. 2002. *Wittins Blads*. http://www.lallans.co.uk/furthsettins/info.html#media. (accessed 10 November 2003).

Volosinov, V.N. 1973. *Marxism and the Philosophy of Language*, Cambridge, Mass.: Harvard University Press.

Scottish Political Identity Construction in the Media: Learning and Teaching Questions Around the Theme of Inclusiveness

Neil Blain and Anne Gifford

> *Leon Trotsky claimed that artistic creation is 'a deflection, a changing and a transformation of reality, in accordance with the peculiar laws of art' ... Literature, then, one might say, does not stand in some reflective, symmetrical, one-to-one relation with its object. The object is deformed, refracted, dissolved – reproduced less in the sense that a mirror reproduces its object than, perhaps, in the way that a dramatic performance reproduces that dramatic text, or – if I may risk a more adventurous example – the way in which a car reproduces the materials of which it is built ...*
> (Terry Eagleton, *Marxism and Literary Criticism*)

The genesis of this article was an attempt to discuss the way in which the Scottish Higher Still qualification, generally undertaken by students in the fifth or sometimes sixth year of their secondary school studies, or at college or later, can move across the boundaries of 'literature' as conventionally defined, and into the realm of the media. While the original audience for the paper comprised schoolteachers of English and specialists in Scottish language studies, the article also serves as an introduction for a much broader audience to some themes in the language of Scottish political identity.

1. The Scottish Higher Still: approaches to language

The introduction of the Higher Still Framework for post-sixteen in Scotland has offered new opportunities for learners in secondary schools and further education colleges. The central principle underpinning this curriculum development is the need to provide an appropriately staged approach for learners. The final stage, Advanced Higher, should provide clear articulation with (at least) level one of HEI study.

The Arrangements for English and Communication have undergone a number of revisions since first published in 1997. There has been considerable debate about course content over the last six years: critical listening has now been dropped as an examinable component; oral communication is no longer compulsory and the literature and language balance, always hotly debated in an English curriculum which does not separate the two strands into separately examined courses, shifted in favour of literature. The battle continued over whether Scottish literature should remain as a compulsory element. It was lost and Scot. Lit. falls into the 'recommended' category. Significantly, studying media, which has in various ways, and to varying degrees been undertaken by teachers of English as an 'alternative' dimension, has been more fully embraced at Advanced Higher level.

Advanced Higher English and Communication (more or less equivalent to 'A' level) has extended the areas of study available to students. Two new sections have been introduced, Language and Scottish Language, which offer interesting possibilities for students to engage critically with text in a number of specialist areas. Some examples of topics include: the use of Scots in a particular geographical area; the linguistic characteristics of political communication; the linguistic characteristics of tabloid journalism; and the use of Scots in the media. This sample not only reflects the broader scope of the curriculum but also signals a more politicized agenda.

Unfortunately, there has been a very low uptake by students of these areas of study and the latest round of Scottish Qualification Authority (SQA) revisions will see Language and Scottish Language streamlined into a single Language section (for a report on teaching these new language qualifications, see Rohmer 2002). The two topic areas, linguistic characteristics of tabloid journalism and uses of Scots in the media, are likely to merge into a single topic which has the Scottish press as its focus. However, although this offers opportunities for students to engage critically with an important area of linguistic and cultural study, there is still work to be done to support teachers who have predominantly approached textual analysis from a literary studies perspective. Why should they shift from this tried and tested method? And if they do want to shift, how should they do it?

Why might students choose this topic? Answers might include the fact that it can have both a contemporary and Scottish dimension; it shifts the focus from literature; and it makes use of an attractive interface between English, Cultural, Communication and Media Studies.

What do students need to be able to do? These specimen questions both indicate the parameters and point forward to what we have to say about the language of Scottish identity generally.

1. Discuss and illustrate the ways in which tabloid newspapers describe individuals in terms of general categories such as gender, marital status, race, age.

2. *Tabloid newspapers have to be lively because they offer themselves as a brand of entertainment.* Describe some of the principal linguistic means by which tabloid newspapers present serious issues in lively ways.

3. Read *The Sun* editorial and identify those features of the discourse which are recognisable as tabloid commentary. Explain how these features combine to create a particular voice. Discuss how the commentary establishes a 'dialogue' between the newspaper and its readers. Identify two ideological positions which you believe are evident in the editorial and, with specific reference to the text, describe what these positions are.

How do teachers prepare for this? Chiefly, they re-focus approaches to textual analysis, in other words they shift from a focus on literary appreciation to critical analysis, with a particular focus on form. They provide background reading in sociolinguistics and the language of the press. They source a selection of news stories/ features/editorials which can be presented in various ways *eg* as a single example to explain and illustrate a particular aspect of news discourse; or as a themed grouping to explore, for example, the representation of conflict; or as a 'same story/same day' selection from different newspapers (tabloid and broadsheet publications are a good mix).

A 15 hour programme with roughly five three-hour teaching slots might involve:

- What is news discourse – identifying patterns in text.
- Representation of groups – words (What's in a name?).
- Representation of groups – syntax (Modality, transitivity).
- *The Sun says* ... analysing tabloid commentary: editorials and readers.
- Themed study – Political Identity Construction in the Scottish Press.

What about a critical framework? A possible list might involve:

- *Discourse*: there is a common topic and there are formal links across sentences. Discourses are always socially and culturally situated. Any discussion of the discourse of print journalism must make reference to headlines, sub-heads, use of bold type, use of pictures with text, although the *main focus* of the exam question will be linguistic characteristics.
- *Lexical choice*: naming, category labels and stereotypes.
- *Syntax*: modal verbs (*can*, *shall* and *will*), and transitivity – basically, for any one clause, who (or what) does what to whom (or what)?
- *Mode of address*: (for example) empathy, identification.
- Further categories might be *word play*; and world view, and the considerable topic of *ideology*, which is in focus for much of the rest of this paper. What follows refers to the categories outlined here implicitly to avoid a mechanistic repetition. The analysis below suggests a variety of directions for teaching programmes but it is also in itself a discussion of Scottish identity issues in the media.

2. Political identity? General questions

It is worth beginning with a prime characteristic of political identity in the Scottish press (indeed of all representative processes) and that is to do with *construction*. 'Representation' is no doubt the core term when we're trying to explain how the media deal with the world, a concept also much used both in sociology, where it has a broader meaning, as well as in media and cultural studies.

But there is a longer debate about the passivity of metaphors like reflection and transparence for the way in which both literature and the media deal with the world: reflection here is a 'mirror' metaphor, and transparence a 'window' metaphor. Terry Eagleton and other writers have explored this very helpfully in the context of literary studies (Eagleton 1976), but researchers on the media collectively apply a greater number of conceptual approaches to the question of 'representation', including at more complex levels 'ideology' (suggesting questions about political economy) and 'signification' (emphasizing semiology); and also a less specific group of concepts which seek to illuminate symbolic and other communicative processes in culture, including 'discourse', 'myth', 'narrative' and 'mode of address' (Macdonald: 2003). It is as well to avoid doctrinaire preference for any single approach to the description of symbolic process and, if we use the term 'construction' here, it is to to emphasize the *fabricative* force of media narratives.

The idea of a construction of an identity is quite a fruitful classroom idea, too, because it can be contained in a single lesson, which might address one newspaper editorial or three comparative articles, or run for forty minutes or fifteen hours, or across a particular phase of a particular subject, coming back in and out, perhaps in different contexts, for example different media, and (ideally) even cross-referencing other subjects. There are ways in which the subject of English can refer to the subject of History in the context of constructions – a view of history which has been growing in influence since the 1960s is the idea that history is best seen as a *narrative* (Wright 1985; Hobsbaum and Ranger 1992) so that, for example, recent Scottish history has often taken issue with the construction of Scotland offered by earlier versions of history, the latter sometimes not of Scottish provenance (Beveridge and Turnbull 1989; Kidd 1993).

And history is, of necessity, lying behind discussions of the construction of political identity. Though, of course, there are many potential questions, these opening four extracts from media texts outline some of the background issues for the study of political identity in Scotland:

- (Henry VIII's) real achievement was the creation, almost by accident, of an England that, in terms of kingship and religion, endured for centuries after his death. (www.channel4.com/plus/real_lives/, 2001)
- … after Edward VI died young, order was restored during the long reign of Elizabeth I. The English monarchy and Anglican church, as created by Henry VIII, remained in place for centuries: today, the Queen is still head of the church and bishops still sit in the House of Lords. (www.channel4.com/plus/real_lives/)
- 'On the 20th of June 1982 with Charles by her side, Diana gave birth to a seven and a half pound boy, a future King of England' (Channel 5, 29 May, 2001)
- 'Fifteen years ago we didn't care whether there was any black in the Union Jack. Now not only do we care, we must' (Stuart Hall, *Race, Culture and Difference*)
- 'Commonwealth and colonies were symbols of "Britain"', and that '"Britain" is rather an empty word now that they have gone' (W.J.M. Mackenzie, *Political Identity*)

Before we address the significance of these extracts, let us note that if we talk about political identity in the Scottish press as a topic specifically for English teaching, it is nonetheless a topic which needs some degree of connectedness with other subjects and disciplines. In other words, the topic needs *adjustable subject parameters*. The question of the oppressive aspects of academic disciplines was celebratedly theorized by the French intellectual historian, Michel Foucault, in the 1960s and 1970s; Foucault hears 'discipline' in this sense as a restriction of intellectual space (Foucault 1970; 1977). And indeed discipline boundaries are, when placed beside real life, highly artificial, while also very necessary if you happen to be preparing students for Higher Still English or any other school qualification. How far teachers make a distinction between the syllabus on which students prepare for an exam, and the space available in the classroom for widening the subject boundaries, is a professional decision.

A notably awkward aspect of media and cultural studies is that they insist on dragging in other disciplines, and indeed at the core of the definition of media and cultural studies is the notion of hybridity. Economics, linguistics, semiotics, sociology, history, politics, psychology, legal studies and nowadays information and computing technology can all be pulled in to play and often are, and there has been a proliferation of related fields such as gender studies (gendered language is a central question in the discourse of political identity). So to discuss media texts in the classroom while staying consistently within strict subject parameters is practically very difficult.

The short selection even of very brief extracts above raises a myriad of questions about the depiction of a United Kingdom whose political identities are plural yet contested. The claims from a UK Channel 4 website whose notes accompanied a television series on the Tudor monarchy depict a stable English monarchy which is synonymous only with a white Christian England, which has accommodation neither for Muslims, Sikhs nor other significant religious minorities, nor for the Scots and Welsh. In an interview on his book, *The English: A Portrait of a People*, and after the appearance of national legislatures in Edinburgh and Cardiff, Jeremy Paxman observed that 'Never before have the English had to think about what it really means to be English. In the past, the thoughtless substitution of "British" for English everywhere was representative of a state of mind of what might be called a superiority complex because of England's place as the dominant partner in the Union.' (*Scotland on Sunday*, 18 October 1998, p.13) We see this clearly in that domain in which much of the national dimension discreetly handled elsewhere is made rudely visible, namely sport:

> English commentators refer to English athletes uniquely as British, and to Scottish athletes as both British and Scottish. Scottish commentators, on the other hand, also refer to English athletes uniquely as British, but to Scottish athletes uniquely as Scottish. Thus while Scottish identity is maintained by both sides, English nationality has apparently disappeared, though perhaps this disappearance is indeed only apparent, since it may well be the case that for English commentators Britishness and Englishness are identical. (Blain *et al*, 1993)

In other words, to be Scottish and British constitutes a dual identity, but to be English and British is merely tautological. Returning to the extracts with which we started, 'An England that, in terms of kingship and religion, endured for centuries after (Henry's) death', an English monarchy which 'remained in place for centuries' after Henry's death, are conceptions strangely at odds with historical facts such as the Union of the Crowns between Scotland and England in 1603, and the Union of Parliaments in 1707, neither, after all, so very long after Henry's reign. Yet in the media accounts cited, the union is not linguistically in existence, even in the twenty-first century, since as we also see (*pace* Diana) the London media routinely refer to 'the King of England' and similar nostalgic objects.

Hall's reminder about 'black' in the Union Jack points us toward a whole world of ethnic complications unimagined in the Channel 4 programme notes. If W.J.M. Mackenzie's observations about the disappearance of the British dimension from Scottish and English life suggests that the Scots may not in the end worry too much about the London monarchy being spoken of as merely English, then a much more serious matter is the question of space for multi-cultural Britain in these linguistic formulations of history. This is not of course only an English matter:

> Anti-English racism may not be as obvious as anti-Asian racism, but it comes from the same narrowing of vision that has caused all forms of racism to increase in recent years in Scotland. (Rafferty, 1998)

Scotland and England both require a language in which to enable new and generally dual identities. To an already complex debate about ethnic minority identity in the United Kingdom must therefore now be added a further dimension: if it is increasingly difficult to use the term 'British' of indigenous white English and Scottish majorities, then we must likewise redefine the field of enquiry into what might now be argued as the *post-British* identity of Pakistani-Muslims and other minorities whose identities present especially heightened instances of dynamism and contestation. Working within the 'British' frame of reference, on the other hand, Gilroy (1987) suggests that the construction of British identity frequently excludes minority ethnic groups, while Modood (1994) argues that a new kind of Britishness – a new national identity with a diversity of forms which allows minorities to make a claim upon it rather than conform to a particular cultural norm – needs to be created. Jacobson (1997) observes that British Pakistanis are within a process of redefinition of what it means to be British.

Billig (1987) notes that from a social psychological perspective disputes about national identities can never be finished. In fact, a variety of critiques, aimed, from a range of perspectives, at bemoaning or dethroning the central position of the national dimension within debates about collective identity seem to have left it placed much as it was, though influential commentators on national aspects of collective identity, and on local-global relationships, have taken a wide range of positions on these questions (Gellner 1983; Harvey 1989; Hobsbawm 1990; Nairn 1990, 1998).

Young Glasgwegians with ancestry from Pakistan when given the choice over their self-descriptors tend to choose bi-cultural terms like 'Scottish Pakistani'. The terms widely used by the press and most white Scots, 'Asian' and sometimes 'black' are used significantly less by young Scottish Pakistanis (Saeed *et al* 1999).

The linguistic challenge for inclusion policies and inclusive classroom teaching lies partly in the relative unfamiliarity in the British context of dual national definitions, compared to the American tradition of conceptualizing specific groups as 'Irish American' or 'Italian American'. Apparently comparable British terms (such as 'Anglo-Scot' or 'London Irish') are in fact limited in field of reference and circulation, and there are remarkable omissions in the terminological field – no dual terms to describe people of English or Irish descent or origin living in Scotland, for example, despite the large presence and cultural importance of these groups. Hyphenation is still a much underused resource in the reconfiguration of plural identities in Britain.

Further research needs to be done on semiological questions relating to the distinction between the arguably assimilative trajectory of terms like 'African American', 'Black American' or 'Asian American' – in which 'Black' or 'Asian' apparently operates as a qualification of Americanness – as distinct from, say, 'Scottish Pakistani', which while on the one hand at least also offering a plural identity, on the other provides 'Scottish' only as a qualifier of Pakistani identity.

('British Asian' appears to be doubly unsatisfactory to Scottish Muslims.) Would terms such as the inverted compound 'Muslim Scot', or the adjectival – there is no ungendered noun available in this latter instance – 'Pakistani English' be the mere equivalents of contemporary usages, or an improvement? And by whom might they be offered, and by whom refused?

Unfortunately, observers in the UK are far from being able to worry about these niceties. There is a tradition in Britain, represented vociferously by right-wing politicians such as Lord Tebbitt (*Daily Telegraph* 6.10.97 and 8.10.97; *Independent* 9.10.97), of demanding a straight decision between unitary identities, which represent inclusion or exclusion, a demand which therefore does not constitute, as an offer, any real choice, not least because of the mythic and ideological constitution of large ethnic minorities precisely as unassimilable.

Certainly, one possible way of achieving this would be the legitimization of bi-cultural language, though questions of agency, beyond the scope of this paper, are evidently complex and challenging. As it happens, the term 'Glasgow-Italian' has long operated as a positive identity marker for the substantial Italian-originated population and culture in the city in which this research was based and 'Scottish-Italian' is also an accepted term.

The deployment of terms such as 'Scottish Pakistani' and/or 'Scottish Muslim' would facilitate simultaneously strengthened links to the host culture and to individuals' ethnic group or origin.

3. Broadsheet and tabloid language

With further regard to 'adjustable parameters' in the classroom, if we want to explain differences between views of the Scottish Parliament in the upmarket *Herald* and *Scotsman* newspapers, details of the ownership and editorship of these newspapers are always much to the point. But teachers may have to live without too much detail about that in the classroom. In constructions of political identity in the Scottish press, the left- or right-wing leanings of papers have to be taken into account, as well as their devolutionist or unionist tendencies (teachers may now have to explain these old-fashioned terms like 'left-wing' and 'right-wing' however!); and whether they are broadsheets or tabloids is still very significant for the study of language - *still*, because two things have happened.

One is that the language of the tabloids has tended more and more toward the demotic – the old tabloid *Daily Record* (still published in Glasgow now but under different ownership) was a newspaper which preserved a relative complexity of expression compared to its descendant. Secondly, the broadsheets have moved in the direction of the tabloids linguistically, though – especially in the broadsheets – there is linguistic variation from contributor to contributor, and variation between different kinds of content (reports, features, leaders, reviews and so on). Despite that, the writing of sports reporters and diarists, for example, in the broadsheets, will still differ from the discourse of their counterparts in the tabloids, still sometimes quite markedly

National character isn't the same as political identity or nationalism (Blain *et al* 1993) but it's a closely associated element of political identity. Two features of its media discussion are exemplified here:

> **DON'T CALL SCOTS LOUTS: the *English* are, Mr Mellor**
> Front page headline, *Daily Record,* 15 June 1992
> All it took to change failure to success was a bit more gas in the tank and a whole lot more fire in the belly … Up went the sleeves, in went the tackles, off at the toot went the runners, their legs going like drumsticks, and the hard-earned win was achieved (*Sunday Post,* 17 June 1990: both extracts in Blain and Boyle, 1994).

First of all, there is the essential factor of political identity in Scottish newspapers, which is the page-by-page, sometimes column-by-column insistence that *this is Scotland* and *we're all Scottish* (even if many people aren't!). As always, England, Englishness and English football fans are deployed as a reference point for what Scottishness both is and is not. It still fails to occur to Scottish journalists and editors with sufficient frequency that racism can be a quality as much applicable to writing about English culture as about Muslim culture.

Regionality and urban/rural splits remain a major feature in the media handling of Scottishness and Scottish political identity. Analyzing radio output from 2001, Hugh O'Donnell notes of the west of Scotland commercial station Radio Clyde's *Saturday Super Scoreboard* phone-in programme how the form of Scots still in 2003 used by *The Sunday Post* is an object of humour for the Clyde show's participants:

> However, while the availability of contemporary varieties of Scots, whether urban or rural, is taken for granted by everyone involved, what is quite clearly rejected is the kind of artificial, antiquated Scots which *is* by and large acceptable within certain restricted areas of the educational system, and which belongs to a discourse constructing Scotland as a quaint and nostalgically rustic land. Outside education a major media outlet for this kind of Scots is the Sunday newspaper *The Sunday Post*, whose cartoons 'Oor Wullie' and 'The Broons' have been reproducing this kind of unchanging, folksy Scots for decades. For *Saturday Super Scoreboard* this kind of 'kailyard' Scots is invariably the object of laughter. In one episode commentator Dougie MacDonald was the butt of incessant mockery when he described a particular warm-up routine before a match as 'hunch cuddy hunch', the name for an old Scottish game similar to leap-frog. None of the other panel members had ever heard this word and, amidst their recurring merriment, they eventually decided that it was 'an old Scottish word like *jings*, *crivvens* or *help ma boab*'. This is an amusing counter-attack by the panel against the opponents of contemporary Scots since words such as these – *jings*, *crivvens*, etc – are precisely the kinds of word used by educated elites to denigrate this particular mode of speech, despite the fact that such terms have no real place in it. What are seen as old-fashioned stereotypes invariably evoke mirth. On one occasion there was undisguised hilarity when a caller let it be known that his name was actually William Wallace, whereupon he was invited, in the midst of guffaws, to 'address the nation'. Not

only does *Saturday Super Scoreboard* come out against these 'couthie' discourses of Scottishness, it constantly underlines its own modernity, repeatedly reminding its listeners to consult its website, or to communicate with the panel via e-mail. (O'Donnell, 2003)

Discussing the re-emergence of Scots in some recent comedy output on television, O'Donnell notes that on BBC Radio Scotland's similar *On the Ball*, and on BBC Scotland television's *Off Side*, a demotic football chat show, host Tam Cowan speaks only west of Scotland urban dialect while, on the radio show, Stuart Cosgrove, his fellow presenter, tends to keep to Standard English, or what we might define as Standard Scottish English. O'Donnell points up here the further demographic determinant of class. He points out that on Clyde's show 'it is taken as axiomatic by all concerned that callers can use whatever dialect of English they like (including regional English dialects) with no value judgements of any kind being passed' and he adds a very important point about the politics of class speech:

> As a result, a whole range of individuals who would normally be excluded from any kind of participation in the media are offered a space where not only is their chosen mode of speech not criticized in any way, but where their contribution, providing certain basic rules are observed, is invariably welcome. (O'Donnell, 2003)

This set of political issues about language is one where the observer is left largely – perhaps sadly – commenting on a linguistic absence in the press, by way of an (admittedly rather limited) presence in broadcasting. *The Sunday Post* thereby suggests itself as uniquely fruitful territory for those seeking linguistic contrast along 'national' lines.

When looking abroad, at other nationalities, the language of political discernment in the Scottish tabloids seems sometimes as brutal as that of the London-based papers:

> HERR TODAY, GONE TOMORROW! Mein Gott … Berti takes no prisoners: Germans savage Scotland (*Daily Record* 15 June 1992)

though there may be some degree of difference between the level of degradation of language here and a historical equivalent from the *Sun* (editionized for Scotland, but motivated elsewhere):

> KRAUT OF THIS WORLD: Blitz kids storm through on a Euro glory night (about a Scotland U-21 victory over Germany in 1992)

Again, compare:

> FROGS WON'T CATCH US ON THE HOP AGAIN!" (Scottish *Sun,* 7 November 1992)

with:

> C'est magnifique says Rangers boss: I'M READY FOR YOU". (about Rangers' European opponents Marseille in *Daily Record*, 7 November 1992)

There is an echo here, from the early 1990s, of a once-valid distinction between Scottish and English tabloid language which in the twenty-first century is harder to find. More recent incarnations of the *Record* have seen it intensify its tabloid nature.

We have noted above how 'Scottishness' in the context of multi-cultural developments has become a yet more complex phenomenon. There are signs of a recognition of that fact even here in this most nationalistic of domains, sport, and perhaps a degree of optimism may be permissible given some good-natured media responses to the multicultural world:

> An article in *The Sun* recounts how Coventry's Moroccan star Moustapha Hadji can speak five languages but cannot understand team boss Gordon Strachan's Scottish accent ('No comprendo Strachanese', 16 September 2000). Interestingly, the same day's Scottish edition of the paper runs a story about how Scotland Under-21 defender Lee Wilkie is learning 'the best chat-up lines' from Italian and Spanish stars at Dundee, and is quoted as saying 'They are learning a few English words but maybe it would be better if the Scots boys learned Italian'. (Blain and Boyle 2002)

4. Conclusion

In a short paper, only some teaching and learning directions, and some central identity questions, have been mapped out; and the spirit of this paper so far has been in a sense generic, in so far as a number of the themes here could be swapped for other Scottish themes; and any one of the themes could be illustrated by many other examples. We have not tried to handle the very large and centrally important issue of gendered Scottishness here, preferring on this occasion to concentrate on the ethnic dimension. But the theme of 'Scottish women' and 'Scottish men' is a further topic for fruitful lessons, especially since the insistent Scotticization of everything in the Scottish press necessitates this hybrid category. Of course, this is an economically-driven insistence, because the main thing Scottish papers do to differentiate themselves from English papers is to be as Scottish as possible.

But where we manage to remember the '*constructedness*' of this version of daily events, we will be able to lever up the language and look underneath – for example, is it any more satisfactory to read 'one nation' versions of Scotland ('Scots everywhere today are celebrating' might serve as a generic model) than it is to read 'one nation' versions of the UK?

What is certainly true is this: neither media producers nor educators are helpless in the reformulation of more suitable varieties of language with which to include the human complexity of the contemporary world. Conscious redirections of language – for good reasons such as the removal of stigma from illness, or for indifferent reasons such as mere political correctness – are a feature of contemporary life (Berman 1992; Dunant 1994; Cameron 1995) and should be possible to address, given political will and technical resources, in the arena of ethnic identity. Such a development would make accusations of 'unBritishness', or 'unScottishness', or 'unEnglishness' much harder to substantiate. Work of this kind in the classroom must be as good a way as any of tackling prejudice in the longer term.

References

Berman, P. 1992. *Debating P.C. the Controversy Over Political Correctness on College Campuses*. New York: Delta

Beveridge, C. and Turnbull R. 1989. *The Eclipse of Scottish Culture*. Edinburgh: Polygon

Billig, M. 1987. *Arguing and Thinking*. Cambridge: Cambridge University Press

Blain N., Boyle. R., and O'Donnell, H. 1993. *Sport and National Identity in the European Media*, Leicester: University of Leicester Press

Blain N. and Boyle R. 1994. "Battling along the boundaries: Scottish Identity Marking in Sports Journalism", in eds. Jarvie G. and Walker, G. *Ninety-minute Patriots: Scottish Sport in the Making of a Nation*. Leicester: Leicester University Press. 125-141

Blain, N. and Boyle, R. 2002. "Sport as Real Life: Media Sport and Culture", in eds. A. Briggs and P. Cobley *The Media: an Introduction*, (2nd ed). London: Longman. 415-426

Cameron, D. 1995. *Verbal Hygiene*. London: Routledge

Daily Telegraph 1997 'Tebbit disowned after culture clash warning', 6 October; 'Conservatives at Blackpool: Cheers for Tebbit as he defends Britishness', 8 October

Dunant, S.1994. *The war of the words: the political correctness debate*. London: Virago

Eagleton, T. 1976. *Marxism and Literary Criticism*. London: Routledge

Foucault, M. 1970. *The Order of Things: An Archaeology of the Human Sciences*. New York: Vintage Books.

Foucault, M. 1977. *Discipline and Punish: The Birth of the Prison*, London: Allen Lane

Fowler, R. 1991. *Language in the News: Discourse and Ideology in the Press*. Routledge: London

Gellner, E.1983. *Nations and Nationalisms*. Oxford: Blackwell

Gilroy P.1987. *There Ain't No Black In The Union Jack*. London: Hutchinson

Hall, S. 1992. "New ethnicities", in eds. J. Donald and A. Rattansi *Race, Culture and Difference*. London: Sage

Harvey, D. 1989. *The Condition of Postmodernity: an enquiry into the origins of cultural change*. Oxford: Blackwell

Hobsbawm, E. J. 1990. *Nations and Nationalism Since 1780*. Cambridge: Cambridge University Press

Hobsbawm E. and Ranger T. eds. 1992. *The Invention of Tradition*. Cambridge: Cambridge University Press

Independent (newspaper) 1997 'British Muslims horrified by Tebbit's dark vision', 9 October

Jacobson J. 1997. "Perceptions of Britishness", *Nations and Nationalism*. 3: 2: 181-199

Kidd C. 1993. *Subverting Scotland's Past: Scottish Whig Historians and the Creation of an Anglo-British Identity, 1689-c1830*. Cambridge: Cambridge University Press

Macdonald M. 2003. *Exploring Media Discourse*. London: Edward Arnold

Mackenzie W.J.M. 1978. *Political Identity*. Manchester: Manchester University Press

Modood, T. 1994. *Changing Ethnic Identities*. London: PSI
Montgomery, M. 1985. *An Introduction to Language and Society*. Routledge: London
Nairn, T. 1990. *The Modern Janus – the new age of nations*. London: Radius
Nairn, T. 1998. *Faces of Nationalism*. London: Verso
Paxman, J.1998. *The English: A Portrait of a People*. London: Michael Joseph
O'Donnell, H. 2003. "Fitba Crazy? *Saturday Super Scoreboard* and the Dialectics of Political Debate", in eds. Bernstein A. and Blain N. *Sport, Media, Culture: Global and Local Dimensions*. Frank Cass: London
Reah, D. 2002. *The Language of Newspapers*. London: Routledge
Rohmer, L. 2002. "Specialist Study of Language within the English Higher Curriculum; Approaches to Practice", in eds. Kirk, J.M. and Ó Baoill, D.P. *Language Planning and Education: Linguistic Issues in Northern Ireland, the Republic of Ireland, and Scotland*. Belfast: Cló Ollscoil na Banríona. 212-220.
Saeed, A., Blain, N. and Forbes, D. 1999. "New ethnic and national questions in Scotland: post-British identities among Glasgow Pakistani teenagers", *Ethnic and Racial Studies*, 22:5: 821-844
Scotland On Sunday (newspaper) 1998 'Just answer the question' (William Paul), 18 October
Sunday Times Magazine 1998 'Scotch wrath' (Jean Rafferty), 4 October
Wright, P. 1985. *On Living in an Old Country*. London: Verso

Screivin anent Scots:
A Psychopathological Study o a Puckle Scots Journalism

John Law

I am sayin 'screivin' here in its auld New York, Damon Runyon sense that descrives whit hacks dis for a leivin – fuls newspapers, raither nor its modren uiss in the Scots muvement ti mean juist 'writer', neutral-like. An I am foondin this study on a puckle o whit haes been gaithert in the bygaun at the Scots Language Resource Centre in Perth bi wey o press cuttins the twal year or thareby o oor existence, tho the cuttins thairsels covers a langer time. I can tak a sklent at nae mair nor a smaa swatch o them in the time we hae, for ti deconstruct the connachin o the Scots leid that sindrie screivers uises insteid o the objective reportin thay micht mainage anither day o the week, on anither subject.

I haena attemptit here ti dael wi ither things that cuid hae been howkit, an likely wad be warth howkin at in mair extendit studies o the situation: instances whaur oor papers haes alloued Scots pieces ti be prentit in ful, for example, or whaur reports haes gien positive publicity ti Scots in a mensefu wey. An it wad be guid ti ken juist hou muckle press material ti back up sic faurer studies cuid be brocht ti haun.

Nor dae I try an draw oot onie morals for the Scots language community regairdin chaunces o makkin better uiss o the press – I am fair pessimistic aboot this, I hae ti say, in circumstances whaur eien letters til the Editor in plain Inglis is sub-editit ti utter destruction whyles in monie a paper – tho the wee locals is better aboot this. Nor dae I hae a lot o howp at we'll see Scots columns the like o Robbie Shepherd's in the P&J spreidin til ither titles.

Smilers wi knifes ablo thair cloaks

Ae aerlie cuttin we hae, fair broun wi age, is frae the *Scotsman* o April 23rd 1966,[1] entitelt 'The vanishing Scots tongue', an is a feature piece daelin wi progress at the twa muckle dictionars. A photie o David Murison at 53, an Jack Aitken at 44, is posed ti shaw the baith men in dour dignity, as tho interruptit at thair scholar darg, caain ower a pynt o lear in the papers fornent them. It maks them leuk gey dowie, aiblins disjaskit.

Nou, the harigals o this airticle is aa whit ye wad cry 'responsible journalism', stappit fu o facts on the subject at haun: we can wauger the screiver wis gled ti be speirin at sic weel-informed men, an made maister o aa the details he gies us anent William Craigie an William Grant, an sindrie organisations, dates, volunteers, siller – doun ti sic ferlies as that the Victoria Bowling Club, Kirkcaldy haed pitten in £5 5s til the SND subscreivins.

But as ye micht jalouse frae the teitle an the photie, the heid spin on it is gey caurrie:

> *David Murison stood at the window of his study in Edinburgh's George Square and gazed out at the glass and concrete tower blocks rising from the rubble o the eighteenth-century town houses that used to*

---

[1] *Scotsman*, 23.4.66 – airticle but byline, daelin wi progress at SND an DOST

stand there. "The Square's like the language," he said sadly. "It's being knocked down and demolished."

If Murison is bitter as he sees Scots emasculated by Anglicisation and corrupted by Americanisms, it is hardly surprising. For the Scottish National Dictionary which he has been editing for the past 20 years, is rapidly becoming the record of a dead language.

But 53-year-old Murison may have one consolation denied many other major lexicographers (like the brothers Grimm, whose Dictionary of the German language, begun in 1838, was finished only in 1960). He may live to see his work completed.

Aiblins this micht be fair comment on a something Murison sayed at interview, an on ae aspect o the wey he felt aboot things. But whan we read the hail airticle, we micht wunner whit mair aither Murison or Aitken iver sayed til thon *Scotsman* screiver, in amang aa the purvey o facts, aboot whit thay thocht thairsels the pynt o whit thay war daein wis, or whit thay thocht aboot modren Scots letters, an we can wunner in vain, for in aa the lenth o fower lang column we dinna get telt.

An whan we come til the tail o the blad, we hae this mensefu observation:

> *Dr Johnson's comment after visiting the Highlands was that "tradition is a meteor which, once it falls, cannot be rekindled." The fire is now burning low, but the staffs of the dictionaries are harbouring its last, fading sparks.*

Trig eneuch in its ain orra wey, this picks up on a mention aerlier on in the piece at Boswell haed thocht on makkin a Scots dictionar... but whit a revelation o the screiver's rael opeinion in thon *harbouring*! Dis he mean 'haining', but cuidna mynd the word, or dis he mean bringin thae last lowes ti herbour ti be drount in the watter, or tied up at the scrapyaird quay? Na – he means the Scots language is a creiminal, nane the waur o the hingin his airticle gies it, an Murison an Aitken dangerous men.

Touers o haivers

Stanley Eveling, umquhile TV reviewer o the Scotsman in the edeition o Merch 15t, 1986,[2] gaes on the lenth o three sax-inch column anent Billy Kay's three-pairt series, *Our Mother Tongue*. Here hou he gets roadit:

> *Some people speak perfect English. They rhyme "pass" with "arse" and not with "ass"; they call tatties potatoes and lugs they call ears ...*

He gangs on ti pynt oot hou monie speakers o this orra perfect Inglis bydes in Scotland an says hou *"the long, baneful, linguistic influence of this powerful English lingo is spreading."* He says he likit the programmes fine, an thay war *"richly illustrated by some marvellous chatterings... and full o hame's truths* (sic)." Whit an impaction o patronisin hostility in thon *'marvellous chatterings'*!

---

[2]   *Scotsman*, 15.3.86 – TV review column bi Stanley Eveling, wi philosophisin anent language efter mention o Billy Kay's three-pairt series, *Our Mother Tongue*.

But he lats on neist ti be "*depressed*". Whit he means, it turns oot, is at he nou wants ti treat aabodie til a philosophical excursus aa his ain, pyntin oot whit wey the'r nae need ti fash yersel aboot language daith, an he haes three propones ti pit forrit anent whit he cries "*romantic fallacies to do with words.*"

The first is that it isna true "*that some* [words] *are better than others so that to change from one way of speaking to another is to gain something or to suffer loss.*" Weel, that's the *Scotsman* sub-editor telt, gin his rid pen wis hoverin ower thon *linguistic lingo* abuin.

The saicont fallacy is "*that nature cuts up languages into distinct blocks which define the identity of a nation or a speaker so that loss of it is loss of nationhood or one's inner self.*" An biggin on this siccar foond, he pits the kepstane on it bi annuncin: "*Poetry does not need the past: itself it speaks and spells and its present is now.*" We micht struissle ti see whaur this glamourie can be yokit whan we michtna ken the meanins o some words.

His third fallacy is a true ane: "*that the closer you get to the soil or the terraces the richer the culture, the truer, more honest, more valuable the speech.... you can't be pompous in Scots. You can. Pomposity knows no boundaries.*" It micht be gey pompous ti leuk at thon 'terraces', an wunner gin it wis peasant fermin, raws o hooses, or the fitba staund the man means. As nae dout it wad be aa the same kinna fowk in onie, it canna maiter muckle.

It wad be a peitie no ti quote the peroration:

> *And lastly, I'm depressed because the programme threatens a romantic fallacy of my own. All my life, I've been trying to understand German thoughts, Greek thoughts, Scotch thoughts, French thoughts, Jewish thoughts, Christian thoughts and Hindu thoughts and with these thoughts in mind, to see whether they might not become my thoughts. Not my English thoughts but just mine, the stateless soul who thinks, as the galaxies swim past my window, fenetre, ventana, fenster, of this and that and whose language is just the visible envelope that shrouds the invisible idea. A thought's a thought for all that.*
>
> *There are no languages, only language, parts of which we can speak.*

Humour stumers

Twa instance will hae ti dae for aa the monie entries in oor cuttins archive whaur fell daft reportage, wad-be jokey heidlines an tabloid cantrips cowps whit micht hae been positive stories for Scots the ither wey aboot.

In the *Daily Express*, the 14t Januar 1996,[3] a reporter Neville Rigby taks tent o the Grant's whisky *Unco Sonsie* campaign, an for aince the'r nae faut in the heidline: *Whisky ad cheers revival of Scots language in school*. But the hail airticle collapses the meenit it stcrts wi this dozent first paragraph cttlin ti mak for news value:

> *After generations of disapproval and being written off as a variety of English dialects, Scots has been revived.*

An aa throu the piece, irony an reidicule is laid on wi a nummer seiven shovel, an inaccuracy (*lalands*) tashes the text:

*Next month, with the aroma of haggis still heavy after thousands of
Burns suppers pay homage to the bard's 'lalands' (lowland) tongue, a
Scots language project will be launched by the Scottish Consultative
Council on the Curriculum to distribute teaching materials throughout
Scotland.*

The destruction o airticles wi heidlines hostile til the apparent threid o the writin
wis seen in the *Herald* o 18/12/97,[4] whaur Carlos Alba's piece settin oot the case
pitten forrit in the SLRC paper, *Threapin on Scots*, is wrutten as straucht as we
cuid hae weished, an wins in at the fit o the front page o the paper.

Houiver, some mentality thocht fit ti heid the piece wi this byordnar heidline:

Scots ganging agley, whatever that means

Nou, the paper *Threapin on Scots* disna uise the phrase 'gangin agley'
oniewhaur at I can finnd, sae the bodie that wan at this gloss on the situation haed
ti howk it oot his or her ain heid, syne lat on no ti ken whit it micht mean. The
effect is ti unnermine the airticle Carlos Alba wrate, an no content wi that, the
compositors o the front page thocht fit ti set it aa aff wi a bit cartoon frae Bill,
whaur a cheil wi a rid neb in a snawstorm is walkin by a sign sayin 'Scots language
needs government support' an sayin ti himsel, 'And it's got as much chance of
getting it as a disabled single mother.'

Nou, this wis in a paper that at thon time haed hecht SLRC ti gie us practical
support wi oor campaign for the Scots leid, efter we haed kittilt interest at Board
level in Scottish Media Group. This wis thaim daein thair best for Scots.

Scots as a register o Inglis

The maist sophisticatit attacks on Scots comes frae fowk that haes a hauf-wey
unnerstaunin o it, but no able for ti haunle it wi onie success thairsels, lats on thair
ain condeition is the universal ane. Don Paterson's airticle in *Scotland on Sunday*,
26/3/00,[5] *Haud yer tongue – Why speaking your mind can sometimes leave a bad
taste in the mouth*, gangs throu the hail jing-bang.

*Formed by centuries of hostile invasions conducted in rubbish weather,
the Scots tongue inevitably came to display certain characteristics: it
sounds very grumpy, and involves a lot of phlegm. ... Just as the Inuit
have their 70 words for snow, the Scots Thesaurus lists around 50-odd
different kinds of coughing. Suddenly you understand why Scots is
incapable of supporting an erotic literature.*

Sae here we ar in the ryk o the wad-be lairned, wad-be facetious. But Paterson at
laest awns a Scots Thesaurus, an wants ti offer a puckle sage avisement:

---

[3]   *Daily Express*, 14.1.96 – Neville Rigby, *Whisky ad cheers revival of Scots language in school*
[4]   *Herald*, 18.12.97 – Carlos Alba, *Scots ganging agley, whatever that means*
[5]   *Scotland on Sunday*, 26.3.00 Don Paterson, *Haud yer tongue – Why speaking your mind
can sometimes leave a bad taste in the mouth.*

The subtlety of the Scots we could be speaking now is hinted at when you look at the marvellous fossil-tongue of Scots Law, which, if we were genuinely serious about trying to revive the language, would be a better place to start than introducing the words "mingin" and "barkit" into genteel conversation.
But the truth is that pretty much all the Scots we have in daily use is the language of the street or the farm. This leaves us with precisely two registers: coorse and couthy.

Efter stravaigin in nae parteicular direction roun the topic o place-nems, Paterson haiks awa this road:

If couthy's all we have, though, then couthy it'll have to be. At least Scots seems to be edging its way back into the school curriculum again, even if no-one can really agree on what it actually is... But even if Scots has fallen on hard times, at least we still have the literature: so I was disturbed when a very short friend of mine came home from school recently, spouting not 'The Bonny Broukit Bairn' or 'To a Mountain Daisy' or one of William Soutar's lovely bairnsangs, but the same bloody awful piece of mumsy doggerel I'd been forced to recite 30 years ago. You know. Ye've hurt yer finger, ye puir wee sowel / yer pinkie, dearie me ...

This isna ti refute himsel anent the possible registers o Scots, sen he disna mention a poem at ye cuidna cry couthie – rowth o them tho thare is in the pages o MacDiarmid, Burns or Soutar – but we can jalouse that quaetly intil himsel Don Paterson haes mair ti say aboot Scots nor he will on ane o his facetious days. An at the hin en he eien gies us a prescription whit it micht tak ti revive Scots mensfu-like:

Its fate lies with the aspirant working classes who used Scots in their childhoods, and insist on it as a legitimate means of expression in their adult and professional lives – ie, a great many readers of this newspaper. Of course, it's bound to sound a bit affected to start off with, but in reality, it's a good deal less so than the deliberate adoption of an upwardly mobile accent – and we aw ken fowk who've done that. You can only change a language from within, word by word; we can only reclaim our Scots through the medium of our English.

A smaa nummer o quaistens gaun beggin thare, ye micht think. In parteicular, the idea o 'aspirant working classes' threapin on onie sic a thing as Scots in thair 'professional' lives, laes ye wunnerin dis thaim that didna aspire ti speak ocht but Scots an aye speaks it hae naething uissfu ti say anent it? An ay, it micht be true for Don Paterson at he wad hae ti foond greater uiss o Scots on his ain Inglis. Orra eneuch it micht be, tae. But thare haes ti be something wrang wi a view that says ye can lairn an uise a language bi utterin a puckle o its words amang yer ongaun uiss o the chief killer leid for the ane ye'r ettlin ti beild.

I will leuk last at a piece that for patronisin haes haurdly an equal in oor hail archive, an it is bi the novelist Allan Massie, in the Scotsman, 6/9/2003,[6] ablo the heidline *We Scots have a sober and enlightened nationalism - let's be thankful*. I dinna ken gin Allan Massie is winnin himsel up ti mak a leiterary sally in the style o John Galt, but I mynd a puckle years back he wis writin aboot hou a possible Scots wad juist be a haunfu Scots currans in an Inglis clootie dumplin. As a leiterary maiter, gin a bodie can mak this work – an some fowk dis try an write this wey – we'll advance nae objection here til a beuk that aiblins isna oot yit. Here a flavour o whit Allan Massie says, the heuk o his airticle bein the sweirness o the SNP ti walcome MEP cheils frae the Vlaams Blok til the Scots Pairlament:

> *The fact is that the SNP has never had a linguistic culture to defend. This is a principal difference between it and most European nationalist movements. Of course, many Scottish Nationalists have a certain tenderness for the old languages of our country, Gaelic and Scots. But then so do many Scots who are not nationalists. More to the point, both these languages are far too fragile to have been made the basis of a nationalist movement aimed at securing independence. That was already the case even when the SNP was formed 70 years ago. Occasionally enthusiasts talk of the revival of one of these languages, or indeed both, but few suppose this is a practical proposition.*

The implication wad seem ti be, that gin the SNP wis onie wey foondit on defendin linguistic culture, it wad hae ti be fascist an racist. Weel, this is a leam frae the mynd o ane o the Scottish Tories' twa intellectuals, but as an SNP insider it seems til the present writer that maiters is aathegither the ither wey aboot. The norie that Burns draps the wee bit Augustan Inglis inti Tam o Shanter, hardly able for ti ken the odds in whit he wis daein, gies the bard smaa credit.

> *The Scots of the Enlightenment were not so much bilingual therefore, as capable of moving comfortably between varieties of what was more or less the same language. They did so often scarcely consciously. They did so in writing. Nobody exemplified this easy way with varieties of language better than our National poet Burns. Not only did he, as in Tam O'Shanter, move smoothly from vernacular Scots to standard Augustan English in the passage beginning "But Pleasures are like poppies spread", but the language of some of his finest lyrics may most fairly be described as English with a Scots flavouring.*

The norie that Burns draps the wee bit Augustan Inglis inti Tam o Shanter, hardly able for ti ken the odds in whit he wis daein, gies the bard smaa credit.

> *This is perhaps as much as we can hope for in any attempt to revive Scots: speaking and writing English with a stronger Scots flavouring, by introducing Scots words and phrases to our speech and writing whenever this can be done without awkwardness, quaintness, or the impression of insincerity. There are many words and expressions too*

---

[6] *Scotsman*, 6.9.2003 – Allan Massie, *We Scots have a sober and enlightened nationalism - let's be thankful*

> *good to be allowed to die, and we could certainly refresh our language by making more use of them. This is an achievable aim, because a modest one; far too modest, I jalouse, to be any part of a political programme. Yet it would be sair misguided to regret that Scottish nationalism did not come into being in order, as Brogan put it, to "defend the claims of a linguistic culture". It would be a very different and ill-fa'ard beast had it done so: more like the Vlaams Blok indeed. For once you start by insisting on linguistic purity, you are all but bound to move on to insisting on other sorts of purity too. Such a nationalist movement is likely to become exclusive and consequently intolerant.*

This byordnar line o airgiement wad mak onie threapin on a ful uiss o Scots gey haurd ti pit forrit: we canna afford ti be ill-fa'ard, whitiver that means.

Conclusions

We micht hae gane pickin an walin amang the sources for this essay[7] wi ither pynts ti pruve – that reportage o Scots language issues is aften mair objective an freinlie in the *Press & Journal*, the *Courier*, an the wee local papers, for example. An the SLRC media archive contains ither instance o hamesucken mair felloun bi faur, whaur the screivers concerned wad lour hae the hail o Scots letters tint in a bleeze on the Guy Fawkes bonnie. We micht hae seen hou faur ower monie stories anent Scots byles doun ti *here's a few funny words to amuse you*, wi the Scots aye served up deid in the tangs-grup o Inglis invertit commas. An ower an again, we see an onsiccarness aboot the chances o weans lairnin Inglis successfu, an that is byordnar – for whit wad it tak in the day's warld ti hinner them frae lairnin it?

Discomfort wi Scots, crulgin an cowkin at it, is a kynd o smit, an it is gey common in oor papers. Unnerstaunin o the seikness amang the audience for this paper, fowk that's aa faur ben wi Scots, needs ye ti think whit like ye micht be gin ye war mair in the condeition o bein fair weel-read in Scots, but no able for ti speak it awfu weel, an no able for ti write it. Nouadays, gin ye dinna tak the bus, ye can byde certain bits in Scotland an fail ti hear onie Scots avaa. No aesie ti impruve yer speakin that wey.

An gin it cam ti thinkin on writin, fornent the siccarness ye wad hae settin doun Inglis, kennin bi the beuk whit wey the onie kinch o spellin is sortit oot, aince ye ken whit side the Atlantic ye ar on, an whit is guid gremmar fornent ill, ye wad finnd yersel sair pitten til it. An oniewey – wad yer newspaper or yer publisher lat ye get awa wi mair nor ane or twa Scots currans – a *jalouse* here an a *sair misguided* thare?

An yit, an yit, as yer readin wad aye be tellin ye – ye hae here a guidlie heirskep, anc that ye can fine weel unnerstaun.

Frae here, raither nor lairn a bittie mair an bring on yer Scots language skeils, it is an aesier pad, as the pad o bad faith aye is, ti decide that the language is deid an you entitelt ti craw on its corp, pykin oot dentie bits.

---

[7] Media archive – Scots Language Resource Centre, Perth

Language, Culture and Politics: a Theatrical Perspective

David Grant

In September 2001, I directed a production of *Translations* by Brian Friel for the Hungarian Theatre of Cluj in the northern Romanian province of Transylvania. It was, in effect, a field study into the interrelationship between language, culture and politics. The very existence of a Hungarian-language theatre in a Romanian city is inherently political. The redrawing of borders following the First World War had relocated a substantial Hungarian-speaking population within the new Romania, and in the spirit of the idealism of the Versailles settlement, the old Habsburg Winter and Summer theatres in Koloszvar (the city's Hungarian name) became the Romanian and Hungarian Theatres, respectively. Despite Ceaucescu's concerted efforts to disperse ethnic Hungarians throughout Romania, the theatre continued to flourish, combining the literary values of the Hungarian theatre tradition with the boldly innovative spirit for which Romanian theatre has become internationally recognised. Under the leadership of its current Artistic Director, Gabor Tompa, the Hungarian Theatre has made a particular effort to attract Romanian speakers, with simultaneous translation being offered of all performances. When, therefore, Romanian-speakers attended my production of *Translations,* they listened in Romanian to a translation of a Hungarian version of a play in which they were asked to accept that the characters were speaking either English or Irish (*pace* the occasional passage in Latin or Ancient Greek).

The play's treatment of the relationship between two language cultures had clear resonances for Hungarian-speakers in Cluj/Koloszvar: but I was relieved to discover the sophisticated way in which they processed their understanding of any parallels between the play and their own experience. In particular, they pointed to the robust survival of Hungarian in Romania, in comparison to the marked decline of Irish, which they saw (as the play itself does) as principally the consequence of the commercial power of the English language. The presence of the McDonald's fast food chain and the ubiquity of Internet Cafés in Cluj were vivid indications that this was a continuing phenomenon. What this analysis fails to allow for, however, is the over-riding irony that *Translations*, with its acknowledged status as one of the great plays of the English-language theatrical canon, was written by an Irishman.

This reversal of the colonial process, through which an Irish writer can claim the language of the coloniser as his own, lies at the heart of the international reputation currently enjoyed by Irish dramatists. In the context of the current symposium, this recognition must cast doubt on the wisdom, at least as far as the theatre is concerned, of seeking to assert the separateness of Scots as a distinct language. Unlike Romanian and Hungarian, which share no common linguistic roots, the differentiation of English and Scots seems to be an example of what Freud called "the narcissism of minor difference".

The idea of Scots as a distinct language seems to yearn for a certainty of definition that maps uneasily onto the diverse array of use of words to be found throughout Scotland. As a theatre director, I find this quest for a standard identifiable language especially ironic. Theatre is concerned with the oral use of words. The written word is merely a means to an end and often provides an inadequate record of the sounds it seeks to represent. The certainty to which a 'language' must aspire in order to validate itself politically seems to depend primarily on the written word and to deny the essential fluidity of all language.

The Russian theorist Mikhail Bakhtin makes the distinction between centripetal and centrifugal forces in the evolution of language which, he argues, are in a constant state of dynamic tension.[1] The pressure to conform to a centralised norm is counter-balanced by the consciously subversive attraction of local vocabularies and turns of phrase. It is one way in which communities can assert their diversity within the increasing media-driven universality of standard English as a *lingua franca*. In theatre, it is that decentralising force which is of crucial interest. Local variations and idiosyncracies of language lend colour and vibrancy to dialogue which the written word cannot always capture. This a luxury denied to Hungarians in Romania, for whom the centralised norm is a crucial benchmark against which to measure their authenticity. In Ireland, since at least Joyce, Irishness has been best expressed in the distinctive use of the English 'word-hoard'.[2] And the driving energy of this distinctiveness can be heard in the way in which the words are spoken, not written.

Nor is this a uniquely Irish phenomenon. When a modern director approaches Shakespeare, for instance, one of the greatest challenges is to free oneself up from centuries of learnèd editorship and to remember that Shakespeare's theatre was an essentially oral tradition. The written word took mainly the form of hand written cue scripts, with non-standardised spelling, which if the earliest extant published versions are any guide, contained many useful hints for the actor. So for example if the word *he* appears as *he* and *hee* in the same speech, this may well carry some nuance of meaning which the actor should take on board.[3]

In our modern literate world, this emphasis on orality is hard to grasp. And the urge for spoken language to assert its validity in standardised written forms seems almost irresistible. But in the theatre, different rules have always applied – and nowhere more than in the North of Ireland. Brian Friel himself, who lives, as Paul Durcan so pithily expressed it, in "the part of the South which is more northerly than the North",[4] the Inishowen peninsula of Donegal, has commented on the use of Elizabethan English only fields away from his home.[5] And John B Keane's Kerry English has similarly been described as Elizabethan.[6]

---

[1] Mikhail Bakhtin, *The Dialogic Imagination: Four Essays*, trans. Caryl Emerson and Michael Holquist, University of Texas Press, Austin, 1981, p.271.
[2] A neologism from Seamus Heaney's *Beowulf*
[3] Patrick Tucker, *Secrets of Acting Shakespeare*, Routledge, 2002
[4] from 'Dancing with Brian Friel' in Paul Durcan, *Greetings to Our Friends in Brazil*, The Harvill Press, London 1999, p.158
[5] Brian Friel, Essays, *Diaries, Interviews: 1964-1999* (ed. Christopher Murray), Faber, London, 1999

Drama rejoices in this oral diversity, but in the Irish theatre our interest is not so much in language or even dialect. It is above all with accent and a sense of the vernacular. The driving force behind this interest is the fact that theatre as a living medium depends for its survival on audiences who in the North of Ireland have consistently shown a delight in hearing their own voices on stage. In the early twentieth century, dramatists had to strive to recreate these distinctive local sounds in written form so that they could be shared with actors. But even a brief look at the collected works of one of the most successful Belfast writers in the first half of the last century, St. John Ervine,[7] reveals the pertinent fact that, whereas his first play is written phonetically, all his subsequent plays adopt standard spelling, albeit of a locally specific idiom. The conclusion I draw from this is that the local sounds on which the success of the plays depended had to be discovered by actors in rehearsal. And these actors required a native understanding of the local voice that could not effectively be communicated in print without seeming to be reduced to parody. A layman's response to the contemporary printed form of Ulster Scots is often similar.

But more recent developments in the theatre have altered our understanding of this crucial relationship between the spoken and the written word. The growing importance of community theatre and the devising process have allowed us to rediscover the theatre's oral roots. The Italian Nobel Laureate, Dario Fo, for instance, does not write plays in the conventional sense. He creates a storyboard of images, improvises around these, and only after extensive experiment before an audience, does a written version emerge.[8] And that written text alone is only as efficient a record of the performed event as sheet music is of a symphony. In fact, the symphonic record is more precise having a range of symbols to show dynamic changes which the normal playtext cannot match.

The work of Marie Jones is the best local example of this phenomenon. She began her writing through collaborative projects with Charabanc Theatre Company, whose plays were only committed to the word processor after extensive development in rehearsal. When I was involved with the publication of her first play to appear in print,[9] the manuscript showed a disregard for conventional punctuation that was truly Shakespearean – and all the better for that!

Melissa Sihra, has charted a similar phenomenon in the work of Marina Carr, comparing successive published editions of her play *Portia Coughlan*. In earlier versions a fluid phoneticism prevails, where the very distinction between words breaks down, reminding me more than anything else of the experience of staging sections of James Joyce's *Finnegans Wake*. My main recollection of that rehearsal

---

[6]   Mic Moroney, 'The Twisted Mirror: Landscapes, Mindscapes, Politics and Language on the Irish Stage', in *Druids, Dudes and Beauty Queens* (ed. Dermot Bolger), New Island, Dublin, 2001, p.254

[7]   St. John Ervine, *Selected Plays*, (ed. John Cronin), Colin Smythe Ltd., Gerrards Cross, 1988.

[8]   Ron Jenkins, *Dario Fo & Franca Rame: Artful Laughter,* Aperture, New York, 2001

[9]   Marie Jones, 'The Hamster Wheel', in *The Crack in the Emerald* (ed. David Grant), Nick Hern Books, London, 1990

process was the way in which the seemingly impenetrable text revealed itself most when the actors employed the broadest Dublin accents. Elisions which were hidden from the eye immediately became clear to the ear. In the latest edition of *Portia Coughlan*, standard English spelling has been adopted and Carr comments in the introduction that she has "given a flavour of the text, but the Midland accent is more rebellious than the written word permits". Melissa Sihra concludes that "while the contestation of standard linguistic structure has poetic and political value, the semantic inaccessibility of the early versions of *Portia Coughlan* was in Carr's opinion, self-defeating, especially with regard to non-Irish and non-English speaking practitioners and scholars".[10] The fact remains, however, that the plays were written to be performed – not to excite the scrutiny of scholars. My own point is, *not* that the publication of standardised version is a mistake, but that its existence seems to bear out the unviability of the phonetic rendition of essentially oral material.

So, when I reflect on the significance of the current publication's themes for the theatre, I am unsure how to proceed. The oral emphasis of this theatrical tradition is not served by any attempt to compartmentalise Ireland's oral diversity into a number of distinct languages. Instead, I would prefer to retain the many "flavours" of language (as J.M. Synge put it) within the one broad church of, if it must be so categorised, 'Hiberno-English'. (This is not to discount the significance of Irish-language theatre. I do not feel qualified to comment on this, but I would hope the same principles would apply. The differences between spoken Irish in different parts of Ireland are often commented on by Irish language theatre companies.)

The real theatrical charm of this diversity is that it is not always necessary for the audience to understand the literal meaning of the words to appreciate their theatrical effect. Enda Walsh's densely idiomatic and phonetically written *Disco Pigs* is a good example. When the director Conall Morrison was adapting *Tarry Flynn* for the stage, he listened to recordings at the Ulster Folk and Transport Museum of Cavan farmers unsullied by exposure to decades of television, whose distinctive and to him incomprehensible use of English helped him acquire a better intuitive understanding of the character of, as T.S. Eliot puts it, "the auditory imagination" of the border counties in the 1950s.

And accent can be even more theatrically significant than idiom. In Frank McGuinness' *Observe the Sons of Ulster Marching Towards the Somme*, the diversity of Ulster Protestantism is conveyed by having characters from different parts of Northern Ireland, and of different social class. These distinctions are only partly achieved through vocabulary and syntax. In performance, the crucial semiotic is accent.

With the news that Scotland is soon to invest in a National Theatre which will not be building-based and that will continue to celebrate the country's existing diversity of theatre production, it is to be hoped that this inclusiveness will extend

---

[10] Melissa Sihra, *Landscapes, Voices and Corporeality of Excess in the Theatre of Marina Carr*, unpublished doctoral thesis, Trinity College, Dublin, pp 158-9.

to a new confidence in the vitality and durability of the many distinctive ways in which Scots use the English language. This diversity was evident in Bill Findlay's paper at this symposium where he spoke of the many regional linguistic variations to be found throughout Scotland[11]. However distinctive these may, Scottish theatre is clearly not in a parallel situation to that of the Hungarian Theatre in Cluj where simultaneous translation is the norm. This symposium itself offers empirical proof of this in the lack of use of headsets for contributions offered in Scots.

The example of Ireland and the Abbey Theatre has often been referred to in the long campaign for a Scottish National Theatre. But surely the main lesson to be drawn from Ireland is the way in which Irish writers has colonised the English language and made it their own. The result has been to place Irish drama at the centre of international attention. By contrast, attempt to distinguish the Scottish use of English from the mainstream, can surely only serve to marginalise Scottish drama. That cannot be in the long-term interests of Scotland, its writers or its National Theatre.

---

[11] Bill Findlay, 'Modern Scots Drama and Language Planning: A Context and A Caution', in the present volume.

Language and the Irish Cinema Question

Des O'Rawe

> *If it were all in the script, why make the film?*
> Nicholas Ray

Introduction

In this short presentation, I would like to comment on the role of Irish-language filmmaking in the development of 'contemporary Irish cinema'. By this, I mean an indigenous cinema culture capable of producing films that are intelligent rather than tedious, aesthetically distinctive rather than embarrassingly derivative. In recent years, independent filmmaking throughout Europe has been 'mainstreamed' to the point of virtual extinction. In general, contemporary European cinema has been unsuccessful in its attempts to negotiate indigenous creative and critical space within the vast matrix of industrial and cultural alignments that have occurred as a result of globalization. This malaise is very noticeable within an Irish context, where organizations such as Bord Scannán na hÉireann (Irish Film Board) and the Northern Ireland Film and Television Commission have been forced to formulate and implement policies designed to appease the jealous god of popular entertainment rather than the more courageous goal of artistic innovation.

In reality, a living cinema – a 'critical' cinema – has, with the exception of a brief period during the late 1970s and 1980s, never developed into a robust tradition or significant artistic movement within Irish cultural life. Irish cinema has always largely comprised of European and American co-productions that use 'Ireland' as a location or setting in which to situate this or that prefabricated story or narrative situation. Most contemporary Irish feature film productions and co-productions dutifully follow this trend (for example, *Snakes and Ladders* (MacAdam, 1996), *Waking Ned* (Jones, 1998), *With or Without You* (Forte, 1999), etc., etc.). However, one of the more interesting pockets of resistance to this tendency has been Irish-language film culture and this fact affords us an opportunity to reflect on ways in which language – oddly enough – can sometimes be essential to the future of a cinema.

Images and Words

In other papers at this symposium, an emphasis has been placed on three performance-related activities: acting, scriptwriting, and (less directly) sound and 'soundscapes' (music and song, for example). However, these activities are ultimately incidental to the creation of 'intelligent and aesthetically distinctive' films. Arguably, the cinema has always been more committed to 'non-acting' than to 'acting' *per se*, and its insensitivity towards the feelings of scriptwriters is the stuff of many a Hollywood memoir. Furthermore, throughout the history of avant-garde cinema (from Germaine Dulac to Stan Brakage) sound-montage and the illusion sound-image synchronicity has been treated with scepticism and hostility.

The reason for this deep ambivalence towards the performing arts, and their place in the art of cinema, is worth reiterating: the cinema is committed to privileging the visual over the lexical, images over words. Primarily, it is the art of composing, framing, cutting, and juxtaposing shots. It is a matter of eye, a way of seeing rhythm and texture, line and colour, movement and stillness. Cinema ('the art of the cinematograph') is what it says it is: movement written in light.

Terms such as 'acting', 'script' and 'sound' are actually very problematic – although this view is obviously at odds with the cultural proclivities and production priorities of many contemporary filmmakers and their potential sponsors. Indeed, given this fact alone, we might be inclined to admit defeat, watch the opening sequence from *Blown Away* (Hopkins, 1994) and conclude that contemporary cinema has little to offer the development of *any* language, and cannot but use a lesser-used language in a 'symbolic' or (as in the case of *Blown Away*) shambolic way. However, within an Irish context, such conceptual 'instabilities' (and endless disappointments!) may yet prove instrumental in opening a creative and critical space that can be occupied by an imaginative and committed Irish-language film culture. Certainly, there is a precedent for such a development, and its legacy should not be renounced simply because political forces and cultural managers insist that we equate the modern with the mainstream, the popular with the trivial.

Critical Contexts

Throughout the post-independence period, Irish-language filmmaking was 'documentary' in form and function. In the *Amharc Éireann / A View of Ireland* newsreels of the late 1950s and early 1960s, for example, there is a strong sense that Irish language narration and dialogue is being deployed to add 'documentary' and ethnographic authenticity to the subject matter. However, this should not be allowed to obscure the fact that these shorts were quite innovative for their time. For example, the modernizing implications of the *Amharc Éireann* series differ markedly from the conservative aims and 'hard primitivism' of Robert Flaherty's *Man Of Aran* (1934) (cf. Rockett, Gibbons and Hill 1987: 200-203, McLoone 2000: 38-44). While by no means modernist, many of the *Amharc Éireann* films do seem to possess, what Gerry White has described as, "a very progressive aesthetic [that] often [steers] away from the stagey and manipulative formal strategy favoured by Flaherty" (White 2003: 113). White offers some examples of these 'progressive' formal techniques, pointing out that some of the films were shot in a style that anticipated 'cinéma-vérité', a style that would also characterize Louis Marcus's Gael Linn film, *Fleadh Ceoil / Music Festival* (1966) (White 2003a: 113n6, 121n16).[1] (Incidentally, Marcus, in addition to making and

---

[1] White also discusses George Morrison's *Mise Éire* (1956) *Saoirse?* (1961), arguing that Morrison's films, like the *Amharc Éireann* series, 'aggressively address important contradictions in Griersonian idealism about the civic role of documentary, the problems of writing and visualizing Irish history through a nationalist lens, and the complex place translation plays in the postcolonial world' (White 2003a: 121, cf. O'Brien 2000). Whilst this claim exaggerates the cinematic sophistication and ideological complexity of these films, it is clearly the case that the modest history of Irish language filmmaking has been characterized by some degree of aesthetic innovation (cf. Pettitt 2000: 77-82).

commissioning Irish-language films, has lobbied for many years in support of independent Irish and Irish-language filmmakers.)

Since the mid-1970s, Bob Quinn has emerged as the chief custodian of this tradition. Quinn, a former producer at RTÉ, co-founded Cinegael in 1973 with Seosamh Ó Cuaig and Toni Cristofides (Cinegael 2003). Like Marcus, Quinn has long recognized the need for an independent Irish cinema to take some of its 'counter-cinema' bearings from Irish-language culture. According to one critic, '[Quinn's] commitment to the Irish language flows from the feeling ... that language is not just the repository of a long and radical tradition in Ireland but also the most effective bulwark against being subsumed into an Anglo-American cultural universe' (McLoone 2000: 133-134, cf. White 2003b). In films such as *Caoineadh Airt Uí Laoghaire* / *Lament for Art Ó Laoghaire* (1975) and *Poitín/Poteen* (1978), Quinn broke the traditional bond that had fixed Irish-language films to documentary forms.[2] This is one of the reasons why he continues to be regarded as a central figure in the 'new' Irish cinema movement that emerged in Ireland in the 1970s and 1980s, a movement that included filmmakers such as Kieran Hickey, Thaddeus O'Sullivan, Pat Murphy, Joe Comerford, and Cathal Black. Quinn also injected a spirit of political directness into Irish film culture and he has done as much as any of his peers to assist in the development of a political cinema in Ireland.

Quinn's uncompromising anti-metropolitan ('anti-Temple Bar') socialism has never enjoyed widespread support (and seems increasing irrelevant in these – supposedly halcyon – days at 'the end of history'), but it does posit the possibility of a politically informed and socially engaged film culture. In this regard, films such as *Caoineadh Airt Uí Laoghaire* and *Poitín* remain crucial points of reference in any discussion of indigenous Irish cinema and the spirit of 'critical regionalism' that, at is best, this cinema was been able to generate (cf. McLoone 1994: 156-171). Quinn's Cinegael films are still charged with 'critical' images and dissident ideas that can seem all the more compelling because they are accompanied by Irish dialogue. Quinn's avant-garde credentials have also been reinforced by his experimental use of sound and silence in his short film *Cloch* (1975) and his 16mm feature *Budawanny* (1987).[3]

---

[2] A bond that has of course been restored (and re-imagined) in recent years by filmmakers such as Desmond Bell (*Rotha Mor an t'Saoil/Hard Road to Klondike* (1999), *An Scéalaí Deireanach?* /*The Last Storyteller* (2002)).

[3] A clear sense of Quinn's cultural politics can be gleaned from the pages of *Maverick: A Dissident View of Broadcasting Today*. Regarding the contribution Raidió na Gaeltachta (RnaG) and Teilifís na Gaeilge (TG4) make to Irish cultural life, Quinn states: "In the ecology of Irish broadcasting, RnaG and TG4 may be considered to be the only species that are unique to Ireland, and like any rare species whose cultural hinterland is ever diminishing, they are hanging on by their fingertips. In the ecosystem of sounds, images and ideas which broadcasting should be, there is presently a mono-cultural preponderance of weeds, choking all educative possibilities, asphyxiating our cultural life and slowly toxifying our imagination." (Quinn 2001: 31)

New Initiatives and Old Problems

Recently, the production of Irish language films has been supported by the Oscailt and Lasair schemes. These initiatives offer funding for Irish language shorts and have been widely praised for helping to promote Irish as a modern language while also contributing to the indigenous Irish film culture. However, a recent article on both schemes indicates (albeit inadvertently) the extent to which most of these films have eschewed an experimental aesthetic and have instead reverted to the imitation of mainstream cinema forms (Lysaght 2003). For Ruth Lysaght, the problem is one of writing and narrative exposition rather than one of composing, framing, cutting, and juxtaposing shots: 'For although formal experimentation is important, it is secondary to real stories, to what Lelia Doolan refers to as "gut feeling, creative intelligence [which] reflect the society we're living in"' (Lysaght 2003: 36). In my view, this kind of logic is detrimental to the development of a visually distinctive cinema for Ireland, and I doubt that it has much to offer the promotion and 'modernisation' of the Irish language. However, *Éireville* (Finlan, 2001) appears to be one of Lasair's more intriguing productions: "This version of unreality was shot in colour and transferred to black and white in the edit – an innovation in the digital format." (Lysaght 2003: 37) It has to be said that this film is also an imitation, but at least it is attempting to imitate something worth watching, *Alphaville* (Godard, 1965). Mind you, it was also Jean-Luc Godard who once remarked that "a short film does not have the time to think".

Conclusion

In a famous sequence from *Hush-a-Bye-Baby* (Harkin, 1989), a nationalist youth is bewildered to find himself conversing with a British soldier in Irish. Harkin's film is relentless in its interrogation of prescribed notions of sexual, cultural and political identity. The use of the Irish language in this sequence is very obviously 'symbolic' and absurd, although not so absurd as to deny the spectator an instant of ironic identification. This humorous scene (in a film that ruminates on the politics of language acquisition and that moves between urban and Gaeltacht locations) is just one of several 'gaps' that are allowed to appear throughout the narrative. In a sense, there is an Irish-language film within *Hush-a-Bye-Baby* (within its 'gaps') and this possibility creates a connection between the lesser-used language and the lesser-made cinema. The filmic territory inhabited by Quinn (and visited by others) must be recognised and developed more thoroughly by the present generation of Irish-language filmmakers. This would make a significant contribution to the emergence of independent film culture in Ireland, a film culture that might at least succeed in disassociating some 'contemporary Irish cinema' from most of the mainstream.

References

Cinegael, 2003, *Bob Quinn: Film Maker, Writer, and Photographer*, http://www.conamara.org/filmogr.htm#

Lysaght, Ruth, 2003, 'Súil Nua: Oscailt, Lasair, and Contemporary Irish Language Film', *Film Ireland* 90: 36-37.

McLoone, Martin, 1994, 'National Cinema and Cultural Identity: Ireland and Europe', In eds. John Hill, Martin McLoone and Paul Hainsworth, *Border Crossing: Film in Ireland, Britain and Europe*, Belfast: Institute of Irish Studies. 146-173.

McLoone, Martin, 2000, *Irish Film: The Emergence of a Contemporary Cinema*. London: BFI.

O'Brien, Harvey, 2000, 'Projecting the Past: Historical Documentary in Ireland', *Historical Journal of Film, Radio and Television* 20.3: 335-350.

Pettitt, Lance, 2000, *Screening Ireland: Film and Television Representation*. Manchester: Manchester University Press.

Quinn, Bob, 2001, *Maverick: A Dissident View of Broadcasting Today*, Dingle: Brandon Press.

White, Jerry, 2003a, 'Translating Ireland Back into Éire: Gael Linn and Film Making in Irish', *Éire-Ireland* 37.1/2: 106-122.

White, Jerry, 2003b, 'The Films of Bob Quinn: Towards an Irish Third Cinema', http://www.conamara.org/biogr.htm#

The Coming of the Radio

Alan Titley

Language lives within a sound system. What we hear in our parents first mewings and cooings, and even in the first gurglings and burpings is our first language. It is crackle and hum.

Language is the original glug of the world and its last breath. It is what we do all day and every day. It is the unconscious sea on which we float. It is the gabble in which the least thought-out grunt has the same sound-status as the most profound philosophical probe. It is the unprivileged piffle up and against the royal road of the printed word.

Irish and Scottish Gaelic and Ulsterish were unfortunate, or fortunate, in being bunged into the back. Our languages did not sing on the Kings' or the Protectors' or the Pretenders' or the rePublicans' highways.

They sang in the backwoods and skulked in the alleys. They mirked in the mire and slurrupped in the slurk. They sang songs unsown and savoured the syllables of spinnings and spoots.

But print gave proper standing to their prattle. Print privileged the power-brokers, those who wanted to tie meaning to a tight corner. Books bent meaning to the best of being. Letters gave learning its longed-for grip.

Out of the corners the Bible gave tongue to certainty. Hidden syllables swallowed hard and held their lips. Deep down there glottals stuck as thran as a donkey. They ranthered on with rhyme but no reason. Words craked from culchie to grulshy. We spoke but were not spancelled.

Beyond the blackbible the unechoed utterance spread. Into the schoolroom with feruled regularity; and into the newspaper with neutered narrative; and through the polity with policed meaning.

But without these inpalings, below the stock of dictionaries, beyond the march of townspeak life was lovingly lived. People spoke the spake and crawked the talk. Words whemmled what was writ and werded what was expected. Away out there in the Garden of Gamblers or in Rory's Castle, or beyond in the unimaginative Ballynoo, or below in the blytheless Newbliss people done their doings.

What was right was what was read in the schoolroom, and in the kirk or chapel, imagined in the church. Standards descended from above, from God in his heaven, from what was right with the world. Magic joined the civic dance and diswondered the word.

Grammer laughed in all the books at its new place and status, and then balked and squealed and slowly paled as the regular did tighten. Irish, Ulsterish, bad English felt the prong of paid propriety.

But people still spoke their speech in grammar beyond book and bell and candle. They speechified and spluttered and stutteringly stammered, or if you like, just talked in house and field and haggard.

And when books came down to grab and pierce it, talk wafted into the air and smoked abroad, and thusintegrated out there with the silence. Words ran away from the legal lexicographers, from the lovely lies, from the lying down of the law. Words winged with wonther and with ways. Out there in the sticks what was writ did not run.

The wireless became wordful. Released the ghost from the machine and tore up the page. The primful passed away and we returned to the rough ground. What had been scriptly spiked rang and raired. Parts of speech fled from from chapter and versed in the corner of mountain mouths. What glue had gooed together gums began to take apart. Ourselves we moan and ululate, oursouls we laugh and sing and scotch and scour, and universilly protest eirenicons with others.

Now we can gaelicly gabble across the globe or commune with the next community. We can be somethings to us and something to others. We are vaigs venting our sweetness on the asserted airs. We have wound our voices around our wtongues.

Spiorad

Trevor Ó Clochartaigh

Is onóir mhór dhom go n-iarrfaí orm páipéar a scríobh don ócáid thábhachtach seo. Is oth liom nár fhéad mé a bheith in bhur láthair ach tá súil agam go gcuirfidh mo chuid tuairimí leis an díospóireacht bhríomhar a bhí agaibh.

Cuid lárnach de phobal ar bith ná an 'spiorad' atá acu. Léiríonn spiorad pobail a láidreacht ó thaobh cultúr, teanga, féinmhuinín, omós dá gcúlra agus misneach le tabhairt faoin úireacht. Tá Spiorad na Gaeltachta lagaithe go mór le tamall de bhlianta, spiorad an ghlúin óg ach go h-áirithe. Tá gá le gníomh a dhéanamh le caomhnú a dhéanamh ar an spiorad seo agus sílimse gurb é an mhodh is éifeachtaí leis seo a dhéanamh ná tré mheán na n-ealaíona.

Is gá Spiorad na drámaíochta a neartú, Spiorad na Dearcealaíona, an Cheoil agus na Litríochta. Tríd mheáin na h-ealaíona ardóidh muid meanman agus neart phobal na Gaeltachta agus na nGael ar fud na tíre agus thar lear. Beidh sin mar thaca agus mar eiseamláir dóibh siúd a mhaireann i gcultúir bheaga cosúil linn thar lear. Cothóidh sin ceangal agus comhoibriú leo siúd, ar mhaithe lenár gcultúir go léir.

Crann Taca

I láthair na huaire tá bearna an-mhór idir lucht cruthaithe na n-ealaíon agus a lucht maoinithe. Go minic bíonn an-chuid smaointí, tograí agus gníomhaíochtaí ealaíona ar siúl ach teipeann orthu de bharr easpa cumais, taithí agus spéise le dul i ngleic leis an gcóras maorlathach maoinithe. Tá gá le heagraíocht leis an dá thaobh a thabhairt níos gaire dá chéile má tá todhchaí folláin le bheith ag na healaíon Ghaelacha. Tá gá le h-eagraíochtaí eatramhacha cosúil le Proiseact nan Ealan in Alban le tograí ealaíona a shíolrú agus a chothú tré taithí a chur ar fáil agus iarrataisí ar thacaíocht airgid a réiteach don lucht maoinithe. Tá gá le meascán de thograí a chur ar bun agus iad a fhás chuig staid ina mbéidís mór go leor le seasamh ar a gcosa féin. Tá sé tábhhachtach meas agus omós an lucht maoinithe a fháil tré thograí fuinniúla, samhlaíocha a chur chun cinn agus bunús maith a chur futhú ó thaobh fóirne agus riaradh de. Is crann taca a bheadh ansin a mbeadh ealaíontóirí in ann brath air len iad a thabhairt ar aghaidh ó thaobh saothar agus gairmiúlachta de.

Drochstaid na Gaeilge sna Gaeltachtaí

Tá géarghá faoi láthair ann le gníomhaíocht a dhéanamh maidir le cúrsaí forbartha na Gaeilge i measc an aos-óg. Tá caighdeán na Gaeilge scríofa agus léite ag titim go tubaisteach sna scoileanna agus sna teaghlaigh Ghaeltachta. Tá sé rí-shoiléir go bhfuil ag teip go hiomlán ar an gcóras oideachais an scéal seo a leigheas agus go bhfuil sé riachtanach ag eagraíochtaí cultúrtha agus sóisialta, Údarás na Gaeltachta ach go háirithe, gníomhú chun an an meath seo a cheartú.

Gníomhaíocht Teangan tré mheán na Drámaíochta

De réir an taithí atá agam ag plé le cúrsaí drámaíochta agus na meáin chumarsáide ag leibhéal scoile, pobail agus go gairmiúil feictear dhom nach leor feachtaisí teangabhunaithe leis an Ghaeilge a thárrtháil mar gnáth-theanga labhartha. Foghlamaíonn daoine níos fearr tré páirt a ghlacadh i ngníomhaíocht thaitneamach tré mheán na teangan. Is í an drámaíocht an gníomhaíochtaí is éifeachtaí agus is taitneamhaí chuige seo.

Níl seo fíor i gcomhthéacs na Gaeilge amháin, ach sna mionteangacha thré chéile. Nuair a bheidh gnéithe éagsúla den chleachtas drámaíochta seo forbartha, d'fhéadfaí iad a úsáid in aon áit ar fud an Domhain. Is é sin go bhféadfadh lucht na dteangacha neamhfhorleathana ár sampla a thógáil, an cur chuige a bheadh forbartha againn a ghlacadh agus a gcuid teangacha féin a fhorbairt ar an slí chéanna. Tá sé ciallmhar ceangal a chothú agus tionscnamh a fhorbairt i gcomhair lenár gcomhleacaithe in Albain agus san Bhriotáin, mar shampla.

Níl aon draíocht ná mistéir mór ag baint leis an gcineál seo forbartha. Is tré mheán na drámaíochta, cultúir agus litríochta is mó a tugadh an teanga agus an cultúr atá againn ar lámh ó ghlúin go glúin go dtí seo. Nílimíd ach ag foghlaim ó shainscil ár sinsir. Ag athchothú an 'Spiorad' nádúrtha atá ionainn.

Spiorad na Drámaíochta

Sa drámaíocht tugtar le chéile cuid mhaith de na scileanna a bhíonn sna réimsí ealaíona éagsúla – an litríocht, an taispeántas, dearcealaíon, ceol, an aisteoireacht agus na hilmheáin. Is ealaíon pobail agus poiblí í. Baineann sí le ócáidí agus bailiú slua. Tá sé nádúrtha go dtosófaí ar 'Spiorad' a chothú dtús báire tré mheán na Drámaíochta. Chuige sin is gá cur chuige cuimsitheach agus uilíoch a thógáil leis an drámaíocht a fhorbairt ar gach leibhéal. Is tograí neamhspléacha atá i ngach ceann a luafaidh mé anseo agus d'fhéadfaí tabhairt fúthu ar bhealach céimnithe. Ach tugann gach togra acu tacaíocht dhá chéile agus beidh comhoibriú praicticiúil idir iad agus na daoine a bheidh páirteach iontu.

Feidhm na Drámaíochta

Tá sé thar a bheith soiléir gur bealach iontach taitneamhach í an drámaíocht leis an duine féin a fhorbairt, ó thaobh féinmheas, féinmhuinín, teacht i láthair agus misnigh de. Seo tréithe gur gá dúinn díriú ach go h-áirithe orthu i gcomhthéacs páistí le Gaeilge má theastaíonn uainn go mbeidh siad gníomhach sna pobail dár díobh iad.

Bíonn tionchar i bhfad níos leithne ag an drámaíocht ar dhaoine ná díreach dul chuig, nó páirt a ghlacadh i ndrámaí. Leathnaíonn an drámaíocht tuiscint an duine ar an saol, cothaíonn sé samhlaíocht agus mothúcháin an duine agus is inneall í an drámaíocht leis an scríbhneoireacht, aisteoireacht, dearadh agus léiriú a chur chun cinn.

An Drámaíocht mar Fheithicil

Is feithicil í an drámaíocht inar féidir linn forbairt teangan agus chultúrtha a chur chun cinn. Ach tá bealaigh éagsúla leis an fheithicil céanna a chur ar bóthar. Tá géarghá dar liomsa le meascán de thograí a mbeadh straitéisí éagsúla acu leis an drámaíocht a chothú, a neartú agus a chur chun cinn ag gach leibhéal de phobal na Gaeltachta agus na Gaeilge. Déanfaidh mé cur síos orthu ceann i ndiaidh a chéile.

Drámaíocht Bunscoile

Is dóigh liom go bhfuil faillí iomlán á dhéanamh ag an Roinn Oideachas maidir leis na riachtanais curaclaim i leith na drámaíochta atá leagtha síos acu féin. Ní féidir a bheith ag súil go mbeadh gach múinteoir oilte leis an drámaíocht a theagasc. Is féidir leo roinnt obair a dhéanamh maidir le drámaí Nollaig is eile ach tá gá le speisialtóirí a thabharfadh cuairt ar scoileanna go rialta leis an ndrámaíocht a theagasc.

Dár ndóigh sna Gaeltachtaí agus sna Gaelscoileanna ba chóir go mbeadh an tseirbhís seo ar fáil tré mheán na Gaeilge. Measann muid gur rud ar nós uair a chloig sa tseachtain le gach rang a bheadh i gceist. Bheadh na ranganna bunaithe ar chluichí drámaíochta agus cumadóireachta.

D'éirigh le mo chomhlacht féin, Sin Sin! teo., a mhacasamhail seo a chur ar fáil sna Gaeltachtaí ar fad, ar bhun píolóta ar feadh tamaill, faoi choimirce Údarás na Gaeltachta, agus d'éirigh an-mhaith leis. Tá a leithéad céanna a bheartú ag Pléaráca i mbliana agus guím gach rath orthu, ach tá gá forbairt níos forleithne a dhéanamh ar an gcleachtas.

D'fhéadfadh an-tionchar a bheith ag an gcineál seo oibre an-tapaidh ar chaighdeán Gaeilge na ndaltaí scoile. Seo sampla amháin ó mo thaithí féin leis an tionchar a mhíniú. Thug mé rang uair a chloig amháin i scoil i mbreac Ghaeltacht i nDeisceart Mhaigh Eo. Nuair a chuaigh mé ar ais an tseachtain dár gcionn dúirt an múinteoir leis go raibh na páistí ag spraoi na cluichí a mhúin sé dóibh sa gclós agus go raibh méadú 50% tagtha ar an bhfoclóir Gaeilge a bhí acu taréis rang amháin a dhéanamh leo.

Beidh gá le tacaíocht láidir d'fhorbairt don chineál seo ó thaobh acmhainní daonna agus airgid de ach is fiú an tairbhe an trioblóid. Freisin bheadh gá buíon teagascóirí a oiliúnt don obair már níl na scileanna a theastaíonn forbartha mar is ceart go fóill againn. Ní leor aisteoir a chur isteach i scoil, is gá go mbeadh scil na teagascóireachta forbartha iontu chomh maith.

Drámaíocht san Oideachas (Theatre In Education)

Tá Drámaíocht san Oideachas ar bun in Éirinn le beagnach 30 bliain. Séard is Drámaíocht san Oideachas ann ná drámaíocht a chuireann complachtaí gairmiúla drámaíochta ar fáil i saoráid oideachasúil. Go bunúsach léiríonn an chomhlacht dráma atá dírithe ar aoisghrúpa faoi leith a bhfuil téama oideachasúil leis agus léiríonn siad é i scoileanna. Cuireann Oifigeach Oideachais an chompántais pacáistí d'ábhar oideachasúil ar fáil do na múinteoirí chomh maith.

Is iad na príomhchompántais in Éirinn ná TEAM i mBaile Átha Cliath, Grafitti i gCorcaigh, Barnstorm i gCill Chainnigh agus Replay i dTuaisceart Éireann. Le cüpla nbliain anuas rinne Grafitti (le tacaíocht ó Údarás na Gaeltachta) turais chuig na scoileanna Gaeltachta le leagan Gaeilge do dhráma a forbraíodh i mBéarla. Ba mhaith ann iad. Ach is é an scannal is measa ná nach bhfuil aon Chompántas Drámaíocht san Oideachas ag freastal ar an Iarthar ná ar Iarthuaisceart na tíre, beag ná mór, i mBéarla ná i nGaeilge.

Tá sé riachtanach go mbeadh Drámaíocht san Oideachas (DSO) á sholáthar do scoileanna Gaelacha agus Gaeltachta ar bhonn rialta le go mbeidh deis ag páistí taithí a fháil ar ócáidí amharclainne. Bíonn an ócáid seo ar nós an sorcas ag teacht go dtí an baile, bíonn draíocht iontach ag baint leis, ach freisin is ócáid í inar féidir an Ghaeilge a chur trasna mar theanga bhríomhar, shuimiúil, thaitneamhach. Tugann an DSO eiseamláir iontach d'aisteoirí óga agus fostaíocht dó roinnt mhaith daoine chomh maith.

Drámaíocht Óige / Amharclann na nÓg

Creidim gur cheart go mbeadh an Drámaíocht Bunscoile, mar atá mínithe thuas, ar fáil do gach dalta bunscoile i ngach scoil. Ach nuair a thagann tú chuig aoisghrúpa iarbhunscoile caithfidh tú oibriú le daoine a bhfuil fiorshuim acu san ábhar agus daoine eile nach bhfuil, a ligeann ag plé le gníomhaíochtaí eile. Is dóigh liom gurb é an bealach is éifeachtaí leis seo a dhéanamh ná gréasán de chlubanna drámaíochta nó 'Youth Theatres' as Gaeilge a bhunú sna ceantracha Gaeltachta éagsúla agus ar fud na tíre. Tá a leithéad ar fáil i mBéarla agus iad á riaradh faoi scáth an 'National Association for Youth Drama' sna 26 condae. D'fhéadfaí drámaí, ranganna drámaíochta agus ceardlanna a chur ar fáil do dhaoine sna clubanna seo. D'fhéadfaí smaoiniú ar dhioplóma FETAC/HETAC sa drámaíocht a dhéanamh thar tréimhse dhá bhliain leis na rannpháirtithe le go mbeadh cáilíocht acu. (Déantar seo mar shampla in Galway Youth Theatre).

Lasair / Amharclann Náisiúnta na nÓg

Ba cheart leanacht gach bliain le 'Lasair', Dianchúrsa Aisteoireachta do dhaoine óga idir 18 & 23 bliain d'aois a d'eagraigh Sin Sin! teo. agus Tosg, faoi scáth Iomairt Cholmcille le tacaíocht ó Proiseact nan Ealan. Cuirtear an cúrsa seo ar fáil sa Samhradh ar feadh trí seachtaine, do dhaoine óga as Éireann agus dAlbain agus déantar léiriú poiblí mar chuid den chúrsa. Bíonn sé dírithe ar dhaoine atá ag iarraidh traenáil 'ghairmiúil' sa drámaíocht. Bíonn na léirithe a dhéantar mar eiseamláir do dhaoine óga eile agus thabharfaí sprioc maith dóibh siúd a bheadh sna clubanna drámaíochta chomh maith mar bheidís ag iarraidh a bheith maith go leor le dul ar aghaidh chuige. Freisin cothóidh sé ceangail idir scoth na n-aisteoirí óga ó na Gaeltachtaí éagsúla agus ó Albain.

Oiliúnt Ghairmiúil

Níl aon chúrsa oiliúna Drámaíochta tríú leibhéal i nGaeilge le fáil in aon áit sa tír seo go bhfios dom. Tá sé de cheart ag aisteoirí óga a leithéad a bheith acu. Go deimhin tá a leithéid riachtanach má táimid le teagascóirí, aisteoirí, scríbhneoirí dearthóirí agus léiritheoirí a chothú ar bhonn rialta. Bhí caint ar feadh tamall ar Dioplóma sa Drámaíocht in Ollscoil na hÉireann Gaillimh, chuirfinn fáilte mhór roimhe sin, ach is dóigh liom go bhfuil gá le dioplóma de chineál eile, nach mbeidh an oiread béim ar acadúlacht, macasamhail an chúrsa FETAC/HETAC, a bhféadfadh aon duine cur isteach air, agus ina mbeadh an béim ar obair phraicticiúil agus meastóireacht leanúnach seachas aistí agus scrúdaithe.

Drámaíocht Ghairmiúil

Tá géarghá le forbairt a dhéanamh ar Dhrámaíocht Ghairmiúil tré Ghaeilge. Níl Amharclann De hÍde ag feidhmiú a thuilleadh, tá Aisling Ghéar i mBéal Feirste agus tá roinnt léirithe suntasacha i nGaeilge déanta ag Amharclann na Cathrach, ag Diarmuid De Faoite an Taibhdhearc i nGaillimh agus Amharclann na Mainistreach. Ach is dóigh linn go bhfuil áit ann do chomplacht eile ar mhúnla 'Na Fánaithe' a raibh mé féin páirteach iontu sna 90aí, a bheadh ina bhuíon beag aisteoirí agus dramadóirí an mbeadh an bhéim acu ar dhrámaíocht atá gar don phobal a léiriú

Bheadh compántas gairmiúil ina eiseamláir do dhaoine óga agus aisteoirí. Bheadh sé ábalta scríbhneoireacht úr a ghríosú agus a chothú. Bheadh sé ina dheis fostaíochta freisin dóibh siúd a dteastaíonn uathu an drámaíocht a leanacht mar shlí bheatha.

Focal Scoir

Tá deis iontach againn 'Spiorad' nua a chothú i measc óg agus aosta na Gaeltachta. Tá gá daoine a aimsiú atá sásta tabhairt faoin obair sin agus gá na polasaithe cearta a chur ar bun agus tacaíocht chuí stáit a chinntiú don obair. Más féidir sin a dhéanamh bheadh dóchas níos mó agam don teanga. Muna ndéantar beidh an scéal níos measa faoi cheann deich nó scór bliain eile. Ach is fiú iarracht a dhéanamh ach é a dhéanamh go luath agus go críochnúil.

Ros na Rún: Alternative Gaelic Universe

Gordon McCoy

In this paper, I examine the Irish language soap opera *Ros na Rún*, setting the show within the context of language revivalism in Ireland.[1] The Gaelic movement is caught between two kinds of ideology which inform minority language revivals. Essentialising ideologies maintain that a unique and immutable world-view is borne by each language, reifying and 'freezing' a particular culture. There is a focus on inner purity, boundary maintenance with defined 'Others', and an organisation of semantic maps which 'carve up' reality (Glaser 2002, Street 1993). A distinctive traditional culture is elaborated as the language becomes a link with ancestral life. The problem with such an approach is that it mitigates against individual creativity and promotes inflexibility, artificiality and decay. For example, learners of the language may find difficulty in being accepted as members of the speech community (Glaser 2002: 32-33).

However, individuals are not constructs of culture, but are culturally creative and agents of cultural change (Cohen 1994; Lavie et al. 1993). A dynamic approach to language revival privileges choice, change, hybridity and multiple realities which allow for different ways in which to imagine the language and its speakers. The drawback of this approach is that it can create a cultural free-for-all leading to the loss of distinctiveness, inviting accusations that the language group has no specific culture and is undeserving of public support (Glaser 2002).

Language revivals utilise elements of different ideologies, reconstructing and modifying tradition to meet the demands of modernity; each generation selects, elaborates and transforms the tradition it inherits (May 2001: 14, Lavie et al. 1993: 5). There are both essentialising and dynamic ideologies at work in the Irish language world, but there is an increasing trend towards dynamic, post-modern approaches to the language in the Republic of Ireland in recent years. This reflects growing post-nationalist sentiment in the state and the fact that most speakers of Irish are learners who infuse their language activities with their own urbanised values.[2] Furthermore, native Irish speakers are also keen to demolish 'reservation' stereotypes that set them apart from their English-speaking counterparts. Such stereotypes are intended to eulogise them but often have the opposite effect.

In many ways, *Rós na Rún* is a standard soap opera, which adheres to the conventions of the genre. It has the soap staples of disposable villains, long-lost relatives, issue-led storylines, end-of-series cliffhangers, and even a little product placement.[3] Yet the fact that the show is in the Irish language introduces a surreal element that is sometimes reflected in the storylines.

---

[1] I would like to thank Sinéad Ní Shuinéar for video-recording *Ros na Rún* on my behalf over a long five year period, for sharing with me on 7 June 2002 her interview of 31 May 2002 with Trevor Ó Clochartaigh about *Ros na Rún*, and for all her other help and support in preparing this paper.

[2] In Northern Ireland Irish is essentialised as a symbol of nationalist identity, and pluralist discourses and cultural hybridity are stymied by the cultural conflict.

[3] Eagle-eyed viewers would have noted that in the village bar, locals drank *Beamish* rather than the more popular *Guinness*. In one episode, almost every character was wearing the pink ribbon of the breast cancer awareness campaign. The serial's producer told me campaigners had requested this, and the actors were happy to comply free of charge.

The title of the show is a double-entendre in the language, for *Ros na Rún* means 'Headland of Sweethearts' or 'Headland of Secrets'. The programme is set in a seaside village in the Gaeltacht, or Irish-speaking district, within commuting distance of the university city of Galway. As such, *Ros na Rún* is situated somewhere along the rural-urban continuum, much like the village of Spiddal, where the programme is filmed.

According to essentialists, the Irish language expresses distinctly Irish and anti-English values, which its speakers literally embody. The relationship between nationalism and Irish is naturalised; one becomes more Irish and less English by speaking Irish. Distinctiveness is also expressed by romantic ruralism; the Gaeltacht is represented as a rural idyll in which tradition is unscathed by modern influences, and a mecca for learners seeking pure idiomatic Irish and authentic rural traditions. Irish speakers are portrayed as devout Catholics who play indigenous sports such as hurling and Gaelic football. These views of Irish predominated in the Irish state for many years since its inception. Essentialising ideologies are prescriptive, stressing conformity and silencing dissenting voices; for example, censorship was exercised on sexual topics in Irish language vocabulary and literature.

Yet *Ros na Rún*, a short bus journey from the nightclubs of Galway, is no reservation, and its inhabitants overturn every romantic stereotype of the idealised Gael.

Cultural Purity

Leaving aside issues of language, which are discussed below, *Ros na Rún* is clearly part of the broad, modern world. Racial purity is dramatically challenged by the arrival of a black character who speaks perfect Irish. People dress in modern fashions and their work involves computers and broadcasting technology; they return from long-term residence in England and America with new ideas and values. Life imitates art as the young professionals of *Ros na Rún* are similar to those who are filming them; the creation of the Irish language television channel TG4 led to the creation of 350 jobs and an influx of audio-visual workers (dubbed 'the Connemara 4 set') into Spiddal and its environs. These Gaelic professionals have infused the area with a new generation living and working through Irish (Hegarty 2003b).

The archetypal noble Gael of the past shunned 'foreign' English games such as cricket and soccer. Significantly, when a sports team is organised in *Ros na Rún*, it plays soccer rather than Gaelic football. Yet this is an authentic, if officially unrecognised tradition, in the Gaeltacht because many people living there are enthusiastic about the game after periods spent working in Britain[4].

Religiosity

The archetypal noble Gael is a deeply religious character – a devout Catholic. Yet the only conventionally pious character in the show is gently mocked for her beliefs; her daughter-in-law is horrified when she hangs a Sacred Heart of Jesus

---

[4]   Soccer is increasingly popular in Ireland as a whole due to the successes of the Irish team in the World Cup.

picture in her flat. The scene is a metaphor for the clash of secular and religious Ireland expressed in terms of the generation gap. Another character with 'spiritual' leanings is a new-age hippy, drawn to Celtic mysticism, who wages endless visual war on stereotypical Gaelic dress-sense. The parish priest is a 'non-entity' who makes an annual appearance in connection with ritual weddings and funerals. He is not part of village life and no-one is ever seen going to Mass.

Furthermore, the presence of two openly gay men challenges the sexual hegemony of the church. They are represented as responsible adults; one even becomes the surrogate father of an orphaned nephew. Miraculously, the only homophobe in *Ros na Rún* is the odious publican, Tadhg Ó Díreáin, a character with evil intent of Shakespearean proportions.

Nationalism

For some traditionalist learners of Irish, the language embodies their Irish identity; they learn Irish to become more Irish. Native speakers share the nationalist beliefs of these learners but do not base them upon their less selfconscious use of Irish; for them the language expresses regional identities more often than national ones. Learners of Irish in the Republic have also challenged traditional interpretations of the language. Since the 1980s the association of the Irish language with violent nationalism in Northern Ireland was rejected by many south of the border during a process of redefining Irish national identity (Watson 2003: 69).

As such, the characters of *Ros na Rún* are true to form, as Irish politics is never mentioned. In fact, traditional old-style nationalism has only once been touched upon, when the pious shopkeeper wanted to erect a memorial to her grandfather's heroic role in the war of independence. This provoked a neighbour into revealing that he had, in fact, been an informer for the British authorities. Another romantic myth bites the dust.

Harmony with nature

Ros na Rún is set in a village, not in the rural Gaeltacht, as one might expect. There are only two elderly farmers on the show, who are never actually seen farming. One is an inveterate poacher who has to be restrained by the wildlife service from exterminating a rare bat inhabiting his shed. While the noble Gael of yore may have been presented as nature-loving and even part of nature, the characters of *Ros na Rún* only seem to go on nature walks when they are depressed. There is a particular 'bridge of sorrows', frequented by characters who seem to be contemplating throwing themselves into the water beneath. Basically 'nature' in *Ros na Rún* is a depressing place to be, where characters isolate themselves to brood, only to happen upon others who comfort them and invite them to articulate their distress. This is a standard soap device; the park bench in the English soap *Eastenders* serves the same function.

Egalitarianism and Informality

Soaps tend to have few authority figures as central characters, and party politics are never mentioned; a series is often well in advance of contemporary political events, such as elections. British soaps are often preoccupied with class differences, a recurring theme of British life, but this is not the case in *Ros na Rún*. Rather, the ideal of the classless egalitatarian Ireland is rigorously enforced in the soap, where class snobbery is regularly mocked. Older characters are not presented simply as icons of post-modern irony (Lysaght 2002:2); they rarely teased by younger characters for being out of touch, and locals of all ages socialise together in the pub and café. Authoritarian figures, such as the priest, politicians and policemen, are noticeably absent, presenting a community with little social stratification. Employers and employed socialise and even sleep together. Formal encounters are usually between locals and outside agencies which do not represent the best interests of the community. Thus the general soap trend of omitting authority figures serves an Irish ideal.

Clearly some aspects of tradition are unattractive and best left behind. Tadhg and Angela, the publican and his wife, have a marriage based on the traditional primacy of economic survival rather than contemporary romantic attraction; Angela is constantly attempting to establish her own economic independence, only to be thwarted by Tadhg at every turn. Other characters in the soap, as well as the viewers, are led to view the marriage as a sham, and to wonder what keeps the pair together, considering the level of mistrust between them.

Themes of *Ros na Rún* have included such social issues as tax evasion, drunk driving, wife-beating, and heroin addiction. There have also been personal tragedies such as miscarriage, rape, abortion, infertility, and dilemmas such as dubious paternity and confusion over sexual orientation. Controversial storylines have led to descriptions of *Ros na Rún* such as 'Gomorrah in the Gaeltacht' (Hegarty 2003a).

These issues beg the question as to how real or surreal the soap is. *Ros na Rún* is subtly different from the world we live in. Some of these differences derive from the necessities of the soap opera format. For example, time and memory are 'compressed' as viewers are not expected or required to remember incidents which happened in previous series. In *Ros na Rún* one character 'forgets' her abortion, only to remember it a year later, in time for her to exit the serial on a round-the-world recovery tour.

Another departure from reality is the lack of characterisation and hyperrealism, particularly in regard to the male characters. The evil pub landlord is clearly the villain we love to hate, a two-dimensional stock-in-trade soap character. Yet even his bitterest enemies have to drink in his pub, as he has the only tavern in town, an unlikely prospect in an Irish village! In one storyline, two teenage sisters enter various confusing liaisons with the same boy, resulting in an unwanted pregnancy. The soap focuses on the emotional distress of the girls, but the boy is merely a hapless sideline, whose function is to impregnate the 'wrong' girl, thus setting the scene for inter-familial battles and a 'convenient' miscarriage (keeping both the girls active socially and available for future lovers). The emphasis on the sisters and lack of characterisation of the boyfriend reflects the fact that the core audience for soaps are women.

The lack of authority figures is also conspicuous, as discussed above. The absence of the priest is a nod towards greater secularism, but in reality the priest is still an important member of a rural Irish community, hardly the out-of-touch automaton who makes an annual clockwork appearance in *Ros na Rún*. While the presence of gay people in the Gaeltacht is validated by the soap, their total acceptance in *Ros na Rún*, especially as a live-in couple, may be rather optimistic. Furthermore, one of them is in effect a 'gay dad', which would surely draw the attention of social workers in a real Gaeltacht. Certainly, the gay storylines of *Ros na Rún* have attracted protests from viewers. The show's publicist told me how she arrived at work one morning after the screening of a gay storyline to discover her answering machine full of complaints that the gays ruined the '*iomhá dheas Chaitliceach na Gaeltachta*' ('nice Catholic image of the Gaeltacht').

Ros na Rún creates an alternative universe. The mixture of reality and unreality is in greatest evidence in the linguistic format of the show. In terms of reality, one significant feature is the lack of a uniform or national dialect of Irish - the characters are faithful to their own dialects. In fact the show's writers allow the actors to ad-lib as much as they like. This process creates authentic records of dialects, and even sub-dialects, of Ulster, Connemara, and Munster Irish. English language subtitles help learners and Irish speakers who have problems understanding some of the dialects.[5]

The most striking and realistic feature of the characters is their use of Irish and English. Irish speakers, who are all bilingual, use English words and phrases in their speech to swear, to emphasise a point, to express humour, and to express English-language concepts, such as 'stir-fry' or 'control freak', for which there are no ready Irish equivalents. The following examples will illustrate:

(1)   Tá droch-**feeling** agam
        I have a bad feeling
(2)   Nil ann ach **friggin' bastard**
        He's only a friggin' bastard
(3)   **Will you just** fág é
        Will you just leave it
(4)   An bhfuil tú ag **feel**áil **alright?**
        Are you feeling alright?
(5)   Is dócha nach bhfuil **two out of three** ró-dhona
        I guess two out of three isn't bad
(6)   Tá an Vince sin ar **power trip**
        That Vince is on a power trip
(7)   Tá mé ag **hoover**áil
        I'm hoovering

Furthermore, there is a realistic portrayal of intergenerational differences in the use of Irish and English; the older characters speak a more idiomatic Irish largely unadulterated by English, whereas the younger characters pepper their speech which English words, and use more calques. Native speakers of Irish, when talking to their close friends or colleagues, are not always conscious of switching languages and this is so in *Ros na Rún*. In a way, the series is a soap which happens to be in Irish, not a soap operating as a vehicle for that language. In the show, Irish is not a topic of conversation – it is not an issue.

---

[5] The translations are done with a cavalier informality, often reflecting the English of Galway than standard English; the phrase '*Maith go leor*' (literally 'good enough') was translated as 'Right, so'. One viewer told me that he has noticed how sexual references made by one character have not appeared in the translations.

The use of English in *Ros na Rún* has incensed both Irish language revivalists and   some native speakers, who criticise the show for the use of *Béarlachas* (anglicisms), presenting Irish as a pidgin language with a bad grammar, interpenetrated by English. For some critics, native speakers would or should not use such 'bad' Irish[6]. Others accept *Ros na Rún* Irish as a linguistic reality but object to this being broadcast into homes as an exemplar for learners.

The linguistic laissez-faire of the actors was confronted by official linguistic prescriptivism. The Irish of *Ros na Rún* has been the cause of some debate within TG4 itself, particularly as the soap's sponsors, Foras na Gaeilge, complained about the quality of the language on the serial. The show's producers received a letter from the TG4 management with a series of complaints: the amount of unnatural anglicisms on the serial; the lack of improvement in the Irish of the non-native speaking actors, which renders their Irish difficult to understand; and the lack of Irish to be heard on the set. Copies of the letter were displayed on the set, but some of the cast paid little attention. One actor explained the lack of concern in terms of the generation gap, '*Níor chuir sé isteach ar chuile dhuine. Ní bheadh an tuiscint céanna ag na daoine óga. Maireann siad i saol eile.*' ('It didn't bother everyone. The young people would not understand. They live in another world.') (*Foinse* Deireadh Fómhair 2001, p. 2). Since 2002, however, viewers have noted that the use of English has declined on *Ros na Rún* and purist protests have become less common.

The criticism of purists is reflected in the antics of the sole linguistic authority figure in *Ros na Rún*. This is Labhrás, the absurdly comical figure of the radio station manager. His pedantic insistence on 'proper' grammar and pronunciation alienate not only his employees, one of whom nicknames him 'Mr. Genitive Case', but local people generally.

In one scene, Labhrás offers a classic grammar textbook to Caitríona, an employee of his, implying that her colloquial speech falls short of guidelines set out decades earlier. The authors are the Christian Brothers, a teaching order recently associated with the physical and sexual abuse of the children in their charge. Caitríona refers to this '*drochainm*' ('bad reputation'), rejecting the package deal of theocracy, hypocrisy and cultural immutability Labhrás offers. The scene confronts generations, genders and ideologies as well as linguistic issues. Labhrás presses the book on Caitríona, telling her to ignore media mischief-making, and insisting no-one ever found the Christian Brothers guilty of bad grammar. Caitríona rolls her eyes, a reaction invited of the viewers, who collectively recall their schooldays struggling with Irish grammar and pedantic teachers. To make matters more absurd, Labhrás acquired Irish as a second language, while the employee is a native speaker refusing to conform to imposed notions of purity.

The linguistic premise of *Ros na Rún* is deeply surreal, evoking a Gaelic utopia. The most strikingly unreal aspect of *Ros na Rún* is that the show portrays characters which speak the three main dialects of Irish, yet manage to understand one another without difficulty or comment. This is a ploy designed by the show's

---

[6]   The satirical newspaper column *Ar son na cúise* ('For the sake of the cause') lampooned the language of the show as '*RosnaRúnais*', and announced that language experts had discovered it was related to Irish (*Foinse* 6 Deireadh Fómhair 2002, pg 29).

producers to cater for Irish speakers from all parts of Ireland, thus increasing the audience. But the ease of mutual comprehension is not borne out by reality. The grammar, pronunciation and lexicon of the three main dialects is so different that speakers of different ones sometimes resort to English to communicate.

In such a mixed linguistic situation, one would assume that Irish speakers would adapt their language in order to be understood by others, yet on the show there is absolutely no trace of dialect accommodation or convergence. In the real Gaelic world, Irish speakers often comment on the differences in each other's dialects.[7] Yet in *Ros na Rún* no-one even comments on anybody else's dialect, except Tadhg, the evil pub owner, who mocks his wife's Donegal Irish, which is simply another manifestation of his odiousness.

Also significant is the fact that learners' Irish, spoken by a number of core characters, some of whom are represented as incomers, is given equal validity with all other dialects. The learners are confident and fluent despite their stilted pronunciations, and no one ever teases them. Yet viewers are often amused to hear a strong Dublin accent in Irish and on a website chatroom one fan commented on a character, 'Dave should be selling bananas on Moore Street' (a working-class open air market in Dublin) (*www.rosnarun.com*: accessed 1 July 2002). The Irish language movement has produced, through Gaelic-medium education, a large number of young people who speak fluent, but 'imperfect' Irish, described memorably to me by one teacher as '*Gaeilge líofa lofa*' ('fluent rotten Irish'). The show endorses the place of these young people in the Gaelic world, but spares them the criticism of native speakers who might deter them from speaking Irish.

Ros na Rún is a microcosm of an unproblematically bilingual Ireland in which Irish is unremarkably spoken in *every* context, including by emergency services, hospital and hotel staff, and artists in Dublin art galleries. The reality is very different. It is also extremely unlikely for Irish speakers to address strangers in that language, yet this happens in *Ros na Rún*. Furthermore, leaving aside professional 'strangers', there are few if any communities without English monoglots whose presence forces Irish speakers to switch to English to accommodate them. Yet everyone in *Ros na Rún* speaks Irish.

Tradition and innovation are juxtaposed in many of the serial's themes. An episode screened in June 2002 illustrates this trend, as hidden voices of the Gaelic world come to the fore. The two gay lovers, Tom and Jack, decide to marry, partly because Jack is in danger of losing his life due to a heart complaint. They exchange vows on the beach, a rare moment of happiness on *Ros na Rún* involving a nature scene; yet the privacy of the event hints at the lack of community acceptance. Tom gives Jack his mother's wedding ring, a moment which blends custom and innovation. Jack, switching to English, says the ring 'fits perfectly'. The switch is all the more dramatic as Jack speaks English with a London accent; the character *and* the actor who plays him were reared in an Irish-speaking family in London. Jack's speech incorporates both 'Englishness' (London-accented English) and 'Irishness' (Connemara-accented Irish).[8]

---

[7] This was discovered by an American learner of Irish, who, on noting that most characters in *Ros na Rún* speak Connemara Irish, recounts being told, 'There are a couple of characters from Donegal though. I can't bear to listen to that slag what's-her-name. She sounds like she just walked off a Gaoth Dobhair bog. It's horrible to hear.' (Fallon 2002: 153).

[8] Irish people who speak with English accents are often assumed to have abandoned their Irishness for English values.

In the midst of this contemporary scene there are elements of tradition; Jack reads a centuries-old love poem,[9] and Tom finishes with a traditional toast '*Fad saoil agus bás in Éirinn*' ('Long life and a death in Ireland'). Jack gives Tom his will as their marriage is denied by the state; he wishes to leave his assets to Tom and his 'adopted' son. The scene is certainly novel, as it is the first gay marriage to be screened on Irish television.

Ros na Rún is the flagship series of TG4, a television station which has radically transformed the image of the language. The serial is part of a process of cultural and linguistic hybridity which reconciles the old and the new, English and Irish cultures and languages. The station is influenced by dynamic ideologies of market forces, individualisation, and consumerism. Thus TG4 emphasises drama and popular magazine-style programmes covering leisure and human-interest issues, with 'sexy' presenters and emotive content; English-language subtitles maximise the audience (Watson 2003: 123, 127). Viewers can now see original productions of comedy, the pop charts, cookery shows, an outrageous world travel series, and documentaries on anything from reindeer herders to Chinese politics, as well as dubbed versions of children's programmes including *Pokémon* and *The Muppets*. TG4 uses Irish casually, even allowing mistakes and bad pronunciation; one programme juxtaposes Irish and English, though it is clear which language is there on sufferance (Lysaght 2002: 11).

The fact that these alternatives to traditional models not only exist, but attract a wide audience indicates a revolution in attitudes to the Irish language, no longer the sole preserve of the conservative idealogues or a key to a purer past. Exclusionary prescriptive models are rejected for interaction with the English language and urban values, infusing TG4 with a multitude of voices.

This process has not gone without complaint, as TG4 has been criticised for being aimed at an urban audience and ignoring the concerns of the Gaeltacht (Watson 2003: 123).[10] Irish language broadcasting is caught between a revivalist focus on promoting Irish to English speakers and service provision for existing Irish speakers. Gaeltacht residents criticised TG4 for not having a strong identity, for the use of bad Irish, and for not promoting a positive image of the Gaeltacht, although the station is based in the Galway Gaeltacht (Ó Cinnéide et al 2001: 81).

In 2002, *Ros na Rún* became a teaching tool in the Republic's schools, with videos, worksheets and lesson plans scripts being provided to teachers; the programme is available through the *Ros na Rún* website, *www.rosnarun.com*. In 2003, two hundred secondary schools were using *Ros na Rún* as a tool of instruction, and many teachers have noted an increased interest in visiting the Gaeltacht among their students. The personal and social issues such as teenage pregnancy and drug abuse are very relevant to the teenage viewers, although some teachers are uncomfortable with the ensuing discussions are given advance warning (Holden 2003). The educational system is illustrative of the dominant

---

[9] The poem, '*Ceann Dubh Dílis*' ('Dark True Head') could have a homosexual interpretation, as it relates the passion of a young man who spurns all the girls in a town for a secret love (Ó Tuama and Kinsella 1981: 285).

[10] One complaint that Gaeltacht viewers have is that most TG4 programmes are subtitled in English, which they find distracting; they would prefer subtitles in Irish, which would help them to understand other unfamiliar dialects or unclear speakers. Irish language subtitles are available for *Ros na Rún* on a teletext service.

dynamic between learners and native speakers of Irish. The cultural distance between English and Irish speakers is obscured, as the cultural values accruing to Irish are, for the most part, being transmitted by second language learners (Ó Baoill 1999).

Ros na Rún is certainly popular outside the school domain, attracting 280,000 viewers a week, breaking out of the Irish language 'ghetto' (Holden 2003); in 2001 the *Sunday Times* television critic Liam Fay chose *Ros na Rún* as his favourite serial (Lysaght 2002: 11). The serial is regularly covered in 'soapwatch' columns of the Republic's popular magazines, and in 2003 womens' groups congratulated the serial's producers on a storyline involving wife abuse. These are considerable achievements in Irish language terms, as it is often assumed that anything produced in Irish will be substandard when compared to its English-language equivalent.

Although surreal in terms of creating an Irish language utopia, TG4 is involved in a dialectical relationship with viewers:

> What was first a vision depicted as reality is now becoming more real, as there is a resurgence of interest in language amongst younger people ... [*Ros na Rún*] depicts an Ireland that does not 'really' exist, but is incrementally becoming more plausible (Lysaght 2002: 5, 12)

In terms of cultural politics, the Irish language has two contrasting images in the Republic of Ireland. One is that of officialdom and state cultural restoration, and undoubtedly a state-sponsored Irish language soap is part of this process. Another is that of counter-culture and subversion; a fundamental contradiction in Irish society is that although the state endorses Gaelic revivalism and the constitution recognises Irish as the first official language, Irish speakers are marginalised in many aspects of civil and political culture. As such, Irish speakers often must use minority rights discourses to campaign for the status of the language (Watson 2003). As Irish speakers are minoritised, they can identify with other marginal groups and counter-cultures, challenging prevailing norms in the state. There is also a sense of Irish being a secret or hidden language, enabling speakers to be more controversial in Gaelic (Lysaght 2002: 6); for example, on phone-ins broadcast on the Republic's Irish language radio station, Raidió na Gaeltachta, some callers are blatantly libellous, but the broadcasters are relatively unconcerned, as less people are listening.[11]

As such, *Ros na Rún*, being in Irish, can address controversial themes such as abortion, which its more cautious English-language counterparts in Ireland have avoided[12]. The gay characters and the recent addition of a black character symbolise the identification of liberal Irish speakers with other minorities.[13]

---

[11] In fact Irish language journalists complain that they only seem to have a major 'scoop' when their story is deemed important enough to be translated into English

[12] I note that the Scottish Gaelic soap *Machair* was far more wholesome than *Ros na Rún*; no doubt the producers were aware that the audience for the show was mostly composed of rural Highlanders, who expected Gaelic television to demonstrate a greater degree of propriety.

[13] The Gaelic League is even encouraging immigrants to learn Irish, which 'indigenises' newcomers, who in turn make Irish speakers feel less stigmatised, as they speak one language among many (Heussaff: 2003).

The serial, as *Ros na Rún*'s producer said, is 'skewed slightly to the left' (personal communication to Sinéad Ní Shuinéar, 31 May 2002). The mixture of linguistic and cultural fantasy and reality in *Ros na Rún* reveal the competing essentialising and dynamic ideologies at play in the Irish language movement, and demonstrate a paradigm shift in favour of the latter without entirely deconstructing the former. Tradition and innovation exist concurrently as the cultures of rural native speakers and urban learners meet and create a synthesis, or a least an engaging stand-off, in the effort to represent and revive the Gaelic world.

References

Cohen, A. P. (1994) *Self Consciousness: An Alternative Anthropology of Identity.* Routledge: London and New York.

Fallon, Steve (2002) *Home with Alice: A Journey in Gaelic Ireland.* London: Lonely Planet Publications.

Glaser, Konstanze (2002) *Essentialism and Relativism in Gaelic and Sorbian Language Revival Discourses.* (http://www.arts.ed.ac.uk/celtic/poileasaidh/seminarwebversion2.html)

Hegarty, Shane (2003a) 'Gomorrah in the Gaeltacht' *Irish Times* January 25 2003, p.. 5.

Hegarty, Shane (2003b) 'Is it craic or crass?' *Irish Times* October 31 2003, p 17.

Heusaff, Anna (2003) 'More Irish than the Irish themselves?' *Irish Times* November 26 2003, p. 17.

Holden, Louise (2003) 'Enjoying going to rack and ruin.' *Irish Times* October 22 2003, p. 14.

Lavie, Smadar, Narayan, Kirin, and Rosaldo, Renaldo (eds.) (1993) *Creativity/Anthropology.* Ithaca: Cornell University Press.

Lysaght, Ruth (2002) *Pobal Sobail: Ros na Rún, TG 4 and Reality.* Unpublished paper presented at the UCD/IFC conference 'Keeping it Real', April 2002.

May, Stephen (2001) *Language and Minority Rights: Ethnicity, Nationalism and the Politics of Language.* London: Longman.

Ó Baoill, Dónall (1999) 'Social cultural distance, integrational orientation and the learning of Irish'. In A. Chambers and D. Ó Baoill (eds) *Intercultural Communication and Language Learning.* Dublin: IRAAL/Royal Irish Academy.

Ó Cinnéide, Seosamh, Mac Donnacha, Seosamh, and Ní Chonghaile, Sorcha (2001) *Polasaithe agus Cleachtais Eagraíochtaí Éagsúla le Feidhm sa Ghaeltacht.* Gaillimh: Ollscoil na Gaillimhe.

Ó Tuama, Seán, and Kinsella, Thomas (1981) *An Duanaire 1600-1900: Poems of the Dispossessed.* Portlaoise: Dolmen Press in association with Bord na Gaeilge.

Street, Brian V. (1993) 'Culture is a Verb: Anthropological aspects of language and cultural process.' In D. Graddol, L. Thompson and M. Bryam (eds) *Language and Culture.* Clevedon: BAAL and Multilingual Matters.

Watson, Iarfhlaith (2003) *Broadcasting in Irish: Minority Language, radio, television and identity.* Dublin: Four Courts Press.

Modern Scots Drama and Language Planning:
A Context and A Caution

Bill Findlay

I write with two hats on, so to speak: as someone with an academic interest in Scottish theatre and in drama written in Scots, and as a theatre practitioner who creates Scots translations and versions of foreign drama. My perspective here is therefore at once objective and subjective.

Scotland has a tradition in theatre reaching back to medieval times (see Findlay, 1998); yet, remarkably, the period of the past thirty years has been the richest in that long history for indigenous theatre-making, including for playwriting in Scots.[1] Of particular interest for our purposes here is that playwrights, and play translators, have employed varieties of Scots of a kind, or kinds, that marks a significant change of direction in what had largely, till 1970, been the norm in twentieth-century drama written in Scots.[2] What that norm was, was gently lampooned by John Byrne in 1977 in his play *Writer's Cramp* (Byrne being one of the most important Scottish dramatists of the past thirty years). Alasdair Cameron (1990: xi) comments that Byrne's play "takes a chain-saw to Anglo-Scottish literary pretensions"; it also, in a related way, pokes fun at those who earnestly believe that Lallans - in the twentieth-century neo-Lallans sense of a reconstructed, ideal Scots aspiring to become a national language again3 - is the way forward for Scottish writers. The play centres on the life and work of the late Francis Seneca McDade, who had "injest[ed] [*sic*] the skinny worm of Celtic art" in the hope of "herald[ing] the dawn of a new epoch in Caledonian culture" (Byrne, 1990: 3). Byrne presents us in the play with what his "Narrator" character archly describes as "one of McDade's alas, too rare excursions into the Lallans"; of which the Narrator dryly remarks, after recitation of the poem, "Would there were more" (Byrne, 1990: 22). Why he should pass that double-edged, barbed comment is apparent from the poem, titled 'Dimples':

---

[1] For general discussion of developments since 1970, see Stevenson and Wallace (1996) and Smith (1998: 269-308). For discussion of why the resurgence began in the 1970s, in which playwriting in Scots played a significant part, see Findlay (2001: ix-xxvi).
[2] For discussion of the position with play translations in the period after 1970, see Findlay (1996). See, too, the analysis of language and identity over this period in Paterson (1996).
[3] "Lallans" derives from Scots *Lawlands* 'Lowlands'. As a term referring to Lowland Scots speech it reaches back to the eighteenth century and was used as a name for their medium by poets such as Robert Burns and Alexander Wilson (see *SND*: Vol V, 496). However, in the twentieth century it became identified with, in one helpfully succint definition, "a form of 'plastic Scots' based on the traditional varieties of Older Scots" (Corbett, 1997: 14). The *Scottish National Dictionary* offers a narrower definition still of the term's twentieth-century adoption: "Since c.1940 the name *Lallans* has been *specif.* applied by its exponents to the movement begun by Lewis Spence, Hugh MacDiarmid and others to recreate and extend the range and vocabulary of Scots in literary usage" (*SND*: Vol. V, 496).

Door dreekit Dormley's dimples hing
Roon' his knees in wrinklit rime,
An' aw the Kings graut him a boon
Fur sic a furry woggle true.
Fir maun the clachan gates din clase,
An' Wriggles sclim' abune the wa's.
Desmond grins a couthy grin,
Fur ilky pithy wriggles cringe.
Mickey Moakers an' poakey noakers
Nickit roon' the knickers' rind.
Fit gran' creckles bide a'ben
An' grizzles crackit at the groakit. (Byrne, 1990: 22)

This is, of course, a send-up on John Byrne's part, a parody incorporating cod-Lallans words. In this it can be said to instance a change of sensibility in Scots writing for the stage - a change exemplified by Byrne's *The Slab Boys* trilogy of plays (Byrne, 1987, repr. 1990), written, in contrast with 'Dimples', in modern working-class urban demotic Scots as spoken in Byrne's hometown of Paisley, and in West-Central Scotland more generally.

I will come back to that changed sensibility and consider why it happened and what it constituted. I should first sketch in, because it has a direct bearing on that change, how Scots was used in drama, and the form it took as a stage language, in the six decades of the twentieth century before 1970.

In those decades we find a series of initiatives to establish a national theatre for Scotland.[4] The first significant initiative was the founding of the Glasgow Rep Theatre in 1909, which mutated into the Scottish Repertory Theatre and whose objective was "encouragement of the initiation and development of purely Scottish drama by providing a stage and acting company which will be peculiarly adapted for the production of plays national in character, written by Scottish men and women of letters" (quoted in Hutchison, 1998: 208-209). After this company folded, because the First World War intervened, the baton was taken up in the 1920s by the Scottish National Players, whose founding principles included "to develop Scottish national drama through the productions [...] of plays of Scottish life and character" (quoted in Hutchison, 1998: 221).[5] It is not necessary to run through all of the subsequent companies that shared similar aims to these right through to the 1960s;[6] the point to be made is that, despite their "national" aspirations, held with sincerity and integrity, the companies tended to have a limited sense of "national" when it came to work in a Scots idiom, in that the playwrights avert their gaze from the contemporary industrial and urban reality of Scotland, and therefore from the associated linguistic reality, too. Hence, work in

---

[4]   In the context of this symposium, it is interesting to note that the proponents invariably looked to Ireland as the exemplar; to both the Abbey Theatre in Dublin and to the work in Hiberno-English of Irish playwrights.

[5]   Again in the context of the symposium, it is of interest to note that the producer of the Scottish National Players for a period in the 1920s was the celebrated Irish theatre director Tyrone Guthrie.

[6]   The key companies are discussed in Hutchison, 1998, and Smith, 1998.

Scots typically has country or historical settings; settings where the Scots employed could be a traditional, conservative, country-inflected Scots, or a re-imagined Lallans.[7]

The exception to this stricture was Glasgow Unity Theatre,[8] a left-wing company that flourished in the 1940s and similarly aspired to be a vehicle for a drama that was national: "What we try to create is a native theatre, something which is essentially reflecting the lives of the ordinary people in Scotland" (quoted in Hill, 1977: 63). Glasgow Unity nurtured a school of social realist playwrights who indeed took as subject matter "the lives of the ordinary people of Glasgow", and who, complementary to this, took as their medium the voice of the people - that is, an urban demotic Scots

Glasgow Unity's groundbreaking achievement in those respects was largely forgotten, or at least ignored, after the company's demise in about 1950. But, as the nature of work in Scots after 1970 would show, Unity were before their time, and it is to be regretted that the kind of work they pioneered, particularly linguistically, was not followed up on till twenty and more years later.[9] Instead, what prevailed in Scots-medium playwriting in the 1950s, and for the most part into the1960s, was as instanced by the kind of work discussed in John Thomas Low's essay 'Mid Twentieth Century Drama in Lowland Scots' (cited here because it represents one of the first extended discussions of the use of Scots in modern drama and because its selectivity of focus in itself betrays a blinkered sense of Scots' range in drama). The six featured plays, two of which are translations of Molière, had their respective premieres in 1937, 1947, 1948, 1950, 1953 and 1954, yet no mention is made at all of Glasgow Unity writers' contemporaneous work in a Glasgow-Scots idiom; an omission which is the more striking given the great success enjoyed in the 1940s in Scotland, and indeed in England, by plays such as Robert McLeish's *The Gorbals Story* (1946) (McLeish, 1985) - performed "more than six hundred times in the three years between 1946 and 1949"[10] - and Ena Lamont Stewart's *Men Should Weep* (1947) (Stewart, 1983). Rather, Low's attention is solely on what he describes as "a body of classics of the Scottish theatre", many of which "have their roots in history, legend [...] [or] present

---

[7] For more discussion of this point, see Hutchison, 1998: 224-225; Hutchison, 1977: *passim*. As Hutchison (1977: 57), for example, notes, there are exceptions such as George Reston Malloch's *Soutarness Water* (1926), which has a country setting but is written, as he says, in often "vigorous Scots dialect".

[8] Although it was a short-lived amateur company, Unity had a precursor of sorts in the Bowhill (later, Fife) Miner Players, which toured the work of miner and playwright Joe Corrie to largely working-class audiences in mining communities and variety theatres from the late 1920s until disbanding in 1931. Corrie's best-known play, *In Time o' Strife* (Corrie, 1985), deals with the impact of the General Strike of 1926 and is written in the contemporary Scots speech of mining villages in West Fife.

[9] A qualification here is that the actor and playwright, Roddy McMillan, who was a member of Glasgow Unity and subsequently joined the Citizens' Theatre, had a play, *All in Good Faith* (McMillan, 1979), in Unity's style, and in Glasgow Scots, staged by the Citizens' in 1954 and by the Edinburgh Gateway Company in seasons 1957-58 and 1963-64

[10] The quotation is taken from Linda Mackenney's introduction to McLeish, 1985 (p.9), where she provides further details of the play's popularity in Scotland and England.

dramatic portraits of types or great figures from the past" (Low, 1983: 170). In other words, his chosen plays avoid engagement with modern Scotland, and hence ignore the speech realities of urban Scots. His survey is concerned, he writes, "with plays which use the Lowland Scots tongue as the main linguistic medium" (Low, 1983: 171): one can but assume therefore that omission of mention of plays by Glasgow Unity writers signifies that they do not warrant admission to his categorisation of mid-century drama in "the Lowland Scots tongue".

It is difficult to avoid reading this curious omission as other than reflective of a discriminatory position being adopted over what constitutes "good" versus "bad" Scots (or, at least, of work in Lallans being accorded a privileged status).[11] A. J. Aitken, in teasing out the distinction between "good" and "bad" Scots, concluded of the latter:

> It seems fair to say that, though it is rather less conservative in its characteristics than "genuine" Scots, it is nevertheless undoubtedly a variety of Scots. The labels it commonly attracts include Demotic Scots, urban Scots and working-class Scots; as well as, more pejoratively, corrupt Scots, debased Scots, slovenly Scots, so-called modern Scots, the Glasgow-Irish and Factory Scotch. (Aitken, 1980: 46)

Such pejorative labels can be found having been applied by advocates of Scots, including by writers associated with twentieth-century Lallans. Robert Kemp, for example, one of the three playwrights employing "Lowland Scots" whose work provides the focus for Low's essay (the others are Robert McLellan and Alexander Reid), states in the introduction to his 1951 play The Other Dear Charmer, which centres on Robert Burns's relationship with Clarinda, Mrs Maclehose:

> In Scotland the country speech is the finest speech and holds in it a sense of natural aristocracy. There is nothing slipshod or vulgar about it [...]. (Kemp, 1957: 17)

In insistent repetition of this, he added, in advice to future performers of his play:

> I beseech all concerned not to mistake the music-hall pronunciation of Scots, a by-product of industrialism and slums, for the kind of speech that [Burns] would have used. [...] [T]here is nothing vulgar or slipshod about his speech. (Kemp, 1957: 17, 19)

In such a view, the Scots tongue of the countryside and of the past is under threat from the debased Scots speech of the urban working-classes; one being "good" Scots, the other "bad". Hence, the Scots-medium plays of a dramatist like Robert Kemp, in the conservatism of attitude and idiom betrayed, and in their historical subject matter, represent an attempt to hold back the tide of modernity by means of a "Classical Scots" undefiled by contemporary urban experience.

The tone of regret and lament, and indeed embattlement, that often accompanies such sentiments is also a feature of some academic writing about Scots by scholars of a similar generation to Robert Kemp, such as David Murison, late editor of *The Scottish National Dictionary*, as here:

---

[11] In fairness, elsewhere Dr Low comes close to admitting the validity of contemporary urban accent and dialect, though his recommended playwrights, Alexander Reid and James Bridie, suggest a still-narrow view of Scots-medium playwriting. See Low, 1980: 73, 92.

> Like dialects everywhere, it [Modern Scots] is under the severest
> pressure from the standard language through constant confusion with
> the official speech. Scots and English forms are jumbled up
> haphazardly so that a clear and consistent pattern can no longer be
> traced, and a systematic grammar has gone out of the window. Modern
> Scottish writers, striving for realism, reproduce this speech faithfully,
> but one may question how far it is Scots at all and not merely a broken
> kind of English. This is especially true of the speech of the industrial
> areas, where the influence of Highland and Anglo-Irish dialect, the
> new vocabulary of industrialism imported from England, the general
> currency of standard and substandard and slang English, particularly
> on the social strata of the towns, have all combined to attenuate and
> even obliterate Scots. (Murison, 1977: 56)

A similar view and tone to this was expressed early in the 1970s by a scholar of
Scots of a younger generation, J. Derrick McClure, when he wrote disapprovingly
of "naturalistic writers who are concerned with representing the impoverished and
bastardised Scots spoken in present-day Glasgow rather than with exploiting the
full expressive potential of the Scots language in its entirety" (McClure, n.d.
[?1974]: 62).

What the period from 1970 to the present has done in Scottish theatre has been
to blow apart such anxieties about "good" versus "bad" Scots and to ignore the
prescriptive instincts that invariably flow from them. Ignored, too, has been the
generally prevailing assumption of Lallans playwrights that "debased" and
attenuated contemporary urban Scots speech did not constitute "Scots", properly
speaking, and could not therefore be a fit vehicle for a putative national drama.
Lindsay Paterson, in his essay 'Language and Identity on the Stage', observes:

> It is easy to forget just how stultified Scots-language writing had
> become by the 1960s. Historical plays used a highly artificial form of
> older Scots [...]; contemporary writing used at most a Scottish accent.
> When dramatists such as Hector MacMillan, Tom McGrath, and
> Donald Campbell started writing in a Scots that could be felt to be real,
> they were contributing to that awakening of national self-confidence
> [...] which has now thoroughly reinvented the national identity. The
> first thing these writers did was to harness the sheer energy of
> working-class Scots into a vigorous theatricality in which issues of
> wide social significance could be debated incisively. (Paterson, 1996:
> 75-76)

The necessity for this sea-change in order to liberate Scots-medium playwriting
from its linguistic conservatism and nostalgic subject matter was well-diagnosed
by Edwin Morgan in 1972 when he wrote of "a great deadlock to be broken" in
Scottish theatre:

> Directors and management seem to be hypnotised rigid by the polarity
> of Received Standard versus Costume Scots - neither of which any
> Scotsman actually speaks. Only rarely do Scottish theatre audiences
> hear that modest and unforced reflection of their own living speech-
> habits which English or American audiences take for granted.
> (Morgan, [1972] 1974: 164)

(It was, of course, just that "Costume Scots" that John Byrne was satirising in the poem in cod-Lallans in his 1977 play *Writer's Cramp* cited at the outset.) Edwin Morgan went on to remark that he regretted "heavily entrenched positions regarding language in Scotland", preferring to see the "untidiness" that is the reality acknowledged and given a voice in creative work:

> I would rather see the mixed state that exists being explored and exploited, more truthfully and spontaneously and hence more seriously than at present, by writers [...] [and by] playwrights in particular. It may be that we have a blessing in disguise. But if we want to uncover it we shall have to use our ears more and our grammar books less. (Morgan, [1971] 1974: 156)

Morgan's comments proved prescient because the unprecedented exploration by playwrights over the past thirty years of the creative resources of Scots as a stage language has been characterised by writers ignoring, or being oblivious of, the kind of language planning and standardisation that is suggested by Morgan's reference to "grammar books". Instead, they have used the evidence of their ears and of the "untidiness" of the reality of contemporary speech; and they have done so untroubled by the supposed deficiencies brought about by "bastardisation", "debasement", "vulgarity", and the like dismissive epithets.

For, it is Central-Belt urban Scots, and West-Central and Glaswegian Scots especially, that has generally predominated in the varieties of Scots used by playwrights. This can be seen not just in plays with contemporary or recent-past settings, but in plays with a historical setting, as well as in translations of classic and modern foreign-language drama. An example of one of those history plays is Liz Lochhead's celebrated *Mary Queen of Scots Got Her Head Chopped Off* (Lochhead, 1989), which, in fashioning a non-naturalistic, period-suggestive speech, takes as its base a modern West-Central vernacular Scots which is then aggrandised with words and forms from other regions and from the past. One finds a similar strategy, too, for example, in her Scots translation of Molière's *Tartuffe* (Lochhead, 1985) and in Edwin Morgan's of Edmond Rostand's *Cyrano de Bergerac* (Morgan, 1992). In the introduction to the published edition of the latter, Morgan offers an insight into his how his choice of stage medium was motivated by such an approach (and by a wish to take a different route from Lallans):

> I decided that an urban Glaswegian Scots would offer *the best basis* [my emphasis], since it is widely spoken, can accommodate contemporary reference, is by no means incapable of the lyrical and the poetic, and comes unburdened by the baggage of the older Scots which used to be thought suitable for historical plays. (Morgan, 1992: xi)

As a consequence of the shift that has occurred, so secure has been seizure of the centre ground in modern Scottish theatre by writing using a contemporary urban Scots of the Central Belt - and especially of West-Central Scotland - that that variety of Scots has supplanted the kind of conservative and literary (i.e. "grammar book") Scots synthesised by Lallans writers of an earlier generation or

---

[12] With reference to the surge of work in demotic Scots since 1970, Paterson (1996: 79) argues that "the most innovative development in Scots in the theatre has been its use for purposes that are not realistic at all"; purposes that fuse "the realist tradition in Scottish literature with the fantastic".

two. To put that more bluntly, the once disparaged Scots of the industrial and urban-dwelling working-classes has largely shouldered Lallans to the periphery of our theatre; and, further irony, it has in doing so become a new kind of "standard" Scots, in both naturalistic and non-naturalistic forms,[12] in terms of its ubiquity on our stages and in radio and television comedy and drama (and, indeed, in contemporary literature).[13]

In tandem with the changed sensibility that has brought this about, and the linguistic liberation associated with it, has been an equally unparalleled exploitation of regional varieties of Scots, such as the Scots speech of Caithness, Easter Ross, Aberdeenshire, Angus, Fife, the Lothians, the Borders, Galloway, Ayrshire, Lanarkshire, Stirling, Perthshire - not to mention the urban dialects of the cities of Aberdeen, Dundee, Edinburgh and, of course, Glasgow. In this development one sees, too, a focus on the evidence of ears not grammar books, and an openness to the diversity of real speech.

Randall Stevenson, co-editor of the standard work *Scottish Theatre Since the Seventies*, writes there: "it is probably Scots speech that is the most fundamental influence on the drama" of the period, for "it is a resource which has greatly empowered the progress of Scottish theatre over the past quarter century" (Stevenson and Wallace, 1996: 4, 5). In the majority of cases, the Scots-medium dramatists who have contributed to achieving this have not, in contrast to earlier Lallans writers, seen themselves as agents of language planning, as it were - as shoring up the fragmented ruins of a once-national language in the hope of a better day, or of "raising the status of a marginalized language variety" and "bind[ing] the marginalized speech community together as a homogenous political entity" (Corbett, 2003: 253). What they have added to the modern corpus of Scots writing is substantial, and that contribution may in itself inadvertently help to advance the development and cause of Scots; but for dramatists the work has been the thing, and their use of Scots has, for the most part, sprung from the artistic imperative to find or fashion the most appropriate and most effective stage idiom for their chosen subject matter, and to do so drawing on the close detail of *living* Scottish speech. Thus, modern Scots scripts commonly betray an attention to the minutiae of pronunciation, where sound is regularly phonetically rendered, often idiosyncratically so; indeed, to the extent that, from a language planner's perspective, playwrights' spelling must often appear anarchic and the product of a mindset that is wilfully resistant to standardisation. John Corbett, in his essay 'Language Planning and Modern Scots', has set out a larger context in which this phenomenon can be placed:

> The orthography of Scots will only be fully standardised if there is social pressure on all writers to conform to a fixed set of norms. This pressure is not likely to be felt if Scots is used for literary purposes alone: literature is by its very nature experimental, and its departure from homogeneous norms are often deliberately intended to give a sense of the regional or social specificity of a character or text. It

---

[13] I am, of course, using the word "standard" in a loose sense here in relation to frequency of usage in performance language that can be classified as "Scots"; that is, I do not intend it in the stricter terminological sense as applied in corpus planning (about which, in relation to modern Scots, see Corbett, 2003: 260-262).

follows that Scots orthography will only be standardised if Scots were to be used more widely in functions beyond the literary, and if a standard spelling system were to be taught in schools so that writers could perform the functions adequately. [...] Thanks to the style sheets and the dictionaries, more than at any time in the history of the language, the possibility of training oneself in a more 'focused' Scots spelling is available to committed writers who wish to conform to a normative set of practices. (Corbett, 2003: 261)

Standardisation in spelling, then, is not, nor should it be, the responsibility of the writer, though s/he could of course choose to conform to a provisional or agreed standard. It may be that the past thirty years will prove to be a transitional phase, and that, at some future date, such standardisation is embraced by Scots-medium playwrights of a different generation. As regards the present generations and the dramatic texts produced since 1970, since the nature of their Scots and its orthographic representation is, as has been indicated, partly rooted in a reaction again Lallans and its associated prescriptive tendency, individualism is likely to continue to flourish, partly in the spirit of experimentalism to which Corbett alludes and partly in the spirit of embracing and practising a linguistic pluralism in what constitutes "Scots". It can be argued that, since the survival of Scots has been grounded in, and hangs on, its employment in daily speech, drama, as the most speech-based genre, is particularly deserving of study in relation to corpus planning; the more so when it has, over the past three decades or so, sought to register the linguistic reality of Scotland.[14] Corbett (2003: 271) notes, "research into corpus planning in Scots has hitherto been based on the strategies used by the 'Scots synthesisers' [...] to construct a 'plastic' or 'reintegrated' Scots for use in literature" . He adds: "Much detailed work on the motivations governing the choice of lexis, grammar, orthography and discourse genres of the different generations of Scots writers remains undone". Modern Scots drama, I would argue, has much to offer in this regard as an object of study.

As regards, then, the symposium's theme of how the Performing Arts can contribute to minority language development, it can be argued that beneficial consequences of the quantity and vitality of Scots drama since 1970 are several and significant:

- plays, and translations of plays, in Scots have been produced in remarkable and unrivalled quantity;
- plays, and translations of plays, in Scots have thereby become an established and readily accepted feature of the Scottish theatre scene, from the smallest to the largest professional theatre companies, both touring and building-based;
- theatre managers and artistic directors have recognised that work in Scots is both potential and proven good box office, and that audiences are not resistant to work in Scots but quite the reverse;
- the size of the theatre audience means that work in Scots is reaching much wider numbers than the relatively modest readership there is for published poetry and prose in Scots, and this has made a significant contribution to

---

[14] This last phrase is a reformulation of the title of Edwin Morgan's essay, 'Registering the Reality of Scotland', where he argued for a new openness by writers to the realities of contemporary Scots speech. See Morgan, 1974, 153-157.

consolidating and advancing Scots as an integral and high-profile part of Scottish culture;

• in attending a public performance of a play in Scots, audience members are experiencing in a powerful way a confirmation, and perhaps for many a discovery, of the resources and status of Scots, as well as the sense of shared identity between writer, performer and audience that flows from this.[15]

Language planners can, of course, build on such beneficial consequences; consequences which, in answer to one of the questions that the symposium wished to have addressed, can be said decidedly to signify the expression and substantiation of a culture beyond the merely symbolic. However, if this fruitful exploitation through drama of the diverse resources of Scots speech is to continue, the lesson of the rich and vital output of the past thirty years - set in the context sketched in here of the resistance and rejection that that work represents to the contrasting and would-be prescriptive nature of Lallans writing in earlier decades of the twentieth century - would seem to be: *ca/caa/caw/ca' canny* ('take care') if minded to urge that playwrights adhere to standardisation to assist legitimising a normative "good Scots".

References

Aitken, A.J. 1980. "New Scots: The Problems". In eds. J.D. McClure, A.J. Aitkenand J.T. Low. *The Scots Language: Planning for Modern Usage.* Edinburgh: Ramsay Head Press. 45-63

Byrne, J. 1987, repr. 1990. *The Slab Boys Trilogy.* London: Penguin

Byrne, J. 1990. *Writer's Cramp.* In ed. A. Cameron. *New Scottish Plays.* London: Nick Hern Books. 1-40

Cameron, A. ed. 1990. *Scot-Free: New Scottish Plays.* London: Nick Hern Books

Corbett, J. 1997. *Language and Scottish Literature.* Edinburgh: Edinburgh University Press

Corbett, J. 2003. "Language Planning and Modern Scots". In eds. J. Corbett, J.D. McClure and J. Stuart-Smith. *The Edinburgh Companion to Scots.* Edinburgh: Edinburgh University Press. 251-272

Corrie, J. 1985. *Plays, Poems and Theatre Writings.* Edinburgh: 7:84 Publications

Findlay, B. 1996. "Talking in Tongues: Scottish Translations 1970-1995". In eds. R. Stevenson and G. Wallace. *Scottish Theatre Since the Seventies.* Edinburgh: Edinburgh University Press. 186-197

Findlay, B. ed. 1998. *A History of Scottish Theatre.* Edinburgh: Polygon/ Edinburgh University Press

Findlay, B. ed. 2001. *Scots Plays of the Seventies.* Dalkeith: Scottish Cultural Press

Hill, J. 1977. "Towards a Scottish People's Theatre: The rise and fall of Glasgow Unity". *Theatre Quarterly* 7 (27): 61-70

Hutchison, D. 1977. *The Modern Scottish Theatre.* Glasgow: Molendinar

Hutchison, D. 1998. "1900 to 1950". In ed. B. Findlay. *A History of Scottish Theatre.* Edinburgh: Polygon/Edinburgh University Press. 207-252

Kemp, R. 1957. *The Other Dear Charmer.* London: Duckworth

---

[15] For a discussion of this point in relation to Liz Lochhead's Scots translation of *Tartuffe*, see Stevenson, 1993: 118.

Lochhead, L. trans. 1985. *Tartuffe: A translation into Scots from the original by Molière*. Edinburgh/Glasgow: Polygon/Third Eye Centre

Lochhead, L. 1989. *Mary Queen of Scots Got Her Head Chopped Off and Dracula*. London: Penguin

Low, J.T. 1980. "A Scots Language Policy for Education". In eds. J. D. McClure, A.J. Aitken and J.T. Low. *The Scots Language: Planning for Modern Usage*. Edinburgh: Ramsay Head Press. 67-95

Low, J.T. 1983. "Mid Twentieth Century Drama in Lowland Scots". In ed. J. D. McClure. *Scotland and the Lowland Tongue*. Aberdeen: Aberdeen University Press. 170-194

McClure, J. D. n.d. [?1974]. "Modern Scots Prose Writing". In ed. J.D. McClure. *The Scots Language in Education*. Association for Scottish Literary Studies Occasional Papers Number 3. Aberdeen: Aberdeen College of Education and the Association for Scottish Literary Studies. 54-67

McLeish, R. 1985. *The Gorbals Story*. Edinburgh: 7:84 Publications

McMillan, R. 1979. *All in Good Faith*. Glasgow: Scottish Society of Playwrights

Morgan, E. 1974. *Essays*. Cheadle: Carcanet

Morgan, E. 1983. "Glasgow Speech in Recent Scottish Literature". In ed. J. D. McClure. *Scotland and the Lowland Tongue*. Aberdeen: Aberdeen University Press. 195-208

Morgan, E. trans. 1992. *Cyrano de Bergerac*. Manchester: Carcanet

Murison, D. 1977. *The Guid Scots Tongue*. Edinburgh: Blackwood

Paterson, L. 1996. "Language and Identity on the Stage". In eds. R. Stevenson and G. Wallace. *Scottish Theatre Since the Seventies*. Edinburgh: Edinburgh University Press. 75-83

Smith, D. 1998. "1950 to 1995". In ed. B. Findlay. *A History of Scottish Theatre*. Edinburgh: Polygon/Edinburgh University Press. 253-308

Scottish National Dictionary (SND) 1925-1975. 10 vols., eds. W. Grant and D.D. Murison. Edinburgh: Scottish National Dictionary Association

Stewart, E.L. 1983. *Men Should Weep*. Edinburgh: 7:84 Publications

Stevenson, R. 1993. "Re-enter Houghmagandie: Language as Performance in Liz Lochhead's Tartuffe". In eds. R. Crawford and A. Varty. *Liz Lochhead's Voices*. Edinburgh: Edinburgh University Press. 109-123

Stevenson, R. and G. Wallace eds. 1996. *Scottish Theatre Since the Seventies*. Edinburgh: Edinburgh University Press

Scots and Identity

David Purves

What is Scots? This is a question which cannot be fully explored here, but I would like by way of example, to read a dramatised fragment from 'Beside the Bonnie Briar Bush' by Ian Maclaren. This was a Victorian tear-jerker which sold more than fifty thousand copies before 1895. The conclusion refers to the *Daith o Dr MacLure*, the local doctor. *Dr MacLure is on his daith-bed an he is veisitit bi his auld frein, Drumsheugh.*

Drumsheugh: It's maist awfu ti hear ye speakin aboot deein, Weelum.
MacLure: Na, Na, Paitrick, it's owre late nou. The'r a knock that canna be mistaen, an A heard it lest nicht. A hae focht Daith for ither fowk for mair nor fortie year, but ma ain tyme haes cum at lest. A'm juist fair worn oot, Paitrick: that's ma complaint an it's past curin.
Drumsheugh: Whit wul becum o us when ye'r no here ti gie a haund in tyme o need? We'l tak ill wi a streinger that disna ken yin o us frae anither.
MacLure: It's aw for the best, Paitrick. A'm the lest o the auld skuil, an A've kent for a whylie that ma day is owre, an that ye soud hae a yungir man. Wad ye pit up a bit prayer, Paitrick?
Drumsheugh: A-A-A haena the wurds, Weelum.
MacLure: Juist say whit's in yeir hert! The Almichtie wul ken the lave Himsell.
Drumsheugh: (*kneeling*) Almichtie God, Dinna be haurd on Weelum McLure, kis he haes no been haurd wi oniebodie in Drumtochtie. Be kynd ti him as he haes been til us aw. An Lord, whaur he haes gaen wrang, dinna cuist it up til him! An gie him a walcum hame, for he's sair needin it, eftir aw his wark! Amen!

This, of course, is kailyaird. Some might say pure schmaltz, but *whit brings a tear til grannie's ee, maunna be lichtlied. Whitever, the language is gey close ti the wey ma graundfaither spak.* It would now be difficult, if not impossible, to find a medical practitioner in Scotland who spoke like this: in nothing but Scots. It is now four hundred year since *Jamie the Saxt* ascended the English Throne and also became King of Ireland. After this time, Scots, which had been the State Language, came to be represented in Scottish education as a corrupt kind of English, to be corrected in the classroom, perhaps with the tawse. Since then, generations of Scots have had to come to terms with a situation where at school, their mither tung – the way of speech natural to them, was offically regarded as unacceptable. The psychological consequences of this kind of deracination in Scottish education are incalculable. Following the restoration of a Scottish Parliament, it was reasonable to expect a radical change in public attitudes towards the Scots Language.

Scots, unlike Gaelic, the ancient language of the Scottish Kingdom, has always been closely related to English, although some sentences, such as, *Monie a pikkil maks a mukkil*, or *Guid gear cums in smaw bouk*, might appear incomprehensible to an English person. Nevertheless, when London became Scotland's capital and Scotland became a province, it seemed a natural development that the Scots language should come to be regarded as a provincial variant of the 'proper' English in the new power centre in the south of England. Scotland's first representatives at Westminster had to learn to imitate this model, or continue to be laughed at whenever they opened their mouths in the House of Commons. However, today, we have to address the present situation. Throughout the last century, negative attitudes to the Scots language have gradually diminished, although they have by no means disappeared. As recently as 1983, a case was reported by a Swedish linguist (Sandred 1983) of a girl in Edinburgh whose mother stuck her so hard when she heard her use the word, *ken*, that she lost two front teeth. In 1993, a sheriff in Stirling, reputedly a Burns enthusiast, consigned a man to the cells for using the word, *Ay*, in addressing the bench.

I have been asked to address the questions in the Prospectus in relation to the performing arts in relation to language development. The two questions of particular interest to me are:

How far do minority languages in broadcasting, the press and the performing arts express or substantiate culture, and how far is their use merely symbolic?

How far is the use of minority languages in broadcasting, the press and the performing arts simply an educational issue?

If, by 'minority languages' we mean Scots and Gaelic, these questions are not difficult to answer in relation to Scotland. In general, Gaelic is on a life-support system and while many more Scots spoke Gaelic in Scotland than in Ireland in 1926, this position has now become reversed as a result of Irish independence. As regards Scots, the media in Scotland behave as if the Scots language does not exist, although a majority of the population understand and employ some Scots every day. The pattern is the same in radio and television. In radio, there has been some limited devolution to local radio and to BBC Radio Scotland. However, TV in Scotland is almost entirely London-centred, so that even the small number of dramatic productions originating in Scotland are expected to conform to a pattern set in England. There is, I believe, a head of Drama in BBC Scotland, but serious drama in Scots is non-existent. The creation of an independent Scottish Broadcasting Corporation would be essential before Scots could be given its proper place in radio and television.

In any country which aspires to nationhood, the function of the theatre is to extend awareness at a universal level in the context of the native cultural heritage. There is no doubt that the theatre in Scotland now pays little attention to this objective. In general, it has functioned as a provincial extension of the London theatre. It has just been announced [September 2003] that the Scottish Executive now belatedly intends to proceed with plans to establish A Scottish National Theatre. Presumably one of the objectives of a National Theatre would be to encourage dramatic productions in authentic Scots and Gaelic. We will have to hope that this will lead to some genuine commitment in the theatre to Scotland's indigenous culture. The use of Scots has been an important feature of drama in Scotland for hundreds of years, although by the mid 1930s, its use had become largely confined to comic characters in pantomime. These roles reflect a denigratory attitude to the language. Buttons and the Ugly Sisters, dressed in ludicrous costumes, speak Scots, while Cinderella and the Prince (the serious people) employ quacking ERP accents. However, since the 1930s, there has been some extension of the traditional comic use of Scots in mock-historical plays by

Robert McLellan, for example, in *The Flouers o Edinburgh*, which explored the language problems in Scotland in the eighteenth century. A number of playwrights of merit followed McLellan's example in the post-war period, in writing mock-historical plays in Scots. However, such plays attract criticism by being backward-looking and not being evidently concerned with contemporary issues. It is certainly true that the action in such plays is frozen in historical time. Here we have a closed comical world, populated by *gallus lads, chaumer louns, stickit meinisters an wurthie beylies in buckelt shuin*. This kind of thing gives a skewed image to the Scots Language.

Even after 400 years of cultural represssion, Scots is not just a comic language. It still has the resources to deal with any kind of dramatic situation. My later years have been preoccupied with trying to demonstrate the shamefully-neglected potential for expression in the Scots language in poetry and drama. In writing plays in Scots, I have tried to avoid the mock-historical pantomime image, by taking the action out of historical time, as in *The Puddok an the Princess*, and *The Ill Guidmither*, or by making renderings in Scots of classics like *The Tragedie o Macbeth*, Chekhov's *The Thrie Sisters*, and Strindberg's *The Ootlaw*.

The other question we are asked to consider, concerns the purpose of education. In 1993, all the Scottish education authorities agreed, in partnership with the Scottish Consultative Council on the Curriculum (SCCC) to take part in the Scottish Language Project (Robertson, 1993). This project was launched in 1996, with the object of promoting the use of Scots and Gaelic in primary and secondary schools. It now seems to have been abandoned by the Scottish Executive. The normal way to teach any language, is by reference to the literature in it, and to the idiom, grammar and syntax which the literature exemplifies (Purves, 2002). There is a substantial body of literature in Scots from around 1700 to the present time, which is surprisingly consistent linguistically, and which could provide a useful resource given the will to employ it. Unfortunately, what now survives of spoken Scots has become fragmented and dissociated from this literature. An important challenge in Scottish education is to re-establish the link between the speak of the playground and the body of literature in Scots.

A more recent document entitled, *The National Cultural Strategy*, was published by the Scottish Executive in 2000, but this was dedicated to political correctitude and promised no effective early action. In this blinkered document, Scotland's languages were referred to, but English is the only one specified! The others are grouped as a diverse group of languages, some of which are evidently native, and others associated with ethnic minorities.

The way forward for Scots does not, at present, lie in introducing term like *cludgie, shunkie, duffie, sitooterie* and *lang-bletherer* into the New Parliament building. Nor does it lie in the production of so-called poems in DIY Scots, by writers who have no real command of the language, some of whom, I am vext to say, are cloistered in academic institutions; or in translations into bogus Scots of official documents (Scottish Office, 1997). The notion that 'Freedom Now' should be rendered as, *Unthirldom the-nou!* is as absurd as the late Professor Aitken's joke that *lang-bletherer* should be substituted for 'telephone' in the New Scotland. The way forward requires an educational revolution in which the language is identified as a separate linguistic system from English: a linguistic resource and complement to English, rather than a corrupt form of it.

Both the Scots Language and Scots-English, which has a sound system directly derived from Scots, are important badges of identity, and the continuing erosion of community identity by the tide of globalisation is a serious problem which should receive the attention of the Scottish Parliament and the Government of Northern Ireland. While it would be unwise to expect miracles, what we can reasonably expect, is that Scots will now take its proper place in Scottish education and be recognised by the media and in public life, as a valuable part of our linguistic heritage.

References

Purves, D (2002) *A Scots Grammar – Scots Grammar and Usage* (revised edition), Saltire Society, Edinburgh.

Robertson, R. (1993) 'The Scottish Language Project', in *Chapman* 72: 57.

Sandred, K I (1983) *Good or Bad Scots*, (Uppsala: Acta Universitatis Upsaliensis) Studia Anglistica Upsaliensia 48.

The Scottish Executive (2000) *A National Cultural Strategy*, Edinburgh.

The Scottish Office (1997) *Scotland's Parliament* (Supplement in Scots), Edinburgh.

Whit wey fur no? **Scots and the Scripted Media: Theatre, Radio, TV, Film**

Janet Paisley

I'll start with a story.

While she was terminally ill, my mother and I visited Malta. Despite our shared fear of travelling on water, she was determined to see the garden island of Gozo. On the crowded ferry, a Dutchman made room for her to sit next him. My mother immediately started blethering, in passable English seein she was oot the hoose. The man interrupted with 'I'm sorry, I do not speak English.' My mother reassured him this was okay, as if she thought no less of him for it, and continued to blether away to an increasingly perplexed man. I gied her a dunt. 'Mam,' says I. 'He's just telt ye he doesnae speak English.' 'So,' she nips ma heid aff. 'There's nuthin wrang wi his ears is there?'

Deein, aye, but no deid yit, no by a long chalk. And she wisnae wrang. It's no whether folk kin speak a language whit maitters. It's whether or no they kin unnerstaun it, if they can 'hear' it or no. Ma mither was weel yaist tae folk wha couldnae *speak* the English, at least no very weel seein it's gey haurd fur Scottish tongues tae git roon it, but wha could *unnerstaun* it fur it was aw they could read or write, aw that was in their papers baur the Sunday Post and aw they heard fae their radio, TV and pictur hooses. Whit thon man shoulda said, an whit we should aw be learnt tae say aboot leids we cannae comprehend oan hearin, wis 'I don't understand English.'

In Scotland, maist folk kin unnerstaun English. A wee drappie folk speak it, but no near as mony as ye micht think. In big swatches ae the toons an country, gey near nae English kin be heard oan the streets or in the shops an even less inside the hooses. Adult immigrants micht never hae ony English, speakin their hame language in the hoose an yaisin Scots tae communicate ootside it. Amang the natives, a guid mony think English is whit they speak but it's no. Maist folk swap aboot, yaisin Scots fur the intimate, faimly, neebourly an workie conversations an only yaisin English whaur thur ootae place or speakin tae strangers an foreigners.

It's thon habit, when even twa guid Scots speakers will speak English tae yin anither, whit could mak folk think there's nae muckle Scots yaised. But fae traivellin aw ower Scotland fur twenty five year, meetin and speakin wi a wheen o folk o aw ages, I jalouse there maun be fower million Scots speakers bide in Scotland and the full six million wha understaun it.

In scriptwriting, what matters is whether folk can understand the language they hear. It might be fun to write in Latin and I recently enjoyed three hours of storytelling in Korean. But if you want to speak to the majority, you best do it in their language. The spoken language of the majority of Scotland's inhabitants is Scots. A similar majority understand spoken English. If understanding was the sole aim, scripts could be written and delivered equally in either language. However, in dramatic scripts, understanding is only one requirement of language. Speech is the main element used to carry story and plot. It also conveys a character's age, gender, personality, background, place of origin, attitude, intellect, emotional state and world view. For a scriptwriter, speech is character. Accurate portrayals require the use of speech from the relevant backgrounds and areas. So, maist scripts fur the Scottish media wad obviously dae the job better written in Scots.

But are they? For theatre, writers write as they choose. It's a writer's medium. The script leads the production. Plays are often written in Scots, and are delivered in that tongue, with the aid of voice coaches to assist the actors if the dialect is a minor one. Theatre frequently tours its productions around the UK and abroad. It clearly believes audiences, at home and beyond Scotland's borders, will understand Scottish characters speaking their own tongue.

Radio drama is normally written and delivered in English. Exceptions can be made if the writer feels Scots language is necessary. I was allowed to write one network production in Scots, *A Play for Today* where authenticity was agreed to be important though, in production, the actors had to tone down the very localised dialect to ensure it was widely understood.

Educational radio, where programmes are normally for Scottish use only, is more likely to accept scripts in Scots. I've written three or fower history series, aboot twenty scripts aw in a variety of Scots dialects and aw broadcast brilliantly in they voices. Nae medium does it better. It's just no done often enough. I've also written about two dozen stories, in the required English, for a Moral education series. Drama-documentaries and plays which, unusually, were to be networked, also had to be written in English. Only they scripts wi Scots characters dramatisin a Scottish story staun ony chance o yaisin the Scots language. Scotland's bairns kin huv their history in Scots but morals, an awthing else, come in English.

Radio is still a writer's medium. But naebody has ever come tae me because they want a script in Scots. I ay ask. If the writer doesnae ask, they'll no get and if the show's to be networked, they won't get anyway. Radio is still unconvinced that Scottish audiences understand their own speech and believes those outside Scotland will struggle to understand it.

TV drama is not a writer's medium. Rather like Hollywood, British TV scriptwriters are told what and how to write by many other people: storyliners, script editors, producers, executives, directors and, occasionally, actors. For STV and BBC the language rule is the same. Scripts are written in English. Actors are expected to accent the script so it will sound Scottish without being Scots. Although it isn't the purpose of regional broadcasting, programmes are made with the intention of securing UK distribution and in the hope of worldwide sales. TV doesn't care if Scots understand their own language, it doesn't believe the rest of the world will.

There is no Scottish film industry. Most screenwriters have to leave the country. Big productions require big budgets. That usually means American investment and scripts in English. The wonderfully authentic Ken Loach apart, low budget productions, such as *Orphans* or *My Name is Joe*, made with British backing might be written in light Scots dialect then added to in production by the actors. Short films, the only kind financed by Scotland, which may be given backwater TV screening and have no systematic cinema distribution will be seen by few people, and can be written in Scots – if the writer wants to take the risk.

That risk is if the script can or will actually be read by those who might select it for production. Plays like *Trainspotting*, TV comedy like *Still Game*, and films like *Sweet Sixteen*, have proved that the spoken Scots language can be understood by English-speaking audiences. But most media people, like the general public, have little or no experience of seeing Scots on the page, find it difficult to read and won't try.

Writers also have problems in writing the language. A Scottish education doesn't include literacy in the Scots language. No-one learns how to write it. Although there is remarkable countrywide agreement among practitioners and lay-people, no-one actually knows how to write it. There is no authoritative teaching of contemporary, historic, standard or dialect Scots and writers need all four. Since a standard language arises from spoken language and contains similar structures and vocabulary, it is possible for actors to reverse that process and produce authentic dialect. They often do to deliver dialects of English from that standard. Scripts in standard Scots could be uniform in spelling and grammar and easily read by all involved in production.

The problem is obvious. There is no standard language from which the various Scots dialects can be extracted. That lack of uniformity is an artistic blessing for writers outside the media. Inside, it can be a nightmare. Series TV drama uses teams of writers, each of whom write individual scripts for the same cast of characters. Some broadcasters employ even larger production teams all of whom read the scripts and request changes. Variety of authorial language is seen as hindering that process.

While I was writing, pre-production, for one new Scottish show, and hoping TV had caught up with literature, I wrote my first scripts in the different registers of Scots that suited the characters. Amazingly, the English producer loved 'hearing the characters' voices for the first time'. The other writers were asked to do likewise. All the production team and many of the directors were English. There were some interesting misunderstandings. But they coped. It was an historic shift. TV scripts in Scots.

It didn't last. A new boss arrived from London. The writers were told to stop using 'phonetic' spelling; that actors are responsible for 'accent' not writers; and finally, that Scots dialect looks silly. We argued, as did our English writers who didn't want to lose this effective new tool either. We explained that Scots was not English and why; we argued the need for authenticity; we tried to help by removing Scots forms where we felt the actor would get it anyway; we kept the grammar so that the actor could deliver in Scots. Finally, one of the English writers decided the problem might be the variety of our spellings. We standardised the list of Scots words which had English forms but which we felt had to be in Scots. Words like: *gaunae, hivnae, willnae, tae, oot* etc. At this point, there was no problem with Scots words which don't have English versions. Our list received no response. Instead, the script editors were told to change Scots spelling into English. I had one script returned in which a character, upset, had exclaimed '*Aw, whit!*' to find it now read 'All what!' Eventually, another new boss took over, Scottish this time. The writers were sent the blunt instruction that scripts must be written in standard English.

I write in both languages. For European use, I've translated some of my poems and plays from Scots into English. It's not easy. Translation is a specialist time-consuming art. Actors are not translators. They create accent. Unavoidably, I would speak Russian or German with a Scottish accent. Actors can deliberately make any text sound Irish, French, Jamaican, West or East Coast, Island or Doric by recreating the tune of that speech. But they don't change the language or grammar and can't translate English into Scots. That's why confused voices jar so many dramas pretending to Scottishness. Both languages are used in the wrong places, often during exchanges where the other would surface.

There are also cultural differences in language and how it's used. The BBC in particular, being London based, operates rules that apply to English culture. Words in common use in Scotland are banned. '*Crap*' is not allowed. '*That's crap!*' you might say, but not on BBC before 9.00 pm. In Scotland we use '*bitch*', an offensive word to Londoners, in the same variety of ways that Londoners use 'cow', a far more offensive and also dated word in Scotland. Yet the word 'cow' will be substituted for 'bitch' in scripts for Scottish programmes with no regard for the increased offence or for the cultural interference such enforced changes cause. It's impossible to use English to indicate Scottish speech. What is the English for '*midden*' or '*scunnered*'? '*Going to not do that*' and '*No, I'll not*' don't work. Authentic Scots dialogue must be fully scripted.

Forced to write standard English, writers stop hearing the characters and their schooling takes over. English usage like 'no-one' and 'someone' replaces the Scottish '*nobody*' and '*somebody*'. '*The day*' and '*the morra*' become 'today' and 'tomorrow'. Words instinctively avoided by Scots speakers, like 'little' and 'won't', sneak in. Actors, told by TV executives to keep their Scots 'light', are forced to speak a hybridised, invented language from nowhere. Their characters then sound false and unconvincing. When viewers complain '*I dinnae like the wey they talk; we dinnae speak like that; they soond awfy funny; naebody talks like that*' it's interpreted as a dislike of the Scottish voice rather than a rejection of falseness.

Strange then, that the best-selling shows produced by BBC Scotland are *Rab C. Nesbit* and *Chewing the Fat*. Both are in ripe Glaswegian Scots. Since both are comedy, TV drama would argue that's what sells them. But viewers must understand the language better to realise such comedies than to follow drama, and the language in comedy, like all else in it, is exaggerated for effect. The more subtle language of drama would be even more easily understood. There is no good reason why Scots is not used.

The Scots language is accepted, by the British government and the Council of Europe, as the second largest indigenous language of the UK. Internationally, it's also accepted and even celebrated. Last year yin o ma stories was yaised fur a Russian universities translation competition, fae Scots intae Russian. Sittin in a café in Barcelona, I learnt a Catalan wummin hoo tae speak the Angus Scots poetry o Violet Jacobs so's she could perform it oan stage the next day at an international event. I've hud work requested in Scots fur translation intae Hungarian an yin Bulgarian company turnt doon the offer ae an English translation fur yin play sayin 'we have very good translators because nobody writes anything in Bulgarian.' Gaelic and Scots are the indigenous languages of Scotland. There is no good reason why English is used to broadcast to a nation which does not speak it.

The answer is not to put Scots into the cul-de-sac of minority language broadcasts but to use it in all mainstream home and network productions in the majority quantity that reflects its use in society, moderated only by an accurate percentage of Gaelic programmes with the option of sub-titles for those of us who'd like to understand our second national language better. This applies to news, sport, documentary, comedy and game shows as much as to the tortuous, unreal language of current drama. Scots is uniquely advantaged by its connection with English. The more it's heard outwith Scotland, the more it will be understood.

The answer to the problems of reading and writing it is equally simple. Outside the Gaelic-speaking areas and apart from Gaelic medium education, all schools from infant on should teach Scots side-by-side with English, not just for language lessons but as an equal tool for the teaching of all other subjects. It is a basic human right to speak, read and write your own language and to be taught the language of the community you live in. The Scottish parliament, Scottish education and the British media discriminate against the Scots-speaking community and derogate Scottish culture. They're not alone.

In a land whaur literature is oor maist successful international art form, ye kin walk oantae the concourse o the main railway station in oor capital city an confront a bookshop full ae adverts fur naethin but English books and writers. Ye kin git aw the papers ye like but ye'll no find yin whit gies ye the news in oor ain tongue. Pit oan the radio or TV an ye'll haurly hear a yin that soonds like the folk ye pass every day oan yer road roond tae the local shop. Either ootae ignorance, or feart ye'll think thaim ignorant, the same bodies wad deny speakin ony Scots. Naewhaur else in the warld wad they things happen. Nae ither country denies its ain. Are we waitin fur somebody else tae change that fur us?

The media is a social mirror. Oors lacks the courage tae be authentically Scottish. In that respect, ye couldnae want a mair accurate reflection o oor society. Confidence in yer ain tongue and in yer ain richt tae speak oot yaisin it kin only be learned when ye hear that voice coming back tae ye.

Let me feenish hoo I sterted. In Malta, when the rain came oan, we went tae the supermarket. The checkoot lassie sympathised 'it is a pity about the rain'. 'Yes,' said ma mither. 'And it was keeping up fine too.' I fell oot the shop he-hawin at the lassie's mystified look. In typical Scots-mither style, as if laughin itself was the greatest sin in the book, ma mither demanded tae ken whit wis sae funny. 'I said it in English,' she insisted. 'Naw, mum,' I telt her. 'Sayin it so it soonds English doesnae make it English.'

Noo we maun tell oor media that sayin it so it soonds Scots doesnae mak it Scots either. The misrepresentation of our language, people and culture needs to stop.

Scots in Soaps

Christine Robinson

Since the demise of *Take the High Road*, the only surviving Scottish true soap is *River City* and this paper therefore focuses on that programme. (Occasional drama series such as *Taggart* and *Monarch of the Glen* are fundamentally different from the soap genre and do not come within the scope of this paper.) When this topic was suggested to me, I naturally set about researching it with some enthusiasm. I am grateful to the BBC who supplied me with shooting scripts by three very different writers. All quotations are taken verbatim from these scripts unless otherwise stated. Before I even glanced at these scripts, however, my first step was to record a number of episodes of *River City* and file them under E for *after*. As soon as I had a few free hours and a calm mind, I started playing my way through them and very rapidly came to the conclusion that a paper with the title *Scots in Soaps* would be a very short paper indeed unless I interpreted that as including the Scots that was conspicuous by its absence. So part of this paper is a catalogue of lost opportunities.

Before listening to these episodes, I had no idea which writer wrote which episodes. But I rapidly began to be reasonably confident about my ability to tell which were written by English writers and which were written by writers with a knowledge of Scots, or at least with SSE as a first language rather than South British English (SBrE), in spite of the actors' best efforts to achieve consistency. A large part of this paper consists of me trying to work out what lay behind these summary, instinctive judgements.

To do this, I turned my attention to the scripts and examined their language in some detail.

My findings are assembled more or less under the following broad headings:
- vocabulary which can be considered as particularly Scots
- vocabulary where the relationship to SSE or SBrE cognates are easily demonstrable through regular sound changes. With this I have included spellings which represent informal regional pronunciations.
- syntax and inflectional morphology which overlap a bit with idiom
- cultural references which impinge on language
- tag-like terms of address

The first script was by Naylah Ahmed, an English writer from Birmingham who is particularly involved when storylines concern the Asian Malik family, to ensure that cultural references are accurate. Good. A point to the BBC. But, as we shall see, their concern for ethnic differences is limited - no such overt and deliberate care is demonstrated to ensure that elements of Scottish culture are accurately represented.

What I have to say about Naylah Ahmed's script is not intended as a critique of her as a writer; in this series, she is at a linguistic disadvantage. Her Scots vocabulary is limited and consists entirely of seven occurrences of the interjection *ach;* three occurrences of *aye* in the sense of *yes*; and three occurrences of *wee*. But let us not be downhearted. We all know that the vast majority of English words are available to Scots, at least as alternatives to specifically Scots lexical items.

While there is little in this that we can claim as exclusively Scots, there is nothing much in the script that we would reject as exclusively English. Some attempt is made to hint at a Scots accent with *gonnae* which reappears as *gonna* a little further down the same page and a later *gonna* towards the end of the script which would seem to negate the first hypothesis that sprang to mind that *gonna* might have been a typo. *Gonnae no dae that missus.* Another hint at accent produced one occurrence of *ya* as a second person pronoun in unstressed position.

Where I really began to feel uneasy with this script was when I started looking at syntax. Again, it was not so much a case of anything being particularly un-Scots or even un-SSE but in the use of negatives; while *He isn't going* and *He's not going* are acceptable in Scots, SSE and South British English (SBrE), Scots and SSE have preference for the latter: *He's not going.* SBrE tends to prefer the former: *He isn't going.* This writer did use the preferred Scots form and, on three occasions, even used *no* rather than *not.* But, although the vast majority of her negatives follow the Scots pattern, there are still rather more English constructions than might be expected, and her overuse of the enclitic *-n't* began to have an English feel to my SSE ears. Predictably, although she used *never*, she never used it to negate a single occurrence. She always used it in a sense where it could be interpreted as *never-ever.*

Further examples of what I could describe 'SBrEnglishness by default' lie in her *how* and *why* interrogatives (she always uses *why* for reason and keeps *how* for manner) and in her relative pronouns (*who* and *which* are preferred to *that*). For example, consider:

(1a)   I'm the one who's supposed to have a fella

It is possible in SSE, but you would be more likely to hear

(1b)   I'm the one THAT's supposed to have a fella

north of the border. Another usage that is predominantly English is to be found in the following:

(2a)   I have responsibilities towards it ... and so does Nazir.

Native SSE speakers would more naturally use *has* instead of *does*:

(2b)   SBrE: I have responsibilities towards it ... and so does Nazir.
(2c)   SSE: I have responsibilities towards it ... and so has Nazir.

There were a couple of syntactically rather odd and unexpected sentences:

(3a)   He's a pain in the backside is what he is
(4a)   It never was the talking you were good at.

I would not personally regard (3a) as well-formed, although I have asked native speakers of SBrE who do not seem to have quite as much agin it as I have. And (4a) I might well expect to hear in Highland English. I checked with a Gaelic speaker who informed me that they were both consistent with Gaelic syntax. Now that is weird, considering that Naylah, from Birmingham, makes so very little attempt to conform to Scots syntactic preferences elsewhere in the script. Is it really likely that she would be reading *Para Handy* to get into the groove? Another thought occurred to me. Mamta Kash who plays Hana Malik has a Liverpool Asian accent. Could there be any influence of Irish Gaelic on Liverpudlian that Naylah was tapping into? I have been unable to find any evidence to support this, although I would welcome comments on this point, and these lines were not spoken by that character anyway but by two of the supposed Glaswegians. I remain baffled. On the night, the actors who were landed with these oddities simply changed them to:

(3b)   He's a pain in the backside, that's what he is.
(4b)   You were never very good at talking

As regards the use of terms of address, this author uses *love* and *pet*. Again, one is not aghast, or even particularly surprised to hear them, but they are not to be found in the scripts by Scottish writers, when *hen* and *son* are the preferred options, and by the use of *hen* and *son* they firmly place the dialogue in a Scottish context, without any conceivable loss of intelligibility. The actors too must have been a bit uncomfortable with the proliferation of *love* and *pet* since the majority of them were omitted in performance. A notable exception is the character Moira who uses *pet* to her daughter, as a special 'pet' name for her and her alone. The 'hen' is more distant, less loving. It can be used to strangers. I spoke to Jo Cameron Brown who plays Moira and she explained why her character's use of *pet* is so very clearly the exception that proves the rule, underlining the different way in which we use *pet* and *hen*.

My last gripe with Naylah's script is again a matter of probability rather than absolute rights and wrongs. I know that Scottish eating habits are in the process of change, but in the community depicted in this programme, what would a schoolgirl call her midday meal? And her evening meal? Would Kirsty really say:

(5) ... So as well as tonight's dinner, I got lunch too!

The balance of probabilities suggests otherwise. The *dinner ticket* has not yet been replaced by the *luncheon voucher* in schools.

Now, although individually these tendencies and preferences are trivial, collectively, they begin to add up to a discernibly non-Scottish piece of writing.

By contrast, a script by Jim McRoberts has a much more identifiable sense of place. While much of his vocabulary is general Scots: *daft* (4), *wee* (12), *aye* (8), and single occurrences of *afore, simmer, sassenach, lassie, sweeties, thegither, the night, slainte, haver* and *boak,* there are one or two things that begin to narrow the location down to the west a bit. *Weans* is in there, for example, although this is less regionally restricted than it used to be and has already spread over most of Scotland, and *maw* as a term of address for the female parent. The socially challenged Shellsuit Bob's use of rhyming slang puts us in an urban setting when he describes himself as *Hank Marvin* and recommends that Derek punish an assailant with 'a *swift kick in the haw maws*'. His variant of the interjection expressing scunner is *och!* (1) or *uch!* (4) rather than the preceding writer's *ach!*

When it came to spelling representations of Scots words with easily recognisable English cognates, he included *whit* (10), *dae* (2) *gonnae* (8), *naw* (6), *oot* (3), *naethin* (4), *wi* (4) and the possessive *ma* (4). *O* from *of* by V-deletion features only twice and we get *gie* twice. *Tae* replaces *too* only once. We also had single occurrences of *ye, yer, Ah, ma, granda, auld, doon, heid, hoose, haud, noo, nae* and the exclamation *Aw!* Clearly the use of Scots spellings are there to give a suggestion of Scotsness to an English orthography.

The present participle inflection appeared as <in> rather than <ing> only six times, a very small number in comparison with the actual occurrences of the participle.

From Shellsuit Bob, we get an example of the second person pronoun *yous*.

Syntactically, the cliticisation of the verb with *-n't* is generally avoided and the resultant form appears with *no* rather than *not* a resounding 28 times. Compare the relative Scottishness versus Englishness of the following:

(6a)   And d'you not think they look good together?
(6b)   And don't you think they look good together?

This writer goes for the first option consistent with SSE preference. However, when he is writing for the English speaking Asian lady, he mixes in the form that he deselects for Scots speakers or SSE speakers, and so she says:

(7)   Declaring yourself to be a Muslim isn't the most popular thing you can do these days.

This would seem to imply that Mr McRoberts is either a knowledgeable dialectologist or he has a sensitive ear. Perhaps both. He obviously hears the different speech characteristics of each of the characters and includes more or less Scots as appropriate.

Other negatives are expressed using the *-nae* forms: *cannae, didnae, wouldnae, couldnae, disnae* and *shouldnae*.

And from this writer we find one incontrovertible use of *never* as a one occasion negation:

(8)   Ma maw never had anything in the hoose to eat this morning. No 'never-ever' about that. Another example of the same thing is very clear when seen in the context of the action. Shellsuit Bob has just grabbed sweeties off three passing children and he tells them:

(9)   Right, beat it – count yourselves lucky I never took yer money.

When it comes to interrogatives, we get the typical blurring of the distinction between *why* and *how*. He uses *How no?* when the speaker is quite clearly demanding a reason.

Further Scotticisms include the unmarked plural following a numeral in *seventy-odd mile* and the use of a determiner where you would not expect to find one in SBr E: *your dinner.*

Phrases which I would identify as adding to the sense of place include:

yer at yer aunties (an invitation to eat up)

by the way (as an almost throw away tag)

a pure waste of space

eh, big man?

In the name o the wee man (as an expression of astonishment).

Moving on to his cultural references, Jim McRoberts does indeed refer to the evening meal as 'tea': *Tea's early the night*. Although, just to prove that the times are changing, the very same meal is the one referred to by the very same character in 'your dinner's oot', but there is no mistaking the Scottishness of his reference to the *playpiece*.

The last script I looked at was by Janet Paisley, and I must acknowledge the tremendous help she has given me in early stages of preparation of this paper. She has obviously thought deeply about the language to be used and had made up a list of spelling and usage recommendations. As you would expect, she includes quite a bit of Scots in her scripts but has been told to write in English, since the script editors are English and can't be expected to understand Scots. I get the impression that she sometimes tests the boundaries. The vocabulary that she manages to smuggle past the language police in a one episode script are: *wean, hackit, aye* 'yes', *ay* 'always', *plooky, but* (as a tag), *fair* (as an adverb), *ben, yin, the day, loon, mind* 'remember' *scunner, lassie, yer man* 'husband', *chapped, afore, anyroad, daud, ken, wee, thegither, the morra, daft, close, backside furrit, dunderheid* and *numpty*. In addition, she adds such Scots features as *nae* and *tae* – a big favourite at 23 occurrences – *gonny/gonnae, oot, aw* 'all', *aw* 'Oh!', *no* 'not' *noo, fer* 'for', *naw, kin* 'can', *jist, dae, ower, an* 'and', *wi, mair, heid, wummin, haud, eejit,* and *polis*.

She includes the distinctively Scots phrases:

A piece in a poke (a much more honest description than *a packed lunch*, and one that brought back memories of my schooldays)

I'm away without an explicit verb of motion

Can I no jist!

Put his gas at a peep,

See women!

The other road round.

Her pronouns include frequent use of *ye* for the second person singular. *Yeese* and *youse* appear, if rarely, for the second person plural. *Ma* and *yer* appear as possessives and *yoursell* and *thersells* as reflexives, The distal demonstratives include *they* (*thae*) and both *thon* and *yon*. Verb morphology approximates to realism with *done* as the past tense as in *he done that* and *stole* as a passive participle as in *that got stole*. Scots negatives with *not* or *no* abound and *–nae* forms, *wasnae, doesnae, didnae, wouldae, willnae, cannae*. One of the neddish characters, Deke, even treats us to a double negative. Note too the absence of the preposition that SSE would demand in :

(10)   I have just sat and ate something you scraped out a crack in the close.

As regards the cultural issue of meals, Nazir, the businessman, eats *lunch*, he talks of *working lunches*. You can see clearly how a change in working patterns is impinging on the language we use. The same family that used *tea* and *dinner* interchangeably in Jim McRobert's script find the terms equally synonymous in Janet's script:

George: if ye call abandoning me to get my own tea all right then she's doing fine.
Moira: she went out?
George: hours ago and there's no dinner on or anywhere near it.
Moira: I'll get the dinner on
[Note that determiner]
Did she say where she was going?
George:
I think we can guess, don't you?
Derek: Ma tea ready? I'm starving?

Interestingly, the actors rationalise this themselves and alter *dinner* to *tea* through this particular exchange.

So Janet's script contains a fair bit of Scots. Some characters are given more than others – Deke, for example, tends to be quite broad. A character who appears in this episode is Rosine, who quite clearly originates from Aberdeen, and Janet Paisley inserts North-East vocabulary items like *loon* in her dialogue. The actress, Joyce Falconer, who plays Rosine is a native speaker of North East Scots and, although she occasionally uses a form that might be more associated with Glasgow, her character very definitely remains an incomer into the city. Janet often remembers to write this in with the likes of *dinna* instead of *dinnae*, but if she slips up, Joyce usually goes her ain wey. She sticks to the script for one occurrence of *yin* but substitutes *een* on another occasion. Rosine is much more inclined than other members of the cast to substitute a more distinctively Scots form or lexical item. I'll come back to what the actors do with the scripts in a moment but, to just sum up what is happening with the writers, I would suggest very strongly that English writers cannot completely capture the Scots or SSE idiom in their writing. Scots writers, on the other hand, can write an English script that the actors can take into Scots without any difficulty. And even Janet's script, enriched as it is by Scots vocabulary and idiom is still overwhelmingly SSE, not Glasgow regional Scots. Remember that the items that I have described are all that there is in a half-hour episode. The rest is written in English. The token *taes* and *daes* are no more than that – a smattering, a quick salting and peppering to give a Scots flavour to an English text. This is a limitation that has been set upon her and we may see this as an opportunity to create a genuinely Scots programme thrown to the winds by a production team lacking in linguistic insight.

I wondered what was going on and so I e-mailed Stuart Doherty the producer. I had heard that there had been some upheavals in the production team, and that the Scots members of the writing team had also been removed – highly respected writers like Janet and Jim and Ian Heggie, writers that, frankly, they were lucky to have. I know that Janet Paisley was reinstated, and I believe there have been one or two others. Anyway, I was aware that there may be some sensitive internal politics, and I therefore approached with great caution indicating my genuinely unbiased academic interest in the linguistic facts. I received the following reply from Mr Doherty:

To be honest, I don't think there's a lot of point in meeting. We're not trying to conform to any linguistic pattern whatsoever, nor does the Scots language (about which I know nothing) have any influence on what we do. We're simply trying to make drama that will attract as many viewers as possible.

Having looked at *River City* from the writers' point of view, and having failed to be given more than a glimpse of the production point of view, I turned my attention to the actors. I spoke to several actors and the majority expressed a preference for scripts to be written in English, giving them autonomy to deliver the lines in the appropriate accent. And this is precisely what happens with Naylah Ahmed's scripts: whatever realism, whatever sense of Glasgow there is, comes entirely from the creativity of the actors. I did suggest earlier that, in the case of a script devoid of Scots vocabulary and idiom, that reliance on actors is not always enough. It seemed to me that the compromise of Jim McRoberts of writing in English but with Scots vocabulary and idiom included gave the actors the freedom they like but gave them superior material to work with. The younger actors all come from the Glasgow area and do a very good job on such details as the replacement of the velar nasal with alveolar nasal – this is only suggested very occasionally in the spelling the scripts but is heard frequently from the actors, with a very naturalistic variation in its frequency depending on sociolinguistic factors, TH-deletion again *with* is only occasionally written as *wi*, V-deletion: *have becomes hae* and so on, L-vocalisation of *all > aw* and so on, homorganic consonants are lost as in /nd/ >/n/, use of the glottal stop, use of appropriate Scots vowels including the typically Glasgow unrounding after /w/ as in *want* and so on, keeping the extent of these variants consistent with what might be expected of their character. Hence Shellsuit Bob and Deke have the most distinctively Glasgow features in their speech. The girls, as sociolinguistic studies would predict, are more likely to vary their speech depending on which of the other characters they are speaking to a very naturalistic touch.

One much written about feature of the speech of many young Glasgow speakers that tends to provoke a bit of a reaction from many older speakers is TH-fronting. It does not feature largely in the speech of the young actors. So we don't hear pronunciations like *nufin*. Instead, we get the traditional Scots variant /h/ as in *nuhin*.

I asked actors what guidance on accent they had been given. Apparently, in this and other programmes, the general (and often the only guidance) was 'we love your Scottish accent but can you either tone it down or try to be clearer'. Jo Cameron Brown (who plays Moira) made the point strongly, that 'toning down' was not what was required, and that Scots could be perfectly comprehensible to a wide audience, provided that clarity was the watchword. As she pointed out, this is NOT reality. In reality, speech is often slovenly and difficult to make out. This is acting, and the words are there to be heard and understood.

I haven't dealt with *Take the High Road* in this paper, mainly because it does not seem to have aroused the same kind of controversy as *River City*, but I did have a word with Eileen MacCallum, who confirmed that there was the same lack of guidance there, too. There was a general consensus among the more experienced actors to settle on a kind of general west-ish rural Scots, but younger actors inclined more towards urban Glasgow. At least *High Road* had a strong sense of location and community. She pointed out that soaps are made to a tight schedule and a tight budget with nothing to spare for voice-coaching as there would be for a drama series. It was listening to her that made me realise an essential truth: soaps are ephemera – if you could wrap your fish supper in last week's episode, that's exactly what you would do.

To return to what actors do under these trying circumstances as well as using appropriate pronunciation on their own initiative, the actors often deviate from the script. There may be a number of reasons for this – imperfect learning of lines when working under extreme pressure of time, for example. But another reason can be because the lines are hard to say (which incidentally makes them hard to memorise). Jo Cameron Brown explained to me that she changed:

(11a)   It's only been a year since losing her father
to
(11b)   It only been a year since she loast her father

because she did not feel the first construction was natural to a Scots or SSE speaker.

Comparing Riz Abbasi's version of his character of Nazir's dialogue with the text, he too will alter lines to a more naturally Scots syntax. Occasionally vocabulary items are changed and this can happen in both directions. Rosine alters words to accord with her own dialect and occasionally substitutes a Scots word for an English one, but this is rarer among the other characters. In fact there is the occasional translation of a Scots word into English: *plooky* in Janet's script metamorphosed into *spotty* in transmission. One of the younger actors, Gordon McCorkell, who plays Derek aka Deke, and a Glaswegian himself, was kind enough to let me ask him a few questions, and he admitted that his knowledge of Scots vocabulary is not extensive. He is not alone in that, particularly among younger speakers.

The following excerpt will provide some idea of the extent to which the script can be altered:

Kirsty:
Script: Thought ye'd like everybody to know you're still the wean.
Performance: Thought ye'd like people to know you're still the wean.
Hazel:
Golden Oldie me.
Brian:
Happy birthday
Kirsty:
Script: Soon as ma mum gets this room fumigated for hackit crabs, it will be. Cheers Brian.
Performance: Yea it will be when ma mum gets this room fumigated for hackit crabs.
Cheers Brian
Brian:
You're aw right. No gonny put then up

Kirsty:
Script: Seeing it's ma birthday, I'll just no answer that, will I?
Performance: Seeing it's ma birthday, I'll just no answer that, OK?
Brian: What's up wi her?
Hazel:
Script: Feelin her age. Young folk these days, eh?
Performance: Feelin her age I suppose. Young folk these days, eh?

Which brings us on to the point of view of the viewers. I have heard rather a lot of adverse criticism on the subject of accents in *River City*, from non-linguists. None of these have complained about intelligibility. What they do complain about is a perceived lack of 'Glaswegianness'. I am told the the accents are 'all over the place.' Well, go to any big city and listen. You can play 'spot the Edinburgher' in Edinburgh. There's not a lot of them about. The older Maliks, the parents, are obviously incomers to Glasgow. As I said before, the mother has a Liverpool Asian accent. The young Maliks are died in the wool Glaswegians. Nazir has probably the most recognisably Glasgow accent after Shellsuit Bob and Deke. Riz Abbasi probably does the most work on turning the Englishness of the script into a regional accent. The Malik girls use less Scots to their parents and more among themselves and with their contemporaries. Rosine has an Aberdeen accent you could cut with a knife. It would be absurd to suggest that there is anything amiss with her acting skills. She's not meant to be Glasgow. Believe it or not, I have spoken to several people who have not realised that she is simply playing another incomer to the city. Actually, her character is the one that people seem either to love or hate – depending on whether or not they like her voice. My older daughter, who couldn't be persuaded to open a book until she discovered *Sunset Song*, is a now complete north-east-ophile and irritates us no end with her Rosine impressions. But Rosine does bring some humour to her part and at least she stimulates a reaction.

Gordon McCorkell is quite happy with the authenticity of the accents. He is aware that there has been criticism but, as he pointed out, people don't always like to hear themselves as ithers hear them. I think he has a good point there.

The accents are Glaswegian but they are not the steorotypical music hall Glaswegian that has continued down through Francie and Josie and Rab C. They even lack the homogeneity that *Taggart* manages to achieve. What you have, accentwise, in *River City*, is a much broader spectrum. Glasgow has not just one accent. In real life, it has many variations, refinements and shades overlaid on certain widespread features depending on age, gender, the social class of this speaker and the social situation the speaker is in at the moment. This returns us to the difference between real life and drama. In reality, we have time to work out who belongs where in a social group. In drama, we want it writ large. I'm not saying for a moment that *River City* should use some kind of music hall accent, but I do think that a more positive use of Scots would incline to that sense of place that *Taggart* has and this programme so desperately lacks. Then I wouldn't hear comments like '*River City*? Where is that set? Is it Glasgow?' And in order to do that, there has to be some kind of language policy for the programme.

To give an example, as Jo Cameron Brown explained to me, one of the relationships that was going to be explored in *River City* was the relationship between Moira and George, representing an older, more traditional style of marriage in the light of changing social mores. Moira was to be seen as a woman who could have been an achiever, she could have gone places. George, slightly threatened by this, puts her down and makes a point of keeping her in her place. He wants his tea (or breakfast) on the table when he's ready for it, and it's her job to make sure it's there.

> *Nae breakfast*
> *Yer Bran's in the box*
> *You're no talking tae a horse*

Jo Cameron Brown could see the linguistic possibilities in this kind of relationship, and she said early on that they were there, but the whole notion of examining the relationship seems to have gone down the said river and taken the differences in George's and Moira's language along with it. (Actually a large part of their interaction seems to centre around his demands for food.)

So what can we say about a programme that sets out to explore the life of a community and ignores the language of that community. In this paper, I have used the phrase 'a sense of place' on several occasions, because language is such a major contributor to that sense of belonging. A community has a sense of place. *River City* has not. That is certainly one of the reasons why it is a 24 carat bubblyjock.

The Scots Leid in the Performing Airts the Day

Sheila Douglas

In the warld o the tradeetional performin airts at praisent, the Scots leid is whit maks their growthe come awa. It maun be said at this pynt that Scots is no a minority leid in Scotland for it is spakken or uptakken by maist fowk. Sae it is no the media or the eddication system or the airts warld that eik tae the fowk's abeelity tae yaise the leid, but raither the conter. The leid is the grund o oor leeterature, oor muisic and oor theatre.

I hae haed lang expairience o performin the tradeetional airts, tellin cracks and singin ballants and sangs, as weel as scrievin in Scots. Ony skeel I may hae in yaisin Scots for ony o thir haes been hailly ma ain love darg. Ony kep I hae had tae pass on Scots as ane o ma mither tungs, I hae made muckle o. But ye cannae learn fowk tae yaise a leid in a vawcum, but only throu whit fowk dae wi it. Singers, makars and shennachies aa yaise the leid tae perform their airt. Een instrumental muisic lippens tae the vyce and twang o the leid. There are fowk galore pittin their backs intae this, but their ettles arenae uphauden aither politically or financially. We micht hae expeckit wi oor Pairliament reconvenit and the airts bein ane o the devolved maitters it is mintit tae owresee, that we wad get a better deal for thae tradeetional airts. But it seems that tae be uphaudit wi siller, ye hae tae spick or sing in English (or Italian or French or German).

The trauchle is that the tradeetional airts are grundit in a leid that the Scottish Executive thrawnly winna haud wi or awn. They say it's ower deefficult tae mak a defineetion o it (for thaim it may be sae) and therefore cannae gie it offeecial recogneetion. They hear it aa aroon them ilka day o life, yet they aye fin it aisier tae trowe that Gaelic desairves millions o pun o siller tae uphaud it, een tho its spakken by less nor 2% o the fowk, gaun by the last Census feegurs, an the maist raicent scance o the seetuation. The Executive aye denies whit maist Scots, whether or no they yaise the leid or vallae it, ken tae be the truith. They dae this in spite o the fack that we hae at least sax hunner year o Scots leeterature, which is maistly mislippen by the eddication system that learns oor bairns language and literature are pit unner the heidin o "English". The Executive dis this in spite o the fack that onyb'dy can hear the leid spakken onywhaur in the kintrae. It dis this tae in spite o the fack that onyb'dy wha switches on *Holyrood Live* on televeesion can hear the soun o Scots daily frae the flair of the chaumer. Mony politeecians o coorse are weel-kent for haein claith lugs, blin een and selective memories.

I misdoot but that the Scottish Executive doesnae gie a thocht tae whether it is aisy or no tae fin a defineetion o Scots. The truith is they haena takken tent o the fack that Scotland is and has lang been, a kintrae wi no wan, no twa, but three leids, aa rowed in thegither. They see it throu the een o Westminster whaur Scots is descreived as "jist a form o English" yet they let on they cannae unnerstaun it when they hear it spakken. At the ruit, o coorse, it's a question o siller. Gin they gien it recogneetion as the leid o atween a hauf and twa thairds o the population, *they wad hae tae pey for it.*

Gainstaunin this stane waa o nay-say is the growthe o Scots culter, wi the performin airts weel tae the fore. In Scotland the day there is a dirlin ootwardluikin warld o muisic, wi a wheen o tradeetional performers whase names are kent aa owre the warld. There is forby a braw network o fowk clubs, sessions and festivals. Ane o the maist wechty o ongaun moyens on the girss ruit performance o tradeetional muisic and sang in Scotland haes been the Fowk Revival o the 1960s an 70s. That may hae been langsyne but its effecks were lang-lestand. At the time it wis a tippie fassoun, like the norie the noo for whit is aften gey dootsomely caaed Celtic muisic. The kinch o fassouns is that they gae by. But the Fowk Revival was a muivement that rowed in sae mony "ordinary" fowk that it chyngit the perceptioun o Scots for aye. *We reddit oorsels o the tartan toorie!* It led tae a re-findin o the Scots tradeetion, throu the leid, which maist fowk spak or unnerstude. Tradeetion is cairried on by a swairm o fowk performin, no by a haunfu o byordinar "stars". This is whit the Fowk Revival wis aboot., *whit Hamish Henderson cried "the carrying stream".* It wis by a mischance that fowk music becam mercat-like and this bealin conter-influence noo hi-jacks what shuid be the heirship o ilka Scot.

The Royal Scottish Academy o Music and Drama in Glesca noo haes a Scottish muisic degree coorse and some gey braw performers are graduatin fae it and becomin weel-kent. As ane o the coorse tutors, wha are aa practeecians o Scots culture, I hae ettled tae kythe hou the Scots leid is conneckit wi the muisic coorse the students are follaein. I hae recordit stories and ballants, for HOTBED, the RSAMD's electronic teachin/learnin projeck wi a password that gies an ingait til't, whase acronym stauns for "haunin on tradeetion by electronic dissemination".

The RSAMD's Drama School pits a gey muckle vailye on upbringin actors tae yaise sindry forms o Scots, no juist the yaisual caricature Glaswegian. I hae whyles supplied the actors' vyce coach Ros Steen, wi taped swatches o parteecular forms o Scots speak tae help her in her wark. But aa that disnae chynge the fack that the tradeetional airts, like the airts in general, want for siller in Scotland.

Storytellin in Scotland has raicently been gien a heize and has been weel-hained wi siller. I first brocht it intae the Perth Fowk Festival in 1973 and stairtit a competeetion for a caup at the Tradeetional Muisic and Sang Associations's Festival at Kinross in 1974 and sinsyne it haes become a pairt o maist TMSA festivals as weel as ither fowk festivals. The modern mistak tae think o it as a ploy for bairns haes been bainished by the settin up o a Scottish Storytelling Centre in Edinburgh's High Street, which is noo hoosit in a Lottery-fundit biggin, neist tae the Netherbow Airts Centre. The Scottish Storytelling Forum, o which I am a foonder member, rins an annual festival at the en o October, a monthly Storytellin Club caaed the Guid Crack Club and haes a trainin scheme wi coorses and warkshops for storytellers. The Directory it prents gies leets and parteeculars o storytellers aa ower Scotland, mony o them wi a guid Scots tung in their heid.

Only the fack that there are eneuch fowk *spickin* Scots tae mak the leid the medium o the sangs sung and the stories telt, hauds the tradcetion gaun. Whit maun be is for the status o this majority leid tae be gien a heize and ae wey o daein this is by its bein gien recogneetion by the Scottish Executive. I speir at my students hou they ken a tune is Scottish when they hear it. The answer is that it is foondit on the lilt and tune o the leid. These language pattrens are lang-kent tae the lugs o Scots fowk, een gin they are scantlins ware o't. Scots aye leives in the performin airts, thanks tae the voluntar chave o fowk wha are browdent on't, but nae thanks tae the politeecians.

The Scots Language in the Performing Arts Today

In the world of the performing arts today, the Scots language is what makes their development increase. It has to be said at this point that Scots is not a minority language in Scotland, for it is spoken or understood by the majority of people, even though some of them curiously deny it. It is not therefore the media or the education system or the arts world that make the language grow, but rather the opposite. The language is the foundation of our literature, our music and our theatre.

I have had many years of experience of performing in the traditional arts, telling stories and singing ballads, as well as writing and teaching Scots. Any skill I may have in using Scots for any of these purposes has been acquired purely by my own efforts. Any opportunity I have had to pass on Scots as one of my mother tongues, I have made the most of in all of my activities. But you cannot teach language in a vacuum, but only through how people use different forms to embody it. Singers, poets and storytellers all use the language to practise their art. Even instrumental music is based on the speech rhythms and intonations of the language. There are plenty of people working hard at this, but their efforts are not supported either politically or financially. We might expect, with our Parliament reconvened and the arts being one of the devolved matters it is supposed to oversee, that we would get a better deal for the traditional arts. But only arts that are expressed through English (or Italian or German or French) seem to qualify for funding.

The trouble is that our arts are rooted in a language that the Scottish Executive refuses to recognise or even to admit exists. They say it is too difficult to define (which it may be for them) and therefore they cannot give it official recognition. They hear it all around them every day, yet they find it easier to believe that Gaelic is important enough to warrant millions of pounds of funding even though, according to the Census 2001 figures, it is spoken by less than 2% of the population. It is not used by more than a very few of our leading poets, novelists and dramatists. They deny what most Scots, whether they use the language or value it, know to be the truth. They do this in spite of the fact that we have at least six hundred years of Scots literature, which is all but ignored by the education system that teaches our children language and literature under the heading of "English". They do this in spite of the fact that anyone can hear the language spoken everywhere in the country. They do this in spite of the fact that anyone who switches on *Holyrood Live* (live Parliamentary proceedings) on television, can hear the sound of Scots daily from the floor of the chamber. Many politicians of course are renowned for having cloth ears, blind eyes and selective memories.

I do not believe the Scottish Executive gives a thought to whether it is easy or difficult to define Scots. The truth is they have not taken into consideration the fact that Scotland is a trilingual country: it has not one, not two, but three languages and has had for a very long time, and these languages are inextricably bound up with one another. They see it through the eyes of Westminster where Scots is described as "just a form of English" yet they claim they cannot understand it when they hear it spoken. The bottom line, of course, is money. If they gave it proper recognition as the language of between half and two-thirds of the population, *they would have to fund it*!

Against this stone wall of denial, the living growth of Scottish culture is a flourishing contradiction, with the performing arts well to the fore. In Scotland today there is a lively outward looking world of music of all kinds, with a galaxy of traditional performers known worldwide. There is a fine network of folk clubs, sessions and festivals. One of the most important influences on the grass roots performance of traditional music and song was the Folk Revival of the 1960s and 70s. That may have been a long time ago but its effects were long lasting. At the time it was a trendy fashion, like the one at present for what is often very dubiously called Celtic music. The trouble with fashions is that they pass. But the Folk Revival was a movement that involved so many so-called "ordinary" people that it changed the perception of things Scottish forever. We got rid of the tartan toorie! It led to a rediscovery of the Scots tradition through the language, which most people spoke or understood. Tradition is carried on by a mass of people performing, not by a handful of "stars". This is what the Folk Revival was about, showing us we are all part of what Hamish Henderson called "the carrying stream".

Storytelling in Scotland has recently been given a financial boost. I first brought it into the Perth Folk Festival in 1973 and started a TMSA competition for a cup at Kinross Festival in 1974. Since then it has become a part of most TMSA festivals as well as of other folk festivals. The mistaken idea that it is just an amusement for children has been banished by the setting up of a Scottish Storytelling Centre in Edinburgh's High Street, recently been housed in a Lottery-funded building next door to the Netherbow Arts Centre. The Scottish Storytelling Forum, of which I am a founder member, runs an annual festival at the end of October, a monthly story telling club called the Guid Crack Club and has a training scheme with courses and workshops for storytellers. The Directory it prints gives lists and details of storytellers all over Scotland, many of them with a guid Scots tung in their heid. Only the fact that there are enough people speaking Scots to make the language the medium of the songs stories, holds the tradition together. What needs to happen is for this the status of this majority language to be raised and one way of doing this is for it to be given recognition by the Scottish Executive.

The Royal Scottish Academy of Music and Drama in Glasgow now has a Scottish Music Degree Course and some very fine performers are graduating from it and becoming well known. As one of the course tutors, who are all practitioners of Scottish culture, I have tried to show how the Scots language is connected with the music course the students are following. I have recorded stories and ballads for HOTBED, the RSAMD's electronic teaching/learning system, with a password that enables students to access it. The acronym stands for "handing on tradition by electronic dissemination". The RSAMD's Drama School puts a very high value on training actors to us different forms of Scots, not just the usual caricature Glaswegian, that is now out-dated. I have from time to time supplied the actors' voice coach, Ros Steen, with taped excerpts of particular forms of Scots to help her in her work. But all that does not alter the fact that the traditional arts are seriously under-funded in Scotland. I ask my students how they know a tune is Scottish when they hear it. The answer is because it is rooted in the language: it reflects the lilt of it. These language patterns are familiar to the ears of Scots people, even though they may be scarcely aware of it. Scots still lives in the performing arts, thanks to the voluntary or low-paid work of the people who are enthusiastic about it, but no thanks to the politicians.

Scots in the Public Sphere

John Corbett and Fiona Douglas

1. Introduction

This paper is the result of a dialogue that brings together the authors' various interests in the language of the media, language planning, political language in Scotland, and in the establishment of an electronic text archive of present-day writing and speech in Scotland. One of the authors completed a PhD on the use of Scots vocabulary in the press (Douglas, 2000) and the other contributed a chapter on language planning for the *Edinburgh Companion to Scots,* launched at the Belfast Symposium (Corbett, 2003). One observation that has struck us from these activities is the pace of change in post-devolutionary Scotland, and this paper has allowed us to stand back, pause for breath, and make a provisional assessment of recent developments in the public domain use of Scots.

2. Language Planning for Public Domain Scots, or Checking the Boxes

Language planning contradicts some of the cherished tenets of linguistics insofar as it eschews the principle of objective description in favour of intervention and prescription. Scots language activism can draw upon the now extensive literature and experience of language planning elsewhere, with the result that linguists cannot simply observe a naturally occurring situation and determine, say, in which domains Scots is or is not being used in. Activists can prepare the ground in accordance with models of language planning, in the interests of making a case for broader acceptance of their preferred medium. This is an interesting situation, not least for descriptive linguists, who find themselves, willingly or not, implicated in the processes that they are objectively trying to portray.

For example, the target domains for a 'full national language' were codified in the 1960s by linguists such as Stewart (1968), since when they have achieved a relatively wide currency in language planning circles. Stewart asks a set of questions that can be answered with reference to a growing body of 'public domain Scots':

1. Official, e.g. is the language used as an official language by the governing authorities?
Until the establishment of a Scottish Parliament in 1999, there was no attempt to use modern Scots as an official language. Since then, a breakthrough has been achieved with the publication in Scots (and other languages) of a Report of the Education, Culture and Sport Committee into Scots, Gaelic and minority languages in Scotland, sometimes called the 'McGugan Report' (McGugan, 2003). This has been followed by a Scots version of a public information leaflet, *Makkin your voice heard in the Scottish Pairliament,* and a pamphlet by the Cross-Pairty Group on the Scots Language, *Scots: A Statement of Principles,* based on the Universal Declaration of Human Rights (Donati et al, 2003). A popular history

of self-government in Scotland, *A Scots Parliament* by James Robertson, written in Scots throughout, is on sale in the Scottish Parliament bookshop (Robertson, 2002). These publications are written in a thin, accessible but nevertheless distinctive medium – which might be dubbed 'Civil Service Scots'.

2. Provincial: is the language used as an official language by part of the nation?
So far, these initiatives at national level have not been replicated by local authorities, although some, like Perth and Kinross, have a record of support for the Scots language.

3. Lingua franca: is the language used for wider communication amongst different speech communities in the nation?
Although it is difficult to give evidence that Scots is used as a public domain *lingua franca* in Scotland, it is occasionally used as a medium to present talks to speakers of Gaelic, Irish, English and Scots at the Belfast Symposium – usually without simultaneous translation. We can point, then, to at least one situation where Scots is regularly used to fulfil this function.

4. International: is the language used for diplomatic relations, foreign trade, tourism, etc?
Although instances are few and far between, there are examples that Scots can be used in international contexts. At an exhibition of Scottish arts and crafts held in the Smithsonian Institute, Washington DC, in the summer of 2003, there was signage in English, Gaelic and Scots – the Scots provided by Dr Sheila Douglas, the folk historian and singer. And, again in 2003, the British Council Scotland approached one of the authors of this paper, John Corbett, to ask him to furnish a Scots version of the Council's mission statement, to put on its website, once more alongside English and Gaelic paraphrases (see http://www.britishcouncil.org/Scotland).

5. Capital: is the language the major medium of communication in the capital city?
The answer to this question depends on the definition of 'Scots' to which you adhere, a definition that tends towards the 'dense Scots' end of the language continuum, or one that favours a 'thin Scots' that is heavily anglicised. How the population of Edinburgh, and elsewhere in Scotland, self-identifies its speech habits awaits the inclusion of a Scots question in a national census.

6. Group: is the language the major means of communication amongst a particular social or ethnic group?
This question is easier to answer: it is certainly possible to indicate certain social groups, such as working-class urban Scots, rural workers, or inhabitants of the islands of Orkney and Shetland, whose use of Scots is relatively dense and distinctive. Arguably, though research is needed to provide evidence of this, Scots is regularly used as a means of everyday communication by particular social groups in Scotland.

7. Education: is the language the medium of communication in primary, secondary and/or higher education?

There are now many more resources than there have been for several decades to support the use of Scots as a spoken – and written – medium of communication in schools, colleges and universities. *The Kist Anthology* broke new ground in the 5-14 curriculum in the 1990s, the introduction to the teacher's workbook giving advice (in Scots) about using Scots in the classroom. Since then, other publications by Merlin Press and most recently Itchy Coo Publishers deliver a range of materials for primary and secondary schoolchildren (see www.itchy-coo.com). Scottish Language Dictionaries' educational outreach website, the 'Scuil Wab,' is set to be relaunched with some activities that encourage the use of Scots across the curriculum (see www.sldl.org.uk in due course). At the 2002 Belfast Symposium, the *Luath Scots Language Learner* was launched, a textbook with the innovative aim of teaching the auld tongue to non-native speakers (Wilson, 2002).

In higher education, there are several instances of students at Glasgow University using Scots as a medium of written communication, usually for assignments and essays in Scottish Literature or English Language, and one Glasgow graduate did go on to complete a PhD in and on Scots at Aberdeen University (Allan, 1998). Aberdeen Scots Leid Quorum was also responsible for compiling and publishing two issues of *Cairn,* an academic journal of Scottish History, written entirely in Scots under the editorship of Dauvit Horsbroch. From the very start of the Belfast Symposia, certain articles in the proceedings have also been published in Scots.

8. School: is the language studied as part of the school or university curriculum?
The advent of Higher Still in Scotland opened the door to the formal study of 'Scottish Language' at school and college level, though the take-up for SQA Advanced Higher 'Language' options remains disappointingly low, particularly compared with the substantial uptake in England, Wales and Northern Ireland for GCE 'English Language' A-levels. For many years now, Scots has been a regular part of undergraduate study and/or postgraduate research at institutions such as Aberdeen, Edinburgh and Glasgow Universities, as well as overseas institutions such as the University of Helsinki, home of the Helsinki Corpus of Older Scots.

9. Literary: is the language used for literary purposes?
A constant throughout the history of the Scots language has been its use in literary expression, most usually in poetry and drama in the modern period. There is still abundant evidence of activity in this domain. More recently, there has been a move towards extended prose in Scots in popular genres such as the science fiction novel, *But n Ben a-Go-Go,* by Matthew Fitt (Fitt, 2000).

10. Religion: is the language used in the rituals of a particular religion?
There is certainly the potential for the use of Scots in Christian religious ceremonies, with various versions of Biblical texts now available – from William Lorimer's *New Testament in Scots,* reprinted as a Canongate Classic (Lorimer, 2001 [1983]), to Jamie Stuart's more colloquial *A Glasgow Bible* (Stuart, 1997). Advance publicity at the 2003 Belfast Symposium promises the imminent publication of a new four-volume version of the complete Bible, in a pared-down Scots based on Ogden's Basic English vocabulary – a Scots version of the Bible

that, in the blurb at least, is reminiscent of the functional 'Civil Service Scots' mentioned above (Falconer and Arthur, forthcoming). There was also mention at the Symposium of the new version being 'tested' in kirks – so presumably such texts are being used here and there by congregations – and the publication of research into the response would be illuminating.

Like all lists, Stewart's 1968 one is provisional and can be added to. One surprising omission that it would be necessary to include today is:

11. Media: is the language the medium of mass communication in the national newspapers, or electronic media (television, radio, internet)?
As in the case of the capital city, this question is not an easy one to answer. At the 2003 Belfast Symposium (see this volume), Maggie Cunningham, BBC Scotland's Head of Radio, argued that supporting the Doric reminiscences of Robbie Shepherd and the urban banter of Tam Cowan and Stuart Cosgrove amounted to a shift towards Scots programming, supplemented by a list of fifty Scots words that BBC Radio Scotland presenters were encouraged to use. Across the water, BBC Radio Ulster's arts magazine *A Kist o Wurds* is clearly a pioneer in the use of a fairly dense Ulster-Scotch as the regular medium of communication in a topical radio magazine programme (samples can be downloaded from ulsterscotsagency.com/ Audiolanguage.asp) (see Chris Spurr, also in this volume). In other media, the use of Scots is even patchier – there has been very little dense Scots used in national newspapers, apart from the very occasional article on the Scots language. There are, however, various websites that utilise varieties of Scots (e.g. www.scots-online.org), and Scots appears infrequently in television programmes – usually in comedy or social-realist drama. A few advertising companies have utilised Scots, one of the highest profile campaigns in recent years being the Grants whisky billboard and television advertisements, featuring the slogans 'Unco Sonsie', 'Ilka dram a ferlie', and 'Hae a drap at gloamin-shot' amongst others. Grants' use of dense Scots in its campaign was somewhat mitigated by the fact that the accompanying television commercials all played on the assumption that the Scots used on the billboards was unintelligible.

Patchiness notwithstanding, it is impressive how many of these public domains now have at least some evidence of activity in Scots. In 1968, when Stewart's list of target domains was published, Scots was being used in few of them. Varieties of the language were certainly being used for literary purposes, and they were arguably a major means of communication between members of certain social groups – as they still are today. Scots was also present in the school curriculum in ways that are possibly undervalued – a staple of modern Scottish literature is the stereotype of weans being skited on the lugs for using Scots in class – but examination of classroom practices will show that Scots was, for many pupils, used expressively in poetry and music classes – often in relation to the poems and songs of Robert Burns or Walter Scott (see Corbett 2003). Scots has also had a minor but reasonably constant place in the curriculum of several universities, notably Aberdeen, Edinburgh and Glasgow. But you could hardly argue that Scots was the medium of communication in education, even if it was studied and even celebrated here and there, and until recent years the presence of Scots in domains such as the media and in government has generally been negligible to non-existent.

3. Beyond 'check-box culture'

If we are to indulge in a spirit of 'checking the boxes', then, we can point to Stewart's criteria and say that the number of target domains in which Scots is used has increased from, say, three out of eleven to potentially eight out of eleven – and we have the texts, the websites and the educational resources to prove it. Can we therefore argue that Scots today is closer to being a full national language than it was in 1968 – have three and a half centuries of decline and language shift towards English been slowed and even reversed?

There is no doubt that the fact we can even point to eight out of eleven domains and say that there is at least potential for Scots to be used there today – and resources to support that use – is a remarkable and heartening achievement. The problem is that to arrive at an accurate picture of language use, we have to look beyond the presence of texts and resources and consider how they are used. There needs to be research into issues such as the following:

• the long-term impact of Scots educational resources in the classroom – in particular, the impact on attitudes and competence of learners
• the impact of the presence of Scots language versions of political documents on the attitudes and reading competence of the general public
• the response to the use (if any) of Scots religious texts with Scottish congregations
• the market response to advertisements in Scots (e.g. the Grants whisky campaign)

Some of these research questions are to do with language attitudes, which are usually researched in a snapshot way by lone postgraduates, and others are to do with linguistic competence: e.g. how well do Scottish readers understand and respond to the new 'Civil Service Scots' of the 'McGugan Report' or pamphlets such as *Makkin yer voice heard*? Researchers need to be able to have the resources to identify and work with representative focus groups throughout the country. Such sustained research would have to be properly funded and coordinated – there is at present no mechanism for doing this, though the proposed Institute for the Languages of Scotland might provide such a mechanism.

4. The Rise of 'Civil Service Scots'

Another avenue for research is, of course, the evolution of a twenty-first century 'Civil Service Scots'. It is possibly a consequence of the influence of language planning that the extension of Scots into non-literary target domains is at the expense of literary Scots, which is explicitly avoided and even downgraded. It is remarkable that the advance publicity for the imminent version of the Bible in Scots takes as a selling-point that it is 'refreshingly free from literary pretension' and one of the authors of this paper has attended meetings to promote Scots where literary Scots was explicitly treated with considerable reservation. It is useful to consider why literary Scots, so long the vanguard of Scots language activism, might now be treated with suspicion:

• literature is expressive, playful and symbolic. It is not practical, hard-headed or message-oriented. Cooper (1989:115) is one of many who argue that language planning that rests on literary activity is doomed to failure:

languages revive not when poets and novelists use the medium, but when those such as civil servants use it. Therefore, the argument goes, literary Scots should be avoided in favour of a purely functional prose.

• literature is by nature linguistically deviant and authority-resistant. For example, it is notoriously difficult to get poets, dramatists and novelists to agree on a spelling system because they demand the right to articulate their individual identities, to play with the full range of expressive possibilities, and snub their nose at such self-styled linguistic dictators as lexicographers and grammarians.

'Civil Service Scots' is different. It is not expressive; it is message-oriented. You do not read a Scottish Executive information leaflet for its fine sense of rhythm or the subtle light that it casts on the Scottish character. 'Civil Service Scots' has to be linguistically accessible, codified and fixed so as to be teachable to all those who have to draft and read leaflets and reports. It is well to remember that Sir Ernest Arthur Gowers, author of style bibles such as *Plain Words: A Guide to the Use of English,* and *The ABC of Plain Words* (cf. Gowers, 1987) was himself a civil servant, Chairman of the Board of the Inland Revenue, and that he turned to writing at the invitation of the Treasury, which saw a demand for efficient writers of official documents.

'Civil Service Scots' is a new, indeed nascent, phenomenon, 15th-16th century antecedents notwithstanding. Although it seems to stand apart from literary Scots, there are some interesting parallels with the Lallans movement of the post-war period:

• Like the Lallans writers, the writers of 'Civil Service Scots' are currently a coterie, not on the whole civil servants themselves, but mainly a small band of poets and novelists who are also active in Scots language planning (e.g. James Robertson, Matthew Fitt and Colin Donati, to name a few). Their considerable linguistic skills are hired out to the civil servants, although a few, such as Andrew Philp, actively participate in the drafting of Scots prose. There is also a diaspora of linguists who contribute – for example, the lexicographers at Scottish Language Dictionaries are consulted on spellings for the Scots Hansard.

• Like the Lallans writers, the writers of 'Civil Service Scots' are ettling to 'write a nation into existence', not only by inventing a synthetic language that will represent it across regions and social classes, but employing such a language in official, public domains. That such documents exist is redolent of nationhood.

• Like some forms of literature, even 'Civil Service Scots' prose does fulfil a symbolic, identity-celebrating function. Indeed it might be argued that the Scots versions of official documents disappear like snaw aff a dyke not because they are better written than their English counterparts but because they have, in stylistic terminology, a 'secondary poetic function' (Corbett 1997, 22-8). Official documents do not need to be written in Scots in order to be understood (all literate Scots read English, after all), so if a document *is* written in Scots, it attracts an extra significance, namely that author(s) and readers are affirming a mutual national difference from other English-users.

Neither is 'Civil Service Scots' free from the codification controversies that dogged and continue to dog the Lallans movement – issues of spelling, appropriate vocabulary, grammar and pragmatics. Soon after *Makkin yer voice heard in the Scottish Pairlament* was published, the Cross-Party Group email forum featured a query from an overseas research student about particular expressions in the leaflet that depart from the usages recommended in the Scots dictionaries and David Purves' *A Scots Grammar.* The forum was also able to consider the Executive's response to the query, which noted in effect that even 'Civil Service Scots' is speech-based and still subject to greater variability than a fixed written standard.

Meanwhile, authoritative voices continue to be raised, questioning the validity of the whole enterprise of raising the status of Scots and extending its domains of usage. Jones (2002: 6-7) argues that the scant lexical resources for translations into Scots of technical and bureaucratic documents results in a medium that simply does not carry the authority that 300 years of written standard English can take for granted:

> Very often the effects of language change on regional dialects has meant that original vocabularies have become severely depleted – words for new concepts and technologies have to be taken from a related, but perceived as more culturally dominant language. Language planners very often solve this problem by putting older vocabulary to new, modern use, but this often has the effect of de-intellectualising the language, making it in the process unattractive to users of the standard. One ends up very often with what looks like 'hamely tongue', one which fails to be taken completely seriously when used in scientific and other specialised contexts.

A reasonable academic anxiety that might prompt Professor Jones' argument seems to be that too much scholarly and popular attention can be directed, or arguably misdirected, towards the presence of occasional 'spectacular' texts in Scots that suggest that more activity is going on than there in fact might be. How many people in Scotland are *really* aware of the fascinating but few examples of bureaucratic Scots prose? How do they respond to these examples? How many copies of the *Kist* lie unused in school libraries? How often are Scots Bibles used in kirks? Where such texts are used enthusiastically, what is the effect on readers' linguistic competence and confidence? Despite the fact that such 'spectacular' texts as the McGugan Report often attract media attention, favourable and hostile, this attention is usually short-lived and the complex issues of long-term impact are simply under-researched, which is surprising because public money has been involved in the production of many of the texts and resources.

If scholarly and popular discussions of the use of Scots in the public domain are in danger of being hijacked by the presence of a few spectacular texts of undetermined impact, what could we focus on otherwise? Scots language activists sometimes deride the use of occasional Scots expressions in otherwise English discourse as 'the currants in the dumpling' – however, the nature of interaction between the Scots and English linguistic systems in Scotland is a neglected topic that offers an alternative way of exploring the place of Scots in the public domain.

5. Scots in the Press

Newspapers, simply because they are published and consumed on a daily basis, are one sensitive indicator and creator of 'public domain language'. They are important because they both reflect and intervene in the construction of the language of the public sphere. Newspapers also define themselves partly by the language they use – one dominant myth is that that newspapers 'speak the language of the readers' and individuals can define themselves and others by the newspapers they read – thus slogans such as 'Real Scots Read the Record'.

Although newspapers seldom use the kind of dense Scots associated with the 'Civil Service Scots' idiom, there are clearly elements of Scots in the press. The most obvious element of Scots in the press is lexical. Douglas' (2000) lexical analysis of the Scottish national press during 1995 suggested that such elements of Scots language as were included were usually highly restricted.

First of all, restricted in terms of whereabouts in the newspaper they occurred with feature and sport articles predictably being the most likely to use Scots words. It can be argued that Scots is more acceptable here as these are less formal parts of the newspaper, are designed to 'entertain' and are not concerned with 'hard news'. These article types are more likely to foreground the persona and opinions of the columnist, and hence the use of Scots here is less likely to interfere with the impersonal institutional authoritative voice of the newspaper. Thus there are fairly defined contexts where the use of Scots is deemed to be more or less appropriate – an appropriacy in which both the newspapers and their readerships probably collude – no doubt there would be many letters of complaint if the *Scotsman* decided to publish its front page in Scots. Thus the prevailing hegemony of English for formal and public discourse is maintained rather than threatened by the use of Scots in these contexts.

Secondly, the use of Scots is restricted in terms of the permissible subject matter. The old truism that Scots is mainly used in the public domain for humorous purposes holds true. The *Herald* and *Scotsman* Diaries are frequent users of 'comic' Scots. We may argue that this devalues Scots, that it undermines its language status, and contributes to the maintenance of rigid appropriacy constraints but, nevertheless, it is an important and popular outlet for Scots and is very effective in creating a sense of a shared Scottish community. We understand the words, get the joke, and thereby we have membership of the exclusive Scottish community. For example, in a recent issue of the *Sunday Herald* (07.09.03) Peter Ross interviews actress Dawn Steele about her change in role from Sunday soap *Monarch of the Glen* to midweek socialist drama, *The Key:*

> *Dawn explains that she signed herself on for* The Key *because she wanted to shake herself out of her* Monarch *induced torpor; it was to be a dwam-buster.*

There were, however, occasional occurrences of Scots in hard news stories and these make interesting exceptions. For example, in the *Scottish Sun*'s coverage of the 1996 Dunblane school shootings, there was a noticeable increase in the use of Scots vocabulary with expressions like *wee bairns* included in serious reporting. On the occasion of a national Scottish tragedy, use of overt scotticisms again has an in-group, solidarity function.

Thirdly, Scots in the national press is restricted in density. In the newspapers examined by Douglas (the *Herald*, the *Scotsman*, the *Daily Record* and the *Scottish Sun*), there were very few instances of an entire article written in the kind of Scots that is akin to the 'Civil Service Scots' already discussed. Usage is generally confined to fairly thin Scottish English rather than extended passages of dense Scots. The few examples of dense Scots that did occur were in articles concerned with the language itself, Scottish culture or education. These articles were usually written by language activists rather than regular staff journalists, and interestingly only tended to appear in the broadsheets – resulting in a situation not unlike language activists drafting documents for civil servants.

There is a paradox here, if we adopt the admittedly crude distinction of saying that the broadsheet press identifies with a predominantly middle-class readership while the tabloids attempt to construct an 'authentic' working-class identity. Scots, after all, is associated now largely with urban and rural working-class speech, but it is the broadsheets that occasionally champion its denser written forms. Middle-class oriented broadsheets distance a potential working-class readership either by mocking their use of urban, spoken Scots, or by using a literary Scots with which they do not self-identify.

To return to a point made above, there could be a 'check-box' mentality about the occasional inclusion of dense, formal Scots articles on restricted topics in the Scottish press. You can certainly point to occasional – arguably token – examples of dense Scots in the broadsheet press, but we have little information on the impact of such articles on the attitudes and speech of the largely middle-class readership. The fact that, to date [Autumn 2003], tabloids do not go in for this kind of dense Scots (and may indeed be hostile to it) suggests that writing in formal 'Civil Service Scots' is – like the writing of all standard languages – perceived as a middle-class activity.

In fact, the newspapers' use of Scots generally tends to reinforce existing class boundaries. This was clear in the qualitative difference in the Scots vocabulary items favoured by the broadsheet and tabloid press. Whilst there was a body of shared vocabulary, there were also noticeable differences with the broadsheets using some items of archaic or literary Scots such as *kenspeckle, flyte, Lallans* and *makar* which were entirely absent from the tabloid *Record*. The *Record* avoided certain terms like *keelie, lad o'pairts* and *Jock Tamson's bairns* which arguably presuppose a middle-class perspective, but there was a comparatively high incidence of urban Scots terms such as *blootered* (in both the drunk and football senses) and *bevvy*. There is of course, a correlation between subject matter and vocabulary and so if the broadsheets discuss Scottish literature, arguably they are more likely to use literary Scots lexis, but that notwithstanding, there was a perceptible polarisation in the language of the broadsheets and tabloids

The interesting thing, then, is that 'Scots' in the press does not have a stable set of meanings – its signification depends on a range of factors. It can signify in-group identity – *we're all Jock Tamson's bairns* – or it can be used to distance writer and reader from an out-group. For example, the tabloid aversion to dense Scots marginalises this idiom as 'inauthentic' or 'artificial' – 'real' *Record*-reading Scots don't speak (or write) like this. Furthermore, the broadsheets can easily stigmatise a working-class Scot by phonetically rendering his or her accent, or using an urban Scots term or grammatical feature. Scots can therefore be a marker of distance as well as solidarity.

6. Politics, Language and Citizen Kane

The variable nature of the meanings of Scots in the public sphere is vividly illustrated by the treatment of the Scottish Socialist Party, and particularly Rosie Kane, MSP, in different newspapers. The case of 'Citizen Kane', as some in the press have dubbed her, is particularly interesting for a number of reasons:

- Politics is 'hard news'
- Ms Kane's activities are equally covered by tabloid and broadsheet papers
  The SSP take a nationalist as well as a socialist political position, arguing for an independent Scottish socialist republic
- Their socialist orientation aligns them strongly with urban Scots, which occasionally features in their campaign material and public utterances (opposing parties' policies were at one point compared to pizzas: the SNP's were 'half-baked' while Labour's were 'greasy, cheesy and full of mince')

Rosie Kane's attire and conduct at the swearing-in ceremony that began the second session of the new Parliament made her a figure of particular notoriety. Alan Cochrane writing in the *Telegraph* on 8 May 2003 is very disparaging of her conduct, describing her as the "wee burd" – an interesting example of a Scots form in an otherwise standard English article in the English press. Andrew Wilson, writing in the *Sunday Mail* on 11 May 2003, uses Scots expressions more extensively, not to show solidarity with Rosie but to attack her.

> *So I simply cannot believe that the so-called radicals of the Scottish Socialist Party seem to believe that playing the fool while the Emperor looks and laughs is "the gemme". The antics of Tommy Sheridan's team of Trots last week in the Scottish Parliament is playing right into the hands of the establishment. Either they are too stupid to see it or are happy to play their part. ... Yes Rosie Kane, be gallus and loud. All the above and more. But show some respect for the people who elected you and the fledgling democracy you are now part of. ... I could easy forgive the passion of election night and the calls to make the Parly seem like the "Big Brother Hoose". But the fact they still seem intent on it gives me the dry boak. ... The London-owned media establishment leapt all over it as evidence that the 'Scotch' can't be trusted to govern their own lives. How many of our own people felt the same? ... Indeed, when I was a student, the Militants and the Socialist Workers who sold their daft papers called on us not to desert the working class of England. ... How long before everyone in Scotland realises the great irony of Tommy's party is that they have deserted the working class, too? ... While they dance, sing and pretend to speak for the poor, the government has not changed.*

The linguistic issues at stake here are complex. In the wake of a disappointing election result, the SNP might feel that the SSP has stolen its policies, and that it is successfully using a populist form of the Scots language to express them. Wilson's use of Scots here has a double signification: in his use of it, he shows that he, too, can juggle the tokens of Scottish identity, but his choice of expressions (and his use of inverted commas around the more stigmatised expressions) distances Rosie Kane as 'common'. A key expression here is the ambiguous term, *gallus*, which can have positive or negative associations, of boldness or vulgarity. Wilson uses this term without scare quotes, apparently encouraging Kane to speak up for herself; however, the subtext is that her behaviour and speech betray a feckless and irresponsible class position from which the readership is encouraged to distance itself.

Apparently verbatim reports of Rosie Kane's speech accentuate her Scots usages: e.g.

> *"The tide has changed a wee bit and it's like I cannae breathe."*
> *"I'm no' a political anorak. I don't know what Marx said at 4pm in the Kremlin, I have no idea, nor do I seek to know, all I know is thinks like they're building a big, f***ing motorway through the community I'm living in and it's minging."*
> *"Aye he's gorgeous, aye he's magic." (Sunday Herald, 3 August 2003)*

> *"I didn't want anybody to see me no managing well, no coping."*
> *(Sunday Herald, 11 May 2003)*

In the same article, in which reporter Vicky Allan "meets SSP MSP Rosie Kane, the mistress of the stooshie", the interviewer writes that "Kane is not the most rhetorically eloquent speaker. She speaks in long, funny, rambling, colourful sentences, slipping between subjects, inventing new adjectives [*sic*] such as 'combat-trooserness'.

The press's treatment of Rosie Kane further illuminates issues of the written representation of spoken Scots. The transformation of the spoken medium into its written form is not a transparent process – not every Scots speaker is represented as speaking Scots in the press. In other words, unless the journalist wishes to make a point, the spoken Scots of many interviewees is silently transformed into standard English in press reports, as is shown by the comparison of television interviews and their newspaper counterparts. Nor is the response to such Scots usages as feature in the press necessarily predictable for individual readers. Is Vicky Allan's use of Scots in a Sunday broadsheet mocking her working-class interviewee, or showing solidarity with her? The answer lies in the mind-set of the readers as much as in the language itself. The ambivalence of Vicky Allan's use of Scots in an interview with a working-class heroine, published in a middle-class broadsheet like the *Sunday Herald* can be compared with the less ambiguous use of Scots in a reader's letter to the *Scottish Socialist Voice* (Issue 136, 21 May 2003)

> *Denim dichotomy*
> *So what if Rosie Kane wisnae wearing a vest when she took her oath of disloyalty to an alien English Queen? So what if arch loyalist, Helen Liddell, wore a lampshade oan her heid and an electric iron roon her neck when she made her Westmeenster oath of fealty against the Scottish people? Would it have made any difference to Scotland's misrule? Which is the "craziest" felon in Scottish history? Republican Rosie did more to highlight Scotland's miserable plight in one day than a hundred years of Labour's miserable history. If you were poor and*

> *Scottish who would you choose: <u>Rosie frae Pollok, or Helen of Croy</u>,* <u>*tae*</u> *launch a thousand quips at Labour's Royal Unionist and capitalist Establishment. Second hand Rose jeans, or Loyalist <u>rid trooser suit</u> bought and paid for by the taxpayers? Pollok Free Stater or Coatbridge traitor? Some choice, unless you happen to be a Great British Nationalist, terrified of losing your most gullible and richest colony and most expendable cannon fodder.* (Donald Anderson, Glasgow)

Given the context of this letter – an approving reader writing in an explicitly socialist publication – the urban Scots used here is in solidarity with Rosie and her anti-authoritarian stance. The writer draws on clichés, the working-class interviewee's lack of a 'vest' perhaps recalling the sartorial attributes of Rab C. Nesbitt. Even so, the Scots is comic in a witty sense – the word-play celebrates the writer's and subject's use of language – and there is no implication that the Scots is being used to distance the writer from his subject or to mock her.

An examination of the kind of Scots used in the press shows that likening Scots terms in an otherwise English texts to 'currants in the dumpling' is a misleading metaphor. In a normal dumpling, the currants are randomly and evenly distributed, and they should all taste pretty much the same. The Scots expressions we find in newspapers are not randomly distributed, and their potential as markers of national, regional and class solidarity depends, not only on the terms chosen, but on the ideological positions of the newspaper, writer, subject and perceived readership. For example, if Rosie Kane used the term 'weans' in an interview, in part to identify with her working-class constituency, this might be reported verbatim as a marker of distance or solidarity, depending on the class orientation of the newspaper in which the interview appeared.

7. Conclusion

To sum up, any discussion of Scots in the public domain should take into consideration the following points:
- Elements of Scots are already in the public domain, e.g. in newspaper articles
- Scots does 'ideological work' in complex ways
- Attempts to introduce 'Civil Service Scots' into the linguistic system must take account of the still under-researched ways in which Scots | works in the public sphere

Scots is present in the public domain in several manifestations – from the new 'Civil Service Scots' to the working-class speech reported (or not) in the press – and each manifestation merits research. The language activism of the past decades has borne fruit, but further investigation is required to see how far beyond the cosmetic the new brands of 'Civil Service Scots' in particular go. Scots still has the power to signify social, national, class and other ideological positions in non-literary public texts, and where and how this happens also merits further study. Given that the Scots element in public discourse is usually widely dispersed, we need large-scale and coordinated research into the general impact of language planning initiatives and the variable functions of Scots in the public domain.

References

Allan, A. 1998. *New Founs fae Auld Larachs: Leid-Plannin for Scots*. University of Aberdeen: Unpublished PhD thesis

Cooper, R.L. 1989. *Language Planning and Social Change*. Cambridge: Cambridge University Press

Corbett, J. 1997. *Language and Scottish Literature*. Edinburgh: Edinburgh University Press

Corbett, J. 2003. 'Language Planning and Modern Scots' in J. Corbett, J.D. McClure and J. Stuart-Smith, eds. *The Edinburgh Companion to Scots*. Edinburgh: Edinburgh University Press, pp. 251-73

Donati, C., J. Hendry, J. Robertson and P.H. Scott. 2003. *Scots: A Statement of Principles: A Road Forrit for the Scots Language in a Multilingual Scotland*. Edinburgh: The Scots Pairlament Cross-Pairty Group on the Scots Leid <www.Scottish.parliament.uk/msps/cpg/cpg-scots.html>

Douglas, F. 2000. *The Role of Lexis in Scottish Newspapers*. University of Glasgow: Unpublished PhD thesis

Falconer, G and R.G. Arthur. Forthcoming. *The Basic Scots Bible*, 4 volumes. Belfast: Cló Ollscoil na Banríona

Fitt, M 2000. *But n Ben a-Go-Go*. Edinburgh: Luath Press

Gowers, E. 1987. *The Complete Plain Words*. Harmondsworth: Penguin

Jones, C. 2002. *The English Language in Scotland*. Edinburgh: Tuckwell

Lorimer, W. 2001 [1983]. *The New Testament in Scots*. Edinburgh: Canongate

McGugan, I. 2003. *Inquiry into the role of educational and cultural policy in supporting and developing Gaelic, Scots and minority languages in Scotland*. Edinburgh: The Scottish Parliament Education, Culture and Sport Committee

Public Information Service. 2003. *Makkin yer voice heard in the Scottish Pairlament*. Edinburgh: The Scottish Parliament Public Information Service

Robertson, J. 2002. *A Scots Parliament*. Edinburgh: Itchy-Coo/Black and White

Scottish Consultative Council on the Curriculum. 1996. *The Kist Anthology*. Dundee: SCCC/Nelson

Stewart, W. 1968. 'A Sociolinguistic Typology for Describing National Multilingualism' in J.A. Fishman, ed. *Readings in the Sociology of Language*. The Hague: Mouton, pp. 531-45

Stuart, J. 1997. *A Glasgow Bible*. Edinburgh: St Andrew Press

Wilson, L.C. 2002. *The Luath Scots Language Learner*. Edinburgh: Luath Press

Wad the Ulster-Scots Tongue Richtlie be Gan Foreairt?

Ian James Parsley

A bodie speirt at me twa dey syne, whaur A wad see Ulster Scots 50 yeir frae nou. A niver swithert: 'Deid'.

For thon wad be the lyke outcum o an ongan policie the lyke o whit we haes in Norlin Airlan thenou. Think on the rich traditions o a leid at wis here 400-500 yeir juist bean tint, for a want o will for tae uise fowk wi the linguistic an strategic ken as wad mak the leid sicar.

Thrie yeir syne, A cam tae this confeerance an put fore the notion at the steerars wisna representan thaim as taaks the leid forordinar, an at thaim as taaks the leid forordinar haen nae interest for a leid ats oncum wisna in thair haunds. Hou wad thay? Thair ain leid in prent thay niver kent haaf the tyme! An A wis thinkan this wis maistlie acause Ulster Scots wis cam a pairt o the political balance in Norlin Airlan, an at sicna politicisation wad be the deith o the leid. No muckle is chynged.

A Unionist Leid for a Unionist Fowk

For near the haill debate anent the oncum o the Scots leid in Norlin Airlan – lyke the maist fek debates in this auldfarrant laund – wad be a scunnersom, political ane. Fowk caas for 'coequalitie wi the Earse', a policie at bears the gree lane for hinneran an switheran the wark richtlie a-needan for tae mak the baith leids sicar here. For lea us mak ae thing clear tae aa: thar juist nae parallel atween the Earse an the Ulster Scots! Thay wad be twa leids at gey differan levels o oncum. The Earse haes a status as a national leid, a wheen taakars as kens richtlie thair ain leid (an taakan an in prent), an a weel-kent literar tradition raxan bak tae the first millennium. The Ulster Scots haes nae sic status (an nae status ava in the Republic Airlan), nae 'commontie o taakars' (ein gif steerars wad allou it), an a near hidden literar tradition at maist o thaim as taaks the leid forordinar wadna ken ava. Then pit in at the Earse bes frae a differan brainch o the Indo-European faimlie, whaur Scots faas athin the shaddae o thon *superpower* o leids: Inglis. (An wha decid Ulster Scots wis a Unionist leid oniehou? Wad leids no belang thaim as taaks thaim?)

An Ill-foundit Biggin

Siclyke juist deflects frae whit bes richtlie a-wantan for tae bring on the uiss o the Scots in Airlan. Whit we ar shuirlie richtlie needan wad bc a piogram o lear, forder an apen research tae the heichmaist academic stannarts. Siclyke kythed in the first corporate ploy o the Ulster-Scots Agentrie, but thon wis an attempt at biggan the house afore the founs. Smaa wunner fowk gat thaimsels aa fasht afore the first breek wis put doun!

But midst this midden o ill-biggit ploys, thar a wee bit guid news. A program o lear wis begoud the yeir past at Stranmillis. Tho the initial ettle o this program buid tae be brocht bak a wee bit – for ye canna gae aroun the schuils tellan weans whitwey thay sud taak thair ain leid – thar a wee bit evidence at fowk wi a richt sympathie an unnerstaundin for the subject bes haean an inpit. But thay canna gae the haill gait thair lane!

Forder o Linguistic Ken A-needan

The forder o the leid – an o the braid issue o langage – wad be at the mids o onie attempt for tae mak the Scots leid sicar. In the UK an Airlan we ar gey puir no juist at learnan leids, but at unnerstaundin the wey leids bes claucht tae ane anither. For ensample, a bodie speirt at me twathrie yeir syne, whit wis the Ulster-Scots wird for 'ginger'. 'Ginger', says A. '*So there's no Ulster-Scots word for it, then*', says she. 'Thar is ay', says A, 'the Ulster-Scots wird wad be ginger an aa'. Pynt bean, we ar at the stage yet, whaur haean the ae wird in Scots an Inglis haes the maist fek fowk thinkan 'Thar nae Scots wird', an no juist 'the Inglis an Scots wird bes the same'. Sicna want o ken about langage itssel maks the forder o the Scots leid sweir eneuch, ein afore ye taks in the bodies as wad allou things about Scots as juist besna richt!

For fowk maun hae access tae wittins thay can lippen tae anent the leid an aa. Allouan aa kins wild things wi a want o richt research – the lyke o 'crak' bean nae dout an 'Ulster-Scots' wird – juist gars fowk gree. Giean the richt wittins out, aiblans ein haean the mense for tae say 'We dinna juist knaw' or 'We arna richtlie shuir' the orra tyme, brings fowk onsyde strecht aff.

Role o the Govrenment

A am laith tae criticise the govrenment, for thar eneuch fowk daean that aaricht – but unfortunatelik A maun dae it oniehou. A policie o juist heiran tae thaim as gullers the maist juist disna ansuer the needs o the leid. The govrenment maun faa tae unnerstaundan wha wad be pittan foreairt realistic ploys. For ein wi a fair bit siller apen tae it, we ar efter seean nae progress wi realistic owreaa ploys an visions for the leid – the Agentrie niver daen it, the Future Search niver daen it – acause the process wis niver led frae fowk as haen a winnable vision an as kent linguistic plannin, an cud pit thon knawledge tae best uiss in the Norlin Airlan context.

Laith Bean Associate

The new Academie cud, an put in the richt haunds an takan tent o the lenth we ar yet tae traivel, be the scraich o dawn for the richt oncum o the leid, efter thrie tint yeir. Wirkan alang wi Stranmillis, the Institute o Ulster-Scots Studies an the richt PR fowk, the posltiun o the leid in lear an academia, amang the public, an maist ava amang thaim as taaks it deyandeilie, cud cum sicar.

For a situation whaur fowk lyke masel bes laith for tae be associate wi Ulster Scots juist canna gae on, an the lane wey for tae bring thon situation tae an end wad be, weel, lyke A sayed thrie yeir syne, bringan in fowk as haes a richt ken o the minoritie-leid issues, an a richt feel for langage itsel.

A div richtlie hate sayan A telt yis sae!

From Antagonism to Convergence: Economics and Linguistic Diversity

François Grin

1. Introduction

The discourses extolling the importance of "languages" and "diversity" on the one hand, and of "economic activity" or "prosperity" on the other hand, have a history in which mutual estrangement and distrust dominate.

Roughly summarising things, the opposition between them can be characterised as follows: from the "languages" side, economic activity and development were seen as the grave-diggers of small languages.[1] The associated tendency (visible, among other examples, in much of the Irish language preservation movement well into the 1970s) was then to appeal to a set of values constructed as *antithetic* to the crass materialism of economic activity: these values included tradition, community, authenticity, etc. and were therefore seen as the safe haven or fortress in which small languages could endure.

Reciprocally, proponents of economic development tended to dismiss small languages, as well as efforts made to preserve them, as expressions of a hopelessly misguided backwardness[2]. There would be a lot to say about the variants of such representations, including more refined lines of arguments in which the protection and promotion of minority languages is portrayed as little else than a ploy by local elites (sometimes called "ethnic entrepreneurs") to restrict access to material success and socio-cultural enlightenment – thus allowing proponents of dominant languages, rather paradoxically, to don the mantle of defenders of the oppressed.

In recent years, however, what was a fairly clear ideological divide has begun to fade away. On the one hand, advocates of small languages have decided (in large part for well-advised *strategic* reasons), that they would no longer concede to their opponents what amounted to a quasi-monopoly on modernist discourse. Staking a claim on modernity, on behalf of minority languages, logically implied insisting that economic development could very well take place through the medium of these languages, or even be *enhanced* by using them. This change of tack dovetailed nicely, on the other hand, with a line of discourse (hailing, in fact, from business administration more than from fundamental economic theory), which from the late 1980s on started to praise diversity (albeit in rather vague terms) as a source of creativity – and hence of superior economic performance.

We now seem to be reaching a point where the traditional antagonism between "small languages" and "economic development" has been superseded, opening the way to a more balanced and constructive view of the relationship (perhaps even a *partnership*) between minority language protection and promotion on the one hand, and economic development and prosperity on the other hand. This cheerful

---

[1] See e.g. Prattis (1981), on Scottish Gaelic in Lewis.

[2] This issue is discussed by many classics in sociolinguistics, including Fishman (1989); for a discussion in the Scottish Gaelic case, see McLeod (2001); for a good historical perspective, see Ricento (2000); for a comprehensive recent reader, see May (2001).

optimism is exemplified by a booklet published in 1997 by the European Bureau for Lesser Used Languages under the title of *The Diversity Dividend* (Price, 1997). The fact that Article 13 of the *European Charter for Regional or Minority Languages* is devoted to "economic and social life" could, of course, be interpreted as a sign that this partnership is not self-evident (otherwise, why bother spelling out measures in this respect?). Reciprocally, it can be read as a sign that such a linkage, which would have been considered absurd a few decades ago, is now well established in mainstream perceptions.

However, there are reasons to think that the issue is far from settled – possibly, as we shall see later on in this paper, because it has migrated to another plane. In fact, many aspects of the causal links through which language processes and economic processes influence each other remain very little known. Depending on how the study of these processes is operationalised through a choice of critical variables, and which aspects of this relationship are considered, rather different conclusions may be reached.

Teasing apart the various levels of the issues at hand is useful for the growing debate on worldwide linguistic diversity and linguistic justice – a theme area which should be seen as one of the crucially important ones of the 21st century, on par with environmental protection and large-scale public health issues.

The rest of this paper is devoted to two types of questions. First, I would like to sort out some of the very different ways in which this linkage between language variables on the one hand, and economic variables on the other hand, can be understood. As part of this overview, I shall try to clarify the extent to which convergence between them can be seen as an averred fact, a plausible assumption, or a highly conjectural wish. This line of inquiry focuses on what is known as "resource allocation" and essentially asks whether doing things in minority languages (or advocating such behaviour and devising policy measures to this effect) constitutes a sound allocation of scarce resources.

However, it is important to recall that economics, properly understood, is not confined to matters of efficient allocation of scarce resources. The founding fathers of the discipline, notably Walras, insisted that economics is also about the distribution of resources (Bürgenmeier, 1994) — that is, how the value of economic production is ultimately distributed across individuals and groups. The study of "resource distribution" is closely related to issues of equity and fairness studied in normative political theory, as well as in policy analysis; it asks whether a particular allocation of resources (which may result from policy choices) can be considered "fair" or not – therefore raising the question of its social acceptability, which is part and parcel of proper economic analysis.

2. Language and Economics: The Allocative Debate

The notion that there exists some kind of convergence, or harmony, between minority languages and economic development finds expression in very different types of contributions.

At one end of the spectrum, we find very general statements which, in their simplest form, take the form of well-intentioned, but rather vague claims that linguistic diversity (or such-and-such a language) is a "treasure", an "asset" or a form of "wealth" that must, as such, be preserved. This type of discourse presents two interconnected weaknesses: first, owing to its very generality, it is less likely to be based on a cogent, powerful demonstration (in fact, this line of argument can easily be knocked down by a junior debater, using the "preference revelation argument" that we shall return to at the end of this section); second, possibly as a direct consequence, it will generally fail to impress those who did not agree in the first place – therefore, it essentially comes down to preaching to the converted.

At the other end of the spectrum, some in-depth research has developed in recent years, producing tightly argued contributions, some of them backed up with a large array of figures, and documenting a positive linkage between, say, the use of a minority language on the one hand, and certain manifestations of economic activity on the other hand. There is, in fact, a distinguished tradition of work on such questions in Ireland and Scotland, since early contributions by Ó Cinnéide and Keane (1988) or Sproull and Ashcroft (1993). This tradition is being continued by Chalmers (2003) in his recent analysis of the economic significance of Gaelic language, arts and culture.

More generally, the slow but steady development of language economics (as an interdisciplinary field of research) regularly delivers findings which tend to support the claim that there is economic value in linguistic diversity in general, and in small languages in particular (see Grin, 2003b for a review).

However, as I have suggested earlier, it would be premature for advocates of small languages to claim victory and *decree* the case closed. The problem is that even the carefully researched papers and reports which support this positive relationship tend to focus on subsets of the broader issue. Precisely because they are precise and focused, it is often difficult to generalise their findings. Putting it differently, there is, to my knowledge, no published work, in language economics or in any other field of research, that offers a full-fledged, *general* allocative argument showing that linguistic diversity in general — or the preservation of a language in particular as a component of this diversity — is economically good (or bad) and that we ought to seek more (or less) of it, and for what precise economic reasons.

It is important to note the statements encountered in the literature (along with a more or less developed conceptual or statistical apparatus) have a very differentiated logical standing. Consider the following statements:

A. "cultural diversity reinforces creativity, which in turn enhances productivity at work";
B. "in region R, many economic activities take place in language L, and this activity represents X million Euros per year";
C. (or a related variant:) "every Euro invested in region R in the promotion of language L generates a multiple of this investment through knock-on effects on the regional economy";
D. "knowing a certain language L gives people access to certain jobs that would not be accessible to them without such knowledge";
E. "knowing language L at competence level K gives access to a wage premium of $x\%$".

First, these claims may all be true, but they address specific, and different, aspects of reality; it follows that, for example, the fact that statement B is true does not mean that statement D will be too, and vice-versa. Second and more importantly, none of these findings, even if convincingly established, would amount to a full-fledged proof that linguistic diversity in the aggregate is economically good (or that the protection and promotion of a particular language is economically good) and that *as a consequence*, linguistic diversity (or a particular language) should be supported through policy measures. We have strong arguments, but not iron-clad proof.

Even when focusing on a specific dimension of reality, developing strong arguments requires the explicit identification of the *counterfactual*, i.e., "that against which what one evaluates is being contrasted" (Grin, 2003a); generally, this effort will be well-rewarded, because it will force the analyst to consider the full range of the benefits as well as the costs of alternatives at hand. This leads us turn to the next difficulty, namely, what exactly we use as an indicator of the economic effects considered — and for what reasons.

Let us, for the sake of the example, define "linguistic diversity" (as distinct from, say, the survival of a specific language) as that whose economic significance must be evaluated. Much of what can be said about "linguistic diversity" tends to be true about individual languages, because the latter are, by definition, components of the former. Furthermore, developing this idea in terms of diversity helps to broaden the scope of the argument, and lessens the risk of being accused of pandering to special interests.

It would not be possible here to review the literature on the value of linguistic diversity as opposed to uniformity, but some of the main directions of research can be mentioned.

1. Some models (e.g. Breton, 1964; Church and King, 1993) examine language-learning decisions in bi- or multilingual settings; they conclude that it is more economical to encourage minorities to learn the majority language than any other solution, which amounts to advocating a form of uniformity through the hegemony of the majority language. However, this result is predicated on a number of assumptions, the main one being that benefits result exclusively from communication, that communication is nothing but information transfer, and that the costs of different strategies boil down to language learning expenses that may befall a larger or a smaller number of people.

2. Other models, as developed in particular by Pool (1991b) and Selten and Pool (1997), yield significantly more nuanced results by taking account of differential language learning costs between individuals. Because linguistic hegemony is often ascribed to network effects (in which actors' decentralised decision-making can actually reinforce the hegemony of a language whose learning is comparatively costly), this type of model also allows for the possibility that through coordinated action, social actors may decide to adopt, as a common language, one whose average learning cost is lower than for any other. One important result is that linguistic uniformity, *even if the benefits of alternative options are confined to communication*, is not necessarily the best option, and this result obtains *even when language is seen as no more than a tool for communication*.

3. However, for this very reason (that is, this exclusive focus on communication benefits), this class of models does not amount to a full-fledged policy analysis perspective. Tentative steps in this direction, incorporating a wider range of benefits, also suggest that linguistic

uniformity is not the generally best solution – except, precisely, when narrow restrictions apply (e.g. Pool, 1996, on the official languages of the European Union).

Despite such results, many observers dispute the notion that linguistic diversity is, literally, "worth" maintaining, and they keep claiming that the cost of diversity far exceeds its possible benefits. Jones (2000) is an interesting example, because his paper is one of the few that purports to offer a general assessment. Though the paper claims to address the arguments of proponents of diversity (and to expose alleged fallacies in them), it contains a number of non-sequiturs and logical leaps (for example, he mistakes the promotion of minority languages for constraints on majority languages, and seems unaware of the fact that a phenomenon like bilingualism opens up a whole range of options). Yet it is illustrative of widely held opinions. They can only be countered with more elaborate arguments than simple assertions to the effect that diversity is good. Thus, there is no alternative to the painstaking identification and measurement of complex and interdependent benefits and costs in line with standard policy analysis theory.

Although there is no general model of the economic value of linguistic diversity – and, in fact, no such model of the value of a given language either – there is a framework that can serve to structure the analysis. More specifically, it can help in the identification and measurement of benefits and costs of linguistic diversity (Grin and Vaillancourt, 1997).

The approach rests on a breakdown benefits and costs along two dimensions, namely *market versus non-market value* on the one hand and *private versus social value* on the other hand. This breakdown is summarised in Figure 1.

FIGURE 1: ELEMENTS OF NET VALUE
(BENEFITS, COSTS, BENEFITS MINUS COSTS)

	PRIVATE	SOCIAL
MARKET	A	B
NON-MARKET	C	D

For the most part, these four elements of value are only partly identified, even less evaluated. The only component known with some degree of precision can be located in cell A, owing to a large body of research on the rates of return on second language skills[3].

The preceding discussion is enough to suggest that we have little to go on for establishing, in terms of overall resource allocation, the economic merits of linguistic diversity and linguistic uniformity. Most importantly, there is no empirical evidence regarding non-market value, such as the direct enjoyment derived from linguistic diversity and, conversely, the lack that may be experienced if a small language is squeezed out of existence. The still unsettled character of analytical and conceptual results, coupled with absence of empirical evidence, certainly does *not* mean that linguistic diversity is, per se, worthless. What it means, however, is that it is more of an uphill battle to convince people that public policy should be favourable to linguistic diversity.

Some listeners might rightly raise the following question: why should the burden of proof fall on the advocates of diversity or on the defenders of small languages? Why shouldn't proponents of linguistic uniformity and of dominant languages be held to the same standard of proof? The point is well taken, but there are two answers to this. The first is that exemption from the burden of proof is a mere reflection of power (an issue that we shall return to in the following section). The second is based on core microeconomic theory: when people consider something to be valuable, they are willing, without being nudged or forced to do so, to spend resources on this "something" – and therefore to give something else up. People give up far-away holidays in order to afford a nicer home, which proves that a nice home is valuable in an economic sense; others may scrimp on food in order to spend money on costly opera tickets, which proves that an opera performance is valuable in an economic sense. Hence, if people are unwilling to devote time and money to learning a small language, on what grounds should we claim that this language is valuable in an economic sense?

From a public policy standpoint, the only truly convincing refutation of this argument requires us to show that languages (and linguistic diversity) are public goods and that they must, as such, be supported through public policy – and in this case, the burden of proof is on those who advocate this intervention.

Pursuing along those lines, and given strong parallels between linguistic diversity and environmental quality, it has been suggested (Grin, 1994) to assess the non market value of diversity through contingent valuation method (Kahneman and Knetsch, 1992) — analysing this dimension would be one of the top priorities of an investigation of the net value of policy options.

Even if the many problems posed by the identification and measurement of private value were solved, another formidable problem arises, namely, that of moving from individual-level estimations of benefits and costs to the corresponding social aggregate. For complex commodities like a certain (more or less diverse) linguistic environment, aggregation requires more than a simple sum of private values. This stems from the fact that many of the language decisions made by actor x may affect the value of the language skills of another actor y. Even when the benefits associated with one or another language environment are

---

[3] Even then, limitations exist: these rates of return simply tell us that people who have certain language skills earn more than people who do not, after controlling for standard determinants of labour income. Let us consider the case of rates of return on English. Only Canada (Vaillancourt, 1996) and Switzerland (Grin, 1999) have data about English as a *second* language for a non-immigrant population; in the Swiss case, data on other second or foreign languages makes it possible to assess the relative value of English as an internationally dominant language. It is important to observe that this is a case quite different from that of the market value of English-language skills for immigrants in a predominantly English-speaking country like the United States or Australia (Chiswick and Miller, 1995), which yield the rather unsurprising result that in such a context, English is valuable indeed. However, even if similar research in other non-English speaking countries were to show that the rates of return on English language skills are higher than for other second languages, this would not suffice to ground a case in favour of linguistic hegemony, whether the *hegemon* is English, or any other language. The fact that a language gives access to higher earnings is no doubt likely to be the *result* of its hegemonic position, which is not at all the same thing as constituting a *reason* for this language to be given this hegemonic position.

defined only in terms of communication (as in Church and King, 1993), decentralised decisions by actors can fail to deliver a social optimum; the same problem is even more likely to arise when a broader range of benefits is taken into account.

Summing up, the case that there is economic value in linguistic diversity is gaining in plausibility – and, therefore, in popularity. However, this case needs to be strengthened before one can persuasively argue that social resources should be used, through public policy, in order to protect and promote small languages and linguistic diversity.

3. The Distributive Dimension

Let us now turn to the distributive side of the argument. The question no longer is one of efficient allocation of scarce resources, but of the distribution of net value across society.

More simply, let us ask ourselves who are the winners, and who are the losers, when a certain linguistic situation develops. How much do the winners win, how much do the losers lose, and is this redistribution between members of society acceptable — or, to use a term favoured by normative political theorists, is it "just"? Given that a linguistic situation can be defined as more or less diverse, and that it may be more or less favourable to the maintenance of small languages, these interrogations raise the question of the link between linguistic diversity and social justice, and the impact of language policy on social justice.

It may be, for example, that the policy that seems best from a resource allocation standpoint has unacceptable distributive effects. Then, the option of choosing this policy would be predicated on the possibility of building, preferably into the policy design itself, a system of transfers from the winners to the losers. In the absence of such a scheme (let alone if such a compensation appears not to be possible at all), the policy should be rejected, despite its status as the allocatively optimal one.

When studying the distributional aspects of policy choices, the costs and benefits that need to be taken into account are those that are distributed *unevenly* across members of society, or across groups that make up society.

This does not pose any major conceptual problem if we are concerned about distributive effects between *individuals*, because an individual is a fairly easily identified unit. However, other questions immediately arise if we are concerned about transfers between *groups*: along what criteria are these groups defined — or, putting it differently, what are the *relevant* criteria for identifying groups between which more or less redistribution would occur as a result of language policy: socio-economic status? Gender? Race? Eye colour? Age? L1? Sexual orientation? And which of these groups is it reasonable and legitimate to refer to in an assessment of the redistributive effects?[4]

Again, these questions have not been the object of a full-fledged treatment in the literature, although solid leads can be found in Pool (1991a) and Van Parijs (2001). In the sphere of language, these otherwise thoroughly analysed matters of equity and justice are only beginning to be understood in policy perspective, although they have long been, in many ways, familiar to speakers of regional or minority languages.

Let us again, as we did in the previous section, define the "language" side of the "language € economics" link as "linguistic diversity", and take a closer look at the inequalities that may result from the imposition of a dominant or majority language on others. The list of sources of inequality, as well as the order of magnitude of such inequalities, depends, of course, on the type and context of language dominance considered, but keeping to a high level of generality, five main types of effects can be distinguished (mentioned here without any particular ranking in mind):

- the "privileged market effect": native speakers of the dominant language enjoy a quasi-monopoly over the markets for translation and interpretation *into* the dominant language, the market for second language instruction above a certain level, and the market for language editing — all of which are tasks in which native-level skills are typically required;

- the "communication savings effect": native speakers of the dominant language are spared the effort to translate messages directed to them by speakers of other languages, since the latter will have made the effort to utter them in the dominant language in the first place; reciprocally, native speakers of the dominant language do not need to translate their messages into other languages;

- the "language learning savings effect": native speakers of the dominant language do not need to invest time and effort into learning other languages; this amounts to a considerable savings. Despite massive spending in countries that *do* teach foreign languages, foreign language education typically represents a total, over one's pre-university school years, of about 1,500 to 2,000 hours of instruction and exposure (including homework); the results achieved are accordingly modest, since an estimated minimum of 12,000 hours of instruction and exposure would be needed, on average, to reach native-like (though still not perfect) fluency in a foreign language such as English (Piron, 1994);

- the "alternative human capital investment effect": the money *not* invested in foreign language acquisition can be diverted to other forms of human capital

---

[4] Let us also note, at this juncture, that it is not enough to define justice in terms of equal or equitable access to a certain opportunity set (or, simplifying matters, of access to the same opportunity set) by members of different groups. This point is best explained with reference to the position of bilinguals in society. It is often true that *ceteris paribus* (especially in the absence of discrimination on the basis of one's first language), bilinguals have more opportunities than unilinguals. This may be the case even when bilinguals are native speakers of a minority language (say, *X*) who have had to acquire the majority language (*Y*). Some may be tempted to interpret such a situation as a downright advantage accruing to bilinguals; the existence of such an advantage would therefore exempt the state from any particular obligation towards the minority language – that is, it would exempt the state from taking steps to protect or promote the minority language as an element of cultural diversity. However, this "advantage" is usually dearly bought though various forms of financial and symbolic cost; the dominance of a language can in fact impose considerable costs on speakers of other languages, which, on balance, may more than offset the wider range of opportunities available to them as bilinguals. Whether we are talking, on balance, of a "welfare" deficit or of an "opportunity" deficit makes little difference from an economic (welfare theory) standpoint, although the situations are different in practice.

investment and give native speakers of the dominant language an edge in other areas;

- the "legitimacy and rhetorical effect": native speakers of the dominant language will generally have an edge in negotiations or arguments with non-native speakers, because these always take place in their language.

At this time, these various effects have not been evaluated in terms of cost. Only rough estimates and extrapolations are available; however, they suggest that the effects concerned are significant. For the purposes of this paper, I shall confine myself to just one example concerning the "language learning savings effect", and instead of considering this effect in the context of a country with a majority and a minority language, I shall consider the case of English as a *lingua franca*.

One result of this state of affairs is that English-speaking countries can afford to neglect the teaching of other languages, whereas other countries invest massively, publicly and privately, in the teaching and learning of English. A rough estimation of the savings made by the USA by confining themselves to a comparatively limited foreign language teaching effort at primary (elementary) and secondary (intermediate and high) school levels[5] suggests that these savings are considerable. Given an enrolment of approximately 38m pupils in elementary and secondary schools, the savings to the US education system is a hefty $ 16bn a year (Grin, 2003d). This represents about a third of yearly public spending on research and development in the US (in both cases, figures refer to 1993/94); in other words, the rest of the world is, through language, indirectly subsidising US investment in research, and transfers of this magnitude are perfectly relevant concerns for economic inquiry.

Clearly, the above example makes immediate sense when the counterfactual is defined as "balanced multilingualism" (in which *everybody* makes a roughly similar effort to learn at least one other language — possibly an artificial language like Esperanto). Therefore, some might object that in the case of regional or minority languages, balanced multilingualism is a pipe dream, and that the above calculation is not relevant.

I am ready to accept that majorities cannot be expected to learn regional or minority languages to recreate some kind of balance, particularly in the case of very small minority languages. However, the massive cost, borne by the minority, still exists, and this, in public policy perspective, deserves compensation. One important observation can be derived from the preceding: contrary to what many people confidently assert, it is not the case that, through promotional measures in favour of small languages, majorities are paying for minorities. In fact, because of the very fact that majority languages play a hegemonic role, it is still the case that most of the time, minorities are paying for majorities.

As the above example has shown, however, the issue of linguistic justice can no longer be confined to traditional majority-minority relations (Grin, 2003c). Because of the increasingly hegemonic role of English internationally, one of the most important aspects of the language € economy link, namely, its distributive dimension, is no longer a concern solely for users of regional or minority

---

[5] By 2002, 41 States had no explicit mention of foreign language requirements for graduation from high school, whether in general or for a so-called standard diploma (see http://www.ecs.org/clearinghouse/39/22/3922.htm).

languages — increasingly, it should be a concern for mankind as a whole. This is why I observed, at the beginning of this paper, that some of the key issues in the relationship between language and the economy had "migrated" to another plane.

4. Conclusion

Our overview of key findings on the relationship between linguistic diversity and economic activity indicates that there is strong circumstantial evidence to the effect that in terms of resource allocation (independently of any considerations of distributive justice), the benefits of linguistic diversity exceed its costs, and that society would be well-advised to devote resources to the protection and promotion of linguistic diversity, which implies the protection and promotion of small languages as key components of diversity.

Once we bring in the other (often neglected) side of economic analysis, namely, the distributive aspect, it becomes manifest that linguistic diversity is a matter of socio-economic justice. Of course, it is perfectly possible for a democratic society to decide that net allocative benefits are highest if one language is granted a privileged, possibly hegemonic status. But then this would require appropriate compensation to flow from the native speakers of the hegemonic language to the native speakers of non-hegemonic languages.

Much research work remains to be done in order to deepen our understanding of the language-economy link. However, I believe that some of the analytical distinctions discussed today can help us in this enterprise. Allocation v. distribution, market and non-market value, private and social value, etc., certainly are very broad notions. But when applied to the issue of linguistic diversity, they strongly suggest that from an economic standpoint, linguistic diversity is well worth cultivating.

References

Breton, A. 1964. "The economics of nationalism". *Journal of Political Economy* 62: 376-86.

Bürgenmeier, B. 1994. "The Misperception of Walras". *American Economic Review* 84: 342-52.

Chalmers, D. 2003. "Economic Impact of Gaelic Arts and Culture". PhD thesis, Glasgow Caledonian University.

Chiswick, B. and P. Miller 1995. "The endogeneity between language and earnings: international analyses". *Journal of Labor Economics* 13: 246-88.

Church, J. and I. King 1993. "Bilingualism and Network Externalities", *Canadian Journal of Economics* 26, 337-345.

Fishman, J. 1989. *Language and Ethnicity in Minority Sociolinguistic Perspective*. Clevedon: Multilingual Matters.

Grin, F. 1994. "L'identification des bénéfices de l'aménagement linguistique: la langue comme actif naturel". In ed. C. Phlipponneau and A. Boudreau. *Sociolinguistique et aménagement des langues*. Moncton (New Brunswick): Centre de recherche en linguistique appliquée. 67-101.

Grin, F. 1999. *Compétences et récompenses. La valeur des langues en Suisse*. Fribourg : Éditions Universitaires.

Grin, F. 2003a. *Language Policy and Evaluation and the European Charter for Regional or Minority Languages*. London: Palgrave.

Grin, F. 2003b. "Language Planning and Economics", *Current Issues in Language Planning* 4, in press.

Grin, F. 2003c. "Diversity as paradigm, analytical device, and policy goal". In ed. W. Kymlicka and A. Patten. *Language Rights and Political Theory*. Oxford: Oxford University Press. 169-188.

Grin, F. 2003d. "La société plurilingue: coûts, benefices et équité". *Actes du Colloque 'Viersprachig, mehrsprachig, vielsprachig'*. Berne: Académie suisse des sciences humaines et sociales. 41-55.

Grin, F. and F. Vaillancourt 1997. The Economics of Multilingualism: Overview of the Literature and Analytical Framework. In ed. W. Grabe. *Multilingualism and Multilingual Communities*. Cambridge [MA.]: Cambridge University Press. 43-65

Jones, E. 2000. "The Case for a Shared World Language". In eds. M. Casson and A. Godley. *Cultural Factors in Economic Growth*. Berlin: Springer. 210-235.

Kahneman, D. and J. Knetsch 1992. "Valuing public goods: the purchase of moral satisfaction". *Journal of Environmental Economics and Management*, 22: 57-70.

May, S. 2001. *Language and Minority Rights*. Harlow: Pearson.

McLeod, W. 2001. "Gaelic in the new Scotland: Politics, Rhetoric and Public Discourse". *Journal of Ethnopolitcs and Minority Issues in Europe*, published on-line on: http://www.ecmi.de/publications/jemie/index.html.

Ó Cinnéide, M. and M. Keane 1988. *Local Socio-Economic Impacts Associated with the Galway Gaeltacht*. Galway: Coláiste na hOllscoile Gaillimhe.

Piron, C. 1994. *Le défi des langues. Du gâchis au bon sens*. Paris: L'Harmattan.

Pool, J. 1991a. "The Official Language Problem". *American Political Science Review* 85: 495-514.

Pool, J. 1991b. "The World Language Problem". *Rationality and Society* 3: 21-31.

Pool, J. 1996. "Optimal Language Regimes for the European Union". *International Journal of the Sociology of Language* 121: 159-179.

Prattis, J.I. 1981. "Industrialisation and Minority-Language Loyalty: The Example of Lewis". In ed E. Haugen *et al.*, *Minority Languages Today*. Edinburgh: Edinburgh University Press. 21-31.

Price, A. *et al.* 1997. *The Diversity Dividend*. Brussels: European Bureau for Lesser-Used Languages.

Ricento, T. 2000. "Historical and Theoretical Perspectives in Language Policy and Planning. In ed. T. Ricento. *Ideology, Politics and Language Policies*. Amsterdam: John Benjamins. 9-24.

Selten, R. and J. Pool, 1997. "Is it worth it to learn Esperanto? Introduction to Game Theory". In ed. Selten, Reinhard, *The Costs of European Linguistic Non Integration*. Romc: Esperanto Radikala Asocio. 114-149.

Sproull, A. and B. Ashcroft 1993. *The Economics of Gaelic Language Development*. Glasgow: Glasgow Caledonian University.

Van Parijs, P. 2001. "Linguistic Justice". *Politics, Philosophy and Economics* 1: 59-74.

Not such a big deal? The Economy-Language interaction

Esmond Birnie, MLA and Steven King

Introduction

In tackling this subject, we agree with the observation made by the main speaker, Professor Grin (2001), that, whereas formerly discussion of language policy had largely ignored the economic aspect, this aspect is now rightly getting increasing attention. Professor Grin himself, as one of the most prolific writers in this field, deserves some credit for this turn around.

How does the economy affect the development of minority languages?

History might suggest that the effect has been negative. Certainly, the last three of four centuries have seen minority languages decline in usage relative to English within the British Isles. Similarly, there has been marked decline of the minority languages throughout most of Continental Europe.

Earlier work by the main speaker (Grin 1992 and 2001) points to possible (micro-) economic explanations of such decline. Learning a language is part of the investment in one's human capital. The return to individuals from learning English has increased relative to that from using a minority language. Professor Grin (1992), along with others, further argues that language decline may be subject to threshold or cumulative effects. In other words, as the number of speakers of a minority language decrease the costs of using that language are increased for those who are left.

At the same time, minority language decline may have been influenced by factors of modernisation, which are broader than simply economic growth. For example, Scots may have been in decline from as early as the 1600s (i.e. more than a century before the industrial revolution) and was this caused by the shift in the Stuart royal court from Edinburgh to London?[1] Similarly, Welsh may have held up better in the pre-industrial period than Scots or Scottish Gaelidh and Irish Gaelic.[2] Was this because the Protestant churches in Wales unlike their counterparts in Scotland and Ireland adopted a relatively favourable approach to use of Bible translations in languages other than English? Some would apply Ernest Gellner's notion of modernisation and national building and would argue that monolingualism was part of the process of establishing modern industrial states (Gellner 1983). There seem to have been cases where it was the promotion of a (then) minority language (e.g. Hebrew, Czech, Norwegian or possibly even Irish post-1922) that was part of the forging of a new state/nation. Here in Northern Ireland investments in Ulster-Scots in recent years are sometimes derided as a prop to something artificial. Well, many of the languages of modern Europe have something of "invented tradition" about them, we would note.

---

[1] Davies (1999: 780) argues so.
[2] The view of Hastings (1997: 73) and Harvie (2002: 94).

What does the Charter say with respect to how economic activity (and its regulation) should impact on languages?

With Part 3 Status (and so far this has applied only to Irish and not yet Ulster-Scots though there may be a parity or equality case for this to change) comes Article 13. Article 13.1 is largely about avoiding the negative; the UK government with respect to the whole of the UK is to avoid legislative provisions that would hinder the Part 3 language. Article 13.2 is more detailed and positive in terms of economic regulations and languages (about, for example, banking, health care, safety and consumer information). It is, however, important to note there are qualifications on the responsibilities of the authorities. Firstly, these apply only as far as public authorities (as opposed to the private sector) have competence. Second, those authorities should act as far as is, "reasonably possible". This parallels the section in the Council of Europe's 1995 *Framework Convention for Protection of National Minorities* which similarly talks about, "as far as possible". We do think, as would our Party, that such qualifications are valid.

   We discuss below how far there is a positive case (economic or otherwise) for promotion of linguistic diversity but at this point we will make the point that any regulative burden imposed on the private and public sectors should in some sense be proportional to the genuine level of demand for services in the minority language. The 1998 Belfast Agreement did similarly and rightly speak of UK government promotion of Irish "where appropriate". This qualification was inserted by the Ulster Unionist Party into the text in the final hours before the Agreement was done on 10th April 1998.

What is the impact of languages on the economy?

More specifically, we were asked whether such an impact was greater than that felt on and through the arts, media and broadcasting? Our brief answers are: yes, there is some positive impact, such an impact is probably not that large when measured in, say, Pounds Sterling or percent of GDP (Professor Grin's paper is entirely right to argue that many statements made about the size of the language sector do not really indicate its net economic benefit to the economy) and, yes, that impact does reach beyond the three sectors specified in Article 12 but, we would argue, probably not much further (tourism?). Any economic activity generated in or spun-off by the minority language sector would then have to be compared to the "costs" of maintaining such linguistic diversity. Such costs could be considered as one of a number of transactions costs that are imposed on economic exchange. We doubt if such language-based transactions costs are large in the case of Northern Ireland. Professor Grin (1992) has argued that no framework had yet been developed to rigorously assess the costs and benefits linguistic diversity relative to monolingualism (though he did refer to a study by Vaillancourt (1987) which estimated that the cost of the pro-French language policies in Quebec in 1977 would initially be equivalent to 2 percent of provincial GNP albeit this figure would then taper away over time). In this conference paper Professor Grin argues that we are still unable to really quantify the impact of language policy. He is probably right about this but we think what we can tentatively conclude in the case of Northern Ireland is that *existing* policy on Scots and Irish probably yield economic gains *and* costs each of a few tens of million Pounds. Such figures look large in absolute terms but are small proportionally compared to a regional GDP of about £20,000 million or devolved public spending of more than £8,000 million. And we do not think we can be sure which figure, the one for costs or benefits, is larger.

Conclusions

First: This session and, indeed, the body of work produced by Prof. Grin in particular over recent years, has performed the valuable role of emphasising that there is an economic aspect to language policy. At the same time, and being realistic, the economics often may not be the most important explanation of policy. Since the ending of the Cold War, in a world of "clashing civilisations" (Samuel Huntington, 2000) ethnic division may be the main driver of conflict. In turn, for such conflicts to be resolved, policies may be required which need to address concerns regarding linguistic diversity. For example, in its 1990 Copenhagen Declaration the OSCE/CSCE argued that the protection of national minorities, "is an essential factor for peace, stability and democracy". It is now clear that Northern Ireland is not unique within even western and central Europe in terms of having a minority problem: consider Catalonia, the Basque country, Gibraltar, Corsica, Montenegro, Kosovo, Cyprus, Istria and the Alto Adige. In most of these cases there is a language aspect. *If* it promotes peace then it will be worth spending *something* on linguistic diversity notwithstanding our continuing uncertainty as to the total economic effect.

Second: Professor Grin (2001) argued for linguistic diversity as a "good" in its own right (Article 7 of the Charter refers to "cultural wealth" and the Belfast Agreement used similar words). His conference paper can be read as a very strong plea for government action to promote such diversity. There seem to be three strands to his case but how strong are these?

(a) Prof. Grin argues for language policy because of the impact on resource allocation (i.e. economic growth will be enhanced through diversity and hence there will be more resources to pay for language policy or, indeed, other socially desirable goals). Professor Grin admits his evidence for this is still partly circumstantial. As we have already argued, we certainly accept that language policy has generated some economic activity but whether there is a gain net of the cost we are much less clear about (another way of putting this question is: "let's say that about £ 10 m. of public money is spent on Irish and Scots in Northern Ireland and this has generated X jobs is it not possible that the £ 10 m spent in another way might have generated Y jobs with Y being larger than X?").

(b) Further, Prof. Grin argues for language policy because smaller languages are a public good. At the philosophical level, we are happy to endorse this. It is probably a good thing to have linguistic diversity just as it is to have biodiversity. But, how much is that diversity worth? We really need to remind ourselves of the opportunity cost of the language policy. The public money so spent could have been spent elsewhere with other desirable effects. As Professor Grin put it in his 1997 paper (with Vaillancourt), the optimal degree of multilingualism is likely to be greater than zero but much less than the very large number corresponding to the total number of languages in the world.

(c) Moreover, Prof. Grin argues for language policy because the promotion of linguistic diversity is held to be part of distributional justice. Economists conventionally have dealt with social justice in terms of how levels of income and wealth should be moved around between individuals. Is Professor Grin right to treat "language rights" as analogous to income and wealth? We think only partly so. To a certain degree language skills, like general education and health, could be considered as part of the capabilities that an individual has to operate within the economy. Given this society has introduced notions such as guaranteed minimum levels of provision and equality of opportunity in access to such capabilities. Can this be read across to the case of minority languages?

Some caution is in fact necessary because language skills are not just economic capabilities but also a reflection of individual cultural preferences. How far is the state duty bound to underwrite diverse cultural preferences? The response might be that language is a matter of fundamental human rights. Yes, that is true, but how far are those rights to be applied in the economic sphere given that there is a cost applied? By applying the language of distributional justice Professor Grin's analysis when applied to Northern Ireland would seem to imply that the English-speaking majority needs to do right by the Irish- and Scots-speaking minorities. This is a laudable objective but surely the social contract aspect of this is that obligations are mutual? Yes, the majority should accept *some* measures in favour of the minority but equally the minority should accept that they are a small minority and therefore there is a limit to what can reasonably be done. We do not find an "historic wrong" response to such questions very helpful. We are where we are in 2003. Perhaps the distribution of political power did influence the distribution of language rights in, say, 1703 or 1803 but we do not think it practical or helpful for present generations to spend large sums of money to try to compensate for wrongs in the past.

In short, we support the measured and proportional approach towards minority languages implied by the Charter, the Framework and the Agreement, etc. There probably are political and cultural benefits from linguistic diversity. Whether there is an equally strong economic case is much less clear to us.

References

Davies, N. 1999.*The Isles A History*. London: Macmillan
Gellner, E. 1983. *Nations and Nationalism*. Oxford: Blackwell
Grin, F. 1992. "Towards a threshold theory of minority language survival". *Kyklos* 45:69-113

Grin, F. 2001. "English as economic value: facts and fallacies". *World Englishes* 20:65-78

Grin, F. and Vaillancourt, F. 1997. "The economics of multilingualism: Overview and analytical framework". *Annual Review of Applied Languages*. 17: 43-65

Harvie, C. 2002. *Scotland A Short History*. Oxford: Oxford University Press

Hastings, A. 1997. *The Consideration of Nationhood: Ethnicity, Religion and Nationalism*. Cambridge: Cambridge University Press

Hobsbawm, E.J. and Ranger, T. 1983. *The Invention of Tradition*. Cambridge: Cambridge University Press

Huntington, S. 2000. *The Clash of Civilizations*. Harmondsworth: Penguin

Vaillancourt, F. 1978. "*La Charte de la langue francaise au Quebec: un essai d'analyse*". *Canada Public Policy*. 4: 284-308

Teanga, Cultúr agus Forbairt i gCás na hÉireann: i dTreo Cur Chuige Nua

John Walsh

Cé go bhfuil plé acadúil éigin ar bun le tamall de bhlianta anuas faoi na ceangail chúisíocha idir próisis theanga agus próisis eacnamaíochta, a scríobhann François Grin ina pháipéar sa chnuasach seo, tá go leor taighde le déanamh fós ar roinnt mhaith gnéithe den cheangal seo. Is lú agus is teirce fós an plé seo in Éirinn, agus is bídeach ar fad í an obair theoiriciúil a deineadh faoi na ceangail idir teanga agus eacnamaíocht. Tá cur chuige an pháipéir seo beagán éagsúil; seachas geilleagar nó eacnamaíocht amháin, pléifear an caidreamh idir teanga, cultúr agus forbairt shoch-eacnamaíoch.

Ar dtús, déanfar léirmheas ar chuid de na húdair Éireannacha a ghlac páirt i gcibé plé a tharla faoin gceist. In ainneoin go bhfuil cúlraí éagsúla ag na húdair seo, creideann siad ar fad go bhfuil tionchar leathan ag na nGaeilge ar an tsochaí seachas ról cumarsáide amháin. Is minic nach mbíonn bunús láidir teoiriciúil ag na húdair seo, áfach, bunús a chabhródh linn an caidreamh seo idir teanga, cultúr agus forbairt a thuiscint. Chun iarracht a dhéanamh an bhearna theoiriciúil seo a líonadh, scrúdaítear cuid de na teoirící a tháinig chun cinn go hidirnáisiúnta, i réimsí na sochtheangeolaíochta, na forbartha agus an chultúir. Caitear súil ina dhiaidh sin ar na luachanna atá taobh thiar den chur chuige oifigiúil forbartha in Éirinn agus ar an neamhaird a dhéanann siadsan de chultúr agus de theanga thraidisiúnta. Ar deireadh, áitítear go dtugann an Ghaeilge deis dúinn in Éirinn cur chuige nua forbartha a aimsiú, cur chuige atá préamhaithe i dteanga agus cultúr pobal a bhí faoi chois go stairiúil.

Nuair a d'iompaigh muintir na hÉireann ar an mBéarla, a scríobh Tomás Dáibhis in 1841, chuadar i mbun aithrise ar Shasana agus dá bhrí sin, bhaineadar an bonn dá gcumas nuálaíochta, cumas a chabhródh leo dul i mbun forbartha (O'Donoghue, 1974: 97, 103, 107). In 1892, ina aitheasc "The Necessity for De-Anglicising Ireland", phléigh Dúbhglas de hÍde ról an chultúir Ghaelaigh, an Ghaeilge san áireamh, sa phróiseas náisiúnta athbheochana. Dar le de hÍde, bhí an Ghaeilge ar cheann amháin de réimse gnéithe cultúrtha a d'fhéadfadh spiorad náisiúnta a chothú chun an náisiún a thógáil agus a chinntiú nach mbeifí i muinín Shasana feasta. Níorbh ionann forbairt agus a bheith 'fat, wealthy and populous, but with all our characteristics gone' (Hyde, 1894: 123). Cé gur cáineadh de hÍde faoi bheith in aghaidh na nua-aimsearthachta (Foster, 1988: 448) nó frith-ábharaíoch (Lee, 1989a: 138), bhí a chuid cainte réabhlóideach i ndáiríre mar bhí sé ag áiteamh, den chéad uair, gur teanga bheo chumarsáide í an Ghaeilge, arbh fhéidir í a láidriú mar chuid den athshlánú náisiúnta.

In 1900, d'fhill an t-irıseoir, D.P. Moran ar Éirinn ó Shasana chun a nuachtán féin, *The Leader*, a bhunú. Ba dhuine spleodrach é Moran a d'áitigh arís agus arís eile gur cheart an Ghaeilge a cheangal leis an bpróiseas náisiúnta athshlánaithe. Ina leabhar clúiteach, *The Philosophy of Irish Ireland* (1905), filleann Moran ar an dtéama a luaigh Tomás Dáibhis seasca éigin bliain roimhe sin:

> If you have to begin with a self-distrusting people who are afraid to rely on their own judgment, who have learnt by a long and reluctant effort to imitate a rich and highly-developed people foreign to their

genius, to conceive a mean and cringing opinion of themselves, you will never get much economic initiative out of them. (Moran 1905: 111)

Ní mhíníonn Dáibhis, Moran ná de hÍde conas go díreach a chuireann slánú na Gaeilge le forbairt na tíre. Is ceist í seo nár aimsíodh freagra fós uirthi. Ina ainneoin sin, áfach, tá a gcuid scríbhinní an-tábhachtach mar gur léiriú iad ar díospóireacht bhríomar faoin nGaeilge céad bliain ó shin, díospóireacht ar dheacair í a shamhlú anois.

Chuir Seán de Fréine leis an díospóireacht sna leabhair thábhachtacha *Saoirse gan Só* (1960) agus leagan Béarla de, *The Great Silence* (1965). Tá anailís dhúshlánach aige ar an gceangal idir an Ghaeilge agus an rud go dtugtar "national [and] social well-being" air (1965: 5). Tá argóintí de Fréine bunaithe ar theoiricí na socheolaíochta a áitíonn gur cuid riachtanach den iompar sóisialta is ea teanga, agus ní córas cumarsáide amháin. Tá ról láidir síceolaíoch ag teanga i bpobal, is í an nasc is láidre í sa phobal agus is siombal í dá chultúr agus cosaint air. Má chuirtear isteach ar an nasc, an ghné riachtanach seo, titfidh an tsochaí as a chéile. Áitíonn de Fréine, mar sin, gur spreag meath obainn na Gaeilge sa 19ú haois díothú cultúrtha agus réimse fadhbanna soch-eacnamaíochta, an imirce ina measc (1965: 222)

Cheithre bliana déag ó shin, chuir an staraí Joe Lee leis an bplé ina leabhar *Ireland 1912-1985: Politics and Society*. Dar leis go mb'fhéidir go bhfuil nasc idir slánú na teanga dúchasaí agus an fhorbairt shoch-eacnamaíoch: i gcás na Danmhairge agus na Fionnlainne, níor iompaíodh ar theanga neamhdhúchasach mar chuid den iarracht náisiúnta forbartha agus bunaíodh an fhorbairt sin ar fhéiniúlacht láidir:

it is quite possible that the manner in which the language was lost has damaged Irish potential for self-respect, with all the psychological consequences for behaviour patterns that flow from that, even in the purely material sphere ... Identity cannot be divorced from the general level of national performance. (Lee, 1989: 674)

An ceangal a ndéanann na húdair seo cur síos air, is féidir tuiscint níos doimhne a fháil air i gcomhthéacs roinnt teoiricí atá tagtha chun cinn go hidirnáisiúnta. I dtosach, pléimis an tsochtheangeolaíocht. Cé nach mbíonn cúrsaí forbartha á bplé ag an tsochtheangeolaíocht, mínítear an nasc idir teanga agus cultúr nó idir teanga agus cognaíocht. Scrúdaíonn Joshua Fishman an ceangal siombalach idir teanga agus cultúr: seasaíonn an teanga do chultúr na ndaoine a labhraíonn í. Tá nasc idir an siombalachas seo agus stádas na teanga nó meon na ndaoine a labhraíonn í nó, go deimhin, an staid shoch-eacnamaíoch ina bhfuil siad. Dá bhrí sin, tá tionchar láidir ag toscaí soch-eacnamaíocha ar an gceangal siombalach idir cultúr agus teanga: ní haon ábhar iontais é gurb é an Béarla teanga cheannasach an domhain, de bhrí go mbaineann sé le tíortha láidre eacnamaíocha. Dá leithne agus dá idirdhisciplíní í mar ábhar, is é laige na sochtheangeolaíochta nach ndéanann sí anailís ar fhorbairt shocheacnamaíoch. In *Reversing Language Shift*, áfach, téann Fishman céim níos faide: má dhéanaimid iarracht meath teanga a chur ar gcúl, a áitíonn sé, táimid ag dul i ngleic le fadhbanna cultúrtha na linne seo:

Reversing language shift deals with a "good problem" because it is itself a potential contribution to overcoming some of the endemic sociocultural dislocation of society. In this sense, then, RLS is a contribution to many of the central problems that eat away at modern life, at modern man and at modern society. (Fishman 1991: 7) Próiseas a phleanálann athrú sóisialta agus cultúrtha atá in *reversing language shift*, dar le Fishman. Déanann sé iarracht díothú na gcultúr traidisiúnta a chur droim as ais agus tugann sé dúshlán an cheannais shoch-eacnamaíoch. Dá bhrí sin, creidim go bhféadfadh impleachtaí móra a bheith aige do chúrsaí forbartha agus, dá réir sin, go bhfuil an-luach in obair Fishman maidir le cás na hÉireann.

Seachas Bord na Gaeilge sna 1980í, ní dócha gur thug aon dream eile mórán airde ar Fishman in Éirinn. Tá cur chuige eile, seachas an tsochtheangeolaíocht, áfach, a thugann aird ar an ngné chultúrtha den bhforbairt agus ar tugadh droim láimhe di in Éirinn chomh maith. Tugaim an "cur chuige soch-chultúrtha" air seo agus, go hachomair, tá dhá ghné i gceist. I dtosach, tá "an fhorbairt dhaonna", téarma de chuid na Náisiún Aontaithe. Coincheap a chuir Clár Forbartha na Náisiún Aontaithe chun cinn le 15 bliana anuas atá i gceist le "forbairt dhaonna". Tá fás eacnamaíochta tábhachtach ach leis féin, ní bhainfidh sé forbairt dhaonna amach. Níl sa bhfás ach bealach chun an leas sóisialta a chur chun cinn: breis roghanna a thabhairt do dhaoine agus a gcaighdeán saoil a fheabhsú (UNDP, 1999: 12). Tá tagairtí fánacha don chultúr agus do theanga, fiú, ag na Náisiúin Aontaithe chomh maith, i dtaca leis an bhforbairt dhaonna: '[h]uman development necessarily involves a concern with culture - the ways people choose to live together - for it is the sense of social cohesion based on culture and shared values and beliefs that shapes human development' (UNDP, 1996: 55). Tíortha ilteangacha go dtugtar stádas do na teangacha éagsúla iontu, a deir na Náisiúin Aontaithe, is minic a éiríonn go maith leo ó thaobh na forbartha daonna (UNDP, 1996: 4, 62).

An dara cuid den chur chuige soch-chultúrtha, "eacnamaíocht pholaitiúil chultúrtha na forbartha" atá i gceist: conas a théann cultúr i bhfeidhm ar eacnamaíocht pholaitiúil na forbartha (is é sin, na bealaí ina mbíonn an stát, an tsochaí agus an margadh ag idirghníomhú chun forbairt a bhaint amach). Tá sé seo bunaithe cuid mhaith ar shaothar Thierry Verhelst (1987) agus ar scríbhinní Vincent Tucker, nach maireann, ó Ollscoil Chorcaí (1997 & 1997a). Áitíonn Tucker go bhfuil ceangal cúisíoch idir féiniúlacht chultúrtha pobail agus forbairt shoch-eacnamaíoch an phobail sin: ní tharlaíonn forbairt muna gcuirtear luachanna, nósanna, féiniúlacht pobail san áireamh:

> When a people is stripped of its identity it is no longer capable of self-determination, they become subject peoples whose future and whose past is shaped by others, and whose projects, dreams, values and meanings are supplied by others. In the eyes of the developers their societies are stagnant and fossilised, incapable of self-directed development and portrayed as obstacles to development' (Tucker, 1997: 6-7).

An fhorbairt mar a thuigtear go coitianta í, ón dearcadh Eorpach, tugann Tucker a dhúshlán agus díríonn a aird ar chultúir na bpobal a dúradh a bhí tearcfhorbartha. Tá sé de laige ag Tucker, áfach, ná a laghad plé a dhéantar ar theanga agus forbairt: luann Tucker teangacha (1997: 10), ach ní mhíníonn sé an bhaint atá idir iad agus cultúr ná forbairt.

Muna dtugtar mórán airde in Éirinn ar na teoiricí seo, cén cur chuige forbartha atá in úsáid? Tugaimse "cur chuige an nua-aimsearthaithe" air. Go stairiúil, glacadh leis go coitianta agus go forleathan gurbh ionann forbairt agus fás eacnamaíoch, tionsclú, nua-aimsearthú agus dul chun cinn sóisialta agus, go ginearálta, níorbh aon eisceacht í Éire. De na coincheapa seo ar fad, creidim go dtugann an nua-aimsearthú an léargas is soiléire dúinn ar cheisteanna maidir le cultúr agus forbairt. Tá préamhacha an nua-aimsearthaithe i leabhar clúiteach Adam Smith, *The Wealth of Nations* (1776) agus in Eagnaíocht na hAlban trí chéile, áit ar tugadh tús áite don eacnamaíocht *laissez-faire* - is é sin, nár cheart don rialtas idirghabháil a dhéanamh sa mhargadh mar go dtabharfaidh an margadh aire do riachtanais an duine aonair sa tsochaí. D'fhág teacht chun cinn na heolaíochta go raibh an lámh in uachtar ag an réasúnachas ar an anord, agus ag an nua-aimsearthacht ar an dtraidisiún. Tá sé tábhachtach gur Albannach ab ea Smith, mar bhí an Eagnaíocht Albanach préamhaithe san achrann idir Gael agus Gall agus idir Gaeilge agus Béarla. Chas Smith agus a lucht leanúna droim leis na Garbhchríocha agus a gcultúr traidisiúnta Gaelach agus thug aghaidh ar Londain na tráchtála, na heolaíochta agus an Bhéarla. Tugadh le fios nach bhféadfadh cultúr traidisiúnta dul chun cinn a dhéanamh agus gur teanga "réasúnach" ab ea Béarla trína bhféadfaí idirbhearta eacnamaíocha a dhéanamh (Gibbons, 2003). Bhí na cultúir seo - na Gaeil in Albain agus in Éirinn, na Bascaigh nó na Briotánaigh sa bhFrainc - mar bhac in aghaidh na forbartha (May, 2001: 159). Creidim chomh maith áfach, gur cur chuige thar a bheith cultúrtha ann féin atá sa nua-aimsearthú: trí dhiúltú do chultúir agus do theangacha laga, "traidisiúnta", cuireann sé béim ar an gcultúr atá fite fuaite leis féin: cultúr an réasúnachais eolaíochta. Áitím, mar sin, go bhfuil cath á agairt ag an nua-aimsearthú ar chultúir agus ar theangacha traidisiúnta, cath chun "dul chun cinn" a bhaint amach bunaithe ar bhrú faoi chois na gcultúr seo. Tá sé seo préamhaithe i dtuiscintí comhaimseartha den nua-aimsearthú, san eacnamaíocht mar a léiríodh i gcás na hEagnaíochta, agus sa tsocheolaíocht chomh maith, i scríbhinní leithéidí Talcott Parsons agus Clarence Ayers (Walsh, 2002).

Cad is brí leis seo ar fad i gcás na hÉireann, na Gaeilge agus na forbartha? Tá an nua-aimsearthú - réasúnachas seachas anord, eolaíocht seachas traidisiún, fás in ioncam *per capita* seachas leas coiteann an phobail - naimhdeach do theangacha ar nós na Gaeilge, ach tá an nua-aimsearthú seo fite fuaite le polasaí forbartha an iarthair agus le polasaí forbartha na hÉireann. Bunaithe ar na teoiricí idirnáisiúnta a pléadh sa pháipéar seo - sa tsochtheangeolaíocht, i staidéar na forbartha agus san eacnamaíocht pholaitiúil chultúrtha - áitím gur féidir cur chuige nua a aimsiú a dhíríonn aird shonrach ar thábhacht an chultúir agus na teanga traidisiúnta i bpróiseas rathúil forbartha.

Buíochas

Ba mhaith liom buíochas a ghabháil leis an Dr. Peadar Kirby, Scoil Dlí agus Rialtais, Ollscoil Chathair Bhaile Átha Cliath, as a chuid comhairle agus an páipéar seo á ullmhú agam.

Liosta Tagairtí

De Fréine, S. 1960. *Saoirse gan Só*. Dublin: FNT.

De Fréine, S. 1965. *The Great Silence*. Dublin: FNT.

Fishman, J. 1991. *Reversing Language Shift: Theoretical and Empirical Foundations of Assistance to Threatened Languages*. Clevedon, England: Multilingual Matters.

Foster, R.F. 1988. *Modern Ireland: 1600-1972*. London: Penguin.

Gibbons, L. 2003. "Towards a Postcolonial Enlightenment: The United Irishmen, Cultural Diversity and the Public Sphere". In Carroll, C. and P. King eds. *Ireland and Postcolonial Theory*. Cork: Cork University Press, 81-91.

Hyde, D. 1894. "The Necessity for De-Anglicising Ireland". In *The Revival of Irish Literature: addresses by Sir Charles Gavan Duffy, Dr. George Sigerson and Dr. Douglas Hyde*. London: Fisher Unwin.

Lee, J.J. 1989. *Ireland 1912-1985: Politics and Society*. Cambridge: Cambridge University Press.

Lee, J.J. 1989a. *The Modernisation of Irish Society: 1848-1918* (2nd edition). Dublin: Gill & Macmillan.

May, S. 2001. *Language and Minority Rights: Ethnicity, Nationalism and the Politics of Language*. Harlow: Pearson Education Limited.

Moran, D.P. 1905. *The Philosophy of Irish Ireland* (2nd edition). Dublin: James Duffy & Co., M.H. Gill & Son and The Leader.

O'Donoghue, D.J. ed. 1974 (1914). *Essays of Thomas Davis: Centenary Edition*. New York: Lemma Publishing Corporation (Dundalk: Dundalgan Press).

Tucker, V. 1997. "Introduction: a Cultural Perspective on Development". In Tucker, V. ed. *Cultural Perspectives on Development*. London: Frank Cass, 1-21.

Tucker, V. 1997a. "Health, Medicine and Development: A Field of Cultural Struggle". In Tucker, V. ed. *Cultural Perspectives on Development*. London: Frank Cass, 110-28.

United Nations Development Programme, 1996. *Human Development Report 1996*. New York and Oxford: Oxford University Press.

United Nations Development Programme, 1999. *Human Development Report 1999*. New York and Oxford: Oxford University Press.

Verhelst, T. 1990. *No Life Without Roots: Culture and Development*. London: Zed Books.

Walsh, J. 2002. "Language, Culture and Development: the Gaeltacht Commissions 1926 and 2002". In Kirk, J.M. and D.P. Ó Baoill eds. *Language Planning and Education: Linguistic Issues in Northern Ireland, the Republic of Ireland, and Scotland*. Belfast: Cló Ollscoil na Ríona, 300-318.

Is acmhainn luachmhar eacnamaíochta í an Ghaeilge do Phobal na hÉireann ar fad

Seosamh Mac Donncha

Aithnítear anois gur acmhainn luachmhar í gach teanga atá á labhairt ar fud an domhain agus go dtugann gach teanga léargas ar leith dúinn ar an saol. Aithnítear bás teanga mar ghníomh faillí arb ionann é agus tragóid dhomhanda. Go deimhin is féidir a rá gur acmhainn nádúrtha agus náisiúnta í an Ghaeilge agus má ligtear don teanga bás a fháil, imeoidh ceann de na teangacha is sine san Eoraip agus teanga dhúchais na hÉireann.

Bunaíodh Foras an Gaeilge ar an 2ú Nollaig, 1999, faoi choimirce Chomhaontú Aoine an Chéasta leis an nGaeilge a chur chun cinn ar fud na hÉireann ar fad. Chomh maith le cúraimí Bhord na Gaeilge, a bhí ann ó 1978, tugadh cúraimí breise don Fhoras le cur lena éifeacht an teanga a chur chun cinn, mar shampla, i gcúrsaí oideachais agus téarmaíochta. Aistríodh feidhmeanna foilsitheoireachta an Ghúim agus an Choiste Téarmaíochta chuig Foras na Gaeilge.

Is iad feidhmeanna reachtúla Fhoras na Gaeilge ná:
* Cur chun cinn na Gaeilge ar fud an oileáin.
* Labhairt agus scríobh an Gaeilge a éascú agus a spreagadh sa láthair phoiblí agus phríobháideach i bPoblacht na hÉireann agus, i gcomhthéacs Chuid 3 de Chairt Chomhairle na hEorpa um Theangacha Réigiúnacha nó Mionlaigh, i dTuaisceart na hÉireann nuair atá éileamh iomchuí uirthi.
* Comhairle a chur ar an dá fheidhmeannas, ar fhorais phoiblí agus ar ghrúpaí eile sna réimsí poiblí agus príobháideacha.
* Tabhairt faoi eagraíochtaí, thograí agus ghníomhaíochtaí Gaeilge a mhaoiniú.
* Tabhairt faoi thaighde, fheachtais chur chun cinn agus chaidreamh preasa agus poiblí.
* Forbairt foclóirí agus téarmaíochta.
* Tacú le hoideachas trí mhéan na Gaeilge agus le múineadh na Gaeilge.

Nuair a bunaíodh Foras na Gaeilge thionscain an eagraíocht próiseas pleanála straitéisí agus sa bhliain 2001 cuireadh Plean Forbartha Straitéiseach deich mbliana ar fáil don Fhoras. Sa phlean straitéiseach sin aithníodh an tábhacht a bhain leis an nGaeilge i gcomhthéacs na heacnamaíochta agus na margaíochta. Dá thoradh sin, beartaíodh rannóg láidir chumarsáide agus mhargaíochta a bhunú chun freastal ar an riachtanas áirithe sin. Tá Foras na Gaeilge ag cur tús anois i láthair na huaire le próiseas earcaíochta chun rannóg dá leithéid a thógáil.

Is léir go n-aithníonn eagraíochtaí gnó gur acmhainn eacnamaíochta an Ghaeilge a úsáid mar chuid dá ngnó. Tá an tuiscint sin bunaithe ar an bhfealsúnacht go:
   (a) dtugann úsáid na teanga breis luacha don ghnó.
   (b) bhfeabhsaíonn sé seirbhísí do chustaiméirí.
   (c) léiríonn úsáid na teanga meas don phobal.
   (d) meallann a húsáid custaiméirí nua.
   (e) dtreisíonn a húsáid dílseacht na gcustaiméirí.
   (f) dtarraingíonn sí aird.

Is í sin an teachtaireacht shoiléir atá le cloisteáil ó phríomhcheannairí gnó agus tionsclaithe. Is dóigh gurb é an sampla is fearr de seo atá le fáil ná an sár-obair atá déanta ag "Gaillimh le Gaeilge " i measc lucht gnó na cathrach sin le roinnt mhaith blianta.

De réir ráiteas ón Aire Éamonn Ó Cuív, T.D. agus é ag seoladh Tuarascáil Bhliantúil "Gaillimh le Gaeilge" i mí Bealtaine, 2000, dúirt sé gurbh fhiú 64 Milliún sa bhliain an Ghaeilge do chathair na Gaillimhe. I suirbhé a rinneadh taca an ama sin, dúirt 86% de thurasóirí go raibh an cultúr an-tábhachtach dá dturas go Gaillimh.

Ó thaobh fostaíochta agus postanna de, tá ard-chumas sa Ghaeilge mar bhuntáiste i gcónaí san Earnáil Phoiblí. Níl amhras ach go dtreiseoidh an t-éileamh ar dhaoine le cumas sa Ghaeilge i bhfianaise achtú Acht na dTeangacha Oifigiúla 2003, níos luaithe i mbliana. Breathnaítear uirthi mar bhuntáiste breise i gcomhar le scileanna agus cáilíochtaí eile idir ghairmiúil agus phearsanta. Tuigtear dúinn go bhfuil ganntanas i gcónaí sna rannóga teicniúla do dhaoine atá in ann an obair theicniúil a stiúradh agus a chur i gcrích trí mheán na Gaeilge. Is féidir cúrsaí theicneolaíocht an eolais, ríomhaireachta agus cánach a áireamh i measc na réimsí sin chomh maith a bhfuil ganntanas daoine iontu le cumas Gaeilge.

Mar is eol don saol mór, tá Ranna Stáit agus rialtais ann ina bhfuil ard-chumas sa Ghaeilge riachtanach. Ina measc siúd tá an Roinn Gnóthaí Pobail, Tuaithe agus Gaeltachta, Institiúid Teangeolaíochta Éireann, Foras na Gaeilge, An Gúm, An Coiste Téarmaíochta, Rannóg an Aistriúcháin sa Dáil, An Roinn Oideachais agus Eolaíochta, Coimisiún na Logainmneacha, An Iarsmalann agus an Leabharlann Náisiúnta, gan ach roinnt a lua.

Tá an Rialtas Áitiúil ar cheann de na fostóirí is mó i bPoblacht na hÉireann, le thart ar 40,000 fostaí i ngach gné de sheirbhísí agus riaracháin phoiblí. Mar a luadh cheana féin i gcomhthéacs achtú Acht na dTeangacha Oifigiúla 2003, beidh an Ghaeilge ina buntáiste suntasach d'fhostaíocht faoin Rialtas Áitiúil amach anseo.

Le roinnt blianta, tá an earnáil seo tar éis imeachtaí cultúrtha, staire agus ealaíne samhailtí a sheoladh ar bhonn áitiúil a thugann buntáiste fostaíochta do dhaoine le Gaeilge. I láthair na huairc tá Foras na Gaeilge ag cur cómhaoiniú ar fáil do na hÚdaráis Áitiúla agus do na Boird Sláinte chun Oifigigh Forbartha Gaeilge a fhostú agus tá 14 oifigeach fostaithe faoin scéim go dtí seo. Tá sé beartaithe an scéim a leathnú go dtí Tuaisceart na hÉireann go gairid.

Nuair a luaitear na himpleachtaí a bheas ag Acht na dTeangacha Oifigiúla 2003 i leith na fostaíochta, mar a mheabhraíonn an tAire Ó Cuív dúinn go minic, ní miste a lua go mbeidh éileamh an-mhór ar úsáid na Gaeilge agus ar dhaoine le cumas sa Ghaeilge ar bhonn dlí. Gan dabht, is athrú chun feabhais a bheas anseo do phobal labhartha na Gaeilge sa nGaeltacht agus taobh amuigh di. Is léir go dtiocfaidh méadú thar cuimse ar earnáil an aistriúcháin agus is tráthúil atá na hinstitiúidí tríú leibhéal ag cur dlús le soláthar cúrsaí sa réimse seo.

Bhí agus tá an Ghaeilge fós riachtanach do na Gardaí Síochana agus na Fórsaí Cosanta. Tá an scrúdú cainte sa nGaeilge tábhachtach ó tharla go mbíonn go leor gardaí ag obair sna ceantair Ghaeltachta. Ní amháin sin, ach tá buntáiste airgeadais ann chomh maith mar go bhfaigheann siad 10% breis thuarastail ach iad a bheith ag freastal ar phobal na Gaeltachta.

Bhí clú agus cáil ariamh ar an arm, go háirithe ar an gColáiste Míleata, maidir le húsáid na Gaeilge go gairmiúil. Leanann an traidisiún sin ar aghaidh go dtí an lá inniu san Arm, sa tSlua Muirí agus san Aer-Chór agus nach iomaí scéal atá cloiste againn faoin arm a bheith ag úsáid na Gaeilge mar theanga rúnda eatarthu féin agus iad i gcéin!

Ó thaobh na múinteoireachta de, tá tábhacht ar leith ag baint fós le cumas sa nGaeilge. Is bunriachtanas fós é go mbeadh cumas sa nGaeilge ag múinteoirí atá ag teagasc i mbunscoileanna taobh amuigh agus taobh istigh den Ghaeltacht.

Ag an bpointe seo, ní miste ról Údarás na Gaeltachta a lua i leith chruthú agus chothú na fostaíochta sa nGaeltacht. In imeacht na mblianta, tá an tÚdarás tar éis líon mór postanna a chruthú sa nGaeltacht agus cúrsaí oiliúna éagsúla a reáchtáil chun freastal ar na héilimh fhostaíochta a chruthaíodar. In ainneoin na ndeacrachtaí a bhíonn ag an Údarás ó am go ham ag cruthú na fostaíochta i gceantair atá chomh himeallach leis na ceantair Ghaeltachta, níl dabht ach go bhfuil éacht déanta acu thar na blianta.

Dar ndóigh tá athrú suntasach tagtha ar shlite beatha agus ar na gairmeacha traidisiúnta a bhíodh á gcleachtadh sa nGaeltacht. Tá cúl á thabhairt do na bealaigh traidisiúnta feirmeoireachta, iascaireachta agus ceirdeanna.

Tá meáin chumarsáide mar Raidió na Gaeltachta agus TG 4 tar éis gníomhaíochtaí agus cláir Ghaeilge-lárnaithe agus Ghaeltacht-lárnaithe a chur os comhair an phobail agus i lár an mhargaidh. Tá an fhostaíocht atá á cruthú ag na tionscail chumarsáide seo ag cabhrú le caomhnú agus leathnú na Gaeilge sna meáin chumarsáide agus sa bpobal féin. Dá thoradh seo ar fad táthar ag cur go mór le stádas na Gaeilge agus ag cothú measa ar an teanga.

Tá gá leanúnach le daoine a bhfuil scileanna éagsúla acu – idir scileanna láimhe scileanna teicniúla, scileanna riaracháin agus scileanna bainistíochta. Is ábhar muiníne dúinn ar fad go bhfuil Údarás na Gaeltachta agus Institiúidí éagsúla tríú leibhéal ag leanacht ar aghaidh ag freastal ar na riachtanais seo. Deirtear linn go bhfuilimid ag maireachtáil anois i ré shochaí an eolais. Mar bharr air sin, tá ré na teicneolaíochta eolais faoi lán seoil. Deireann saineolaithe áirithe teangeolaíochta linn, mar an tOllamh Mart Rannut ón Eastóin, nach mairfidh teanga ar bith mura gcuireann siad iad féin in oiriúint don teicneolaíocht teanga. Ní miste dúinn é sin a mheabhrú agus muid ag pleanáil do thodhchaí na Gaeilge. Is cúis misnigh dúinn go bhfuil Údarás na Gaeltachta ag díriú ar thograí teanga-lárnaithe agus iad ag breathnú chun cinn chun féidearthachtaí fostaíochta a scrúdú don Ghaeltacht. Go deimhin, táimid féin i bhForas na Gaeilge ag tacú agus ag maoiniú tograí atá ag plé leis an teicneolaíocht teanga thuasluaite.

Ag an bpointe seo, ba mhaith liom díriú ar Thuaisceart na hÉireann. Is eol dúinn ar fad go bhfuil cúinsí difriúla ar fad i gceist agus muid ag caint faoi chomhthéacs agus thimpeallacht chur chun cinn na Gaeilge sa Tuaisceart. Ó thaobh Fhoras na Gaeilge de, is ar bhonn cearta daonna, cearta teanga, cearta comhionannais agus comhthéacs na Cairte Eorpaí atáimid ag feidhmiú ó thuaidh. Is cúis áthais dúinn a bheith ag cur na Gaeilge chun cinn ar bhonn uile-Éireann, uile-oileánda don chéad uair ariamh. Tugann sé deis dúinn an Ghaeilge a fhorbairt i gcomhthéacs aontaithe Ghaeltachtaí agus Ghaeilgeoirí an oileáin ar fad. Don chéad uair ariamh, táthar in ann plé le Gaeilgeoirí agus le pobail Ghaeilge na hÉireann mar ghréasán aontaithe teanga.

Níl amhras ach gurb é fás líon na nGaeilgeoirí i dTuaisceart na hÉireann an fhorbairt is mó uchtaigh do phobal na Gaeilge le fada. Ní fás thar oíche a bhí ann ach forbairt a d'eascair as tiomantas daoine deonacha, cróga a raibh fís acu agus a d'fhíoraigh an fhís sin de bharr oibre straitéisí chéimnithe.

Tá borradh ollmhór tagtha ar earnáil na gaelscolaíochta ó thuaidh le fiche bliain anuas. A bhuíochas sin d'eagraíochtaí mar Ghaeloiliúint agus anois do na heagrais reachtúla, Comhairle na Gaelscolaíochta agus Iontaobhas na Gaelscolaíochta. Mar bharr air sin tá béim ar leith curtha ar bhunú scoil-phobail thart ar na hionaid oideachais agus níl dabht ach go gcothóidh an cur chuige seo dúshraith láidir d'fhorbairt na Gaeilge mar theanga phobail amach anseo.

I láthair na huaire tá pobail láidre teanga cruthaithe thart ar Chultúrlann Bhéal Feirste agus Ghaeláras Dhoire. Is eiseamláirí iad araon den toradh is féidir a bhaint amach ach pleanáil straitéiseach chéimnithe teanga a chur i gcrích.

Faoi láthair i dTuaisceart na hÉireann tá suas le 200 duine fostaithe leis an nGaeilge taobh amuigh de chúrsaí oideachais. Is daoine iad sin atá ag saothrú a gcodach leis an teanga – ag aistriú, ag scríobh, ag craoladh, ag déanamh cláracha Gaeilge don teilifís agus don raidió, ag aisteoireacht, ag forbairt teanga agus pobail. Is cúis áthais dom a rá go bhfuil Foras na Gaeilge ag cabhrú le agus ag maoiniú go leor de na tograí seo agus is léir go bhfuil rath ar a saothar.

Tá tábhacht ar leith le cúrsaí eacnamaíochta/fostaíochta i gcomhthéacs na Gaeilge ó thuaidh. Ní féidir dul chun cinn substaintiúil a dhéanamh don teanga gan cúrsaí eacnamaíochta/fostaíochta a bheith fite fuaite lenár bpleananna.

Má chuirtear straitéisí teanga chun cinn agus béim ar an ngné eacnamaíoch, beidh sé níos éasca tuilleadh daoine a thabhairt linn agus a mhealladh isteach in earnáil na Gaeilge. Is furasta cur i gcoinne deontais, abair, d'fhiontar Gaeilge. Níl sé chomh furasta céanna cur i gcoinne fiontair a chuireann postanna agus oiliúint ar fáil agus seirbhís don phobal ag an am céanna.

Sin í an aidhm atá leis na deontais agus leis an maoiniú a thugann muidne amach i bhForas na Gaeilge. Is é sin an rud atá na deontais sin againne ag déanamh agus luaim arís samplaí mar Ghaeláras Dhoire, Chultúrlann Bhéal Feirste, agus Chomhairle na Gaelscolaíochta. Is amhlaidh cás le Forbairt Feirste, Comhchoiste Aontroim Thuaidh agus maoiniú na gcomhlachtaí aistriúcháin.

Is sócmhainn eacnamaíoch, chultúrtha, ealaíne agus shóisialta í an Ghaeilge. Is sócmhainn ag an tsochaí mar sin an cainteoir Gaeilge.

Ach fiú mura bhfuil luach eacnamaíoch leis an teanga, rud nach gcreidim go pearsanta, caithfidh muid smaoineamh ar an saibhreas a chaillfeadh muid dá ligfeadh muid di bás a fháil – stair 2000 bliain, tuiscint ar an tír agus ar ár bhféiniúlacht.

Gàidhlig agus an Eaconamaidh: Nàdar nan Deasbadan ann an Alba An-Diugh

Wilson McLeod

Anns a' phàipear bhrìoghmhor aige rinn François Grin tòrr phuingean ùidheachail agus smuaineachail a bheir solas air suidheachadh na Gàidhlig ann an Alba anns an latha an diugh. Tha e gu math furasta aithneachadh gu bheil ceistean eaconamach air a bhith glè chudromach anns na deasbadan poballach a bhios a' dol air adhart a thaobh leasachadh na Gàidhlig, ged a tha cuid de na ceistean seo air am falach mar as trice. Cha bhi e nam ruighinn an seo ach geàrr-chunntas a thoirt air nàdar nan deasbadan seo ann an Alba – na deasbadan a tha a' dol air adhart taobh a-staigh saoghal na Gàidhlig fhèin agus tha na deasbadan a tha gan cumail aig ìre fharsaing, nàiseanta.

Ged a tha sàr-obair ga dèanamh leis na meadhanan Gàidhlig, gu sònraichte BBC Radio nan Gaidheal, ann an bith ag aithris bheachdan agus dheasbadan air iomairt na Gàidhlig agus air ceistean poileasaidh cànain ann an Alba, anns a' chumantas – is e sin ri ràdh, am measg luchd nam meadhanan Beurla agus am measg luchd na Beurla anns an fharsaingeachd — is e deasbad gu math seasg, tana, amh a tha ri chluinntinn a thaobh na Gàidhlig ann an Alba. Is e glè bheag de dh'eòlas a tha aig luchd nam meadhanan agus aig a' mhòr-mhòrchuid de luchd-poileataigs air a' Ghàidhlig, agus gu tric tha e follaiseach nach eil mòran diù aca dhi. Chan ann tric idir a thèid cùisean na Gàidhlig a mhìneachadh no a dheasbad anns na meadhanan Beurla ann an Alba, agus gu h-àbhaisteach is e ceistean bunaiteach, toiseach-tòiseachaidh, seach ceistean mionaideach no domhainn, a thèid a sgrùdadh, cleas:

- carson a tha sinn a' buadraigeadh le rudeigin cho suarach ris a' Ghàidhlig co-dhiù, nuair a tha na h-uiread de dhuilgheadasan mòra rim fuasgladh?
- nach eil a' Ghàidhlig a' bàsachadh a dh'aindeoin nan iomairtean cosgail a thathas a' cur an sàs air a son? nach eil sinn dìreach a' caitheamh airgead ann a bhith ga cumail air seòrsa de '*life-support machine*'?

agus gu sònraichte:

- carson a tha 'sinne' a' cosg na h-uiread de dh'airgead air a' Ghàidhlig, nuair a tha 'iadsan', .i. luchd-labhairt a' chànain, cho gann?

Mar a dh'ionnsaich sinn aig François Grin, tha a leithid de cheistean, a leithid de mhì-thuigse, ri chluinntinn ann an iomadach dùthaich. Gu mì-fhortanach, ann an Alba, tha sinn fhathast aig a' chiad ìre den deasbad, a' dol mun cuairt cearcaill: bidh luchd mì-rùn na Gàidhlig a' gearain mu 'shubsadaidhean' oillteil, agus bidh luchd dìon na Gàidhlig a' mìneachadh gu bheil an t-suim airgid a tha ga cosg air innleachdan Gàidhlig fìor bheag, agus nach e 'subsadaidh' a tha ann co-dhiù. Cha bhi an deasbad a' dol air adhart idir oir bidh e a' tòiseachadh as ùr, aig an aon ìre de dh'aineolas is de dh'an-abaicheachd, gach turas; thèid an aon deasbad faoin a chumail nuair a nochdas an ath airteagal anns na pàipearan-naidheachd no an ath phrògram air an rèidio no air an telebhisean. Is e cearcall gu math sgìtheil a tha ann.

Mar a mhìnich an t-Ollamh Grin, tha rannsachadh air iomadachd chànanach agus an eaconamaidh a' toirt a-steach grunn cheistean bunaiteach: ceistean mu dheidhinn feallsanachd phoilitigeach agus ceartas sòisealta, mu dheidhinn còraichean a' mhion-shluaigh agus fallaineachd a' mhòr-shluaigh. Feumar aithneachadh agus aideachadh nach eil na meadhanan agus an luchd-poileataigs ann an Alba cleachdte ri bhith a' meòrachadh air ceistean mar seo, eu-coltach ri dùthchannan leithid Chanada far a bheil an deasbad mu ioma-chultaras, mun chaidreabh eadar am mòr-shluagh agus na mion-shlòigh (an dà chuid mion-shlòigh "dhùthchasach" agus mion-shlòigh "ùra") fada nas adhartaiche. Ann an Alba tha sinn fhathast aig ìre nam "pàipearan beaga" (na *tabloids*), gu mì-fhortanach, gun doimhneachd argamaid no smaoineachaidh (McLeod 2001).

An rud as dòrainniche a thaobh ceist na Gàidhlig is e gu bheil an sgaradh bunaiteach eadar am mòr-shluagh agus am mion-shluagh gu math làidir fhathast ann an inntinn dhaoine, is e sin ri ràdh an sgaradh eadar "sinne", .i. am mòr-shluagh a tha (mas fhìor) a' pàigheadh nan cìsean, agus "iadsan", .i. an fheadhainn a tha (mas fhìor) a' faighinn nan "subsadaidhean". Is dòcha nach deach an argamaid aig an Ollamh Grin a thaobh luach iomadachd chànanach mar *"public good"* a mhìneachadh agus a sgaoileadh ann an Alba mar bu chòir; gun teagamh, chan eil a' mhòrchuid a' gabhail ris gu bheil taiceadh na Gàidhlig a' leasachadh Alba gu lèir, gu bheil muinntir Alba air fad a' faighinn bhuannachdan à leasachadh na Gàidhlig.

Mar sin, ma tha beachd sam bith aig a' mhòrchuid de dhaoine ann an Alba a thaobh a' cheangail eadar a' Ghàidhlig agus gnothaichean eaconamach, is ann mu dheidhinn ìre na taice poballaich agus ìre nan "subsadaidhean" a tha a' bharail sin. Ach ann an dòigh, tha seo a' ciallachadh gun do rinneadh seòrsa de dh'adhartas co-dhiù, oir cha robh taic phoballach don Ghàidhlig ann idir gus bho chionn ghoirid. Mar sin is ann ri linn soirbheas iomairt na Gàidhlig gu bheil na "subsadaidhean" ann anns a' chiad dol-a-mach, gun do ràinig an deasbad an ìre seo. Gu tradiseanta, an aon bheachd a bha aig daoine a thaobh Gàidhlig agus an eaconamaidh is e nach robh luach pragtaigeach aice idir, gum feumte faighinn cuidhteas i a chum leasachadh eaconamach na Gàidhealtachd agus nan Gàidheal, gu robh adhartas an crochadh air ionnsachadh agus cleachdadh na Beurla. Bha am beachd sin cumanta am measg an dà chuid Gall is Gàidheal (ga chur an cèill ann an abairtean leithid *"Gaelic won't buy you one pound of sausages once you cross the Minch"*). A-rithist, mar a mhìnich an t-Ollamh Grin, chan ann ainneamh a bhios argamaidean agus reatraic mar sin gan cluinntinn a thaobh mhion-chànan: seo seann sgeulachd. Is dòcha gu bheil an seann bheachd seo beò fhathast ann an Alba, ach chan eil e cho làidir 's a bha e, agus is e ceist nan "subsadaidhean" a tha air mullach a' chlàir a-nis.

Tha e coltach gu bheil an Riaghaltas gu math mothachail air an deasbad seo, agus iad a' gabhail sìor-iomagain gum faighear *"backlash"* uabhasach ma nì iad cus airson na Gàidhlig. Tha an tuigse seo ri faireachdainn anns an dreachd Bile Gàidhlig a leig iad mu sgaoil anns an Damhair 2003, bile lag uireasbhach a bhris iomadach dùil am measg luchd na Gàidhlig (Riaghaltas na h-Alba 2003; faic cuideachd Gordon 2003).

Bidh mi a-nis a' toirt sùil air taobh eile den deasbad a thaobh Gàidhlig agus an eaconamaidh ann an Alba, còmhradh a bhios, gu ìre mhòir, a' dol air adhart am measg luchd na Gàidhlig agus luchd-taice na Gàidhlig a-mhàin, deasbad nach cluinnear ach glè ainneamh anns na meadhanan Beurla agus nach eil, gu mì-fhortanach, a' toirt mòran buaidh air tuigsean a' mhòr-shluaigh. Airson fichead bliadhna is còrr, tha luchd-iomairt na Gàidhlig air a bhith a' mìneachadh gu bheil leasachadh na Gàidhlig math airson eaconamaidh na Gàidhealtachd, gu bheil an t-airgead poballach a tha ga chosg air pròiseactan agus innleachdan Gàidhlig (anns na meadhanan agus na h-ealain gu sònraichte) air leth luachmhor don sgìre, gu bheil iad a' cruthachadh obraichean agus a' brosnachadh ghnìomhachasan nach biodh ann às aonais na taice sònraichte seo (m.e. Iomairt na Gaidhealtachd 1993). Tha na h-argamaidean seo stèidhte air rannsachadh acadamaigeach de dh'àrd inbhe: na sgrùdaidhean aig Alan Sproull, Douglas Chalmers agus mar sin air adhart (Sproull agus Ashcroft 1993, Sproull 1996, Sproull agus Chalmers 1998, Pedersen 2000, Chalmers 2003). Gu deimhinne, tha an tuigse ùr seo a' dol calgdhìreach an aghaidh na seann tuigse gu robh a' Ghàidhlig na bacadh do leasachadh na Gàidhealtachd, agus tha i air a bhith cudromach ann a bhith ag atharrachadh nam beachdan a tha aig cuid de dhaoine mu luach agus feum na Gàidhlig. Mar a mhìnich an t-Ollamh Grin, tha na h-argamaidean ùra seo air nochdadh ann an iomadach dùthaich, agus luchd nam mion-chànan "[*unwilling to*] *concede to their opponents what amounted to a quasi-monopoly on modernist discourse*".

Chan eil mi idir airson an iomairt inntleachdail seo a chàineadh, oir tha na h-argamaidean seo stèidhte air prionnsapalan a tha reusanta agus daingeann agus air rannsachadh a tha faiceallach agus susbainteach. Ach feumaidh sinn aideachadh nach eil a' mhòrchuid gan creidsinn fhathast — nach eil iad deònach an cur an gnìomh co-dhiù.[1] Tha sinn air tòrr a chluinntinn mun "eaconamaidh Ghàidhlig" thairis air na beagan bhliadhnaichean a dh'fhalbh, ach càite a bheil e ri lorg? Cò mheud duine ann an Alba — fiù's anns na h-Eileanan Siar — a tha a' cleachdadh Gàidhlig mar phrìomh chànan na h-obrach? Cò mheud buidheann phoblach? Cò mheud companaidh phrìobhaideach?

Rinn mi-fhìn beagan rannsachaidh air na ceistean seo bho chionn ghoirid — ach feumaidh mi aideachadh gur e rannsachadh gu math sìmplidh a bha ann, agus nach eil mise nam eaconamaiche co-dhiù — agus fhuair mi a-mach gu robh nas lugha na 5% de na sanasan-obrach a nochd anns na pàipearan-naidheachd ann an cridhe na Gàidhealtachd (.i. na h-Eileanan Siar agus an t-Eilean Sgitheanach) ann an 2001-02 a' cur an cèill gu robh sgilean Gàidhlig riatanach no fiù's feumail airson coilionadh na h-obrach a bha fo cheist (McLeod 2001b). A bharrachd air sin, bha cha mhòr a h-uile dreuchd "Ghàidhlig" suidhichte anns an raon phoballach (ged a bha a' mhòr-mhòrchuid de na sanasan a chaidh fhoillseachadh le buidhnean poballach sgrìobhte ann am Beurla a-mhàin agus gu tur tostach mun Ghàidhlig).[2] A rèir coltais is gann gu robh companaidhean prìobhaideach,

---

[1] Mar eisimpleir, a rèir rannsachaidh a rinneadh ann an 2003 am measg muinntir Alba air fad leis a' chompanaidh Market Research UK Ltd, bha 43% den luchd-fhreagairt ag aontachadh "*learning Gaelic is not of great value in today's society as there is seldom the need or the opportunity to use it*", ged a bha direach 13% den luchd-fhreagairt a' dol an aghaidh a' bheachd fharsaing "*Gaelic is an important part of Scottish life and needs to be promoted*".

[2] Ged a tha an dreachd Bile Gàidhlig aig an Riaghaltas a' cur uallach air buidhnean poballach na h-Alba a bhith "a' co-dhùnadh . . . a bheil e iomchaidh plana-cànain Gàidhlig ullachadh agus fhoillseachadh" (earrann 5(1)), chan eil am Bile a' sònrachadh nan cuspairean mionaideach a bu chòir dèiligeadh riutha anns na planaichean-cànain seo. Mar sin, chan eil e riatanach gum biodh na buidhnean seo a' dèanamh atharrachadh sam bith air na poileasaidhean fastaidh agus sgiobachd aca gus Gàidhlig a chleachdadh mar chànan

prothaideach a' toirt aire sam bith don Ghàidhlig mar chànan obrach. Gu ìre mhòir mhòir, is ann tro mheadhan na Beurla a-mhàin a tha eaconamaidh na Gàidhealtachd ag obair, agus tha a' Ghàidhlig fhathast air iomall an iomaill. Tha an t-iomallachadh seo fhathast ga mheas "nàdarra" ann an inntinn daoine.

Gu ruige seo, tha a' mhòrchuid de sgoilearan agus luchd-leasachaidh air a bhith a' bruidhinn mun "eaconamaidh Ghàidhlig" mar roinn air leth ann an eaconamaidh Bheurla, gun a bhith a' dèanamh fòcas air a' Ghàidhlig mar chànan obrach. An àite sin, thathas a' cur cuideam air gnothaichean a bhuineas ris a' chànan fhèin, gnothaichean cultarach gu sònraichte, a' tomhas agus a' measadh luach a' bhathair "Ghàidhlig" a tha gan reic agus nan seirbhisean "Gàidhlig" a tha gan lìbhrigeadh (McLeod 2002).[3]

Ach a bheil ceangal ann eadar leasachadh na "roinne Gàidhlig" seo agus neartachadh na Gàidhlig ann am beatha eaconamach na h-Alba? Is e fìrinn na cùise gu bheil tòrr rudan a tha co-cheangailte ri cultar na Gàidhlig gan dèanamh tro mheadhan na Beurla às leth luchd-ceannachd gun Ghàidhlig. Tha fios aig duine sam bith a tha eòlach air suidheachadh na Gàidhlig gu bheil tòrr dhaoine gun Ghàidhlig a' faighinn beòshlaint às na meadhanan Gàidhlig agus às na h-ealain Ghàidhlig, mar eisimpleir. Uime sin chan eil e idir follaiseach gu bheil leasachadh na "roinne Gàidhlig" seo gu mòran diofar a thaobh cleachdadh a'

---

[2]obrach. Air an làimh eile, bha aguisean don bhile (mhì-shoirbheachail) aig Michael Russell BPA anns a' chiad Phàrlamaid, Bile Cànan na Gàidhlig (Alba), a' cur an cèill gu soilleir gum biodh planaichean-cànain nam buidhnean poballach a' toirt a-steach poileasaidhean fastaidh agus sgiobachd. Tha e coltach nach robh an Riaghaltas deònach dol an taobh seo; co-dhùnadh a tha a' lagachadh buaidh phragtaigeach a' Bhile aca gu mòr.

[3] Am mìneachadh aig Sproull:

> From the standpoint of macroeconomics, it makes little sense to define [the Gaelic] economy in terms of the acts of production and exchange that are conducted through the medium of Gaelic [. . .] Taken to its extreme, the adoption of this approach would imply that if someone made a purchase in a local store and the transaction was conducted in Gaelic it would count as part of the "Gaelic economy", yet if the next customer purchased the same item through the medium of English it would be part of the "English" economy. The Gaelic economy cannot, therefore, be meaningfully defined in terms of the language of transaction. The same problems emerge in any macroeconomic definition of the "Gaelic economy" that focuses on the linguistic competence of the producers of goods and services. Examining only jobs in which Gaelic competence is required or desirable will fail to pick up some activities that are totally concerned with the production of Gaelic products or services, yet some or all employees of which may have no Gaelic. In the same way, it will include activities that could not be described as the provision of Gaelic-related goods and services, yet the employees of which may speak Gaelic and the language be useful in the conduct of business. . . . In general terms, the supply-side of the Gaelic economy could be defined as "all those activities (and jobs) whose principal purpose is the provision of Gaelic-related goods and services, including the promotion of the Gaelic culture and language". It is likely that for persons holding jobs associated with these activities, Gaelic proficiency will be either essential or desirable, although it need not be so.

(Sproull 1996: 99; faic cuideachd Sproull & Ashcroft 1993: 4-6).

chànain agus slàinte a' chànain anns an fharsaingeachd (McLeod 2002).
Chan e "roinn Ghàidhlig" ach eaconamaidh Ghàidhlig a tha a dhìth, is e sin ri
ràdh eaconamaidh anns a bheil cùisean gan dèanamh tro mheadhan na Gàidhlig.
Tha fada bharrachd fa-near do luchd-labhairt na Gàidhlig mar "actairean
eaconamach" seach cultar na Gàidhlig fhèin: tha iad a' ceannach àirneis agus
uinneagan dùbailte, chompiùtairean agus àrachas, gnothaichean a tha gu math
àbhaisteach, saoghalta. Gu ruige seo, tha a' mhòrchuid dìreach a' gabhail ris gur
ann tro mheadhan na Beurla a thèid na rudan seo a dhèanamh; chan eileas fiù's a'
ceasnachadh nan àbhaistean a tha air a bhith ann fad iomadach bliadhna. Tha na
tuigsean seo agus na cleachdaidhean seo a' mùchadh a' chànain, mean air mhean.
Ma tha sinn airson eaconamaidh Ghàidhlig a thogail, tha tòrr, tòrr obrach a dhìth,
agus tha an deasbad, an obair togalach, dìreach a' tòiseachadh. Ach a thaobh cor
a' chànain agus a shlàinte anns na bliadhnaichean ri teachd, is dòcha gur e seo an
iomairt as cudromaiche air fad.

Iomraidhean

Chalmers, Douglas (2003). 'The Economic Impact of Gaelic Arts and Culture'.
Tràchdas PhD neo-fhoillsichte, Glasgow Caledonian University.
Gordon, Cosmo (2003). 'A' tarraing air an aon ràmh: pulling together for Gaelic
in the new Scotland'. *Edinburgh Review*, 112, 76-85.
Iomairt na Gaidhealtachd agus nan Eilean / Highlands and Islands Enterprise
(1993). *Ro-Innleachd na Gàidhlig aig Lìonbheairt Iomairt na Gàidhealtachd
/ Iomairt na Gàidhlig: A Strategy for Gaelic Development in the Highlands
and Islands of Scotland*. Inbhir Nis: Iomairt na Gaidhealtachd agus nan Eilean.
McLeod, Wilson (2001a). 'Gaelic in the New Scotland: Politics, Rhetoric, and
Public Discourse', *Journal on Ethnopolitics and Minority Issues in Europe* (ri
fhaighinn air an Eadar-lìon aig http://www.ecmi.de/jemie/download/
JEMIE02MacLeod28-11-01.pdf)
McLeod, Wilson (2001b). *The State of the 'Gaelic Economy': A Research Report*.
Dùn Èideann: Roinn na Ceiltis agus Eòlas na h-Alba, Oilthigh Dhùn Èideann
(ri fhaighinn air an Eadar-lìon aig www.arts.ed.ac.uk/celtic/poileasaidh/
GAELJOBSREP3.htm)
McLeod, Wilson (2002). 'Language Planning as Regional Development: The
Growth of the Gaelic Economy'. *Scottish Affairs*, 38, 51-72 (ri fhaighinn air an
Eadar-lìon aig http://www.arts.ed.ac.uk/celtic/papers/gaeliceconomy.html)
Pedersen, Roy (2000). The Gaelic Economy', ann an *New Directions in Celtic
Studies*, deasaichte le Amy Hale agus Philip Payton, 152-66. Exeter:
University of Exeter Press.
Riaghaltas na h-Alba / The Scottish Executive (2003). *Bile na Gàidhlig: Pàipear
Comhairleachaidh / The Gaelic Language Bill: Consultation Paper*. Dùn
Èideann: Riaghaltas na h-Alba / The Scottish Executive.
Sproull, Alan, agus Brian Ashcroft (1993). *The Economics of Gaelic Language
Development: A Research Report for Highlands and Islands Enterprise and
the Gaelic Television Committee with Comunn na Gàidhlig*. Glaschu: Glasgow
Caledonian University.
Sproull, Alan (1996). 'Regional economic development and minority language
use: the case of Gaelic Scotland'. *International Journal of the Sociology of
Language*, 121, 93-117.

Sproull, Alan, agus Douglas Chalmers (1998). *The Demand for Gaelic Artistic and Cultural Products and Services: Patterns and Impacts*. Glaschu: Glasgow Caledonian University.

Resumé

Economic questions have been important in debates about Gaelic development in Scotland, both within the Gaelic community and at the wider national level, even if reporting on these isses in the English-language media is generally superficial. Gaelic affairs are covered only sporadically in the English-language media, and usually the questions tackled are highly predictable, e.g.
* isn't Gaelic dying anyway despite all these expensive interventions? why waste money keeping the language on a life-support machine, when there are all sorts of serious problems that require attention?
* we are 'we' spending so much money on 'them', the Gaelic-speakers, when there's so few of them left anyway?
Misconceived questions like this can be heard in many countries, but in Scotland the public debate seems to move in circles. Although the topic of linguistic diversity and the economy implicates a number of fundamental questions, as explained in François Grin's paper, opinion-formers and policy-makers in Scotland are not accustomed to serious reflection on such questions, in contrast to countries like Canada where the debate about the relationship between the majority and different minority groups is much more advanced. In Scotland, the traditional dichotomy between majority and minority is still very much alive in people's minds — the supposed distinction between 'us', the majority who pay the taxes, and 'them', the ones who (supposedly) receive the 'subsidies'. The majority have not yet been persuaded that supporting Gaelic benefits Scotland as a whole, that the Scottish people as a whole benefit from Gaelic development.

But the so-called subsidies are a new phenomenon; traditionally, the only opinion people (Gaels and non-Gaels alike) would have expressed with regard to Gaelic and the economy was that the language had no practical value, that progress depended on learning and using English. Views like this have dissipated but not disappeared.

At the same time, another debate has been going on within Gaelic circles, although rarely noticed by the mainstream media. For a number of years, scholars and development agencies have been demonstrating that the public money spent on Gaelic projects and initiatives is very valuable to the Gàidhealtachd, stimulating businesses and creating jobs that would otherwise not exist. This new perception refutes the old view that Gaelic was a hindrance to the economic development of the Gàidhealtachd, and it has been important in changing some minds with regard to the usefulness of Gaelic.

Despite these valuable efforts, the majority have not yet been truly convinced — they are not willing to take these arguments on board in their own lives at any rate. Where exactly can we see this new 'Gaelic economy'? How many people in Scotland use Gaelic as their main language at work? How many public bodies work primarily through the medium of Gaelic? How many private companies?

According to my research less than 5% of the jobs advertised in local newspapers in Skye and the Western Isles in 2002 were designaed as Gaelic-essential or Gaelic-desirable. To an overwhelming extent, the economy of the Gàidhealtachd remains an English-only economy, and Gaelic remains on the periphery of the periphery. This kind of marginalisation is still taken for granted as something 'natural' in most people's minds — an approach that is slowly suffocating the language. A fundamentally new approach to these questions is necessary: the health of the language in the coming years may well depend upon it.

The Economic Impact of Gaelic Arts and Culture: A Response to François Grin

Douglas Chalmers

As an economist, I always approach such multi-disciplinary conferences or gatherings with some trepidation, given my profession's reputation as the 'dismal science' and the reputation of economists as being those (to paraphrase Oscar Wilde) who know the price of everything and the value of nothing. Or as one of my students put it to me rather brutally recently 'economists are people who don't have the charisma to become accountants'.

However, it is a pleasure to follow a presentation such as François Grin' given his long record of work, which I believe goes a long way, in the eyes of non-economists, to rehabilitate and revalidate the science in a multi-disciplinary context. And this evening as expected, we have heard a stimulating and well-focused approach to the thorny issue of Linguistic Diversity and Economic Activity.

Importantly, François Grin has posed a question to those of us involved in the field. How can one strengthen the *economic* case for linguistic diversity? He suggests *inter alia* three research priorities – the issue of language and linguistic diversity as public goods; the need to deepen our conceptual understanding of the non-market benefits of diversity; and finally how might one assess the benefits and costs at a social level? In addition to these three challenges, we should also bear in mind the organisers' definitional question in regard to the economy – in this field, can the 'economy' be simply reduced to the media and performing arts?

In considering the benefits of linguistic diversity, François Grin reminds us that the literature still lacks a "fully fledged *general* allocative argument" showing that linguistic diversity in general is economically good (and consequently that one therefore *ought* to seek more of it per se).

I would like this to be my point of entry into the debate. Whilst I agree that we do not possess the reassurance that might be proffered by a general allocative argument, I would suggest this need not be a matter for major concern. There may be some benefits in seeking out such a Holy Grail – though its possession has so far eluded us – but I think more benefit actually lies in adopting a different approach. To borrow from another discipline for a moment, I would suggest more benefit is to be gained when arguing the economic benefits of linguistic diversity if we adopt the Gramscian approach of seeing the process (and the arguments) as more of a 'war of position' rather than a 'war of movement'[1].

Although we may not yet have the comfort of a general allocative model behind us, we do have a growing body of evidence which suggests that irrespective of the theoretically elegant allocative models which may lie behind a *business oriented* or market approach, an increasing consensus is developing that business oriented strategies are *failing to work* in peripheral geographical areas (Fasenfest

---

[1] Gramsci the Italian philosopher and politician likened the battle for strategic political supremacy to a long term war of manoeuvre rather than a once and for all victory achieved from a sudden full frontal assault.

1993: 10; Highlands and Islands Enterprise 1996: 9). And some of these areas are ones in which linguistic diversity exists, the potential of which is only beginning to be tapped, but where clear positive indications of benefit are emerging. In short we ought not to undersell the significance of the positive (albeit at present limited), data and results now beginning to emerge.

In focusing on François Grin's and the organisers' questions, I wish to introduce some of the findings of my own work on the *Economic Impact of Gaelic Arts and Culture* dealing with the impact of artistic and cultural attributes of Scottish Gaelic on the 'Gaelic Economy', essentially the Outer and Inner Hebrides of Scotland.[2]

This is an economic area where 'market failure' is acknowledged by government established economic development bodies as long existing (Highlands and Islands Enterprise 1996: 9). It is also an area where over decades a whole progression of economic 'initiatives' can be documented, ranging from the 'modernist' approach of encouraging mass emigration in the nineteenth century to last century's more enlightened approaches. These have included selective regional aid, the Keynesian 'carrot and stick' approach of the 50s and 60s, attempts to create large scale, industrial 'growth poles'[3] and finally 'enterprise oriented strategies', none of which have successfully solved the fundamental long terms issues facing such a geographically peripheral area.

Increasingly enterprise bodies are recognising the benefits of a 'joined up' approach, acknowledging the need to *explicitly utilise the potential of Gaelic language, art and culture related activities.* (Highlands and Islands Enterprise 2002: 10) It was this approach that my research sought to investigate.

Undertaking a large scale and very comprehensive survey of one in four of the electorate of the 'Gaelic Economy' with a subsequent response rate of approximately 25 per cent of those contacted, together with parallel investigations of the 'supply side' of the Gaelic related artistic and cultural industry, it was possible to collect robust data measuring the direct and indirect economic impact of the spend on such activities. Thus it was possible to indicate that such activity created between 214 and 230 full time equivalent jobs – a not insignificant impact in peripheral areas.

While this is certainly laudable and significant, François Grin asks us to consider the wider issue of the impact of 'non-market' benefits. It is this that I would therefore like to concentrate on.

A key area of interest in my research was the effect of 'consuming' Gaelic related artistic and cultural products and services and its possible impact on a whole series of longer-term variables that might affect the economy. The 'consumption' in question included amongst other activities the attending of musical events; visiting Gaelic historical projects and theatre; the buying of Gaelic books and videos and watching Gaelic TV and listening to Gaelic language radio – in short it was hoped to encompass the widest range of experience possible in terms of Gaelic related artistic and cultural consumption.

The resultant impact analysed consisted of the perceived consequences of such

---

[2] "The spatial area which stands to gain measurable economic benefits from the further development of the language" (Sproull and Ashcroft 1993)

[3] Such as the ill fated aluminium smelter at Invergordon, near Inverness

consumption in terms of a series of variables, including the cultural distinctiveness of the area; the self confidence of individuals and communities; the desirability of residence in the local area; the attachment of young people to their community; migration rates from and into the area; impact on tourism in the local area; the willingness of businesses to use Gaelic related goods and services in the process of their own production. A whole range of additional questions was also investigated including the subsequent willingness of individuals to purchase Gaelic related goods, and to consider educating their children in Gaelic medium schools.

Testing our sample of respondents against the general characteristics of the population (found through examination of the most recent census), confirmed that our sample was very close to the general population in key characteristics such as age, gender and location, and indeed if anything was *under represented* in attributes (such as fluency) which intuitively might be expected to favourably bias the results.

It does need to be acknowledged however, that unlike some of the 'hard data' in terms of jobs created, the information gathered in developing and analysing this latter part of the research was necessarily 'softer' in nature – dealing with perceptions and opinions.

Nevertheless, a very large-scale picture of substantial perceived impact was constructed, which tended to validate much of the intuitively held belief regarding the potential of the Gaelic artistic and cultural sector to positively impact the health of the local economy. A fuller report of the outcomes is available on request[4], however a few notable examples here may help illustrate the positive outcomes of the surveys.

Amongst the findings that were very clearly indicated amongst the general population were the following impacts of consumption of Gaelic related goods and services:

Firstly, a clear perception existed that community confidence had increased – a necessary (if not in itself sufficient) factor in helping create business confidence (60 per cent of those responding agreed, or strongly agreed that this was the case). Secondly, the desirability of residence in the local area had increased. Thirdly, the attachment of young people to their community (or their wish to return to their community) had increased (46 per cent agreed or strongly agreed that this was the case, whilst just under a third disagreed, and 21 per cent had no firm opinion). Both of these issues of course, are at the heart of the important problem of de-population that tends to be endemic in peripheral or under developed areas.

In the longer term, although most individuals felt it difficult to quantify at present, it was felt that migration from the area would be lessened and tourism would continue to be enhanced.[5]

In terms of overall beliefs regarding impacts, 69 per cent of those replying agreed or strongly agreed that the regeneration of Gaelic language, art and culture was 'essential' for the future *social* development of their own area, whilst 61 per

---

[4] Chalmers, D. *The Economic Impact of Gaelic Arts and Culture*. Unpublished PhD thesis (2003), Glasgow Caledonian University

[5] This was despite the historical neglect by tourism authorities of the potential of cultural difference, now partially ameliorated by the belated introduction (July 2002) of an integrated Gaelic Scotland official tourism portal http://www.gaelic.scotland.co.uk

cent agreed or strongly agreed that it was 'essential' for the future *economic* development of their own area.

These positive perceptions and indicators (notwithstanding the difficulty of measuring these indicators in 'hard' terms) illustrate a potentially rich area for further investigation in other minority language communities. As an economist I would suggest they are undoubtedly part of what differentiates *development* from *growth*, and therefore ought to be welcomed if the aim is to qualitatively improve the social and economic well being of minority language and other peripheral communities.

Without labouring the point unduly, the existing difficulties of using GDP (a money measure) as the sole measure of economic success are well known, if not always acknowledged. Thus in GDP terms, a car crash adds to growth, if it leads to increased medical care, and replacement vehicles – a result which surely illustrates why conventional indicators have not proven satisfactory or adequate when dealing with complex societal factors, such as the sustainable and long term health of a community.

Thankfully in this area, there is an increasing body of literature considering new approaches – such as the United Nations Human Development Index which seeks to take a wider, more holistic view of economic development and change. This is an area which potentially offers much benefit to minority language theorists and where potential allies may perhaps be sought.

I think therefore, to return to François Grin' questions, where research is done, evidence can be found of the non-market benefits of diversity, in a way which also answers the organisers' query as to whether the economy is synonymous with arts and culture for those interested in minority languages. Given the demonstrable impact that I have sought to illustrate on larger societal questions such as community confidence and migration it would clearly be self limiting to reduce the language/ economics link or impact to this area alone.

A final allied point of interest: Despite this positive portrayal of the potential economic impact of such artistic and cultural activity, are these perceptions limited to those using the minority language? Evidence in the research certainly suggested not.

Using log-linear (logit) analysis the data collected for the purpose of this exercise was further analysed to isolate the factors behind demand for Gaelic related goods and services.

Crucially it was possible to show that while fluency was understandably a factor in whether individuals wished to consume Gaelic related goods and services, this was only one of several factors behind consumption.

Analysis indicated that other key issues were income, gender, age and location, with a *rural location, a higher income, greater fluency and female gender* tending to increase the likelihood of consumption.

Shortness of time precludes the possibility of considering the very important implications of this. However, in brief it would suggest that the issue of increasing demand for minority language related goods and can no longer now be regarded as an issue solely for the minority community itself. It is clearly one for the wider population as a whole, and furthermore it is an issue that can no longer be restricted to the prism of language promotion alone – key though that may be, especially in terms of desired outcomes.

References

Chalmers, D   (2003) *The Economic Impact of Gaelic Arts and Culture.* Unpublished PhD thesis, Glasgow Caledonian University

Fasenfest, D.E. (1993) *Community Economic Development.* London: Macmillan

Highlands and Islands Enterprise (1996) *The Rationale for Highlands and Islands Enterprise's Activities.* Edinburgh HMSO

Highlands and Islands Enterprise (2002) *Smart Successful Scotland – the Highlands and Islands Dimension.* Inverness

Sproull, A and B Ashcroft (1993) *The Economics of Gaelic Language Development*, Glasgow Caledonian University

Celtic Languages in the 2001 Census: How Population Censuses Bury Celtic Speakers

Kenneth MacKinnon

Introduction

Questions on Celtic languages have featured on U.K. population Censuses since 1851 for Irish, 1881 for Gaelic and 1891 for Welsh. From 1921 age-analysis of speakers has been presented, but with the partition of Ireland at that time, no information on Irish speakers in Northern Ireland was sought from that Census until 1991. Since 1971, data on reading and writing abilities have been sought and, in 2001, for the first time, ability to understand these languages. The Census question has been limited to the countries in question and the Census authorities have resisted requests to seek information on abilities in Celtic languages throughout the U.K.

Disparities in the language question over this period (seeking response on whether the person can speak Gaelic or Irish, but does the person speak Welsh) were resolved in 2001 with the adoption of *can* as the operative question in all cases. Actual numbers of Welsh speakers may thus have been tacitly depressed in previous   censuses.

This paper reviews the resources of the three national census authorities with regard to results published to date (September 2003) on the distribution of abilities in the three Celtic languages – Welsh, Gaelic and Irish in Northern Ireland – by:

- Office for National Statistics for England and Wales (ONS);
- General Register Office for Scotland (GROS); and
- The Northern Ireland Statistics and Research Agency (NISRA)

These results relating to Celtic languages are presented in:

- univariate tables, which detail totals of speakers and other language skills;
- standard tables, which detail speakers and other combinations of abilities by age and sex, together with a further factor (such as country of birth, general health and limiting long-term illness, etc.);
- theme tables, which detail age and sex breakdown of speakers or persons with any language abilities aggregated either in terms of numbers and/or percentages in terms of a range of social, economic and demographic factors; and
- key statistics tables, which are generally outline tables of specific factors (e.g. aggregate of language abilities) as percentage of total populations of areas.

Although there has been some measure of common practice between these authorities, there is nevertheless a considerable degree of disparity between them in the way in which they present language data, such that it is often very difficult to use them to ascertain actual numbers of speakers, and to compare these languages in their respective societies in meaningful ways. For example, age-groups do not always 'map' or are not always consistent between tables of a given national Census authority, nor between comparable tables of different authorities.

In some cases, detailed below, numbers of actual speakers are aggregated into an 'other combinations' category, which makes totaling actual numbers of speakers impossible. Consistent practice with previous Censuses has not always been followed, which makes trend analysis particularly difficult. The tables for the 2001 census published or announced by September 2003 are reviewed below.

Welsh Language in the 2001 Census

Data on Welsh language abilities are available in the following published tables.
- Univariate table UV84 presents totals of speaker aged 3+ (total for Wales = 582,368), and the three other language abilities separately for Wales and local authority areas. There is, of course, an unknown overlap between them, and it would be helpful for the 16 combinations of the four language abilities to have been detailed.
- Standard table S133 details sex and age by country of birth and knowledgeof Welsh, with 12 age-categories (3-4, 5-9, 10-14, 15, 16-19, 20-24, 25-34,35-49, 50-59, 60-64, 65-74, 75+), and 6 ability categories. Welsh speakers in Wales total 575,640, and it is clear that a total of 6,728 Welsh speakers are contained in the 'Other Combinations' category and are thus inaccessible or unanalysable. (Results for 1991 census were presented in LBS Table 67W in age-categories 3-4, 5-10, 11-15, 16-17, 18-19 thence quinquennially to 85+) Finesse in comparison of age-structures is thereby reduced.
- Standard table S137 details language abilities, sex age, limiting long term illness and general health. There are four age categories (3-15, 16-44, 45-64 and 65+). There are five language abilities categories including an 'Other Combinations' category which contains an undisclosed 6,728 Welsh speakers nationally. The national total of speakers adds up to 575,640.
- Standard table S143 presents data on children speaking Welsh in Welsh-speaking households. Similar tables for Gaelic and Irish would have been an excellent idea.. In 1991, Topic Monitors for Welsh and Gaelic did in fact do so – and included the cases of Welsh and Gaelic speaking ability amongst children whose parents did not speak the language.
- Theme table T15 aggregates all Welsh language abilities into a single category, totalling 797,717 for Wales as a whole. Analysis is in terms of 7 age-categories (3-4, 5-15, 16-19, 20-44, 45-64, 65-74, 75+). Cross-tabulation is presented in terms of 17 demographic, social and economic factors: sex, accommodation, occupancy, amenities, central heating, car or van, living arrangements, family type, economic activity, country of birth, ethnic group, general health, long-term illness, qualifications, industry, and socio-economic class. These details enable a way-of-life / quality of life analysis to be undertaken.
- Theme table T39 more usefully cross-tabulates all actual Welsh speakers aged 3+ (= 582,368 for Wales as a whole) in terms of the same categories as T15.
- Key statistics table KS25 details numbers and percentages of Welsh speakers (=575,640 for Wales as a whole) for Wales and local authority

areas. There are 6 skills categories which again contain 6,728 Welsh speakers in the 'Other Combinations' category.
- A ranking table of local authorities in terms of percentage of population with one or more Welsh language skills was published at an early stage.

It would have been extremely helpful if the definition of 'Welsh speaker' adopted for the univariate tables had been used throughout. This would enable analysis of Welsh speakers to include all instead of the 98.8% of such which feature in tables S133, S137 and KS25. Table T39, which does include all Welsh speakers, is limited to 7 age-categories only.

Gaelic Language in the 2001 Census

Data on Gaelic language is available in the following published tables.
- Univariate table UV12 presents totals of all persons with 9 combinations of language abilities. The 'Other combinations of skills in Gaelic' category is, in fact, the total of persons who can speak and write but cannot read Gaelic. It is thus possible to derive totals of all Gaelic speakers from this table. The total is 58,969 for Scotland as a whole. It must be emphasized that this total is for all people and includes those aged 0-2 years. Data is available for Scotland as a whole and all local authority areas.
- Standard table S206 details Gaelic speaking abilities by age, sex and whether or not born in Scotland. There are 7 ability categories from which it is possible to derive totals of actual speakers as such, persons without speaking skills but ability to read and/or write Gaelic, and persons with understanding ability only. There are 20 age-categories (0-2, 3-4, 5-11, 12-15, 16-19, thence quinquennially to 90+). Similar age-categorisation would have been desirable in the case of Celtic languages in the other national censuses.
- Theme table T27 presents data on Gaelic speakers as such in comparable terms to the ONS tables T15 for all Welsh language skills and T39 for all Welsh speakers. This will enable some valuable comparative analysis to be undertaken on Welsh and Gaelic speakers. The age-ranges are useful but could be more detailed. This cannot be attempted for Irish in Northern Ireland as things stand, since the theme table categories for Irish in T32 do not match those for Welsh and Gaelic.
- The Key Statistics table KS06 presents a total of all persons with Gaelic language skills as a single grouping and whether or not born in Scotland as percentages of total populations of Scotland and local authority areas.
- A Gaelic language table features in the Registrar General's Report to the Scottish Parliament, Table RG10. This presents data on totals of persons able to speak Gaelic, speak, read or write Gaelic in 1991 and 2001, and all persons able to speak, read, write or understand Gaelic in 2001 for Scotland and local authority areas. The table totals 58,652 actual speakers, some fewer than the UV12 total of 58,969. The category of 'speaks, and writes but does not read Gaelic' is obviously (and inexplicably) omitted.

- There is also a table on aggregates of all Gaelic abilities, and whether born in Scotland as a percentage and as numbers for about 630 major towns and settlements.

As published to date, the GROS data on Gaelic is more finely tuned and more consistent than corresponding Welsh data. There is a specific table for Welsh in the family which would be valuable too for Gaelic in line with 1991.

Irish Language in Northern Ireland

Initial data on Irish language became available in 2002. The published tables were not comparable in detail with the five tables published in the 1991 Irish Language Report. These tables were in terms of 8 ability categories from which actual numbers of speakers could be totalled. The tables comprised:-

- Table 1: Age table at province and district levels (single years of age to 24 years, thence quinary age-groups to 95+); and at provincial level only.
- Table 2: Religion and sex by knowledge of Irish; and for the 16+ population.
- Table 3: Qualifications by knowledge of Irish.
- Table 4: Economic activity, by sex and knowledge of Irish.
- Table 5: Social class by sex and knowledge of Irish.

Continuity with these tables would have been useful. What is currently available comprises:-

- Univariate table UV14 detailing the full 16 categories of Irish language abilities. This is available at provincial and district levels – and will be available down to neighbourhood (output area) levels in terms of a simplified 9 category breakdown, comparable to the Gaelic Table UV12. The total of actual Irish speakers which can be derived from UV14 is 115,731 (compared with 131,974 in 1991).
- Standard table S372 details sex and age by knowledge of Irish. The 7 Irish language skills categories include a 'some knowledge of Irish' category, and an 'Other Combinations' category, which totals 24,167 for the province, and would seem to contain 15,280 actual speakers. There are 7 age-categories: 3-11, 12–15, 16-24, 25-30, 40-50, 60-74, 75+. These are far less detailed than the 1991 Table 1, and only allow for the most 'broad brush' trends analysis. (**See Figure 1**) The lack of single years of age for Irish speakers under 25 means that any assessment of success or effects of Irish-medium school level education will be extremely limited, with very little possibility of finesse.
- Standard table S373 details sex and age by knowledge of Irish and country of birth. Language ability is a simple dichotomy: any knowledge of Irish or none. There are 4 country of birth categories: Northern Ireland, Republic of Ireland, Ireland part unspecified, and elsewhere. The 7 age categories are as in S372.
- Standard table S374 details sex and highest level of qualifications by knowledge of Irish for persons aged 16-74 only, as a single group. There are 5 qualification levels and age categories as in S372, which does not enable actual numbers of speakers to be inferred

- Standard table S375 details sex and age by knowledge of Irish and 'Community Background' (Religion or Religion brought up in). Language abilities are a simple dichotomy of any knowledge of Irish or none, with 7 age-categories as in S372. There are 4 Community Background categories: Catholic, Protestant including other Christian and related, Other religions and philosophies, and none. This categorization is supplemented by a more specific range in:
- Standard Table S375A details sex and age by knowledge of Irish and Religion. Ability and age categories are as in S375, but the religious affinities are detailed as: Catholic, Presbyterian, Church of Ireland, Methodist, Other Christian and related, Other religions and philosophies, No religion or not stated. It is not possible to infer actual speakers from S375 and S375A – although the broad age-structures may enable some analysis of differential language-transmission rates to be attempted between the various community and religious groups..
- Theme table T32 on Irish language presents a simple dichotomy of any knowledge of Irish or none – and not in terms of actual speakers as do comparable theme tables for Welsh T29, and Gaelic T27. The common age-categorisation of these tables is not followed for Irish, which is: 3-11, 12-15, 16-24, 25-39, 40-59, 60-74, 75+.. The only category which matches the Welsh and Gaelic theme tables is the 75+ group, so it is not possible to attempt any comparative analysis of social, economic, way-of-life or quality-of-life characteristics of the three UK Celtic language groups. There are 17 social and economic factors, which include 'Community Background'. There is no Ethnic Group category – as this was not asked in Northern Ireland.
- Key statistics table KS24 details knowledge of Irish in terms of numbers and percentages, by province, district, education and health board areas, and parliamentary constituencies. There are 7 language ability categories as in tables S372 and S374, from which it is not possible to infer actual numbers of speakers.

There is a clear need for tables to total actual numbers of speakers as such, as well as understanders, readers and writers of Irish. Age tables of Irish speakers for single years of age to 24 years (and quinary age-groups thereafter) for the four basic language skills at least, at Education Board level would be invaluable in order to monitor the effectiveness of Irish-medium school-level education. An Irish language theme table in terms of actual speakers as for Welsh and Gaelic, and in terms of the actual age-categorisation used for those languages as a standard UK practice would be highly desirable. So, too, would be a table on Irish in the family and household structures on the lines of Welsh language table S143.

Applications and difficulties: age-analysis

The population Census represents an invaluable resource for studying the incidence of the language abilities in these three cases, and the social and economic characteristics of these three language-groups. It is a great pity that the shortcomings identified above make much of this work difficult.

For example, comparison of Irish speakers in 1991 and 2001 is, strictly speaking, impossible to illustrate. The 37 age-categories in 1991 can largely be mapped to the 7 in 2001 but there is considerable loss of detail. **See Figure 1** as compared with **Figure 3**. Single year of age data to age 24 for 1991 do, however, make the production of 3-11 and 12–15 age-groups possible to compare with these groups in 2001. However from age-related data so far published it is not possible to produce actual numbers of speakers as such for 2001. For this value, **Figure 1** actually presents totals of the columns with speaker combinations in Table S372, and shows this together with the 'Other Combinations' column which does contain speakers as a separate estimate of numbers of speakers. The truth lies somewhere between them. This is probably the best possible job that can be done with the published results to date – but it is very unsatisfactory. Moreover, the age-categories are irregular, covering cohorts of 9, 4, 9, 15, 20, 15 years in the under-75 years range. This grossly distorts visual impression, thus making the understanding of language data, and language planning both very difficult.

Similar difficulties affect the comparison of Welsh speakers between 1991 and 2001. Again, the best source (Table S133) omits 6,728 Welsh speakers. The table has 11 age categories under 75 years, with cohort sizes of : 2, 4, 5, 1, 4, 5, 10, 15, 10, 5, and 10 years. Illustrating these data as they stand again produces gross visual distortion of the impression of age-distribution of speakers. **Figure 2** attempts to overcome this by aggregating into cohorts of 13, 9, 10, 15, 10, and 15 years. It is still unsatisfactory and cannot really be compared with the age-distribution for Irish in Northern Ireland. The lack of single year of age data for under 24s means that the age-groups of 3-4, 5-10, 11-15 years in 1991 cannot very satisfactorily be mapped onto the age-groups of 3-4, 5-9, 10-14, and 15 years in 2001.

It is possible to produce a detailed comparison of age-distribution of Gaelic speakers between the 1991 and 2001 censuses from Gaelic language data in the 1991 Census tables LBS 67S and the 2001 table S206. This is shown as **Figure 3**. These age data are much more satisfactory than corresponding Welsh or Irish data, in that the age groups of 3-4, 5-11, 12-15 in the 1991 table LBS 67S match those in the 2001 table S206. It is a pity that data so far available for Irish in Northern Ireland or Welsh in Wales do not enable a comparable picture to be presented. It would obviously enable a better evaluation to be made of the relative effectiveness of Welsh-, Gaelic- and Irish-medium educational practice, and the comparative viability over age of these three language groups.

The inclusive character of all Gaelic speakers in the data on Gaelic language in Table S206 also enables the incidence of language abilities to be graphically illustrated, as in **Figure 4**. Actual speakers can be totalled, as can non-speaker readers and/or writers, and understanders. The Gaelic data are available in 20 age-categories, compared with 12 for Welsh and 7 for Irish. A far more detailed and discriminating picture can be presented for Gaelic language abilities than can be done either for Welsh or for Irish. It would be valuable to be able to undertake this level of analysis for these two languages also.

It is readily apparent from **Figures 3** and **4** that there has been a very marked effect of increases of Gaelic speakers in the primary education age-group. The fact that Gaelic-medium education has not been carried on into the secondary stage is again very obvious. Weaknesses in the 16-19 age-group, which result from this, also show up very conspicuously.

Reversing Language-Shift

Census data also enable measures of language maintenance, language vitality and reversing language-shift to be derived. These are invaluable as a means of comparing the situation in different areas – and could even be a means of comparing the fortunes of the different language groups in their respective countries. **Figures 5–9** indicate some of the applications which are possible.

United Kingdom census data can be used to operationalise Joshua Fishman's (1991, 2001) concept of 'reversing language-shift' (RLS) by comparing mean values of language ability data for the parental and childhood generations. A measure entitled Intergenerational Gain / Loss has been derived from the proportion of minority language speakers of the parental age–range in a particular population, compared with a similar calculation of the proportion of minority language speakers within the age-group of childhood. The salience of each age-group within a specific population is thus compared. Positive values indicate language gain and negative values indicate loss. This assumes some stability of populations which, today, is generally very far from being the case. The measure does, however, indicate salience of the language-group in local populations. A more reliable measure is Intergenerational Ratio which compares mean numbers as a single year-of-age in each age-group as a ratio of the numbers of speakers within the age-group of childhood to those within the parental generation. Values above unity indicate outright gain, and values below unity indicate actual loss, irrespective of other societal factors.

It is possible to plot both values graphically, as in **Figures 4, 5** and **6**. **Figure 5** compares the various Celtic language-groups with each other, and between the 1991 and 2001 censuses, thus indicating trends. It has been possible to compare corresponding age-groups for language-groups as a whole and between the two censuses, namely 5-15 and 20-44s. Again, the 2001 values for Irish speakers aggregates 'speakers' as such with 'other combinations' and is therefore not accurate. It is a great pity that the Irish language theme table T32 did not enumerate totals of actual speakers as did its Welsh language counterpart T39. Moreover, the available age-tables (e.g. S372) do not enable age-groups of Irish speakers to be matched with the other Celtic languages. So the illustration can be impressionistic only – rather than strictly comparable or accurate.

Figures 6 and **7** illustrate Gaelic and Welsh speakers by local authority area in 2001 only. The stronger and weaker cases can be readily compared. The difficulties here arise from the non-comparability of age-groups owing to discrepancies of age-groups between the Gaelic table S206 which was available for council areas, and the most closely comparabe Welsh table which was similarly available at the time, S137. When – or if - T39 becomes available at local authority levels, this could be rectified.

This exercise also enabled mapping to be attempted, and distribution maps for Intergenerational Gain and Intergenerational Ratio for Welsh in 2001 are shown as **Figures 8** and **9**. The considerable gains in numbers of Welsh speakers owing to educational policies stand out very clearly – especially in anglicized southeast and south Wales. Similar mapping has been undertaken for Gaelic but, until more reliable Figures for Irish speakers by age and local areas are forthcoming, this is not really possible for Irish in Northern Ireland.

Recommendations

*   Include all Welsh speakers in Welsh language tables S133, S137 and KS25
*   Similarly include all Gaelic speakers in Table RG10.
*   In Northern Ireland, present actual numbers of Irish speakers in all Irish language tables. In particular:
*   In Irish-language theme table T32, show all actual speakers, and use same age-categories as Gaelic T32 and Welsh T39 theme tables.
*   Standardise all Welsh, Gaelic and Irish theme table age-categories. The following categorisation is recommended: 3-4 Pre-school, 5-11 Primary, 12-15 Secondary, 16-24 FE/HE/Young adult, 25-34 Younger parents, 35-44 Older parents, 45-54 Early Middle-age, 55-64 Older Middle-age, 65-74 semi/early retired, 75+ older. These categories more adequately reflect life stages and are more regular or even than the existing categories.
*   Age-breakdowns for standard tables: 5 year age-groups – or where impracticable as for theme tables (as recommended above.) Use GROS standard table S206 as a model.
*   In Northern Ireland, an age-table for Irish speakers by single years of age for under-25s as in 1991. Table 1 would enable effects of Irish-medium schooling to be effectively assessed. Similar single year-of-age tables for speakers under-25 for Welsh and Gaelic would do likewise. Standardise on best practice.
*   For language-ability categories in univariate tables, present the full 16 categories in each case, i.e. standardise on the recently-announced Irish-language model for higher levels of Census geography (NI UV14). A nine-category model as for GROS UV12 for lower levels would be useful where the 16 categories are impracticable.
*   In other tables with language-ability categories, enable all speakers to be identified. At the minimum, enable all speakers, readers, writers and understanders to be totalled, and similarly also all readers, writers and understanders without speaking ability. Produce tables on Gaelic and Irish in family / household structures on similar lines to Welsh data – and in line with 1991 tables in Topic Monitors.
*   Produce special topic reports / monitors on the three language-groups in comparable methodology, incorporating the above recommendations.

References and Sources

Fishman, Joshua A. (1991) *Reversing Language Shift*, Clevedon: Multilingual Matters.

Fishman, Joshua A. (ed.) (2001) *Can Threatened Languages be Saved?* Clevedon: Multilingual Matters.

General Register Office for Scotland, Edinburgh: 1991 Census Table LBS 67S; 2001 Census tables: KS06, S206, T27, UV12, Registrar General's Report to the Scottish Parliament, Table RG10.

Northern Ireland Statistical Research Agency, Belfast, 2001 Census tables KS24, S372, S373, S374, S375, S375A T32, UV14.

Office for National Statistics for England and Wales, Titchfield, Fareham, Hants., 1991 Census table: LBS 67W; 2001 Census tables: KS25, S133, S137, S143, T15, T39, UV 84.
Registrar General Northern Ireland (1993) *The Northern Ireland Census 1991: Irish Language Report*, Belfast: Her Majesty's Stationery Office.

Figure 1: Irish speakers in N. I. by age: comparison of numbers in 1991 and 2001

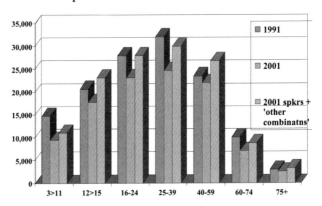

Figure 2: Welsh speakers by age: comparison of numbers in 1991 and 2001

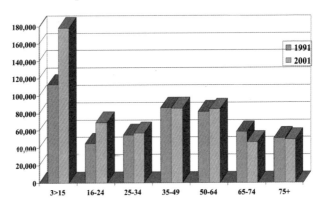

Figure 3: Gaelic speakers by age: comparison of numbers in 1991 and 2001

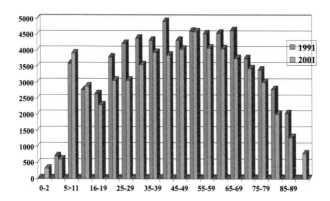

Figure 4: Gaelic language abilities: Scotland 2001

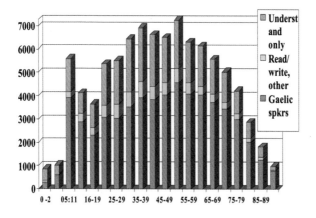

Figure 5: Reversing Language Shift 1991, 2001

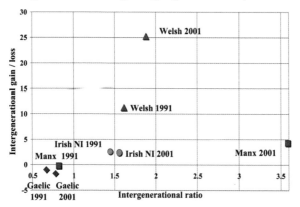

Figure 6: Comparison of Gaelic speakers in 5-15 and 20-44 age-groups: Intergenerational gain / loss, Intergenerational ratio

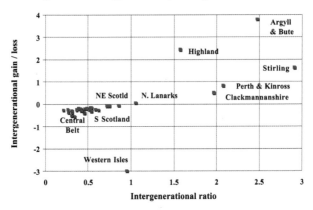

Figure 7: Comparison of Welsh speakers in 3-15 and 16-44 age-groups: Intergenerational gain / intergenerational ratio

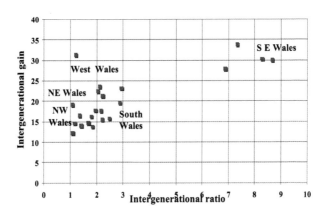

Figure 8: Welsh: intergenerational gain 2001

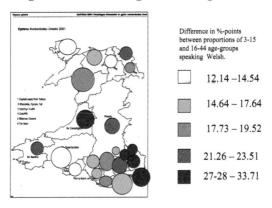

Figure 9: Welsh: intergenerational ratio 2001

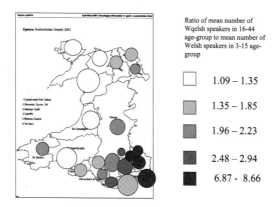

Ratio of mean number of Wqelsh speakers in 16-44 age-group to mean number of Welsh speakers in 3-15 age-group

☐ 1.09 – 1.35

▨ 1.35 – 1.85

■ 1.96 – 2.23

■ 2.48 – 2.94

■ 6.87 - 8.66

Celtic languages in the 2001 Census: how population censuses bury Celtic speakers

Data sources:
- ∨ **Figure 1:** NISRA 2001 Census S372;
- ∨ **Figure 2:** ONS England & Wales 2001 Census S133;
- ∨ **Figure 3:** GROS 1991 Census LBS 67S, 2001 Census S206;
- ∨ **Figure 4:** GROS S206;
- ∨ **Figure 5:** OPCS England & Wales 1991 Census LBS 67W;
  ONS England & Wales 2001 Census T39;
  GROS 1991 Census LBS 67S; 2001 Census S206;
  RGNI 1991 Irish Language Report, Table 1;
  NISRA 2001 Census, S372;
  IOM 1991 Census Report, Vol 1, Table 3, Special tabln 19.05.98;
  IOM 2001 Census Special tabulation 11.08.03;
- ∨ **Figure 6:** GROS 2001 Census S206;
- ∨ **Figures 7, 8 and 9:** ONS England & Wales S137.

A Comment on the Presentation of the Results of the Irish Language Question in the 2001 Census of Northern Ireland

Ciarán Ó Duibhín

I agree with Professor MacKinnon (see this volume) that the presentation of the results of the Irish language question in the 2001 Census of Northern Ireland, as published to date, has not been satisfactory. Issues raised by Professor MacKinnon, such as the adequacy of the age breakdown, are obviously very important for the education sector but, personally, I am concerned only with the most basic analysis of the language question – how many people have a knowledge of Gaelic, and how do their numbers break down in terms of aural skills (understanding and speaking) and visual skills (reading and writing). Even in such a simple matter as this, there is a problem with the published results of the 2001 Census.

In the 1991 Census of Northern Ireland, the language question – to be answered by those aged three or over – was structured as three independent questions: do you speak Irish, read Irish, write Irish? For three two-valued questions, there are eight possible responses, as shown below. It is helpful to look at the three questions as representing active aural skill (speak), passive visual skill (read) and active visual skill (write). Not all the eight answers make sense, though all occur: e.g. write but not read.

Speak	- + - - + + - +	Aural active
Read	- - + - + - + +	Visual passive
Write	- - - + - + + +	Visual active

Table 23 of the Summary Report is a typical results table from the 1991 Census. The eight possible responses are counted in separate columns, together with "not stated" and the total. A slight problem was the absence of a column giving the total number of people who claimed any form of knowledge of Irish; to obtain this, it was necessary to add seven of the eight response columns together. This addition gives, for Northern Ireland as a whole, 142,003 persons, or 9.46 per cent of the population aged three or over. It is simple and enlightening to produce a 2x2 table of aural skill by visual skill for this data.

	Speak Irish	Not speak Irish
Read and/or write Irish	86,636 (5.77%)	10,029 (0.67%)
Not read and/or write Irish	45,338 (3.02%)	1,320,657 (87.90%)
No response to the question (not included in table):		39,725 (2.64%)

Moving on to the 2001 Census, a welcome development is the addition of a fourth question: do you understand spoken Irish (passive aural skill). Four questions means 16 responses to count. It also introduces the possibility of further "meaningless" responses, e.g. speak but not understand.

Understand	- + - - - + + + - - - + + + - +	Aural passive
Speak	- - + - - + - - - + + - + + - + +	Aural active
Read	- - - + - - + - + - + + - + + +	Visual passive
Write	- - - - + - - - + - + + - + + + +	Visual active
	6 1 2 5 5 2 5 5 3 5 5 3 5 5 5 4	Published column

For 2001, the Northern Ireland Statistics and Research Agency (NISRA) have produced tables such as Table S372. An improvement over 1991 is the inclusion of a column for total of positive responses ("has some knowledge of Irish"). However, NISRA appear to have considered that 16 responses are too many to tabulate in separate columns, especially when seven of them are of the absurd variety, and have amalgamated the responses into six columns (as shown by the row of numbers under the table above). Column 5 is a catch-all, "other combinations of skills", which, unfortunately for us, includes both people whose skill is purely visual, and people whose skill is both aural and visual.

Now when we try to make our 2x2 skills table, only an incomplete table can be constructed.

	Understand and/or speak Irish	Not understand and/or speak Irish
Read and/or write Irish	82,308 (5.09%)	0 (0.00%)
Not read and/or write Irish	61,015 (3.77%)	1,450,467 (89.64%)

The contents of column 5, viz. 24,167 (1.49%), should be added to the upper row, but it is not known how they should be apportioned between the two cells.

I brought this deficiency to the attention of NISRA, independently of Professor MacKinnon, and I have to say they have been very receptive to my comments. They provided me with 16-column counts, for Northern Ireland as a whole and for district council areas, and they are to publish these counts in the future. This enabled me to complete the 2x2 table.

	Understand and/or speak Irish	Not understand and/or speak Irish
Read and/or write Irish	95,752 (5.92%)	10,723 (0.66%)
Not read and/or write Irish	61,015 (3.77%)	1,450,467 (89.64%)

For smaller geographical units, NISRA are concerned about maintaining anonymity, and have proposed a 9-column scheme for these smaller areas. I am still hoping to persuade them either to tabulate all the responses in 16 columns, or to use a reduced number of columns which will maintain distinctions between aural and visual skill and between active and passive skill, while amalgamating each "meaningless" response with the most appropriate meaningful response. In 2001, the total number of persons aged three or over in Northern Ireland with some skill in Irish is 167,490 or 10.35 per cent of the population. In comparing this with the 1991 result, two facts have to be borne in mind: 1. the 2001 figure contains 36,479 people who understand Irish only – a question not asked in 1991;

and 2. the "not stated" responses are integrated directly into the 2001 table responses for them have been imputed by NISRA on the basis of responses made by similar persons.

So, my own difficulty with the tables published thus far for the 2001 Census has been the categorization of language skills. Other users of the results of the language question may find that breakdowns of language skill by other variables (such as age, district, or educational level) are published at a level of detail which is insufficient or inappropriate for their purpose.

It is important, therefore, for Gaelic agencies to be aware of this issue, and to ensure that they get the statistics needed for their planning. It is obviously better to be involved before results are published rather than afterwards, so I would urge organisations in Northern Ireland to make themselves known to the Census Statistical Support section of NISRA, as potential users of the results of the Irish language question, and therefore as people whose views may be sought whenever the form of the published results is being considered.

Basque and Language Rights

Eduardo J. Ruiz Vieytez

Summary

0.   Introduction.
1.   Preliminary reflection: Linguistic Rights and Human Rights.
2.   The case of the Basque Language: legal protection and social reality;
2.1.   The Basque Country: a conflictive framework;
2.2.   Institutional organisation and political conflict;
2.3.   The Basque Language: description and sociolinguistic reality.
2.4.   Legal Framework for the Basque Language:
        a)   Northern Basque Country (French Law);
        b)   Southern Basque Country (Spanish Law);
             1) Basque Autonomous Community;
             2) Autonomous Community of Navarra;
2.5.   Social Situation of the Basque Language:
        a)   Public Administration and Justice;
        b)   Education;
        c)   Mass Media;
        d)   Other Cultural Aspects;
2.6.   Trends and Tendencies.
3.   Basque and Irish: minority languages in comparison.
        Basque and Irish: Similarities:
        a)   Sociolinguistic elements;
        b)   Political factors;
        c)   Legal status.
        Basque and Irish: Differences:
        a)   Sociolinguistic elements;
        b)   Political factors;
        c)   Legal status.
4.   Conclusions.
5.   Bibliography.

0. Introduction

In this paper, we aim to provide a useful analysis on the current situation of the Basque language as a European minority language. The final goal of this descriptive analysis is to find some elements that could be of relevance for the perspective of the Irish Gaelic language in both the Republic of Ireland and Northern Ireland. In this sense, a great part of the paper will be devoted to the description and critics of the social situation and legal framework for the Basque language, but there will be some place for a direct comparison of the previously described reality with that one of the Irish language. In any case, we understand that, as a reflection on minority languages and linguistic rights, we are obliged to begin with a more general and deep consideration about the real nature of these so-called linguistic rights. Our position, from the very beginning in the line of defending and developing the cultural and linguistic diversity of Europe, will be that of understanding linguistic rights and faculties as a substantial part of the core concept of human rights. In this sense, we reject the consideration of this set of rights as a kind of additional or optional complement of a more basic and unquestionable standard of human rights.

1. Preliminary Reflection: Linguistic Rights and Human Rights

The formal protection of linguistic minorities in Europe is an extraordinarily recent phenomenon in the sphere of international law. Nevertheless, concern about the existence, tolerance or protection of linguistic minority communities has existed for a long time, but the solutions adopted by different countries for the protection of minority languages have varied widely for social and political reasons. Attention paid to linguistic questions has grown over the last 150 years, in parallel with the development of the Modern State and nationally based ideologies. Indeed, not until the twentieth century was legal recognition of some linguistic rights for minorities incorporated into international treaties.

Nowadays, there is a small set of international binding treaties incorporating specific rights for the linguistic minorities. Apart from the more general clauses on non discrimination, the most relevant provision in this sense is article 27 of the 1966 International Covenant on Civil and Political Rights (in fact ratified by most of the European States). In Europe, there are two relevant treaties, the Framework Convention for the Protection of National Minorities and the European Charter for Regional or Minority Languages. However, not all the European states have ratified these two treaties, being today only seventeen members to the second one. Besides these multilateral treaties, in Europe we can find some other bilateral agreements or treaties with binding effects, as it would be the case of the so-called Good Friday Agreement for Northern Ireland, which also refers to linguistic aspects.

All this means that some linguistic rights are being considered in a growing extent as real human rights and included in this context. We consider linguistic rights as human rights because language is one of the most important aspects of the human identity and a necessary tool for the development of the personality. This entails that a central core of linguistic rights of people derives from the human dignity at the same level of other civil or social basic rights. Indeed, human dignity does not only include a central value of Liberty, but also a sense of Equality. This concept of equality cannot be considered only in a formalistic way (satisfied with the establishment of the same law for everybody) but also in a real and material sense. It should include also the real equality in respect the possibilities of personal development, including of course cultural and linguistic conditions. In this sense, the defence of cultural and linguistic equality of opportunities must be regarded, as it is the idea of promoting equality between men and women or in respect of wealth differences. It is surprising in our societies the number of thinkers and authors who being very progressive in social terms are extremely liberal and non-interventionist in cultural or linguistic issues. It is no by accident that practically all of these are members of the cultural or linguistic majority within their respective states.

The question of minority rights is indeed one of the remaining problems of the definition of human rights. It implies a different perspective in respect to both collective and individual rights and provokes serious controversies when we must deal with rights in conflict. By definition, democracy is not a definitive tool for the solution of the protection and promotion of minorities. To add fuel to the flames, this kind of issues become extremely sensitive in a framework of strongly nationally based states and societies. Identity issues have to do with deep feelings and fears. All this makes the theorisation on minority rights remarkably difficult, but necessary at the same time.

From a human rights perspective it must be defended that people belonging to traditional linguistic minorities share a basic core of linguistic rights that must be considered as human rights. We cannot agree with those positions that speak about minority rights as a kind of "new set" of human rights or rights belonging to the so-called third generation of human rights. On the contrary, we consider linguistic rights as rights of civil, political or cultural nature and, therefore, belonging in any case to the "two first" generations of human rights. Even more, some of the so-considered linguistic rights are in fact already part of traditional civil liberties as freedom of expression or the right to private life. Others, however, are human rights derived from a concrete situation, implying an active role for the public authorities. This would be the case of all the faculties that can be reasonably be demanded to the public sector according to the existing situation of the language. Among these, probably the most important would be the right to get education in or of the minority language in question.

To combat the idea of minority rights as being part of the third generation of rights or new rights, we will also defend that they must be regarded as individual rights of the concrete people, and not so much as collective rights belonging to the linguistic community as a whole. Although this position could appear as less progressive, it is in fact more practical in order to protecting the minority languages and their speakers. Sometimes there is a real confusion between the content of the right or the conditions for its exercise and the definition of the titular. This explains that very often some minority rights are presented as collective rights, but in fact they must not belong to the group itself, although they imply of course collective elements since they derive from the identity, which is created in a given group. In fact, most of the linguistic minorities existing today in Europe do not have demands for constituting a collective subject of political power, but only to the extent is necessary for the protection of their respective identity or language. Even in this case, it is not rare to find linguistic minorities whose members willing to promote and protect their native language are in a minority position inside the group itself. This situation shows that the individual approach to linguistic rights is not only more accurate from a technical point of view, but also more convenient from a practical perspective.

To put it in a nutshell, there is a common core of linguistic rights of the people belonging to linguistic minorities that mist be regarded as human rights. These rights are not in a lower position in respect to other fundamental rights or civil liberties. On the contrary, their recognition and guarantee is a condition sine-qua-non to ensure a real protection of the human dignity of those people. As with other human rights, the public authorities of the State have the responsibility of ensuring the necessary conditions to make possible that members of linguistic minorities enjoy that core of rights and can develop their cultural and linguistic spheres in a proper environment.

2. The Case of the Basque Language: Legal Protection and Social Reality

Before we proceed to the analysis of the current situation of the Basque language, it is convenient to provide some data on the political and institutional reality of the country. The conflictive nature of the relation between the Basque Country and the Spanish State must be understood to get a better idea of the role played by the linguistic aspects within the same framework. Although linguistic and political realities differ in some aspects and evolve with different tendencies, there is still a significant relation among them that cannot be avoided when studying the future of the minority language in the Basque area.

2.1 The Basque Country: a conflictive framework

The Basque Country (*Euskal Herria*) is located in southwestern Europe, at the western corner of the Pyrenees Mountains. Its size is approximately 20,000 square km of which 18,000 in the Southern Basque Country (in Basque *Hegoalde*), within the Spanish Kingdom, and 2,000 in the Northern Basque Country (in Basque *Iparralde*), within the French Republic. Physically, the country is very mountainous, with narrow valleys and very few plains. Some Basque rivers flow into the Atlantic Ocean and others into the Ebro River. Weather is wet and moderate.

Southern Basque Country is divided in four historical territories or provinces: *Bizkaia/Biscay* (capital in *Bilbao*), *Araba/Alava* (capital in *Gasteiz/Vitoria*), *Gipuzkoa/Gipuscoa* (capital in *Donostia/San Sebastián*) and *Nafarroa/Navarra* (capital in *Irunea/Pamplona*). The concept of Basque Country referred initially to the Basque-speaking populations and, subsequently, to the lands occupied by them. In the First century, the Basque-speaking area was much wider than now. By the beginning of the twentieth century, the influence of the Latin languages had reduced the Basque-speaking area down to its present size. Nowadays, the Basque Country is formed by all the political communities where the Basque language (*Euskara*) and culture have remained alive to some extent. However, it is necessary to clarify that there is a strong political opinion stating that Navarra[1] is not a Basque territory. In Navarra itself, the Basque character is not shared by a great part of the population and most of the voters prefer to support Spanish oriented parties rather than Basque ones.

---

[1] In fact, Navarra should also refer to one of the three territories which make up the Northern or French Basque Country. In this case, there is no question about the Basque character of Northern Navarra. However, in the Spanish side, the term Navarra is used to refer to the Spanish province known as such. Although this is not historically correct, it has become the normal use of the term, so we will use it also in this sense.

Map 1: Political map of the Basque Country: BAC, Navarra and Northern.

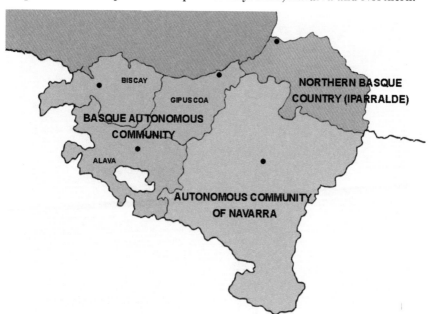

The current population of the whole Basque Country, including that of Navarra, is around 2,800,000, more than 90 per cent of it living within the Southern part. The metropolitan area of Bilbao approximately totals one million people. One third of the actual population moved into the Basque Country from Spanish regions, especially in the sixties. Only one third of the people have native grandparents. There are also significant Basque communities in Latin America and in the American States of Idaho and Nevada. Many of the Basques living in the States are still Basque-speakers.

From an economic point of view, the Basque Country is one of the richest areas of the Spanish State. Economic differences between the Basque country and the poorest areas of Spain are not higher than two to one, but the Basque area remains as one of the most dynamic areas of the State concerning social and cultural aspects. Distribution of wealth is also quite balanced in comparison with other European regions. Northern Basque Country, on the contrary, remains as a rural area living on tourism and on the first sector to a great extent. These socio-economic differences, added to a different age structure of the population will imply serious consequences for the future evolution of the native language on both sides of the Pyrenees.

2.2 Institutional organisation and political conflict

Northern Basque Country is politically located within the 64th administrative division or French Département, under the denomination Atlantic Pyrenees (in French *Pyrénées Atlantiques)*. The population of the Basque area is only 40 per

Map 2: Spain and its 17 Autonomous Communities.

cent of the total population of this Département, whose capital (*Pau*) is located outside the Basque area. The department makes part of the French region of *Aquitaine*, with capital in the city of *Bordeaux*. The regions in France enjoy some administrative competencies but no sort of political autonomy system has been developed in the French Republic. In the last years there has been a significant movement within the Northern Basque Country, with the support of the majority of the municipalities, demanding the creation of a new Basque Department. However, these demands have not been taken into consideration by the successive French governments.

As for Spain, under the 1978 Constitution, the kingdom remains structured as a single unified state, although characterised by a high degree of political decentralisation affecting the whole of the country. In fact, the post-1978 model applied in Spain may be seen as a new departure in terms of the forms of decentralisation of political power and is best described by what has come to be known not as a federal system, but as a complex State. In any case, the 1978 Constitution strongly asserts the principle of national unity as one of its basic mainstays and does not recognise difference among the peoples within the State. At the same time, however, the Constitution acknowledges the existence of "nationalities" and regions within the State and envisages the possibility of territorial self-government for them, without defining a map or definitive model. Constitutional development has given rise to the division of Spanish territory into 17 Autonomous Communities, each endowed with broad legislative and executive powers

Map 3: Basque-phone areas

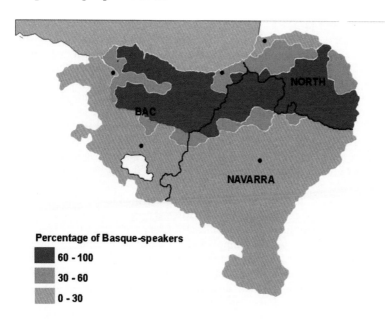

Percentage of Basque-speakers

- 60 - 100
- 30 - 60
- 0 - 30

Following the French model, a Spanish nationally based constitutionalism began to evolve along the 19th century. The attempts politically to unify the kingdom came into conflict with the special political regime of the Basque Provinces. Laws enacted in 1839 and 1876 would suppress the most important aspects of this semi-independent political system. Nationalism was also to develop among the Basques in the late second half of the nineteenth century, creating a political party, the EAJ-PNV,[2] which gained ground rapidly.

In 1931, following the proclamation in Spain of the Second Republic, a system was established in the Constitution to enable some regions to gain autonomy. The Basque Country (without Navarra) elected an autonomous government in 1936 that was suppressed a year later after the conquest of the whole territory by insurgents´ military forces in the Spanish Civil War. The Franco regime period was characterised by a savage repression of the Basque national and linguistic identity. As a counteraction to this repression, new left-leaning nationalist groups sprang up, including in some cases the use of armed struggle to combat the dictatorship. Amongst these groups, ETA[3] was founded in 1962 and still carries out violent action, although popular support to this group within the Basque Country can be considered today as marginal.

---

[2] EAJ-PNV stands for Eusko Alderdi Jeltzalea-Partido Nacionalista Vasco. The meaning of the name in both languages is "Basque Nationalist Party" and "Basque Party of God and Old Laws", respectively (www.eaj-pnv.com).

[3] ETA is the acronym for Euskadi Ta Askatasuna, literally meaning "Basque Fatherland and Freedom".

The present system of autonomy in force for the Southern Basque Country is based on the *Spanish Constitution* of 1978 and the historical rights of the four historical territories or provinces. According to the *Spanish Constitution* of 1978 and *Act on Autonomy for the Basque Country* of 1979, the four territories of the Southern Basque Country have the right to belong to a Basque Autonomous Community (BAC). However, only three of them are integrated in this BAC. Navarra makes a different Autonomous Community with its own Act on Autonomy from 1982. Both communities have their own Parliament elected by universal voting and their respective Governments with legislative and executive powers in different fields like internal security, public health, primary and secondary education, public works, taxes and others. Inside the BAC, every territory has its own Parliament and Government, with some competencies, making up a kind of internal federal system. Besides this, the *Additional Provision to the Act on Autonomy of the Basque Country* states that:

"The acceptance of the system of autonomy established in this Statute does not imply that the Basque People waive the rights that as such may have accrued to them in virtue of their history and which may be updated in accordance with the stipulations of the legal system."

The current Basque conflict has not to do directly with the use of violence, but with the political controversy about the sovereignty and the right to self-determination. In this sense, we can distinguish between the Basque-oriented political parties, in favour of the right to self-determination of the Basque population, and the Spanish-oriented parties, defending the contrary position. At least for the BAC, it seems that there is a social majority in favour of the idea of Basque sovereignty, although this cannot be automatically translated into support for independence. In February 1990, the Basque Parliament approved a political proclaiming the right of the Basque People to self-determination and a proposal for a new deal with the State has been presented by the Basque President in September 2003. Spanish parties, however, have already expressed their opposition to any change of the current *statu quo*.

In the Parliaments of the BAC and Navarra, the distribution of seats as at September 2003 gives the following figures for the different political blocks:

	BAC	Navarra[4]
Basque National Parties[5]	40	8
United Left[6]	3	4
Spanish National Parties	32	38[7]
Total Seats	**75**	**50**

---

[4] The last regional polls in Navarre, took place once after the Basque political Party Batasuna had already been banned.

[5] Apart from PNV, already mentioned, it includes MPs from the banned party Batasuna (only for BAC; see footnote 4), and from the left wing pro-independence party Eusko Alkartasuna (Basque Solidarity) (www.euskoalkartasuna.org).

[6] Although United Left is a coalition of different political groups, some of them State-level-parties, within the Basque Country its position is favorable to the right to self-determination of the Basque people. At the present moment, United Left makes part of the Basque government together with two Basque national parties.

[7] It includes four MPs of the small regional party CDN (Democratic convergence of

The Basque question remains as the most sensitive subject in Spanish politics. In fact, in the Basque Country, being the current political situation extraordinarily tense. Isolated actions of violence carried out by ETA help to distort the political debate on territorial structuring. The Basque question dominates the domestic political agenda in Spain and in the medium term there appears to be no possibility of political agreement between the centralist Spanish parties and those defending the right to self-determination. However, the current system of autonomy does not look to satisfy the demands for self-government of the majority of the population. This is aggravated by the existence of a significant Basque minority in Navarra, where the regional government maintains a conflictive politics in regard to Basque culture and language.

Indeed, this entire conflictive environment affects also the question of the protection of the minority language. There is a clear correlation between Basque speakers and support for Basque national parties, whereas it is still very difficult to listen to talk in this language to the representatives of the Spanish parties. In too many occasions linguistic questions become a political instrument or excuse to show opposition to the adversaries. While quite often linguistic policy developed by the Basque government is regarded by the Spanish Parties as discriminatory, some Basque sectors consider that it is extremely weak for the needs of the language itself. In Navarra, on the contrary, the position of the regional government in respect of the Basque language has been criticised not only by different political and social movements but also by the European Bureau for Lesser-Used Languages as an example of regressive policy.[8] In any case, to a great extent it continues to be a clear link between protection and promotion of the Basque language and political attitudes in favour of self-determination.

2.3 The Basque Language: description and sociolinguistic reality

The Basque language (*Euskara*) has no affiliation with any other language and its origins remain uncertain. *Euskara* is not an Indo-European language although the vocabulary shows a strong influence of Latin, Spanish and French words. The Basque language has some phonetic and semantic characteristics which show that it is a very ancient language. Its grammatical structure belongs to the SOV[9] model. At the same time, it is an agglutinant language, with a nominal declination of fourteen cases. The most complex issue in *Euskera* is the verb, which varies not only according to the subject but also in respect to the direct and indirect objects. Some aspects of Basque phonetics, like having only five vowel sounds, was adopted by Spanish and Gascon (a Roman language spoken in the Southwest of France, variety of Occitan). Nowadays we normally distinguish eight dialects in *Euskera*. It is not always easy for one variety speaker to understand another variety. In 1964, the Academy for the Basque Language (*Euskaltzaindia*) set up the unified Basque (*Euskera Batua*), with a common standard for writing, which

---

Navarra) and 23 from UPN (Union of Navarrese People), a brother party of the Spanish Popular Party, currently at office in Madrid. At the present moment, Navarra has a coalition government made up by these two regional centre-right wing parties.
[8]   Resolution of the Bureau meeting in Helsinki, September 2003.
[9]   Subject/Object/Verb instead of the Subject/Verb/Object (SVO) model characteristics of most European languages.

is the variety used in mass media, education and public administration.

The territory where Basque language is predominant has been reducing at least over the last ten centuries. Along the history, Euskara has very often been spoken in bilingual or plurilingual areas. However, the social position of the language has never been strong and traditionally has remained as a language of rural areas with a very weak literary tradition. The first book published in Basque dates from 1545 and the second one, the New Testament, from 1571.

The actual number of Basque language speakers and their percentage to the total population changes very much depending on the territory we are referring to. Such differences are not only shown in the absolute and relative figures, but also in the different age groups which compose the Basque population. Nowadays, more than 90 per cent of the Basque-speaking people are bilingual and they know Spanish or French as well as *Euskera*. The small percentage of Basque monolingual speakers corresponds to elder people living in rural areas. The Basque language is largely used in the rural zones of Eastern Biscay, most of Gipuscoa, Atlantic Navarra (Northwestern third of the territory) and in the interior of the Northern Basque Country. On the other hand, it is hardly spoken in Alava, Western Biscay, Mediterranean Navarra (Centre and South of this region) and in the metropolitan areas of Bilbao and Bayonne. The approximated figures of Basque language speakers in the different territories as of 1996, are the following:[10]

Territory	Basque Speakers		Passive Knowledge	
ALAVA/ARABA	33,100	13%	27,400	11%
BISCAY/BIZKAIA	219,700	22%	123,700	13%
GIPUZKOA	278,100	48%	55,000	10%
TOTAL BAC[11]	**530,900**	**29%**	**206,100**	**11%**
NAVARRA[12]	55,900	11%	38,000	7%
TOTAL SOUTH	**586,800**	**25%**	**244,100**	**10%**
NORTH(FRANCE)	69,100	26%	15,000	9%
BASQUE COUNTRY	**745,900**	**27%**	**259,100**	**10%**

[10] Different sources provide different data. Percentages can vary between Basque speakers and passive bilinguals. For the BAC, data are taken from the 2001 sociolinguistic survey carried out by the Basque Government. It must be said that these data refer to citizens over the age of fifteen. For Navarra, we show data provided by the Government of this region through the web page. In this case, data refer to people over the age of two. For the Northern Basque Country, figures have been provided directly by the Basque Government.

[11] We could compare these data with the figures referring to the first language of the citizens in the BAC. According to the 2001 census these were: Spanish 76.1 %, Basque 18.8 %; both languages 5.1 %.

[12] According to official data provided by the web page of the Government of Navarra, e percentages for the three linguistic zones are the following:
a) Bascophone area: Basque-speakers   61%   Passive knowledge 13%
b) Mixed area: Basque-speakers   7%   Passive knowledge 9%
c) Non-Bacophone area: Basque-speaking   2%   Passive knowledge 3%

Within this sociolinguistic context, we consider the following as the most relevant data and tendencies concerning the knowledge and social use of the language:

a) There is a strong difference between the Northern Basque Country and the Southern part if we look to the medium age of the Basque speakers. While in the North, the Basque speaking population is quite old and it is not being replaced by the young generations; in the Southern part of the country, we can see a positive evolution of the language especially between the younger groups. This reality has stopped the former tendency to decrease the percentage of speakers at the same time that the age of the population, as it had happened from the 40s. Nowadays, it is no doubt that the educational measures play a very strong role in the increasing of Basque speakers during the last two decades, mainly in the BAC. For the first time in many decades, within the BAC, monolingual speakers are in a minority position among the younger generations. As in Navarra, the official status of the language is reduced to the northern part of the region (the less populated of the territory), the education system plays this promotional role principally in this area and only a little in the central zone of the region.

b) At the same time, we can conclude that there has been a great increase of Basque speakers during the last years in the Southern Basque Country. Again it is necessary to say that the increase has been much more significant in the BAC than in Navarra. According to a comparison of the surveys carried out within the BAC in 1991 and 2001, along this decade there has been a substantial increase of the total number of speakers from 419,200 to 530,900 (meaning in percentages an increase of more than five points (from 24.1 per cent to 29.4 per cent) of people over the age of 15). Within the sector of people between the age of 15 and 24, the increase of active bilinguals for the whole decade dropped from 25 per cent to 48 per cent.

c) There has also been a significant decrease of non-alphabetised Basque speakers both in Navarra and in the BAC. In this case the consequences in both territories are similar because almost all the monolingual Basque speakers of Navarra live in the area covered by the official status of *Euskara*

d) The appearance of a significant and increasing group of passive bilingual people or quasi-speakers is due, on the one hand, to the effort of middle-aged citizens to learn the language even while they live in a Spanish-speaking context. In the figures of quasi-speakers we also find young people whose model of education did not ensure them a good knowledge of the language. On the contrary, this group is not relevant in the Northern Basque Country. This shows very clearly the importance of the social opinion about the language and not only the implementation of the legal framework.

e) From a different point of view, it is remarkable that the condition of a bilingual country (in the sense that almost everybody is able to use the State language) plays against the minority language regarding to the social use of it. This can be seen from the data, which show the relationship between the number of Basque speakers, the number of people who have *Euskara* as their mother tongue and the number of citizens using the Basque language at home. Even in the BAC we can see that only two thirds of the Basque speakers use *Euskara* within their families. Obviously, the social use of the language in the street is even smaller, especially in the places in which bilingual and Spanish monolingual speakers live together, as it happens in all the urban areas over 10,000 inhabitants. It is also remarkable in this sense that the big increase it the number of bilingual speakers has been made mainly among people who express themselves better in Spanish than in Basque, while the percentage of bilingual people with better ability in Basque has hardly varied from 1991 to 2001. Therehas not been a significant change in figures referring to first language of the citizens.

2.4 Legal Framework for the Basque Language

a) Northern Basque Country (French Law)

In *Iparralde*, Basque does not have any official use. It is simply a recognised and tolerated language according to the *Deixonne* Act of 1951, like some other "regional languages" spoken within the French Republic. In this respect, teaching of Basque language can be contemplated in schools, always in an optional manner.

France has always been a very reluctant country to the recognition of national or linguistic minorities. According to this taught policy towards national or linguistic differences, the French Republic has ratified neither the *Framework Convention for the protection of National Minorities* nor the *European Charter for Regional or Minority Languages*. In this latter case, the constitutional court stated in 1999 that ratification of the Charter would be against some of the basic principles of the French Constitution. Therefore, there are no specific legal instruments to promote the use of Basque in the public spheres of the Northern Basque Country.

b) Southern Basque Country (Spanish Law)

The legal framework of the Basque language in the Southern Basque Country varies depending on the Autonomous Community we are speaking about. Indeed, each Autonomous Community has a different Public Law in matters under her competence.

Nevertheless, the *Spanish Constitution* offers a common provision for legal status of languages in Spanish State. Article 3 of the Spanish Constitution of 1978 states that:

1. *Castilian is the official Spanish language of the State. All Spaniards have the duty to know it and the right to use it.*
2. *The other Spanish languages shall also be official in the respective Autonomous Communities in accordance with their Statutes.*
3. *The wealth of the different language variations of Spain is a cultural heritage which shall be the object of special respect and protection.*

This is the second time that Spanish constitutions refer to the linguistic pluralism of the State. The quoted article is very similar to article nine of the *Republican Constitution* of 1931. The actual Spanish Constitution establishes an official status for Spanish language for the whole territory of the State, including also monolingual Catalan, Galician or Basque-speaking rural areas. This means that constitutional provisions consolidate the presence of Spanish everywhere, including an obligation for the citizens (not for foreign residents) to know the language.

In terms of comparative constitutional Law, article three of the Spanish Constitution is very similar to article 68 of the Russian Constitution. A similar model of coexisting one or several regional official languages with one State language in official status through the whole territory is in force in such countries as Italy, the United Kingdom, and Denmark.

It is also important to note that Spain has ratified both the *Framework Convention for the Protection of National Minorities* and the *European Charter for Regional or Minority Languages*. However, in the report sent to the Council of Europe in relation with the former, the State does not make any mention to the existence of linguistic minorities in Spain. As for the Charter, this came into force for Spain in 2001 and currently the first monitoring process is being developed.

b.1) The Basque Autonomous Community

The *Act on Autonomy or Autonomy Statute of the Basque Country* was passed by the Spanish Parliament and approved by the Basque people by referendum in October 1979. Its 6th article refers to the Basque language as follows:

1. *Euskera, the own language of the Basque People, shall, like Spanish, have the status of an official language in Euskadi. All its inhabitants have the right to know and use both languages.*

2. *The common institutions of the Autonomous community, taking into account the socio-linguistic diversity of the Basque Country, shall guarantee the use of both languages, controlling their official status, and shall effect and regulate whatever measures and means are necessary to ensure knowledge of them.*

3. *No one may suffer discrimination for reasons of language.*

4. *The Royal Academy of the Basque Language is the official advisory institution in matters regarding Euskera.*

5. *Given that Euskera is the heritage of other Basque territories and communities, the Autonomous Community of the Basque Country may request the Spanish Government, in addition to whatever ties and correspondence are maintained with academic and cultural institutions, to conclude and, where necessary, to submit to the Spanish State Parliament for authorisation, those treaties or agreements that will make it possible to establish cultural relations with the States where such territories lie and communities reside, with a view to safeguarding and promoting Euskera.*

After analysing these provisions, we can underline three aspects in respect with the new official status for the language:

a) The Act distinguishes between official languages of the BAC (Spanish and Basque) and "own language" of the Basque Country.[13] In the drafts of the Act submitted by the Basque representatives to the Spanish Parliament the terms "national language" and "native language" (*"idioma originario"*) were used. Such a distinction has no legal consequences concerning the status of both

---

[13] We did not find any other word to translate "lengua propia/berezko hizkuntza" into English. That is why we will use forward the expression "own language" even if it is not so suitable.

languages. It remains as a symbolic proclamation to underline the importance of the language for the Basque identity.

b) The Basque language is proclaimed an official language all over the territory of the BAC, even in those zones in which it is hardly spoken or in which it was lost many centuries ago. Therefore, every person, Basque or not, can deal with any public administration located inside the BAC using *Euskara* as the normal language for communication. The official status of one language is a question of Law and it has nothing to do with its social situation.[14]

c) The competencies or powers to monitor the implementation of the language policy correspond to the Basque institutions.

If we analyse the previous drafts of the Act on Autonomy discussed by the Basque representatives, we can also find some interesting aspects that were not accepted by the Spanish parties in the further readings in the Spanish Parliament. In this sense, the two main aspects that were abolished from the draft are the following:

a) The drafts referred to the minority condition and socially difficult situation of the Basque language (*"situation diglósica"*), encouraging the authorities to take in mind such a situation to develop an appropriate language policy.

b) The initial drafts also gave to the BAC the power to maintain formal links with other authorities in Basque-speaking zones. This was supposed to be applied to Navarra, to the Northern Basque Country, and perhaps to the American States with a significant Basque presence. The Spanish Parliament amended this disposition to the extent of the actual redaction, avoiding the possibility given to the BAC to reach its own linguistic and cultural agreements on the international level.

In 1982, the *Act for the Normalisation of the Use of Euskera* was passed by the Basque Parliament with the approval of all the MPs, including those from the Spanish national parties. However, the Spanish Government appealed to the Spanish Constitutional Court on the ground of unconstitutionality of several articles of the Act. In 1986 the Court resolved stating the unconstitutionality of three articles of the Law of minor importance.[15]

This Act develops the provision of the Act on Autonymy proclaiming the official status of the language in the whole territory of the BAC. All aspects of the public sector are included in this Language Act stating the obligation for the public administrations located in the BAC to use, when required, the Basque language, and to go forward in the knowledge of *Euskera* by their respective staffs.

The 1982 Act also sets up two different bodies. On one hand, the Institute for alphabetisation and teaching of adults (*HABE*), which holds financed courses both for adult learners of the language and for non-alphabetised Basque speakers. On the other hand, it set up a Consultative Council for the Basque Language (*Euskararen Aholku Batzordea*), chaired by the president of the Basque Government, and made up by high members of public administration, representatives of Universities and independent experts

---

[14] The Spanish Constitutional Court also underlined this idea in its sentence 82/1986, stating that:

"A language is official when, apart from its reality or social weight, is recognized by the public powers as their normal tool of communication inside them and among them, as well as in their relationships with the private sector and individuals, with full legal force and effects". (our translation from the Spanish official version).

[15] It was the Sentence 82/1986 of the Spanish Constitutional Court.

After the approval of the Language Act in 1982, a vast developing legislation on linguistic matters has been put in force by the Basque government. Among these regulations we can underline the programmes to fund the learning of *Euskara* by teachers and other civil servants and the planning of the Basque administration jobs according to the linguistic requirements of the population. The government has set up a minimum percentage of Basque-speaking civil servants in every administrative unit, depending on the figures of Basque active and passive speakers of the area to be covered by each administration. As a consequence of the implementation of this vast programme, many Basque civil servants have the obligation to show a given standard of competence in Euskara (four different levels have been delimited for the different needs in manual or technical jobs) in a given period.

Within the Basque Government's structure, a General Secretary for Language Policy *(Hizkuntz Politikarako Sailburuordetza)* was set up to deal with every aspect concerning the development, teaching, learning, alphabetising, researching and promoting the Basque language. This General Secretary was directly attached to the president's office, but after 1994 has been depending on the Basque Ministry of Culture and is headed by a deputy minister.

b.2) Autonomous Community of Navarra

The Act on Autonomy for the province of Navarra was passed by the Spanish Parliament in 1982. Because of the different constitutional way employed by Navarra to access to autonomy, the Act on Autonomy was not passed by referendum.

Given that Navarra is a bilingual community, article 3.2 of the Spanish Constitution forced to include some regulation on the linguistic situation. As the Basque language is for the most part presently dealt with in the political opinions, and given the strong opposition of the right-wing sectors of Navarra to Basque nationalism, the regulation of the language status did not follow the standards provided in other Communities as for example the BAC, Catalonia, Galicia or Balearic Islands. Article nine of this Act refers to the Basque language with the following words:

1. *Castilian is the official language of Navarra.*
2. *Basque[16] will enjoy also the official status in the Basque-speaking zones of Navarra. One Statutory Law will determine those zones, will rule the official use of Basque and, inside the general legislation of the State, will organise the teaching of this language.*

---

[16] The Public Law of the Autonomous Community of Navarra does not refer to the Basque language as Euskara (Basque name of the language) nor as "vasco" (Spanish direct translation of "Basque"). They use the term "vascuence" to nominate the language. We cannot find a different word in English to translate it than "Basque", but note that the word used has not exactly the same meaning. Anyway, both in Navarra and in the BAC, people use Euskara to nominate the language when they speak in Spanish. Few people refer to it as "vasco", and you can hardly listen the term "vascuence" in any conversation.

The Navarrese Parliament passed the *Statutory Basque Language Law* of Navarra in 1986. The first important remark to be made is that this Act, differing from those similar Acts from other Autonomous Communities, was not a consequence of a political consensus. Some parties (including the Spanish Socialist Party, which at that moment formed the Navarrese government) voted in favour of the Act, while Basque national parties expressed their refusal, considering it a very restrictive regulation. On the other side of the political debate, the main party of Navarra (a centre-right wing party now, allied to the Spanish Popular Party) abstained because they considered that the Act exaggerated the importance of the Basque language in this region.

The main issues of this Act comparing with that of the BAC are the following:

a) It is proclaimed that both Spanish and Basque are the "own languages" of Navarra. As we said before this statement has no legal consequences but it is of political relevance, specially if we consider that all the other bilingual Communities of the State (BAC, Catalonia, Galicia, Valencia and Balearic iIslands) considered the native language as the unique "own language" of the community.

b) The territory of the Community is divided in three zones: Basque-phone, mixed and non-Basque-phone. Although the Act does not say it clearly, we can conclude that Basque is official in the Basque-phone area, which covers approximately the North-west third of the land of Navarra. The population living in this area is around 11 per cent of the whole Navarrese population. The capital of the region, Pamplona, is located in the so-called mixed zone, which spreads over the central area of the region including 55 per cent of the total population. The remaining 34 per cent of the Navarrese people live in the South and East of the land, the non-Basque-phone area. This means that the capital, in which most of the administrative and judicial units are located, is not included in the official zone of the Basque language. Only some aspects of this status are implemented in the mixed zone, and very few of them in the non-Basque-phone zone.

c) The Act proclaims that the Academy of the Basque Language *(Euskaltzaindia)* is the official consultative body for linguistic matters. This provision, which is also included in the Basque Act on Autonomy, is of a great importance to ensure the unity of the language spoken both in the BAC and in Navarra. Although the Navarrese legislation always refers to the Basque language as *"Vascuence"* and not as *"Euskara"*, the identity in terms of official consultative body certifies the unity of the language over the difference of local dialects.

As in the BAC, many other regulations have been adopted to develop the Language Act's provisions. To implement the linguistic policy of the Navarrese Government a Secretary for Linguistic Policy was set up within the governmental structure. However, this office does not deal exclusively with matters concerning the minority language of Navarra, but also with linguistic issues regarding foreign languages. There is also an administrative unit in Pamplona dealing with official translations.

2.5 Social Situation of the Basque Language

Known the legal framework of the Basque language in the Southern Basque Country, let us have a look at the consequences of this legislation in the social situation of the language. Although the social knowledge and use of a language normally takes very much time to produce significant changes, we can take advantage of the relevant change produced in the legal framework from 1979 to analyse the extent to which legal provisions have helped to the development of the Basque language. This period of two decades should be enough to get some conclusions on the role played by this legislation. Nevertheless, we have to consider that the improving of a minority linguistic situation has many times more to do with the social consideration of the language (including the political feelings and wills of the people) than with the official or institutional regulations. In our case it is really difficult to know which changes in the social situations have been produced mainly due to a protective legislation or to a social collective movement in favour of the language.

a) Public Administration and Justice

The use of the Basque language in public administration largely varies depending on the different zones in the country. Basque is used often in the local and territorial administrations of the Basque-phone zones. The Basque Government, as already explained, is fulfilling a vast program of linguistic adaptation for its staff. However, Spanish, French and Navarrese administrations hardly use Basque and they do not have general plans to develop their linguistic competence. The access to public work in the BAC, except for the Spanish administration includes tests to evaluate the knowledge of Basque for the applicants. Only a few times, knowledge of Basque is considered in Navarre, but never in Iparralde.

The situation in the Justice administration is very bad in the whole country from the linguistic point of view. Basque is hardly used for legal contracts or trials, and there are very few judges able to use Basque in their jobs. If the litigants want to use the Basque language in their appeals, it is required the presence of an official translator. The Spanish Judicial system is based on the unity of jurisdiction.[17] Therefore, judges destined to the Basque Country can come from any other place in the State. Knowledge of Basque language is not always considered to work in the Justice administration, and when it is, it does not play a relevant role.

In the BAC, most of the public signs and panels are written in both official languages, as well as in the Basque-phone area of Navarra. As for the mixed area in Navarra, some of the panels remain bilingual, while many of them are exposed only in Spanish. In Iparralde, very few panels and signs can be seen in both languages.

It is also remarkable to say that in the BAC there have been relatively few complaints and trials dealing with linguistic discrimination. Linguistic conflicts have usually to do with feeling of discrimination by monolingual people when they try to get a position in a public body. In Navarra more problems have arisen dealing with linguistic matters, mainly due to complaints submitted by Basque groups against the linguistic policy of the Navarrese Government.[18]

---

[17] The French system is also based on this principle

[18] Some examples of these conflicts appeared in Navarra are the traditional refusal of the

---

b) Education

The implementation of the Language Act of 1982 included for the educational system the establishment of three linguistic models in Basque schools. Since then, in the BAC *Euskara* is at least a compulsory subject in the basic education. In A model, children receive teaching of Basque language and literature, but the language used for teaching is Spanish.[19] The B model shares the teaching of the different subjects in both languages Basque and Spanish. Finally, the D model includes full Basque-speaking education, except for Spanish language and literature. The so-called X model (all the teaching exclusively in Spanish) disappeared in the four first years of implementation of the new regulations. Some students, due to exceptional reasons as for example a short period of residence within the BAC, can be exempted from the learning of the Basque language.

The offer of the models by the Basque schools is conditioned, on the one hand, by the social demand and, on the other hand, by the capacity of the teachers to use *Euskara*. The evolution during the last 20 years has been extremely positive both in the number of teachers with ability to express themselves in Basque and in the number of children whose learning language is *Euskara*. In the BAC, most of the private educational centres (normally founded by Catholic Church's institutions) receive funds from the Basque Government. In this sense, there is not very much difference in the implementation of the linguistic models between public and private centres, although in general Basque is slightly more used within the public net.

Figures of evolution of the models are very significant. Regarding to basic non-university education, in 1982, 78 per cent of the children were learning in models A or X against 22 per cent in models B or D. By year 2000, models B and D sum up to 60 per cent of the students in the BAC. These figures even grow up to almost 90 per cent when referring to education for children under six years old. In higher schools, although the evolution is also positive, the number of students in A model remains important. In spite of this, the number of teachers in the BAC with knowledge of *Euskara* has had a vast increase since 1980 without equivalent in any other sector of the public administration.

In Navarra, models are offered depending on the zones limited by the Language Act of 1986. In the Basque-phone zone, models A, B and D are available. For mixed zone models A, B, D and G are available (G model corresponds to the disappeared X model of the BAC, that is to say full Spanish teaching). In the non-Basque-phone zone only A and G models enjoy public support. Some Basque-speaking schools are open also in this area, but they are not backed by the public administration.

In academic course 1996-97, 16 per cent of the Navarrese students were following the D model, 11 per cent were in A model and the remaining 73 per cent in G model. Between that time and academic year 2000-01, there was an increase of four points in the percentage of model D students, while model A increased in a more significant proportion. By 2001, models D and B made more than 20 per cent of the Navarrese students, model A reached to 18 per cent, while model G share had decreased to 61 per cent.[20]

Navarrese Government to ensure the view of the Basque television in its region or the denying of any license to a Basque-speaking radio station in Navarra.

[19] This "A" model unfortunately does not ensure a good knowledge of the Basque language for the children at the end of their compulsory education period.

[20] Figures obtained from official data according to the web page of the Government of

In Iparralde only some private schools offer teaching in Basque language for the lower levels. There is no public compulsory learning of *Euskera* in the French system.

Regarding the higher education, in the BAC there are three universities. The University of the Basque Country is the public one and it hosts around 60,000 students in its three different campuses of Bilbao, Vitoria and San Sebastian. The University of Deusto, located mainly in Bilbao, is an old Catholic University with 14,000 students involved in legal and human sciences. Finally, the University of Mondragon is a small centre offering technical studies in connection with the industrial sector of the country. The three of them, specially the public one, offer part of the curriculum in *Euskara*. Several degrees can be fully completed in Basque language. As for Navarra, there are two other universities. The Public University of Navarra is offering only a few degrees in Basque dealing with education matters. As for the University of Navarra, handed by the Catholic institution *Opus Dei*, no degree can be completed in this language. Finally, the so-called Summer Basque University, ruled by a private group, organises short-term courses for university people in the cities of Pamplona and Bayonne.

c) Mass Media

The Basque Government set up in 1982 a public communication body (EITB / Euskal Irrati Telebista) which includes a TV station with two channels, one of which has been broadcasting exclusively in Basque since 1983. It can be watched for the most of the Basque Country[21] and some neighbour areas. Since 1996, it has also been available in other countries by sat. There is also an official radio, with two channels broadcasting only in Basque, one of them dedicated to the young people. At the same time, there are some other private and local radio stations broadcasting in different Basque dialects. Neither the Spanish televisions (both public and commercial) nor the French ones broadcast any programme in the Basque language.[22]

Since 1989, there has been a daily newspaper (*Egunkaria*) published entirely in Basque by a private group, which received some funds from the Basque Ministry of Culture and other public administrations. This daily was closed by judicial resolution in February 2003, as a provisional measure in a criminal proceeding dealing with alleged terrorist offences. The board of the daily, composed by prestigious and well-known people in the scope of the Basque culture, was charged of being supporting ETA through the publication of the newspaper. This action, strongly critiqued by the Basque political parties, got a

---

Navarra: general access at www.cfnavarra.es. Surprisingly, the web page does not offer more updated data.

[21] There have traditionally been some difficulties to catch the Basque television in some areas of Navarra. The government of this region has not yet fully fulfilled the agreements for doing that broadcasting generally available.lan.

[22] The Spanish Constitution states in its 20th article that the public communication bodies (that is to say Spanish public radio and Television Corporation "RTVE" have to take in consideration the linguistic plurality of the State in their broadcasting. In Catalonia, for instance, many programs offered by the Spanish public television are broadcasted in Catalan.

bitter social response and huge demonstrations took place in Bilbao and San Sebastian. With an important popular support, a daily publication was maintained, and nowadays there is a new newspaper published in Basque under the name "Berria" (new/news).

However, the most read newspapers in the Country are written in Spanish. The number of publications and music edited in Basque is not large but it is constantly increasing and it has particularly succeeded in the field of literature for children. Many of these publications have got some public or private funds.

d) Other cultural aspects

The Basque people has jealously conserved folkloric elements such as dancing, singing, cultural demonstrations and other many popular sports and cultural events. All of them are alive and present in the daily life of the People, as can be witnessed in the audience of the typical Basque sport, the *"pelota"*, in both public and commercial television channels. Some of these elements are closely linked with the Basque language, although not always the encouragement or support for them is expressed in Basque. The traditional Basque way of life are often remembered in public cultural gatherings involving all ages all over the country. Even the Basque mythology remains alive and sometimes plays a highly symbolic role. Basque-speaking music groups enjoy also a significant audience. There is some Basque-speaking theatres, traditional dancing academies and cultural associations in the different territories of the country. Most of these linguistic and cultural expressions are financed by Basque public institutions thanks to the regulations that encourage the public sector to promote this kind of events.

The Catholic Church has also played in the past a fundamental role in order to maintain the Basque language. The four Bishops of the Southern Basque Country used to work together, but in recent years, after several new appointments, the bishop of Pamplona (Navarra) has not been a part for common documents. The Southern Basque Church has traditionally been very active in social issues as well as promoting the development of *Euskara*, using it as much as possible. In the same religious context, the Reformation adopted by the ancient royal family of *Albret* in Navarra (16th century) helped the early translation of the New Testament into Basque, which was edited in 1571. This contributed to standardise the written Basque and to use the Basque instead of Latin for religious practice. Until 20th century, most of the writers in Basque have traditionally been members of the clergy.

2.6 Trends and tendencies

As a short conclusion to this overeview, we can state that the evolution of the knowledge of the Basque language during the last years has been negative in the French side of the country, and positive in the South. However, the positive evolution in Navarra is not so brilliant as in the BAC, and it is restricted to the northern half of the region. In both communities the programmes of alphabetisation for Basque speakers have been largely developed. The percentages of people able to use actively the language have been increased in the BAC due both to a social collective mentality in favour of the language and to a promoting legislation, especially in the field of educational system.

The remaining problems for the Basque language in the Southern Basque Country have to do with the following factors:

a) The resistance to adopt and assume Euskara by significant sectors of the population. The political division of the country in some way supports this attitude. The main problem in this sense is that these social sectors perpetuate the actual linguistic situation. Some of them register their children in A model of education, which does not ensure for these children a minimum level of knowledge of the Basque language after finalising their studies. Other parents feel themselves obliged to register their children in bilingual models for practical reasons. The main conflicts in this sense have to do with the access to the civil service in public administrations. The mentality of being discriminated in favour of the Basque-speakers when applying for a public job is widely extended in the Spanish-speaking sectors. Some political parties and social sectors also complain of the large amount of money spent in linguistic policy (public television, linguistic training of civil servants ...). Although no political party has ever proposed that Euskara is not keeping its official status, these attitudes show there is no real assumption of bilinguism as a desirable scenario to be achieved.

b) Globalisation process and impact of new technologies. International communication gets an increasing importance in our societies. Generalisation of communication technologies such as e-mail and internet plays in favour of the English all over the world, but also in favour of the big national languages, such as Spanish or French, when comparing with the minority ones, on the one hand, because it is more difficult or expensive to put in the market such new products in Basque language; but, on the other hand, because it is not easy to encourage the social use of the minority language through these instruments. At the same time, the offer of information via digital television or television by satellite has largely increased the number of channels got at home by the people. This forces the Basque television to share the audience with more Spanish, French or English-speaking corporations.

c) The social use of the language does not correspond with the number and percentage of possible Basque-speakers. This implies that many quasi-speakers have very few opportunities to put in practice their Basque, losing linguistic competence. Some efforts to create Basque-speaking environments inside the Spanish-speaking areas have been tried, demonstrating the difficulties of such an aim. Although the knowledge of the language has clearly increased, the use of it out of the traditional zones remains rare and some times is seen as artificial. On the other hand, in those areas where fifty years ago Basque was the only mean of communication, Spanish can be used today without major difficulties. It is also remarkable that, although significant improvement has been achieved in slowing down the failing of inter-generation transmission of the Basque language, this negative tend has not been totally stopped yet.

d) The difficulties to adopt Basque language for technical questions. Although there is a group of Basque enterprises with the agreement relating internally and among them exclusively in *Euskara*, the Basque language is normally absent of the labour and legal worlds. Commercial and business fields remain as extremely difficult areas for he introduction of Basque language, unless they are developed in a local scale. Sometimes, high-qualified Basque-speaking workers normally miss the vocabulary and the habitude of using Basque in their working life. This sort of problem could be solved after a significant percentage of the younger generations complete their higher studies in Basque language, but the actual situation is still far from that.

As for the current situation of the Basque language, we could conclude that the legislation in force in the BAC is near to the top of its possibilities. The improvement of the social situation of the language will have to be reached more thanks to a social pressure and activity than to a stronger legal framework. Hopefully, in the medium-term, more positive effects will be shown taking account of the massive increase of speakers that is being produced among younger generations. Indeed, very few changes could be reached in the legislation and practice depending on the autonomous powers. On the other hand, Navarrese, Spanish and French authorities should still develop many aspects in favour of the Basque language. Nevertheless, the political confrontation is often a wonderful excuse for these administrations to keep without active plans in favour of the minority language. This passive attitude (when not reluctant) towards Basque language by these administrations is not likely to change at least in the medium term. As a consequence of all this, we can predict that the current three main trends in the evolution of the language health will be reinforced. First, a positive development of the knowledge and use of the minority language within the BAC, possibly expanding also over the northern part of Navarra. Second, little social and institutional presence of the Basque language within the rest of the Autonomous Community of Navarra. Third, a worrying past decade of the linguistic competence in the Northern Basque Country, where the social situation of *Euskara* is likely to become extremely weak and at a great risk within one or two generations.

3. Basque and Irish: Minority Languages in Comparison

When trying to compare the situation of two different minority languages, we find many difficulties. Although some of the conditions in which both languages live can be considered as parallel or similar, it is always true that a great number of factors, economic, social, cultural, political ones, will differ. As a consequence, it will be very difficult to draw an approximate picture if we do not have a deep knowledge of both situations. This is even clearer when the languages in question live in very different conditions themselves, according to various territorial or institutional scopes, as it is the case for Irish Gaelic and Basque.

Knowing these limits from the very beginning, we can try to identify the aspects or elements that would allow us to make a reasonable comparison in between Irish and Basque or, on the contrary, to understand which are the conditions making the difference.

We will organise the similarities and differences between Irish Gaelic and Basque languages by dividing them into three different scopes: sociolinguistic data, political factors and legal framework. Following this scheme, we have identified the following similarities and differences:

3.1 Basque and Irish: Similarities

a) Sociolinguistic elements

1) Linguistic distance: Both Irish and Basque are languages with a significant or dramatic linguistic distance in respect of the majority languages spoken around. There is no possibility of mutual understanding, even in a very basic manner, between Irish and English or between Basque and Spanish or French. For non-speakers, these languages sound impossible to follow and consequently it is extremely difficult for them to feel close to them. This makes a difference in relation with other European minority languages such as, for example, Catalan or Scots. On the contrary, however, due to the short tradition of literature in Basque and Irish, the script used is the Latin alphabet and of course a strong influence of surrounding languages can be noticed in the lexicon.

2) Minority condition: Both Irish and Basque are minority languages within their respective communities. Active or passive speakers of both languages sum up some percentage between one third and the half of the whole population living in Ireland or in the seven Basque provinces.

3) Absence of monolingual speakers: As a result of the evolution of the public sphere along the second half of the 20th century, nowadays we can hardly find monolingual speakers of Basque or Irish. This means that, in a few years, all people belonging to the linguistic minority will be at least bilingual, having a good command of the majority language, making easier the communication with non-speakers of Basque or Irish. This factor also makes the using of minority language less important as a tool of communication, since it is always possible to use the majority language in all kind of groups.

4) Medium-size minority languages: Although Irish Gaelic enjoys of a greater number of speakers than Basque, both languages can be considered as medium-size minority languages within the European framework. This makes a difference with the big minority languages with a large number of speakers (e.g. Catalan, Russian outside the Russian Federation ...), but also with the European linguistic minorities numbering only a few thousands, even hundreds of speakers (e.g. Scottish Gaelic, Ladin, Sorbian, Sater Frisian ...). If we attend to L1 speakers, however, Irish should probably be considered within this latter category.

5) Limited social use of the language: It looks that similar problems arise when considering the social scopes where Irish and Basque are frequently used. Both languages tend to be more used within the familiar and informal relations' environments and for primary education. Access to business and legal worlds seems to be particularly difficult for these minority languages, which are present in a limited scale, in the cultural field.

b) Political factors

6) Politically divided languages: Both Irish and Basque are minority languages within the territory of two different sovereign states. This implies that there is an international border dividing the traditional territory where these languages have been used for centuries. As a consequence of this, we find different legal

status of the same language within the different states and, for the case of Basque, also within the same state. This factor is also important because it makes more difficult the unity of the linguistic community and a normal development of the language.

7) Languages within a conflictive scope: Both Irish and Basque have traditionally lived in a conflictive political framework, at least since the 19th century. Nowadays, for the case of Irish, the conflict can be reduced to the northern part of the island, while in the Basque case, the conflict arises mainly in the southern part of the territory. In any case, the conflictive situation conditions to a considerable extent the social and political positions on the linguistic issue as well as the development of the language itself.

8) Language as an important element of national identity: Languages normally play a very important role in the construction of a national identity. For nations not owing a state, the language remains as one of the most important values of the national community. This was the case of Irish for a long time (although it must be said that religious affiliation also played a significant role), and it is still the case of the Basque language and maybe also of Irish for Northern Ireland. Also due to this political factor, in both cases the identification of the native population with the minority language is by far larger than the real number of speakers, since the maintenance of the language is regarded as one of the key factors for the surviving of the national identity.

9) Languages suffering from the lack of social and political prestige: For many centuries, and as it has happened with many minority languages all over Europe, Irish and Basque were languages without a social and political prestige. Even their own speakers largely considered the use of these languages as a sign of underdevelopment and of lack of culture. Social promotion required a good knowledge of the majority language, when not forgetting about the local one. This tend has been stopped within the last decades, but not in all the areas in which Irish or Basque are used.

10) Existence of self-government powers to endeavour the languages: Nowadays, in both cases exists an institutional framework allowing a certain extent of self-government that can be used for the protection of the minority language. This is clearer in the case of the Republic of Ireland, since it is an independent state with full power to enact and put into practice any kind of legal and political decision on this side. For Northern Ireland, the self-government can be considered as extremely limited. In the Basque case, the political power corresponds to the Basque Autonomous Community and to the Community of Navarra. Certainly, it is not the case for the Northern Basque Country.

11) Positive attitude of the population in respect to linguistic policy: Political surveys made in the Republic of Ireland and in the Basque Autonomous Community show similar results on the popular support for an active linguistic policy. It looks that positive attitudes in the Basque Country are higher than in Ireland, but on the other hand, resistance by some political sector is probably also stronger. In both cases, it seems to be a general support (around 70 per cent of the population of the Republic and the BAC) for a broad framework of measures to be taken by public bodies to endeavour the respective language.

12) Political debate concerning discrimination on the linguistic policy: Although there is a general support for an active linguistic policy in both the Republic and the BAC, it is also true that there is political debate on this policy. This debate deals normally with two different elements: the high cost of the linguistic policy and the possible discrimination suffered by the majority group, in particular at the moment of acceding to positions in the public sector.

c) Legal status

13) Official languages within a limited area: Both Irish and Basque enjoy the legal status of official languages in a given territory. For Irish, this would be the Republic of Ireland and for Basque the BAC and in theory the Northern region of Navarra. Therefore, both languages share also a non-official status in some areas as Northern Ireland,[23] Northern Basque Country and most of Navarra. Irish and Basque are also similar in the fact that their official status is shared with the majority language of the state (although in the case of Irish there is a formal recognition of being the first official language).

14) Languages protected by the European Charter: Both Irish and Basque are today minority languages protected under Part III of the *European Charter for Regional or Minority Languages*, sponsored by the Council of Europe. The protection covers the Irish language in Northern Ireland, but not in the Republic yet. For Basque, the Charter is applied within the Spanish State, but not in the territory under French sovereignty.

15) Existence of Statutory law by consensus: After the approval of the Official Languages Act, both Irish and Basque enjoy protection by an statutory law adopted by political consensus within their respective parliaments. As it happens with the official status, this is valid for the Republic and for the BAC.

16) Statutory law affecting only to public sector: These Acts of protection and promotion of Basque and Irish adopted in the BAC and the Republic have to do mainly with the public bodies, while for the private sector they hardly envisage any sort of obligation.

3.2 Basque and Irish: Differences

a) Sociolinguistic elements

1) Linguistic affiliation: While Irish Gaelic belongs to the Celtic group of language of the Indo-European languages, Basque has no linguistic affiliation with any other language. In this sense, Scottish Gaelic and Manx can be considered as close languages to Irish, whereas there is no language that can be related to Basque.

---

[23] Although in this case, the legal status of Irish Gaelic remains uncertain, due to its formal recognition through the Good Friday Agreement and the European Charter. Indeed, for the UK (apart for Wales) it is very difficult to talk in legal terms about official status of any language, although de facto English is clearly an official language for the whole country. In any case, we consider that Irish Gaelic cannot be considered as official language in Northern Ireland, even if it enjoys some level of protection from the legal framework on force.

2) Amount of native speakers: The number of native speakers of Irish Gaelic is rather low in comparison with that of Basque. On the contrary, there is a much larger community of Irish as second language than that of Basque.

3) Geographical domain or predominance: Irish Gaelic is the predominant language for a very small and scattered territory in the western coast of Ireland. Basque, however, remains widely spoken in a much wider area, comprising many medium-size towns and villages. Although the Basque-phone territory is a continuum, direct communication by land between southern and northern sides of the Pyrenees is not easy.

4) Social use of the language: Due also to its predominance in a wider zone and to the larger number of speakers, Basque seems to be more frequently used and alive in different domains within these territories, than Irish in general.

b) Political factors

5) Independent political framework: While Irish Gaelic happens to be the first official language of an independent state, Basque-speaking community has no kin-state. The existence of a Basque Autonomous Community with wide powers for self-government cannot in any case be compared with the symbolic and political value of an independent state. Politically, this factor is also of a great importance in respect to the position of the speaking community who lives outside the respective framework. While Northern Ireland can enjoy the fact that Irish is the official language of a neighbour European state, the Northern Basque Country has little to win with the official condition of the Basque language within the BAC. The international effect of such a factor is also to be considered.

6) Political attitudes towards the language: The bitter struggle that is currently lived in the Basque Country affects very much the political attitudes in respect to the local language. Whereas in the Republic, all political sectors (albeit some slight differences could also be noted) can consider Irish language as an important element of national heritage, in the Basque case, there is a very different perception of the language according to the origin or political affiliation of the population. This reality, which extends also to Navarra, could perhaps be compared with that of Northern Ireland.

7) Attitude of the Catholic Church regarding to the minority language: Analysing the historical development of both peoples it seems to be a significant difference in the attitude that the Catholic Church has traditionally adopted towards the respective minority language. While in the case of Basque, for many decades local Church has been largely involved in the struggle for the maintenance of the national language, in Ireland most of the religious services were given through the majority language.

c) Legal Status

8) State language status: Being Irish Gaelic official language of an independent state has also some effects at the international level. In this sense, Irish is one of the "treaty-languages" of the European Union, although not at the same practical level of the other state languages. Basque, however, cannot enjoy the same international recognition since it is not the official language of an independent state, but only a regional language, with official status in one part of the state territory.

9) First official language: Irish Gaelic is not only official language of an independent state for the whole territory, but also first official language and national language, according to the *Irish Constitution*. On the contrary, Basque is proclaimed official only for the BAC and Northern part of Navarra. Basque is considered to be the "own language" of the BAC, having this recognition no legal effects. For Navarra, both Basque and Spanish are considered as "own languages" of the region. Official status of Basque in any case can be considered of a superior condition than that of the state language. Even more, any contradiction of interpretation of legal norms, must be resolved in favour of Spanish, unlike in the Irish case.

10) Ombudsman for language: Irish legislation for languages foresees the existence of a specific ombudsman to deal with language complaints. In the Basque Country, there is no institution that could be considered as parallel to this one, apart from the general ombudsman, who should play this role among others. The Basque Act on language creates an Advisory Council of the language, but with very limited powers.

11) Approach of the respective statutory act: Although the contents of both regulations are not so different in practice, the way of approaching to language encouragement is unlike. The Act on normalisation of the Basque language is based on the description of linguistic rights of the citizens. On the contrary, the Irish official Languages Act is drafted from the perspective of the obligations and commitments that have to be fulfilled by the public bodies.

4. Conclusions

Ireland and the Basque Country share a tradition of linguistic diversity that over the centuries has reduced their respective national languages to a minority position. Political and social factors arise in a parallel way for many aspects in both countries. Parallel trends can also be identified in respect to the evolution of the knowledge and social use of both minority languages. Although Basque has a greater amount of L1 speakers in comparison with Irish Gaelic, the current linguistic landscape in most of the Basque Country can be considered as similar to that of Ireland. In particular, looking to the social attitudes and political powers acting in favour of the minority language, situations in the Republic of Ireland and in the Basque Autonomous Community show a significant degree of similarity.

Having more L1 speakers and a wider geographical area where the native language is predominant, Basque language authorities must try to stop the process of loosing the language via intergenerational transmission and protecting the Basque-speaking environments from the input of the state language. For both cases, Basque and Irish, the most important challenge nowadays would be to encourage the social use of the minority language among L2 speakers, providing them the necessary opportunities to get involved in a Basque/Irish linguistic environment. This must be tried not only for the traditional fields of social and familiar relations but also in respect to other aspects of every day's life.

In this sense, legal frameworks play a role. The different perspectives for future that we can appreciate in the case of the Basque language according to the institutional framework applied help to prove this influence of the legal system in protecting a language. However, we cannot underestimate the strength of the social pressure and political consciousness. When analysing the evolution of a given minority language during a certain period, it is not easy at all to identify the impact of the legislation in force and the influence of the citizens' attitudes. In conclusion, both elements have to play at the same time if we want to create positive results. Isolated legal actions or social activity within a restrictive legal framework can do very little to shift or even slow down negative linguistic evolution. This can be proved when comparing the different legal systems and political environments that affect today the Basque language.

In any case, for minority languages as Irish Gaelic and Basque, the future remains uncertain. The large strength of the neighbour languages (English, French and Spanish) does not help the revival of these two small languages. Apart from positive measures and policies adopted both at institutional and social levels within their respective countries, the protection and promotion of minority languages of Europe requires also a different attitude from the rest of the population, mainly from the speakers of majority languages. Linguistic rights must be regarded as fundamental human rights of the people and linguistic promotion policies as a necessary step to ensure the cultural heritage of our continent. In order to achieve this aim, it is necessary to formulate and socialise a theoretical framework on human rights, including those related to linguistic and cultural issues. Thus, protection of linguistic and cultural minorities must be seen as a progressive goal at the same level as today's European societies regard other aspects in social policy. Linguistic rights of people belonging to minorities must be recognised as a central part of the human rights ideology and a necessary element to safeguard the linguistic heritage and richness of Europe.

5. References

Abalain, H. 1989. *Destin des langues celtiques.* Paris: Ophrys

Barandiaran, A. *et alia* 2002. *La situación jurídica del euskera en Navarra.* Pamplona: Euskara Kultur Elkargoa

Basque Government 1995. La continuité de la langue basque. Vitoria-Gasteiz: Basque Government

Cobreros Mendazona, E. ed. 1990. *Jornadas sobre el régimen jurídico del euskera.* Oñati: Basque Institute for Public Administration

Cobreros Mendazona, E. ed. 1989. *El régimen jurídico de la oficialidad del euskera.* Oñati: Basque Institute for Public Administration

De Varennes, F. 1996. *Language, Minorities and Human Rights.* The Hague: Martinus Nijhoff

Dunbar, R. 2003. *La ratificació de la Carta Europea de les Llengües Regionals o Minoritàries per part del Regne Unit.* Barcelona: Mercator-Ciemen

Fossas, E. 1999. *Asymmetry and Plurinationality in Spain.* Barcelona: Institut de Ciències Polítiques i Socials

Intxausti, J. 1989. *Euskara Nafarroan.* Pamplona: Government of Navarra

Intxausti, J. 1990. *Euskara: euskaldunon hizkuntza.* Vitoria-Gasteiz: Basque Government

Jackson, H. and A. McHardy 1995. *The Two Irelands: The Problem of the Double Minority.* 3rd ed., London: Minority Rights Group International

Kirk, J.M. and D.P. Ó Baoill eds. 2000. *Language and Politics. Northern Ireland, the Republic of Ireland, and Scotland.* Belfast: Cló Ollscoil na Branríona

Kirk, J.M. and D.P. Ó Baoill eds. 2001. *Linguistic Politics. Language Policies for Northern Ireland, the Republic of Ireland, and Scotland.* Belfast: Cló Ollscoil na Branríona

Kirk, J.M. and D.P. Ó Baoill eds. 2002. *Language Planning and Education: Linguistic Issues in Northern Ireland, the Republic of Ireland, and Scotland.* Belfast: Cló Ollscoil na Branríona

Letamendia, F. 1995. "Basque Nationalism and the Struggle for Self-Determination in the Basque Country". In Berberoglu, B. ed. *The National Question. Nationalism, Ethnic Conflict and Self-Determination in the 20th Century.* Philadelphia: Temple University Press

Orpustan, J.B. 1994. *La langue Basque parmi les autres. Influences et comparaisons.* Baigorri: Éditions Izpegi

Packer, J. ed. 1999. "Special Issue on the Linguistic Rights of National Minorities". *International Journal on Minority and Group Rights,* vol 6, no 3.

Petschen Verdaguer, S. 1989. *Las minorías lingüísticas de Europa Occidental: documentos (1492-1989).* Vitoria-Gastiez: Basque Parliament

Ruiz Vieytez, E.J. 1999. *The History of Legal Protection of Minorities in Europe (XVIIth-XIXth Centuries).* Derby: Univeristy of Derby

Ruiz Vieytez, E.J. 2002. "Estudio comparado de otros conflictos nacionales". In Etxeberria , X. et alia. *Derecho de autodeterminación y realidad vasca.* Vitoria-Gasteiz: Basque Government

Ryan, S. 1999. "The Northern Ireland case: intercomunal Talks and the re-negotiation of identity". In Turton, T. and J. Gonzalez. *Cultural Identities and Ethnic Minorities in Europe,* Bilbao: University of Deusto

Sellier, J. and A. Sellier, A. 1995. *Atlas des peuples d'Europe occidentale.* Paris: La Découverte

Wilson, R. *et alia* 1999. *No Frontiers. North-South Integration in Ireland* Belfast: Democratic Dialogue

WebPages on the situation of the Basque language:

- Basque Government: www.euskadi.net/euskara
- Ethnologue: www.ethnologue.com/show_language.asp?code=BSQ
- Jaques Leclerc: www.tlfq.ulaval.ca/axl/europe/espagnebasque.htm
- "Behatokia" (Basque Observatory of Linguistic Rights): www.beatokia.org
- "Kontseilua" (The Council of Social Organizations in favour of the Basque •
- Language): www.kontseilua.org
- "Berria"(current Basque daily newspaper): www.bcrria.info
- "Euskaldunon Egunkaria" (former Basque newspaper): www.aurrera.net/Egunkaria/en
- "Argia"(Basque magazin): www.argia.com
- "EITB - Euskal Irrati Telebista" (Basque Public Broadcasting Body): www.eitb.com

Les Langues Moins Répandues l'Exemple du Wallon et du Scots

Jean-Luc Fauconnier

Je tiens à préciser que je m'exprime en mon nom personnel et que je ne suis donc pas ici en tant que porte-parole des instances où j'exerce une fonction. En outre, je ne suis certes pas un spécialiste du scots aussi me contenterai-je ici d'évoquer la problématique des langues collatérales dont le *scots* et le wallon font partie.

Une problématique dont on se soucie depuis peu

La problématique des langues moins répandues est complexe et constitue un vaste sujet qui, pourtant, n'a intéressé les politiques que depuis quelques décennies seulement. C'est qu'autrefois, dans la plupart des grands pays européens, on avait tendance à n'envisager que la notion de langue nationale: en Allemagne, on parle l'allemand, en France, on parle le français. Certes on savait qu'il y avait des nations bilingues et que les accidents de l'histoire pouvaient laisser hors des frontières des locuteurs de la langue nationale, locuteurs que l'on considérait comme de pauvres concitoyens perdus en terre étrangère. La superposition entre langue et nationalité est d'ailleurs à l'origine de quelques conflits marquants; si cette volonté de coïncidence ne fut pas toujours la cause réelle de ces conflits, elle en fut souvent le prétexte. La mise en examen des impérialismes linguistiques constitue d'ailleurs une des tâches de l'Union européenne, du Conseil de l'Europe et de l'UNESCO.

Langues régionales et/ou minoritaires : un projet de typologie

Lorsqu'on examine les différents parlers qui ne correspondent pas à la belle superposition langue / état-nation, on constate que l'on peut les regrouper en trois catégories:

a. Langue d'un état-nation utilisée par une minorité de locuteurs dans un autre état-nation.
Ceci est un cas très fréquent en Europe et ne résulte pas de phénomènes migratoires mais plutôt de circonstances historiques et géographiques. C'est le cas des minorités de langue allemande en Belgique, au Danemark, en France ou en Italie; des minorités de langue suédoise en Finlande; des minorités de langue slovène en Italie ou en Autriche.

Généralement, ces minorités sont bien protégées et reçoivent souvent un double appui: celui de l'état-nation où leur langue est majoritaire et celui de l'état nation où elle est minoritaire mais où, par souci démocratique, on leur veut le plus grand bien. Il est certain que plus l'état-nation du premier type est puissant, plus l'état-nation du second type aura tendance à respecter ces minorités.

Ceci mène parfois à de subtils « marchandages » comme ce fut le cas pour la protection des minorités Danophones d'Allemagne qui fut négociée parallèlement avec celle des minorités germanophones du Danemark. On pourrait évoquer des phénomènes similaires entre la Finlande et la Suède ou entre la Grèce et la Turquie

Il faut aussi évoquer un autre problème: celui de la langue réellement pratiquée. Les Germanophones du Tyrol italien parlent-ils le *Hochdeutsch* ou une variété d'alémanique? Les Valdôtains parlent-ils français ou franco-provençal? Les Alsaciens parlent-ils l'allemand ou une variété de francique ou d'alémanique? Les Néerlandophones du *Westhoek* français usent-ils du flamand occidental ou du néerlandais?   Là encore, se profilent des tendances à une certaine forme d'impérialisme linguistique.

b. Langue non apparentée linguistiquement à une langue d'un état-nation

C'est bien sûr le cas du basque, des langues du groupe rhéto-roman, de la plupart des langues celtiques, du sarde, du frison, du catalan ou encore de l'occitan.

On se trouve là devant des situations très diverses. Le catalan peut-il être considéré comme une langue minoritaire; il n'est pas le vecteur d'un état-nation certes, mais il compte plus de locuteurs que le danois et bénéficie du support inconditionnel d'une puissante instance régionale.

En revanche, que dire du cornique et de ses quelques centaines de locuteurs ou du *sami* qui est pratiqué par une population peu nombreuse et qui, de plus, vit sur d'immenses territoires répartis sur quatre pays.

On pourrait, en outre, inclure dans cette catégorie les langues qui ne relèvent d'aucune structure territoriale: le yiddish, le judéo-espagnol ou encore les différentes langues des "gens du voyage" (Roms, Tziganes, Gitans ...).

c. Langue apparentée linguistiquement à une langue d'un état-nation ou langue collatérale

Nous avons affaire ici à un groupe qui pose tout autant de problèmes que le précédent; les difficultés qui proviennent de l'étiquette qui leur est accolée: *langue* ou *dialecte*. Nous évoquerons ce problème dans quelques instants.

C'est le cas du picard, du normand, du poitevin-saintongeais, du wallon face à la langue soeur, le français; du *scots* face à l'anglais, du bas-saxon face à l'allemand, de l'asturien et de l'aragonais face à l'espagnol ou encore du sicilien, du piémontais ou du vénitien face à l'italien. Leur aspect collatéral a souvent eu pour conséquence qu'on les a assimilés à de simples modalités locales ou régionales de la langue de l'état-nation; ceci eut des conséquences dommageables pour leur statut tant au plan national qu'international.

Une question de vocabulaire : langue collatérale / dialecte

Au départ, ce sont les linguistes qui se sont intéressés à des parlers collatéraux; bien souvent, on les dépréciait en les affublant de dénominations connotées péjorativement: *patois, jargon, dialecte* ... Il faudra attendre la fin du 19e siècle pour que le grand public s'y intéresse.

Sans entrer dans un exposé sémantique, on peut pourtant évoquer rapidement le cas du terme *dialecte* dont la polysémie est particulièrement remarquable et a engendré des discussions souvent fort dommageables; il nous paraît donc utile d'apporter ici quelques précisions lexicales.

Au sens général, qui est d'ailleurs utilisé par la linguistique anglo-saxonne, un *dialecte* est une diversification géographique d'une langue: le français de Liège, l'anglais de Liverpool, l'espagnol du Chili ou l'italien de Rome; il s'agit du *régiolecte* des linguistes. Il arrive que l'on envisage aussi une diversification sociale complémentaire: l'anglais des Américains d'origine africaine (*Black English*), le français des Halles de Paris, etc.; c'est là le *sociolecte* dans le jargon de la linguistique. En France pour ce qui concerne ce sens de dialecte, on se sert souvent de l'adjectif « régional » (le français régional du Québec, le français régional de Belgique ...).

On constatera que l'on peut baptiser « dialecte » bon nombre de parlers; néanmoins le terme sert surtout à désigner des idiomes locaux, d'usage avant tout oral et constituant une variante de la langue officielle d'une nation, mais ce n'est certainement pas le cas du wallon et du *scots*..

Si nous retenons la formulation utilisée par certains: « *Le wallon, dialecte français de Belgique* », nous risquons de confondre la langue wallonne avec une variété régionale du français utilisé en Wallonie (comme le français régional de Liège) et non comme un idiome qui résulte d'une diversification très ancienne du latin parlé à partir de l'ère chrétienne dans ce qui deviendra la Wallonie.

On pourrait tenir exactement le même discours à propos du *scots* et le considérer erronément comme une variété régionale de l'anglais et non comme une langue endogène qui s'est développée spécifiquement à partir d'une source germanique qui est probablement aussi celle de l'anglais.

Ceci a donc mené bon nombre de spécialistes de ces parlers collatéraux à bannir ce terme au profit de l'appellation « langue régionale endogène ».

Une question de vocabulaire qui a des conséquences importantes

Le rapport *Euromosaïc* qui a été subsidié par la Commission européenne et qui a pour but de décrire la mosaïque de langues régionales de l'Europe a exclu, ce n'est qu'un exemple, le wallon de son champ d'étude, considérant que ce n'était pas une langue régionale mais un dialecte.

Ceci est en parfaite contradiction avec les éléments envisagés ci-dessus, avec le sentiment des locuteurs et avec le décret de la Communauté Wallonie-Bruxelles (voir annexes) qui considère le wallon comme une langue coofficielle avec le français. Ceci a des conséquences immédiates sur le statut du wallon au niveau des instances européennes et entre en contradiction avec la Charte européenne pour les Langues régionales ou minoritaires qui n'inclut pas les dialectes – pas plus que les langues des migrants – dans son champ d'application mais laisse aux états membres le soin de décider ce qu'est une langue et un dialecte; je cite:

> « La Charte ne concerne pas les variations locales ou les différents dialectes d'une même langue. Toutefois, elle ne se prononce pas sur le point souvent controversé de savoir à partir de quand les différences d'expression sont telles qu'elles constituent des langues distinctes. Cette question dépend, non seulement de considérations proprement linguistiques, mais aussi de phénomènes psychosociologiques et politiques qui peuvent aboutir, dans chaque cas, à donner une réponse différente. C'est donc au sein de chaque État, dans le cadre des processus démocratiques qui lui sont propres, qu'il reviendra aux autorités concernées de préciser à partir de quand une forme d'expression constitue une langue distincte. »

Le Bureau européen pour les Langues moins répandues (BELMR) a toujours eu, en la matière, une attitude plus démocratique et ceci grâce à celui qui en fut son secrétaire général, mon ami, Donall Ó Riagáin que je remercie publiquement pour la circonstance: ce sont les locuteurs, avant tout, qui décident si leur parler régional doit être perçu ou non comme une langue. Outre cette volonté des locuteurs, le BELMR a pris en compte une série de critères objectifs qui permettent considérer un idiome comme une langue régionale; ces derniers sont les suivants:

- l'existence d'ouvrages lexicographiques et grammaticaux,
- l'existence d'une transcription standardisée,
- l'existence d'un enseignement relatif à l'idiome,
- l'existence d'un enseignement dans cet idiome,
- l'existence de moyens de diffusion (édition, radio, T.V.) et
- l'existence de productions littéraires (poésie, prose, théâtre, chanson).

Il est évident que bon nombre de langues collatérales correspondent à ces critères et, bien sûr, le wallon et le *scots*.

La régionalisation, un espoir pour les langues régionales?

On pourrait considérer que la problématique de la défense et de la promotion des langues régionales et plus particulièrement celle des langues collatérales, passe par l'émergence du pouvoir régionaux. Ce sont en effet, les régions et les autorités locales qui sont les niveaux de pouvoir qui sont les mieux à même d'appréhender cette problématique en raison des facteurs de proximité essentiels en une telle situation.

Il serait pourtant ridicule de faire preuve d'angélisme en la matière en considérant que ces pouvoirs régionaux ou locaux ont toutes les qualités requises en la matière et il conviendrait donc que cette émergence se double d'une intervention des instances internationales pour ce qui concerne bon nombre de langues régionales transfrontalières – elles sont très nombreuses – qui devraient bénéficier de mesures de protection et de promotion harmonisées et cohérentes. On pourrait envisager que ces instances internationales agissent directement avec les régions concernées ; il s'agit là d'un problème important mais nous ne l'aborderons pas ici.

On peut trouver de nombreux exemples de cet aspect transfrontalier:
1. dans le domaine roman, pour les langues d'oïl (France, Belgique, Suisse, Royaume-Uni, Luxembourg, Canada, USA), l'occitan (France, Espagne, Italie), le franco-provençal (France, Italie, Suisse), le rhéto-roman (Suisse, Italie), le catalan (Espagne, France, Italie), et l'aroumain (Albanie, Bulgarie, Croatie, Grèce, Macédoine).
2. dans le domaine germanique, pour le *scots* en Grande-Bretagne et en Irlande, le frison (Pays-Bas, Allemagne, Danemark), et le francique (Allemagne, Luxembourg, France, Belgique), etc.

Le francique constitue d'ailleurs un cas typique de dysharmonie. En effet, le francique, parlé dans quelques villages du nord-est de la Wallonie, est considéré comme une langue régionale endogène; en Communauté flamande où il est largement pratiqué (dans le Limbourg belge), on n'envisage en aucun cas son sort: c'est un dialecte (du néerlandais ou de l'allemand?). En revanche, les Pays-Bas ont inscrit la variété de francique utilisée dans leur province du Limbourg dans leur instrument de ratification de la Charte européenne des Langues régionales ou minoritaires.

Cette attitude de la Communauté flamande a des répercussions fâcheuses pour la signature – et la ratification conséquente – par la Belgique de la Charte européenne des Langues régionales ou minoritaires. En effet, cette Communauté ne manifeste guère d'enthousiasme pour cette signature même si dans l'instrument de ratification belge, on n'envisage que les langues régionales endogènes reconnues par la Communauté Wallonie-Bruxelles. Cette « histoire belge » qui repose sur deux perceptions différentes du concept d'idiome régional dure depuis 1992 et peine bien sûr tous ceux qui militent pour cette signature. Dois-je ajouter que ces derniers sont très heureux que *scots* figure dans l'instrument de ratification britannique de ce document européen?

Cette harmonisation pourrait passer par des accords bilatéraux entre les Régions ou entre les États – ce qui est le cas pour le *scots*, un cas malheureusement trop rare – mais il me semble que ce sont les instances internationales qui pourraient plus efficacement favoriser cette harmonisation. Je pense plus particulièrement à une action en ce sens du Comité des Régions.

Conclusion

Rien ne remplace la motivation et la volonté des locuteurs des langues régionales, motivation et volonté qui ne manqueront pas de trouver un écho auprès des décideurs. Mais il faut se rappeler que les défenseurs des langues régionales sont, pour la plupart, des pacifistes et surtout des idéalistes qui ne peuvent guère compter, en dehors de certaines périodes électorales, sur l'appui des appareils politiques ou syndicaux; ils ne constituent pas un poids économique important et ils développent souvent une argumentation plus passionnelle que rationnelle. Enfin, aux yeux de certains, ils semblent aller à contre-courant du processus de développement socio-économique contemporain.

Prêcher pour la diversité culturelle et linguistique dans un monde dominé par la « pensée unique » n'est pas chose facile. Et pourtant, permettre à un locuteur de se servir de la langue de son choix et de veiller à sa transmission, est-ce si difficile à admettre si l'on se veut démocrate?

Mais pour s'inscrire dans une prospective optimiste, j'affirmerai qu'il y a à peine dix ans d'ici, il aurait été difficilement imaginable qu'un Wallon vienne ici à Belfast, dans la plus franche connivence, évoquer les problèmes communs au *scots* et au wallon, les solutions qu'ont leur a données et les mesures qui restent à entreprendre. Je vous remercie chaleureusement de m'avoir donné l'occasion de le faire et d'avoir pu témoigner qu'au-delà des frontières, nous menons le même combat pour notre dignité et les vraies valeurs humanistes.

Bibliographie

Baggioni, Daniel, *Langues et nations en Europe*, Paris, Payot, 1997.

Bal, Willy, 'A propos de "langues régionales". Notice terminologique.' dans *èl bourdon*. 454.

Giordan, Henri, (sous la direction de -), *Les Minorités en Europe. Droits linguistiques et droits de l'homme*, Paris, Kimé, 1992.

Goetschy, Henri et André-Louis SANGUIN (sous la direction de), *Langues régionales et relations transfrontalières en Europe*, Paris, L'Harmattan, 1995.
Siguan, Miguel, *L'Europe des Langues*, Sprimont, Mardaga, 1996.

Annexes

1. Décret relatif aux langues régionales endogènes de la Communauté française (24 décembre 1990)

Le Conseil de la Communauté française a adopté et Nous, Exécutif, sanctionnons ce qui suit :
Article 1er La Communauté française de Belgique reconnaît en son sein la spécificité linguistique et culturelle de ceux qui usent à la fois d'une langue régionale endogène et du français, langue officielle de la Communauté.
Article 2. Les langues régionales endogènes font partie du patrimoine culturel de la Communauté ; cette dernière a donc le devoir de les préserver, d'en favoriser l'étude scientifique et l'usage, soit comme outil de communication, soit comme moyen d'expression.
Article 3. L'Exécutif de la Communauté française confiera la tâche d'étudier et de proposer toutes les mesures aptes à préserver et à favoriser ces langues régionales endogènes aux organismes consultatifs dont il reconnaît la compétence."

2. Liste des paragraphes ou alinéas choisis par la Communauté française Wallonie-Bruxelles pour figurer dans l'instrument de ratification belge de la Charte

- 10 paragraphes ou alinéas (3 obligations) dans l'article 8 (Enseignement): **1 a iii, 1 a iv, 1 b iv, 1 c iv, 1 d iv, 1 e ii, f ii, 1 g, 1 h et 1 i** ,
- 2 paragraphes ou alinéas (1 obligation) dans l'article 9 (Justice): **1 a ii. et 1 b ii,**
- 6 paragraphes ou alinéas choisis (1 obligation) dans l'article 10 (Autorités administratives et Services publics): **1 a iv, 2 b, 2 e, 2 f, 3 c et 4 c,**
- 9 paragraphes ou alinéas (1 obligation) dans l'article 11 (Médias) : **1 a iii, 1 b, 1 c ii, 1 d, 1 e ii, 1 f ii, 1 g, 2, et 3,**
- 7 paragraphes ou alinéas (3 obligations) dans l'article 12 (Activités et équipements culturels): **1 a, 1 b, 1 c, 1 d, 1 f, 1 g et 1 h,**
- 2 paragraphes ou alinéas (1 obligation) dans l'article 13 (Vie économique et sociale) **2 b et 2 c**, et
- 2 paragraphes ou alinéas (pas d'obligation) dans l'article 14 (Échanges interfrontaliers): **a. et b.**

soit un total de **38 paragraphes ou alinéas (35 obligations)**.

3. Répartition géographique des langues régionales endogènes de la Communauté Wallonie-Bruxelles à joindre à l'instrument de ratification belge de la Charte

Cette répartition se cantonne aux municipalités résultant de la loi de fusion de 1976 et ne prend en compte une section de commune que pour le champenois.

1. langues romanes

champenois: Sugny (Vresse-sur-Semois)
lorrain: arrondissement de Virton
picard: arrondissement d'Ath, arrondissement de Mons, arrondissement de Mouscron, arrondissement de Soignies (excepté Écaussines), arrondissement de Thuin (excepté Anderlues, Froidchapelle, Gozée, Lobbes, Ham-sur-Heure / Nalinnes, Thuin) arrondissement de Tournai, Rebecq
wallon: province du Brabant wallon (excepté Rebecq), province de Luxembourg (excepté les arrondissements d'Arlon et de Virton) province de Namur (excepté Sugny), province de Liège (y compris Malmedy et excepté les municipalités de la Communauté germanophone), arrondissement de Charleroi, Anderlues, Écaussines, Froidchapelle, Gozée, Lobbes, Ham-sur-Heure / Nalinnes, Thuin

2. langue germanique

francique mosellan (luxembourgeois): arrondissement d'Arlon

francique rhénan: Malmedy et Montzen

Walloon and Scots: A Response to Jean-Luc Fauconnier

Dónall Ó Riagáin

The paper we heard from Jean-Luc Fauconnier was indeed very interesting and all the more so when we consider that the speaker has a long track record in language promotion as one of the authors of the *European Charter for Regional or Minority Languages* and later a member (and currently Vice-President) of the European Bureau for Lesser Used Languages.

Some time ago, Ian Parsley and I discussed a suitable term to denote that category of languages described by Jean-Luc Fauconnier. We agreed on the term *hidden languages* as a working title. I subsequently thought of the term *eclipsed languages*. In his presentation, M. Fauconnier has offered us yet another term – *collateral languages*. The word *collateral* sometimes sends a shiver down my spine. When the Americans bomb a hospital or a school, instead of a military target, they describe the destruction caused as 'collateral damage'. On reflection, perhaps the term 'collateral' is not all that inappropriate. Perhaps major languages damage those languages which close to them, not always intentionally, but because of their linguistic proximity.

We all agree that language is a medium of communication. But it is a lot more than that. It is a tool, finely honed over generations, for expressing and recording the ideas, experiences, reflections and emotions of a people. It is a repository in which their genius, their finest feelings, their sadness, their joy and their hopes are stored, not just for one generation but for posterity. Each language offers humankind a unique window on the world. It is no wonder that language acquires enormous symbolic importance.

Languages that can be described as being 'collateral' are no less important in this regard than languages that are decidedly unique. Language distance is an important factor but it is by no means the sole or most important factor. A Walloon-speaking farmer or a Picard-speaking miner looks through a very different window on the world than that of a factory worker in Paris or that of an EU official in Brussels. Likewise a Scots-speaking fisherman from the Ards peninsula or a small shopkeeper from Raphoe will view the world in a different way from a financier in London or a business executive in Birmingham.

I would like to reflect briefly on two aspects of Walloon vis-à-vis Scots in Ulster – that of legal recognition and domain strategy.

Official recognition for Walloon and the other *langues régionales* in the South of Belgium is in the form of a Decree[1] issued in 1990 by the Communauté française in Belgium. Belgium has not signed or ratified the *European Charter for Regional or Minority Languages*.

Recognition for Ulster-Scots came in the *Belfast / Good Friday Agreement* of 1998 and in the UK instrument of ratification of the *European Charter for Regional or Minority Languages* when Part II cover was extended to Scots, including Ulster-Scots.

---

[1] Décret relatif aux langues régionales endogènes de la Communauté française, 24 décembre 1990.

On the question of domain strategy, speakers of the regional languages in Belgium appear to focus their energies on securing a place for their languages in certain domains rather than in all – a modest foothold in the education system and a very definite place in the field of cultural activity.[2] Walloon has a rich tradition of popular theatre and of poetry – a tradition which seems to be flourishing.[3] I have found little evidence of efforts to establish the regional languages in the domains of law, public administration or economic life.

I hope my Ulster-Scots friends will forgive me for saying that it is not yet clear what their priorities are. I hope that the proposed Ulster-Scots Academy will address this issue.

Finally, I suggest that there is a need for a European conference on 'collateral languages'. This conference would cover languages such as Scots, including Ulster-Scots, the *langues d'oïl* in France, the Limbourg language in the Netherlands, Low German, Asturiano and Aragonese in Spain, Scanian in Sweden as well as Piemontese and other eclipsed varieties in Italy. The participants could share information and expertise and hopefully consider a joint strategy to have their voices heard in European institutions. Perhaps the Ulster-Scots community might take the initiative.

---

[2] Michel Francard, *Langues d'Oïl en Wallonie*. Bruxelles, 2000.
[3] Jean-Luc Fauconnier, 'Du Côté des Groupements Littéraires Wallons', in *La Revue Générale*, numéro 5, 1998.

The Walloon–Scots Comparison: Are There Further Parallels with Other *Langues d'Oïl*?

Janice Carruthers

1. Definitional issues

Any attempt to respond to the question posed in the title faces immediately major definitional issues, specifically as regards the notion of 'regional language' as opposed to 'dialect'. As Fauconnier (this volume) points out, the *European Charter for Regional or Minority Languages* considers regional varieties of a given language as 'dialects' ("les variations locales ou les différents dialectes d'une même langue"). Thus, to take the case of French, use of regional lexical items, use of syntactic structures such as the *passé surcomposé*, or neutralisation of phonological oppositions such as [a] and [ɑ] (*patte* vs *pâte*) or [ɛ̃] and [œ̃] (*brin* vs *brun*) would be considered elements of the dialect of particular areas, dialects where the vast bulk of the linguistic characteristics are shared with other dialects of French. The term 'regional language' is more controversial, not least because in addition to linguistic characteristics (at a phonological, morpho-syntactic and lexical level), the Charter provides for speakers and government bodies to have a role in defining what constitutes the psychological and sociological reality of a regional language.

This terminology, while relatively clear in itself, is at odds with most of the literature on the subject in French, where the term 'français régional' is used for what the Charter terms 'dialect'.[1] On the other hand, the term 'dialect' in the literature refers to a linguistic 'level' which is comparable to regional languages, in that it does *not* merely concern regional variation of the type outlined above; rather, different dialects have distinctive morpho-syntactic, lexical and phonological features which constitute linguistic systems in themselves. Indeed the whole tradition of 'dialectology' in France has involved the study of what would be termed 'regional languages' rather than 'dialects' under the Charter. The term 'regional language' is generally reserved for (i) non-romance languages spoken in France and (ii) those romance dialects which have a certain prestige and/or substantial numbers of speakers and/or a literary and grammatical tradition (e.g. Occitan). The term 'patois' on the other hand is employed (sometimes as a derogatory term) to refer to those regional languages or dialects which do not have what could be regarded as 'prestige' associations. This sense of 'dialects' and 'regional languages' being situated on the same linguistic 'level' in relation to the standard (albeit with different sociolinguistic associations) is also clear from Müller's illustration of the evolution of the relationships between (i) 'dialects' and 'regional languages' (both of which are receding), (ii) 'regional French' (i.e. French influenced by the regional language/dialect substratum) and 'ordinary French' from the nineteenth to the twentieth centuries:

---

[1] See for example Tuaillon (1988), Walter (1988), Müller (1985).

Figure 1: Historical Development of French. Adapted from Müller (1985:159)

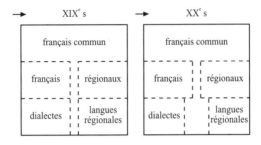

There is thus a very unhelpful clash between the terminology of the Charter and that traditionally used in the literature on France. We shall use exclusively the term *regional languages* and shall leave the term *dialect* to one side. In any case, as regards Walloon, there is a broad consensus that in linguistic terms, it is not French influenced by a substratum (i.e. Müller's *français régional*, the Charter's *dialect*), but rather a language with a distinct morphology, syntax, lexis and phonology.

2. The current linguistic situation in France[2]

Map 1 illustrates the regional languages of France. In broad terms, the languages of the *langue d'oïl* area (of which Walloon is one) are in a greater state of decline than those of the *langue d'oc*, or the non-romance varieties such as Breton and Alsacien. Since many of the *langues d'oïl* were close both geographically and linguistically to what ultimately became 'French', they were more easily 'absorbed', more easily broken down, as it were, by the advance of French as it emerged as the prestige vernacular (from the late Middle Ages onwards), than were the *langues d'oc* or the non-Romance languages, which, to varying degrees, were both linguistically distinct and geographically further from the source of the emerging standard. There were of course other influential factors later in the linguistic history of France which touched the fate of all the regional languages, notably the post-revolutionary policy of linguistic terror, and the advent of compulsory schooling through the medium of French in the nineteenth century. Nonetheless, for the reasons explained, the outlook was and is particularly bleak for the *langues d'oïl*.

That said, one surprising figure which has emerged more recently comes from the National Institute for Demographic Studies' survey of 1999 (known as the 'Enquête famille'), which cites a figure of 570,000 for the number of speakers where a *langue d'oïl* was spoken to them at home habitually (850,000 occasionally).[3] Note, however, that the global picture which emerges from this survey is a rather negative one for all the regional languages, showing a marked decline in the extent to which the languages are spoken in the home across the generations.

---

[2]   An excellent summary of the contemporary situation can be found in Pooley (2000).
[3]   Compare 280,000 (400,000) for Breton, 660,000 (240,000) for Alsacien, for example.

Map 1: The Regional Languages of France, adapted from Ager (1990: 23)[4]

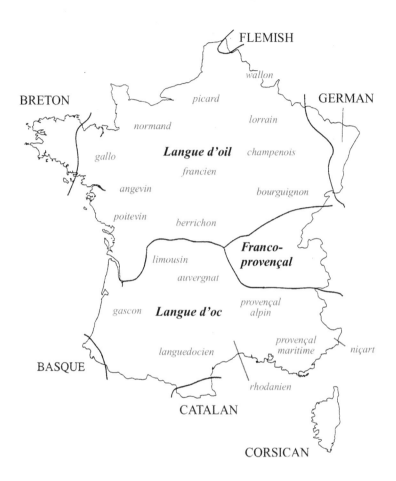

Amongst the *langues d'oïl*, Walloon is an interesting case, because (i) it is geographically one of the more peripheral languages, and linguistically, relatively speaking, one of the more distant from standard French, and thus one of the *langues d'oïl* with a better chance of survival (this is also true of Picard); and (ii) it is spoken across the border in Belgium and thus has a second, potentially more powerful, source of support in political and/or popular terms. For example, there is a substantial literature in the language and a standardised spelling system (devised in the early twentieth century); since 1983, there has been provision for Walloon to be taught in Belgian schools, and there is some media support.[5]

---

[4] This map, adapted from Dennis Ager, *Sociolinguistics and Contemporary French*, is reproduced with permission from Cambridge University Press.
[5] See Price (1988).

In purely linguistic terms, where they exist, all the *langues d'oïl* are *collateral languages* with French, as Scots is a *collateral language* with respect to English; they are endogenous regional languages with their own morpho-syntax, phonology and lexis. In sociolinguistic terms, however, the existence of the type of linguistic infrastructure used by the European Bureau for Lesser Used Languages when considering whether or not a variety is a regional language (the criteria are cited by Fauconnier, this volume), is highly problematic with respect to the vast majority of the *langues d'oïl* in France. None meet the six criteria, and indeed some meet very few criteria: for example, to the best of my knowledge, there is no teaching through the medium of these languages (and indeed very little teaching of the languages), nor is there much if anything by way of media support. A further difficulty is that attitudes in the school system from the nineteenth century onwards, and thus large sections of public opinion in France, are not well disposed to regional languages. This is particulary acute with the *langues d'oïl* (no doubt because of their linguistic proximity to French) which are often regarded as corrupted varieties of French, labelled variously '*français écorché*', '*français abrégé*', '*français déformé*' or '*français 'écrasé*'.[6] There is, moreover, much less sense of these regional languages' association with a strong regional or cultural identity, as is the case for Breton, Occitan or Corsican, for example, or with a rich literary tradition.

3. The political climate

On the whole, it is fair to say that the political climate in France has not been favourable to the regional languages. Although the *Loi Deixonne* of 1951 provided for the teaching of some regional languages in schools, this did not apply to all regional languages (and indeed did not include the *langues d'oïl*), and in any case, was implemented at a point in time where many of the regional languages were already in an advanced state of decline, and it has had limited public and political support. It is Breton which has benefited most from Deixonne and subsequent provision, not least due to a very pro-active Diwan movement, with groups of parents willing to work to set up and support Breton medium schools.[7]

Has the European Charter for Regional or Minority Languages had any positive impact? The initial reports by Poignant and Carcassonne (1998) commissioned by the government in response to the Charter were relatively positive overall, though Poignant did not include the *langues d'oïl* as living languages, and Carcassonne grouped them together under one heading. These reports were followed by the 1999 report commissioned by the *Ministère de la Culture et de la Communication* and carried out by Bernard Cerquiglini (Director of the *Institut national de la langue française*) which highlighted the extreme complexity of the linguistic situation in France when not just indigenous regional languages, but also second generation immigrant languages are taken into account.[8] Indeed, Cerquiglini's list of regional and minority languages totals 75, a

---

[6] Walter (1988:150).
[7] For more details of the subsequent legislation in education and its effects, see Judge (2003).
[8] Cerquiglini's report can be found at www.culture.fr/culture/dglf/lang-reg /rapport_cerquiglini/langues-france.html

figure which is obviously very high. On the one hand, the *langues d'oïl* fare well in his report, as each one is listed separately as a regional language. On the other hand, it was obvious that not all 75 could be supported by the Government as provided for in Part 3 of the Charter, and as a way of determining which languages should benefit, Cerquiglini tentatively recommended considering those which benefit from the Loi Deixonne, a move which would in practice exclude the *langues d'oïl*.

In any case, no such selection took place, since major constitutional issues were raised by the *Conseil Constitutionnel*, centring on the fact that Article 2 of the *French Constitution* states "La langue de la République est le français" ("the language of the Republic is French"), but also raising issues about the "indivisibility" of the French people as articulated in the first article of the Constitution, and the desire not to grant potentially divisive rights to particular minorities within the population.[9] In short, the Charter came up against insuperable constitutional difficulties which meant that it was not ratified in France, and thus the full provisions of Part 3 which would have leant tangible support to minority languages, will not for the foreseeable future be implemented. Note however, that in spite of non-ratification, there is a sense in which awareness of the minority languages has been raised by the discussion which took place around the Charter; a number of positive linguistic measures, including the formation of the *Observatoire des pratiques linguistiques* have been undertaken, and funding for regional cultural activities, including linguistic ones, is available.[10]

4. Conclusions

Our conclusions might thus be summarized as follows:

* There are strong linguistic arguments for extending the comparison with Scots beyond Walloon to other *langues d'oïl* in France;
* Notwithstanding terminological difficulties, the *langues d'oïl*, too, can be classified linguistically as endogenous regional languages which are collateral with French, each having its own morpho-syntax, phonology and lexis;
* The *langues d'oïl* are, however, in an advanced state of decline in France, and it isdifficult to match many of them to the criteria used by the European Bureau for Lesser Used Languages. Both political and linguistic factors have had a hand in this decline;
* Whilst it is difficult to be anything other than pessimistic about the future of the group of *langues d'oïl* in France, Walloon is arguably best placed amongst them to survive, not least because of higher levels of political and popular support in Belgium. In this sense, the majority of the *langues d'oïl* differ from both Walloon and Scots, which both may benefit in the longer term from higher levels of state and/or popular support.

---

[9] The report of the *Conseil Constitutionnel* can be found at www.conseil-constitutionnel.fr/decision/1999/99412.decl.htm

[10] See Judge (2002:62ff.)

References

Ager, D. 1990. *Sociolinguistics and Contemporary French*. Cambridge: CUP.

Héran, F., Filhon, A. and Deprez, C. 2002. "La dynamique des langues en France au fil du 20ème siècle". *Bulletin mensuel d'information de l'institut national d'études démographiques*. No.376.

Judge, A. 2002. "Contemporary issues in French linguistic policies". In ed. K. Salhi. *French in and out of France*. Bern: Lang. 35-72.

Judge, A. 2003. "Linguistic legislation and governmental intervention since the signing of the Charter". Paper given at the *Society for French Studies Annual Conference* 2003.

Müller, B. 1985. *Le Français d'aujourd'hui*. Paris: Klincksieck.

Pooley, T. 2000. "Sociolinguistics, regional varieties of French and regional languages in France". *Journal of French Language Studies* 10/1: 117-157.

Price, G. 1998. "Walloon". In ed. G. Price. *Encyclopedia of the Languages of Europe*.Oxford: Blackwell. 487-488.

Tuaillon, G. 1988. "Le français régional: formes de rencontre". In ed. G. Vermès. *Vingt-cinq communautés linguistiques de la France*. Paris: L'Harmattan.291-299.

Walter, H. (1988). *Le Français dans tous les sens*. Paris: Laffont.